HOPKINS' IDEALISM

Hopkins' Idealism

PHILOSOPHY, PHYSICS, POETRY

DANIEL BROWN

CLARENDON PRESS · OXFORD
1997

Oxford University Press, Walton Street, Oxford OX2 6DP
Oxford New York
Athens Auckland Bangkok Bogota Bombay
Buenos Aires Calcutta Cape Town Dar es Salaam
Delhi Florence Hong Kong Istanbul Karachi
Kuala Lumpur Madras Madrid Melbourne
Mexico City Nairobi Paris Singapore
Taipei Tokyo Toronto
and associated companies in
Berlin Ibadan

Oxford is a trade mark of Oxford University Press

Published in the United States by
Oxford University Press Inc., New York

British Library Cataloguing in Publication Data
Data available

Library of Congress Cataloging-in-Publication Data
Brown, Daniel, *1961–*
Hopkins' idealism : philosophy, physics, poetry / Daniel Brown.
Includes bibliographical references and index.
1. Hopkins, Gerard Manley, 1844–1889—Philosophy. 2. Hopkins,
Gerard Manley, 1844–1889—Knowledge—Science. 3. Literature and
science—England—History—19th century. 4. Philosophy in
literature. 5. Idealism in literature. 6. Physics in literature.
7. Metaphysics in literature. I. Hopkins, Gerard Manley,
1844–1889. II. Title.
PR4803.H44Z596 1996 821'.8—dc20 96-35164
ISBN 0–19–818353–4

1 3 5 7 9 10 8 6 4 2

Typeset by Graphicraft Typesetters Ltd., Hong Kong
Printed in Great Britain
on acid-free paper by
Bookcraft Ltd
Midsomer Norton, Somerset

TO MY PARENTS
Aniko and Kevin Brown

AND IN MEMORY OF
Mary Nemes, Alfred Biddle, and Alice Biddle

Preface

THE historical context in which Hopkins' *Poems* were first received was radically different from that in which they were written. The first edition of the *Poems of Gerard Manley Hopkins* was issued in January 1919 to a prospective readership whose cultural bearings had been transformed by World War I. For many, the Victorian culture within which Hopkins wrote had been not only distanced by the war but devastated and discredited. Yet it was amongst those who repudiated this past most strongly, the modernists, that Hopkins' mature poetry found its first appreciative public, and indeed modernism remains an apt context in which to understand his work. The catastrophist view of artistic and cultural production presupposed by the post-war avant-garde is anticipated by Hopkins, who argues as early as 1864 that progress in the arts occurs 'by a breaking up, a violence' (*J.* 79), and later exemplifies this doctrine with the formal experimentation of 'The Wreck of the *Deutschland*' and its successors.

But it was not only amongst the modernists that the historical Hopkins was fated 'To seem the stranger'. His early following also included admirers of the more conventional poetry of his youth. Many early readers were evidently engaged by the Keatsian romanticism of such poems as 'A Vision of the Mermaids', which was published separately in facsimile in 1929, and the yearning for security, peace, and cosmological certainty that is expressed most directly in 'Heaven-Haven', a poem that was much anthologized from the 1920s to the 1940s. The popularity of such works at this time suggests an element of nostalgia, a modern phenomenon which like that of the avant-garde is founded upon a sense of the present as radically sundered from the past. Such approaches to the poetry, which often dwell upon the historical and biographical cues provided by the early poems, brought such contexts as Tractarianism and English romanticism to the foreground in the formation of a historicizing discourse for Hopkins studies.

The experimentalism of Hopkins' mature poetry that so

excited modernist tastes has been dismissed by a wider readership as eccentric. Many historical studies have sought to counter
this charge and domesticate Hopkins' poetry by placing it within
narratives of cultural continuity, a strategy which is formulated
in the title of W. H. Gardner's pioneering study *Gerard Manley
Hopkins: A Study of Poetic Idiosyncrasy in Relation to Poetic Tradition*
(1944). Such contextual studies have worked to assimilate his
writings within the grand traditions of the English literary canon
and Roman Catholic culture. While this approach has produced
many important and enlightening studies, it has meant that
other contexts, which threaten to enhance Hopkins' reputation for eccentricity and mitigate his claims to canonicity, have
been unjustly neglected.

The following study explores Hopkins' use of early British
idealist thought and energy physics, contexts which Hopkins
scholarship has largely ignored. The conventional picture of the
undergraduate Hopkins as a conservative High-Church ritualist
needs to be supplemented with (or perhaps even supplanted
by) that of the boldly speculative intellectual liberal which the
Oxford and Birmingham writings on philosophy allow us to recover. The implicit consensus amongst many of Hopkins' academic commentators has been that his early thought is, like his
early poetry, immature. There has since the 1930s been a wide-
spread presupposition in Hopkins studies that the doctrine of
'inscape' was formulated clearly and finally only with his discovery of Duns Scotus in 1874; that it, like the new poetry
heralded by 'The Wreck of the *Deutschland*', emerged almost
ex nihilo. The present study examines Hopkins' 1868 notes
on Pre-Socratic philosophy not as the awkward foreshadowing of
his reading of Scotus, an approach that has privileged 'inscape'
(which commentators have often identified with the Scotist *haec-
ceitas*) over the more radical principles of 'stress' and 'instress',
but as an imaginative and syncretic metaphysic which provides
the master discourse for his later writings in theology and poetry.
It is, I argue, by extending his metaphysic of 'stress' to describe
and explain speech and poetic structure that Hopkins arrives at
his distinctive theory and practice of poetry.

A version of this study was submitted as my Ph.D. thesis to the
University of Western Australia in 1992. I would like to thank

the supervisors of my Ph.D., Associate Professor Hilary Fraser and Dr Barry Maund, for their great learning and support. I also wish to thank Dr Catherine Philips and my examiners, Professor Gillian Beer, Dr Norman White, and Professor Frank Turner, for their valuable comments and encouragement.

I am indebted to the Community at Campion Hall for allowing me access to their Hopkins Archive and most particularly to Father Felix Suarez and Father Philip Endeen for their interest and attentiveness in assisting my researches. The Hopkins material used in this book is reproduced by kind permission of the British Province of the Society of Jesus.

Alan Tadiello's kindness and knowledge helped me find my way through the T. H. Green and Jowett collections at Balliol College Library. Dr Robin Darwall-Smith also greatly assisted me in my work on the Jowett Papers. I am grateful to the Master and Fellows of Balliol College for permission to reproduce material from their Green and Jowett archives.

John Burgass of Merton College Library very generously arranged for a copy of F. H. Bradley's notes on T. H. Green's 1867 lectures to be sent to me. My thanks to him and also to the Master and Fellows of Royal Holloway College, London, for permission to publish excerpts from this manuscript.

I wish to thank the staff of the Bodleian Library Oxford, and Henry Wurm and the staff of the Inter-Library Loans department of the Reid Library at the University of Western Australia.

I am grateful to Bert and Barbara Main, Frank Callanan, and Patrick Healy, who have long been to me exemplars of scholarly integrity and friendship. I am especially indebted to Patrick and trace my current interest in philosophy back to our earliest discussions.

Amongst the many and various other debts of gratitude I owe I would like to mention in particular Jason Freeman, Janet Moth, Sophie Goldsworthy, and Sylvia Jaffrey at OUP, Gill Jenkins, Patience Hook, Philippa Bayliss, Claire and Paddy McCarthy, Veronica Brady, Bruce McClintock, Sue Lewis, Bob White, and, most of all, my family.

Contents

List of Figures

List of Poems Cited in the Text

As numbered in *The Poetical Works of Gerard Manley Hopkins*, ed. Norman MacKenzie (Oxford: Clarendon Press, 1990).

Abbreviations

Balliol	Balliol College, Oxford
Bodl.	Bodleian Library, Oxford
Further Letters	*Further Letters of Gerard Manley Hopkins*, ed. Claude Colleer Abbott (London: Oxford University Press, 1959)
Green, *Works*	*Works of T. H. Green*, ed. R. L. Nettleship, 3 vols. (London: Longmans, 1911)
J.	*The Journals and Papers of Gerard Manley Hopkins*, ed. Humphry House and Graham Storey, 2nd edn. (London: Oxford University Press, 1959)
Merton	Merton College, Oxford
No.	Refers to poem numbered as in *The Poetical Works of Gerard Manley Hopkins*, ed. Norman H. MacKenzie (Oxford: Clarendon Press, 1990)
S.	*Sermons and Devotional Writings of Gerard Manley Hopkins*, ed. Christopher Devlin (Oxford: Oxford University Press, 1959)
To Bridges	*The Letters of Gerard Manley Hopkins to Robert Bridges*, ed. Claude Colleer Abbott, 2nd (rev.) impression (London: Oxford University Press, 1955)
To Dixon	*The Correspondence of Gerard Manley Hopkins and Richard Watson Dixon*, ed. Claude Colleer Abbott, 2nd (rev.) impression (London: Oxford University Press, 1955)

1   Hopkins and Oxford

Anyone who writes about philosophy must have his work
judged, not by its relation to the intellectual wants of a
past generation but by its power to meet the wants of the
present time—wants which arise out of the advance of science and the new currents of opinion that are transforming
man's social and religious life.[1]

I

Scientism, which makes empirical science the model for all
knowledge, emerged in the middle of the nineteenth century
with such momentum that it soon appeared to threaten the
entire field of metaphysics: 'The Positivists foretell', writes
Hopkins in 1867, 'and many other people begin to fear, the end
of all metaphysics is at hand' (*J.* 118). The apocalyptic note
which he strikes in this opening sentence of his Oxford undergraduate essay, 'The Probable Future of Metaphysics', indicates
the sense of uncertainty and upheaval felt during the latter half
of the nineteenth century when the dominant metaphysical
tradition of European thought was giving way to our own age in
which science is regarded as the paradigmatic form of knowledge. This is the historical context for the development of
Hopkins' mature thought, which, like that of his religious position, occurs intensively during his years at Oxford, from 1863
to 1867, and is stated definitively in 1868. His efforts in the
undergraduate essays to counter positivism are drawn together
in the idiosyncratic private metaphysic of 'stress', 'instress', and
'inscape' that he formulates early in 1868 in his 'Notes on the

[1] Edward Caird, 'Preface to a Forthcoming Volume of Philosophical Essays to
be Dedicated to the Memory of T. H. G[reen]', Balliol, T. H. Green Papers, MS
II. 1(d), fo. 2.

History of Greek Philosophy'.[2] This doctrine and its distinctive coinages are prompted by Parmenides' 'great text, which',
Hopkins speculates, 'he repeats with religious conviction . . . that
Being is and Not-being is not' (*J.* 127). With these notes
Hopkins clarifies the metaphysical basis of his faith before
embarking, in September 1868, upon his new life in the Society of Jesus.

Positivism, which maintains that only statements grounded in
empirical observation can have meaning, highlights the peculiar
nature and power of nineteenth-century scientism. The 'Positivism' ascribed later in the essay to the second of the 'three
great seasons in the history of philosophy . . . that of Bacon and
physical science' (*J.* 119) consists in the purely scientific application of empiricism which marks the beginning of modern science and provides the intellectual milieu for the great systematic
philosophers from Descartes to Hegel. In Hopkins' day, however, positivistic science often claimed to supersede metaphysics
entirely. The claim is made most clearly by Auguste Comte,
whose positivism systematically elaborates this extreme form
of empiricism into an entire world-view. Comte divides human
history into three successive stages: the religious, the metaphysical, and the positive. In the final stage, which Comte identified
with the nineteenth century, the comprehensiveness of scientific
knowledge is seen to undermine the authority of metaphysics.

It is to this millenarian claim of the 'Positivists' that Hopkins
refers at the beginning of 'The Probable Future of Metaphysics':
'the end of all metaphysics is at hand'. He completes this opening paragraph by introducing 'Purely material psychology' in
terms that suggest the beast of Revelation as 'the τριακτήρ [i.e.
conqueror] foretold and feared' (*J.* 118). Such millenarian
inflections indicate the personal religious and emotional significance that the contemporary predicament of metaphysics

---

[2] All Hopkins' Oxford and Birmingham notebooks other than D. II (which is
in Balliol College) are held at Campion Hall, Oxford. Most are unpublished. They
are listed in the *Journals and Papers* (*J.* 529–35); Anthony Bischoff, 'The Manuscripts of Gerard Manley Hopkins', *Thought*, 26 (1951), 551–80; Carl Schmidt,
'Classical Studies at Balliol in the 1860s: The Undergraduate Essays of Gerard
Manley Hopkins', in John Prest (ed.), *Balliol Studies* (London: Leopard's Head
Press, 1982), 178–81; and Lesley Higgins, 'A New Catalogue of the Hopkins Collection at Campion Hall, Oxford', *Hopkins Quarterly*, 18/1–2 (April–July 1991),
9–44.

had for Hopkins. Britain underwent a millenarian revival in the nineteenth century which intensified during the late 1840s and maintained its momentum well into the 1870s. 'By the late eighteen-fifties . . .', writes Alison Sulloway, 'the outburst of apocalyptic warnings had become a torrent, issuing from prophets of every religious persuasion', including Keble, Newman, Pusey, and Liddon, and she argues that Hopkins too can be regarded as a 'Calamitarian'.[3] Millenarianism is often exacerbated by times of great change, a response that helps to explain the idea's emergence in the rhetoric of Hopkins' essay. That it shapes his approach to the contemporary opposition of metaphysics and positivism indicates the depth of his personal animus towards the latter, the various manifestations of which he identifies as versions of 'materialism'.

Hopkins' perception that 'Purely material psychology' is a decisive threat to metaphysics is corroborated by Wilhelm Windelband who, writing at the end of the century, observed that the changing character of psychology provides an important index of the relations between scientism and philosophy: 'A characteristic change in the general scientific relations during the nineteenth century has been the constantly progressing *loosening and separation of psychology from philosophy*'. The etymological meaning of the word 'psychology' is the science, in the sense of the a priori study, of the soul. By the end of the nineteenth century, however, this conception had been superseded by 'our "psychology without a soul", which is free from all metaphysical assumptions—or means to be'.[4]

The turning point in the fortunes of these conceptions of psychology can be dated to the late 1850s and early 1860s. Gustav Fechner's *Elements of Psychophysiology* (1860) and Darwin's *Origin of Species* (1859) can be singled out as having 'completed the separation of psychology from philosophy'.[5] Physiology

[3] Alison Sulloway, *Gerard Manley Hopkins and the Victorian Temper* (London: Routledge & Kegan Paul, 1972), 165–6, 185. British millenarian movements were especially active during 1867, the year in which Hopkins wrote his essay. See Ernest P. Sandeen, *The Roots of Fundamentalism* (Chicago: Chicago University Press, 1970), 82–3, 88.
[4] Wilhelm Windelband, *A History of Philosophy*, trans. James H. Tufts, 2nd edn. (New York: Macmillan, 1901), 634, 643.
[5] J. C. Flugel, *A Hundred Years of Psychology: 1833–1933* (London: Duckworth, 1933), 72.

became orientated as an experimental study in Germany in the 1830s, and through it developed the materialist approach to psychology, the reductionist idea that mind can be traced to the physical nature of the body. The perception of the nervous system as the intermediary between the brain and the body made neurophysiology central to the emergence of naturalistic psychology. Fechner's book consolidated this experimental and materialist approach.

The continuity that neurophysiology saw to exist between simple neural mechanisms, such as those responsible for reflex actions, and the reasoning brain is corroborated by evolutionary theory in historical terms of the development of simpler into more complex biological forms. This consequence was well recognized prior to the appearance of Darwin's book by Herbert Spencer, who bases his *Principles of Psychology* (1855) upon it, and by T. H. Huxley in his public controversy with the comparative anatomist Richard Owen over the 'Cerebral Structure of Man and the Apes', which took place from 1857 to 1862.[6] The functionalist psychology of the evolutionists is a version of physiological reductionism, a form of materialism: 'we are here primarily concerned', writes Spencer at the beginning of the *Principles*, 'with psychological phenomena as phenomena of Evolution; and, under their objective aspect, these, reduced to their lowest terms, are incidents in the continuous redistribution of Matter and Motion'.[7] Although Darwin is careful in *The Origin of Species* not to draw any conclusions as to the consequences of his theory for human psychology, the scientific respectability that his principle of natural selection afforded the evolutionary hypothesis lent credence to the speculations of Spencer and others. This view traced the traditional

---

[6] Huxley gives 'A succinct History of the Controversy...' in *Man's Place in Nature* (1866); repr. in *Man's Place in Nature and Other Essays* (London: Dent, 1906), 105–10. In this essay, and other writings from the 1860s, Huxley typically draws attention to the specific implications of evolution for the human mind which Darwin had not yet written on: 'I have endeavoured to show that no absolute structural line of demarcation, wider than that between the animals which immediately succeed us in the scale, can be drawn between the animal world and ourselves; and I may add the expression of my belief that the attempt to draw a psychical distinction is equally futile, and that even the highest faculties of feeling and of intellect begin to germinate in lower forms of life' (Huxley, 102).

[7] H. Spencer, *Principles of Psychology*, 3rd edn. (London: Williams & Norgate, 1880), i. 13.

metaphysical concept of 'mind' to functions of the brain that enable an animal to survive the fiercely competitive natural world described by Darwin.

Another decisive factor in the formation and establishment of modern psychology was the associationist doctrine of British empiricism, which, as it is expounded by Locke and Hume, regards all thought as reducible to simple units, discrete states of mind or 'ideas' that correspond to sensations and which combine to form more complex thoughts. In his *Observations on Man* (1749) David Hartley adopts the Newtonian model of vibrations as the neurological parallel to the empiricist 'ideas' of Locke and Hume. Hartley's speculations were seen to receive experimental verification in the following century through Emil Du Bois-Reymond's identification of 'nerve-force' with electricity in 1848, and in the subsequent work of others such as Carl Ludwig and Hermann von Helmholtz, who similarly applied the concepts of physics to physiology. Other contemporary experiments, which identified mental functions with the localized activities of the brain,[8] and the Hartleian legacy of physiological speculation are directly addressed by Hopkins' criticism of the 'Material explanation' of thought: 'it is all to no purpose to show an organ for each faculty and a nerve vibrating for each idea' (*J.* 118).

Hartley's mental doctrine of associationism was notably developed in the nineteenth century by James Mill and later by his son John Stuart Mill, whose *System of Logic* (1843) Hopkins studied at Oxford. Associationism is reunited with physiological speculation in the work of J. S. Mill's friend and collaborator Alexander Bain, who announces in the Preface to *The Senses and the Intellect* (1855) that 'the time has now come when many of the striking discoveries of Physiologists relative to the nervous system should find a recognized place in the Science of Mind'.[9] The book is divided into two main sections: 'Movement, Sense, and Instinct', which summarizes recent findings

[8] These often involved the extirpation of parts of the brain and nervous system of live animals and, following Paul Broca's pioneering of the clinical method in 1861, the post-mortem examination of the brain and nervous system of people whose senses had been impaired.

[9] A. Bain, Preface to the 1st edn., *The Senses and the Intellect*, 3rd edn. (London: Longmans, 1868), p. iii.

in physiology; and 'Intellect', which expounds an associationist theory of mind. This parallelistic approach is further developed in the second part of Bain's work, *The Emotions and the Will* (1859).

Fechner's physiological reductionism, Spencer's functionalism, and Bain's associationism condemn the privileging by metaphysics of reason over other mental and neural activities. By the time that Hopkins wrote 'The Probable Future of Metaphysics' physiological psychology was clearly ascendant and its threatening implications for metaphysics were readily apparent: 'psychology will exercise its own office over almost all the field now held to belong solely to metaphysics' (*J.* 118).

Hopkins also considers 'a second worst forecast': 'Psychology and physiology may withdraw to themselves everything that is special and detailed in the action of the mind and metaphysics will be left as the mode by which we give the bare statement of there being another side than the phenomenal when we regard things'. Although metaphysics would in this case be reduced to 'a bare statement' and 'mere abstraction', Hopkins asserts that 'it is ill-founded' to suppose 'an emptying out and barrenness in metaphysics as a consequence' of psychology's expansion (*J.* 118). The reason for this is simply that positive psychology cannot, according to Hopkins, extricate itself entirely from metaphysics. If the positivists' accretive generalizations 'from the part to the whole' are to be articulated as a science, if meanings are to be derived from the atomistic perceptions of phenomena, they need to be supplemented by the a priori conceptions of metaphysics:

It will always be possible to shew how science is atomic, not to be grasped and held together, 'scopeless', without metaphysics: this alone gives meaning to laws and sequences and causes and developments— things which stand in a position so peculiar that we can neither say of them they hold in nature whether the mind sees them or not nor again that they are found by the mind because it first put them there.

(*J.* 118)

The ultimate sovereignty of apriorism over current science is a methodological consequence of the idealist epistemological principle stated later in the essay: 'the Idea is only given . . . from the whole downwards to the parts'. This principle is invoked by

Hopkins to oppose a central tenet of positivism, 'the prevalent principle that knowledge is from the birth upwards, is a history of growth, and mounts from the part to the whole', which furnishes the methodological presupposition of the Darwinian 'philosophy of flux' (*J.* 120). Darwin's prodigious number of observations of nature led him to emphasize variation in species and so encouraged his theory of the mutability of species. The resultant taxonomy is relativistic and nominalistic: 'To the prevalent philosophy and science', Hopkins writes, 'nature is a string all the differences in which are really chromatic but certain places in it have become accidentally fixed and the series of fixed points becomes an arbitrary scale' (*J.* 120). Hopkins' philosophical writings oppose such tendencies by asserting the ontological primacy of 'type or species', the universal 'Idea' that he believes is instanced by individual creatures.

II

The prescribed essay topic on 'The Probable Future of Metaphysics' highlights the central importance to Oxford classics in the 1860s of philosophy generally and contemporary thought in particular, while the decisive stance that Hopkins takes to the question indicates the extent of his engagement with his studies in these areas. The importance given to the study of philosophy was the main consequence of an Oxford statute of 1850, which set 'to the task of adjusting her [i.e. the University's] curriculum to the requirements of the age'.[10] The arrangement of the classics course was revised so that the philological study of Greek and Latin texts was largely relegated to preparation for the first public examination or 'Moderations', for which candidates could sit after six terms in residence,[11] while the second public examination in Literae Humaniores, 'Final Schools' or 'Greats', became primarily a test in history and philosophy.[12] Studies for

---

[10] 'Literae Humaniores, VII', *Oxford Magazine*, 27/16 (11 Mar. 1909), 247.

[11] James E. Thorold Rogers, *Education at Oxford* (London: Smith, Elder & Co., 1861), 30. Students were also required to sit a minor examination, known as Responsions, soon after entering the University (ibid. 31–2).

[12] Peter Hinchliff, *Benjamin Jowett and the Christian Tradition* (Oxford: Clarendon Press, 1987), 32–3.

Moderations were, according to Mark Pattison, for the most part a continuation of school classics, with the only new area they treated of being logic.[13] He is more enthusiastic about Greats, which he describes in 1868 (the year after Hopkins sat the examination) as the crowning achievement of Oxford education: 'The final examination in the school of Literae Humaniores, as it at present exists, is the heart and life of our system'.[14] He considers it to be the 'most elaborate and intense instance' of the 'educational test of the University of Oxford'.[15]

Hopkins matriculated to Balliol College in April 1863, and sat for Moderations in November 1864, taking advantage of the opportunity for honours it provided by achieving a first class. As well as having to fulfil the pass requirements honours candidates were given an additional paper on logic, which was especially important to their final result. Hopkins, having allowed the maximum number of terms to elapse, took the Finals examination in the middle of Trinity term 1867. Pattison provides a translation of the Oxford statute for this year which prescribes the 'matter of the examination':

The *Literae Humaniores*, for the purposes of this school, we define as, in addition to the Greek and Latin languages, the histories of Greece and Rome, with those handmaids of history—chronology, geography, antiquities, rhetoric, and poetics, and the moral and political sciences, so far as they are derivable from ancient writers. These last, however, we allow from time to time, as shall appear expedient, to be illustrated from modern authors. Dialectic (logic), which we add to the *Literae Humaniores*, as above defined, must always be offered by candidates for a first or second class; and proficiency in logic shall have great weight in the distribution of honours.

Pattison observes that this prescription is substantially the same as the original statute of 1830 and quite inadequate in providing an idea of the practice of the examination in the 1860s.[16]

Although the Vice-Chancellor, the Proctors, and the Examiners in Greats were directed in 1863 to publish a list of classical texts from which Pass candidates were required to

[13] Mark Pattison, *Suggestions on Academical Organisation with Especial Reference to Oxford* (Edinburgh: Edmonston & Douglas, 1868), 271.   [14] Ibid. 287.
[15] Ibid. 289.   [16] Ibid. 287–8.

choose,[17] it would be misleading to say that Literae Humaniores had a formal curriculum. The list of six to eight textbooks which tended to be prescribed in the 1860s proceeded from the vague dictates of the statute, while the approach to these books was determined by the college tutor, whose responsibility it was to prepare the student for the examination. One of Hopkins' early diary entries lists the main texts that he expected to study: 'Greats books. Most of the following. *Aristotle.* Rhetoric, Ethics, Politics. *Plato.* Republic. *Herodotus. Thucydides. Livy,* 10 books. *Tacitus.* Histories or 1st. 12 books of Annals. *Bacon's* "Novum Organon [Scientarum]". *Butler's* Sermons or *Analogy*' (*J.* 49). In the event Hopkins made no formal study of Butler, whose work was falling out of favour at Oxford during the 1860s,[18] or of Aristotle's *Rhetoric* and *Politics.* It is, however, necessary to add to the remaining texts works by the Pre-Socratic philosophers, Sophocles, Demosthenes, Aristophanes, Homer, Cicero, Virgil, Juvenal, Mommsen, and Hegel.[19]

The growth in philosophical studies at the expense of philology, which followed the formal changes imposed by the statute of 1850, is described by Pattison in 1868: 'without altering the "materies examinationis", philosophy was gradually infused into the examinations, till it has become their most material component'.[20] Aristotle's *Ethics,* which had long been a Greats book, and Plato's *Republic,* which Benjamin Jowett lectured upon from the late 1840s,[21] were accordingly studied for their philosophical import. R. L. Nettleship, a friend of Hopkins' at Balliol who like him sat for Greats in 1867, testifies that 'their works had begun to be treated less as instructive analyses or brilliant

---

[17] The list is reproduced in a pamphlet by Revd T. H. Grose, 'Faculty of Arts: Final Examination for the B. A. Degree' (Oxford, 1900), 2 fos. (Bodl., G. A. Oxon. b. 41 (I)): 'GREEK 1. Plato, Apology, Crito, and Phaedo. 2. Herodotus, VII, VIII, IX. 3. Plato, Republic, I–IV. 4. Aristotle, [Nicomachean] Ethics, I (omitting ch. vi), II, III, IV, with chapters vi, vii, viii of Book X. LATIN 1. Tacitus, Annals, I–IV. 2. Cicero, De Officiis. 3. Livy, XXI–XXIV.'

[18] [Charles Alan Fyffe], 'Study and Opinion at Oxford', *Macmillan's Magazine,* 21 (Dec. 1869), 189.

[19] Lesley J. Higgins, 'Hopkins and the "Jowler"', *Texas Studies in Literature and Language,* 31/1 (Spring 1989), 162–4.   [20] Pattison, *Suggestions,* 289.

[21] Frank M. Turner, *The Greek Heritage in Victorian Britain* (New Haven: Yale University Press, 1981), 374. See also R. M. Ogilvie, *Latin and Greek: A Study of the Influence of the Classics on English Life from 1660 to 1918* (London: Routledge & Kegan Paul, 1964), 101.

criticisms of the commonplaces of culture, and more as partial expressions of systematic views of human life and the world'.[22]

There were two parts to the Finals examination that Hopkins sat for. The first required translations from English into Latin, and Latin and Greek composition,[23] while the second, which was taken only by honours candidates,[24] ostensibly drew upon the same recommended texts but demanded a philosophical approach. Thus, as a member of the University senate observed in the year that Hopkins sat for Greats, 'a classical scholar, however eminent in scholarship, is *excluded from honours* in the Final Examination, unless he has given a *considerable time to meta-physics*'.[25] In the second part of the examination 'papers are set severally in Logic, in Moral Philosophy, in Political Philosophy, in the History of Philosophy, [and] in Greek and . . . Roman History and Antiquities'.[26] The importance of 'composition' in the examination can, as Pattison observes, be discounted: 'it exercises little or no influence in the result'.[27] The study of the six to eight prescribed classical texts[28] is seen by Pattison as inadequate and typically neglected by the students. Robert Bridges, in his memoir of Digby Mackworth Dolben, records that Hopkins 'had not read more than half of the nine books [of Herodotus] when he went in for "Greats" '.[29] Pattison offers an explanation for such negligence: 'The reason why the six books offered are so incompletely studied is to be found in the fact that, the greater part of the candidate's effort is given to meet the other half of the test, in the examination in philosophy'.[30]

Although Hopkins did not, as many of the best students did, attempt honours in two schools, this fact detracts neither from his achievement of first-class honours in Greats nor from the qualities that it required of him. Rogers writes that such a first 'denotes years of laborious study, with the possession of extra-ordinary mental powers',[31] while Charles Alan Fyffe, generalizing

---

[22] R. L. Nettleship, 'Memoir', in Green, *Works*, iii, p. lxx.
[23] Rogers, *Education*, 34–5.   [24] Ibid. 38–41; Pattison, *Suggestions*, 289–90.
[25] T. D. Acland, quoted in [Herbert Vaughan], 'English Catholic University Education', *Dublin Review*, 9 (Oct. 1867), 421.   [26] Rogers, *Education*, 39.
[27] Pattison, *Suggestions*, 289.
[28] Cf. ibid. 288. His list coincides in the main with that of Hopkins (*J*. 49).
[29] Cited in G. F. Lahey, *Gerard Manley Hopkins* (London: Oxford University Press, 1930), 18.   [30] Pattison, *Suggestions*, 291.
[31] Rogers, *Education*, 40.

from the experience of Balliol Greats that he shared with Hopkins, attributes it to an intellectual attitude: 'on the whole, the honour-men are those who have, and the pass-men those who have not, sufficient interest in the well-being of their minds to be willing to make some sacrifice of time and pleasure for the mind's sake'.[32]

Hopkins' commitment to his studies is also registered in his weekly essays, the crucial importance of which for the final result was impressed upon him within a few days of his entering Balliol by Benjamin Jowett, the Regius Professor of Greek: 'he advised me to take great pains with this, as on it would depend my success more than on anything else'.[33] Twenty-eight of the thirty-eight surviving Greats essays are, as Schmidt observes, on philosophical topics. While this reflects the nature of Greats in the 1860s as 'overwhelmingly a school of philosophy',[34] it also indicates that the most substantial part of his studies was also that which he found most engaging and valuable, for he appears not to have kept any of the essays from his philological studies of classical literature. Indeed, he does not leave even a record of a single classical essay topic.[35]

III

The Royal Commission appointed in 1850 to reform the universities had, according to Fyffe's 1869 article on 'Study and Opinion in Oxford', 'remodelled Oxford', establishing 'a constitution of things . . . which was to so great a degree an embodiment of the idea that the *raison d'être* of the University was the advancement of learning, that whatever has obviously conflicted with, or had no relation to, that end, has now come to be regarded as an abuse, and doomed to perish'. It was in keeping with this spirit that 'something bearing a resemblance to a philosophic habit of mind has made its way into the study of the

---

[32] Fyffe, 'Study and Opinion', 187. Fyffe entered Balliol in 1864, taking, as Hopkins records (*J.* 159), a first in Greats in Dec. 1867. Hopkins was evidently on friendly terms with him (*J.* 55). Some of Fyffe's recollections of Green's teaching during this period are cited by Nettleship in Green, *Works*, iii, pp. lxiv–v.
[33] 'To His Mother', Apr. 22, 1863, Letter 40, *Further Letters*, 73.
[34] Schmidt, 'Classical Studies', 166.   [35] Ibid. 164.

"Literae Humaniores"'.[36] E. M. Geldart, another of Hopkins' peers at Balliol who also studied Greats from 1863 to 1867, testifies to the general climate of liberalism within the college at this time:

Never was I in an intellectual atmosphere so fearless and so free . . . a lot of men who were some of them Ritualists of the deepest dye, some of them Rationalists, some of them Positivists, some of them Materialists, all eager in advancing their respective views, and yet all ready to listen with courtesy to their opponents. Nobody was shocked or offended by anything; every one was open to argument.[37]

Benjamin Jowett, through his Socratic teaching practices, writings, and campaigning for university reform, was instrumental in establishing the liberal tenor of Greats.[38] Hence it is with some satisfaction that he remarks in 1865 upon the 'great change in education at the Universities, especially at Oxford' that make it 'impossible' to 'return to the old doctrines of authority' which he recalls dominated Greats studies when he was an undergraduate in the late 1830s.[39] '[U]ntil lately', Edwin Hatch writes in 1858, 'the whole tendency of Oxfordism was conservative: it was a perpetual retracing of the old paths: speculation was perilous, originality was heretical.'[40] The superseded pedagogy is consistent with the religious conservatism that J. H. Newman expresses in his Tractarian dictum that 'a rationalistic spirit is the antagonist of Faith'.[41] One of the main aims of the *Tracts for the Times*, which were begun by Newman in Oxford in 1833

[36] Fyffe, 'Study and Opinion', 186, 185. A 'new phase' at Oxford was engendered, which a recent graduate describes in 1858 as 'one of the most hopeful signs of English thought. It is . . . an awakening: it is only twilight, but it is the twilight of dawn' [Edwin Hatch], review article of 'The Ethics of Aristotle . . . By Sir Alexander Grant . . .', *North British Review*, 29 (Aug. 1858), 394–5. Hatch studied Greats at Pembroke College, 1853–7.

[37] Quoted from Geldart's veiled reminiscences, *A Son of Belial*, in Norman White, *Hopkins: A Literary Biography* (Oxford: Clarendon Press, 1992), 60. Hopkins is represented in Geldart's book as his 'Ritualistic friend, Gerontius Manley'.

[38] Evelyn Abbott and Lewis Campbell (eds.), *Life and Letters of Benjamin Jowett* (London: John Murray, 1897), i. 174–84.

[39] Abbott and Campbell, *Life and Letters*, i. 412.

[40] Hatch, review of 'Ethics', 369.

[41] J. H. Newman 'On the Introduction of Rationalistic Principles into Revealed Religion' (1835), in *Essays Critical and Historical* (London: Longmans (1871), 1910), i. 31.

and continued until 1841, was 'to arrest the advance of Liberalism in religious thought'.[42] The implications for religious belief of the abandonment of an authoritarian pedagogy for one of liberalism and rationalism was widely commented upon in the 1860s. Fyffe, for example, commends the liberalism of Greats studies and recognizes in the reactionary clerical response to it an index of its efficacy:

In the extravagance of doubting and criticising all things the young man's mind is fairly shaken out of its dogmatic slumber and set inquiring for a rational point of view, where before he had never felt the need of anything beyond his nursery beliefs . . . [T]here is found an element of reason in his mind which was not there before, which makes him look with wiser eyes upon all his life, upon religion and politics, and upon those that differ from him. The truest testimony to the enlightening influence of the school of Literae Humaniores is the antipathy of that section of the clergy in Oxford which can see in the deepening moral sense of man nothing but a fen-fire that is ever beguiling him further and further from his shelter in the past.[43]

The clerical opposition to intellectual liberalism was of course based upon the fear that this questioning spirit would be directed at the authority of established religion, as indeed it was at the beginning of the decade by Jowett and the other contributors to the *Essays and Reviews*. Through its applications of biblical criticism, which regards the Bible as a literary and historical document akin in these respects to other objects of scholarly study such as the Homeric poems, the *Essays and Reviews* caused a controversy upon its appearance in 1860 which was greater than that which met the publication of Darwin's *Origin of Species* a year earlier. The biblical-critical approach corresponds to one of the consequences of rationalism that Newman had earlier identified: 'it is Rationalism to accept the Revelation, and then to explain it away; to speak of it as the Word of God,

[42] Quoted (from the *Churchman's Guide*, 218) s.v. 'Tract', sb[1] 3b, *OED*, 2nd edn. (Oxford: Clarendon Press, 1989). In making these selective quotations from Newman I do not wish to suggest that he simply represented the old authoritarian pedagogy. His belief that reason should be subordinated to the primarily emotional conviction of faith is well documented in Hilary Fraser's *Beauty and Belief* (Cambridge: Cambridge University Press, 1986), 46–8.
[43] Fyffe, 'Study and Opinion', 189.

and to treat it as the word of man'.[44] Many in the 1860s saw this liberal interpretation of the Bible to have devastating consequences. According to 11,000 Anglican clergymen, signatories to the 'Oxford Declaration' of 1864,[45] if any part of the Bible was seen to be in error then the whole of it could be called into doubt. *Essays and Reviews* was taken as unequivocal evidence that the Broad Church faction teaching at Oxford, particularly Jowett, had moulded modern Greats with the express purpose of encouraging students to reject religious authority.

Not only did Oxford provide most of the contributors to *Essays and Reviews*, but according to Fyffe, 'critical theology' was 'beginning to be taught and studied' in Greats by the late 1860s.[46] The link between the intellectual and theological versions of liberalism was most strongly and publicly represented by Jowett. According to Sulloway the Tractarian priests 'sensed that [in his teaching] Jowett was using Plato to carry on his quarrel with Christian dogma'. Indeed Pusey and some of his associates initiated legal action against him in 1863 over his contribution to *Essays and Reviews* and 'did the best they could to counteract his influence in the lecture halls by their thunderous sermons against the sin of speculative thought'.[47]

While Roman Catholic theologians and clergy were suspicious of the liberal tenor which they perceived in modern education generally, Oxford was, as Pattison observes, especially 'denounced as . . . "dangerous to faith"'. More precisely, 'It is the school of classics (Literae Humaniores) only, and, specifically, the philosophical subjects which have developed themselves within that school, which alarm the church party.'[48] Dr Gillow, a Catholic theologian whom the *Month* regards as the foil to Pattison in the contemporary religious controversy over Oxford education, charges Greats philosophy with being '*limited* to the results of modern thought', which he specifies 'comprise . . . all [the] Atheistical, Rationalistic, Pantheistic, and skeptical

[44] Newman, *Essays Critical and Historical*, 32.
[45] David Oldroyd, *Darwinian Impacts*, 2nd edn. (Sydney: New South Wales University Press, 1983), 246.   [46] Fyffe, 'Study and Opinion', 192.
[47] Sulloway, *Hopkins and the Victorian Temper*, 15.
[48] Pattison, *Suggestions*, 298, 299.

forms of modern unbelief'.[49] The *Dublin Review* of October 1867 writes of 'the terrible and radical danger into which every young Catholic, who goes in for honours in classics is at once necessarily plunged'.[50] '[E]ducation at Oxford', it affirms, 'is infidel to the very core'.[51]

'[T]he fears of the Catholic party' were, according to Pattison's judgement, 'substantially well founded.'[52] In their anxiety over the liberalism of the Broad Churchmen many Catholics were concerned that students who shared the faith and sat for Finals were, as Gillow put it, obliged 'to answer questions on moral philosophy proposed by men whose philosophical views are wholly opposed to the truths of their faith'.[53] Pattison anticipated a 'collision ... impending between the Catholic, or catholicising party, and the liberal party in Oxford, on the subject of the philosophical teaching in the final school'. The Catholic 'party must either conquer, or be content to see all the minds that come under the influence of that training— that is, all the minds of any promise that pass through Oxford— hopelessly lost to them'.[54] In this respect, as in so many others, Hopkins is a remarkable anomaly.

Commentary upon Hopkins' Oxford years almost invariably focuses upon his involvement with Tractarianism and subsequent conversion to Roman Catholicism. There is, however, little evidence to support the common critical assumption that his Tractarianism obliged him to repudiate the intellectual liberalism associated with the Broad Church party. His description of the liberal T. H. Green as 'of a rather offensive style of infidelity',[55] which he made soon after arriving in Oxford and several years before he was taught by him, may be regarded as a Tractarian prejudice. This early opinion may well derive from hearing Green speak at the 'Old Mortality Society', an essay society founded at Balliol in 1856 which provided a forum for liberal and radical speculation at Oxford. Hopkins first came

[49] Quoted in 'Oxford Studies—Mr. Pattison and Dr. Gillow', *The Month*, 11 (July 1869), 103.   [50] Vaughan, 'Eng. Catholic Univ. Education', 421.
[51] Ibid. 419. The opinion is quoted from an anonymous person 'whose authority, gravity, and position in Oxford command the respect of all'.
[52] Pattison, *Suggestions*, 298.
[53] Quoted in 'Oxford Studies—Mr. Pattison and Dr. Gillow', 105.
[54] Pattison, *Suggestions*, 299.
[55] 'To his Mother', 19 Oct. 1863, Letter 43, *Further Letters*, 83.

across Pater at one of these meetings, and appears to have been impressed by his future tutor's 'infidelity' in a paper on, as he told Liddon, 'Fichte's Ideal Student . . . in wh. he denied the Immortality of the soul'.[56] He also heard Pater address the Society later, in May 1866, an occasion which he records simply in his journals as 'Pater talking two hours against Xtianity' (*J.* 138).[57] That he attended this paper, the content of which he found so disagreeable to his faith, nevertheless indicates his intellectual liberalism. The more substantive and consistent evidence of the undergraduate essays and the speculative doctrine of 'instress' and 'inscape' with which they culminate testifies to the deeper and more abiding legacy of Oxford intellectual liberalism. 'A little philosophy', writes Jowett, 'takes us away from God; a great deal brings us back to Him'.[58]

It is clear that, given the nature of Greats during the 1860s, Hopkins could not have achieved his first-class honours without a well developed capacity for free and independent thought. Furthermore, while it is certainly true that Jowett wished to exert a moral influence upon his students and that, especially after the furore over his theological writings, he applied his German-inspired scholarship to the classical texts he taught,[59] it is contrary to the spirit of his liberalism to see it as directed towards compelling students to adopt his Broad Church convictions. Indeed, his practice in tutorials of obscuring his own position so as to encourage independence of thought amongst his students led to a reputation for being contrary: 'to the believer he appeared a sceptic, to the sceptic a believer, to the Humanitarian an Economist, to the Conservative politician, a Socialist, and so forth'.[60]

Although Hopkins did not adopt the Broad Church position it is notable that, according to one of his best friends at Oxford, William Addis, 'He was at first a little tinged with the liberalism prevalent among reading men', and appears to have agreed with at least one application of biblical criticism: 'in a

[56] Quoted from Liddon's diaries, by Jude V. Nixon, *Gerard Manley Hopkins and his Contemporaries: Liddon, Newman, Darwin, and Pater* (New York: Garland, 1994), 170.   [57] See Nixon, *G.M.H. and his Contemporaries*, 173.
[58] *Dialogues of Plato*, trans. Benjamin Jowett, 2nd edn. (Oxford: Clarendon Press, 1875), iv. 158.   [59] Turner, *Greek Heritage*, 416–17.
[60] Abbott and Campbell, *Life and Letters*, i. 391.

walk on Headington Hill he said "I never can believe that the Song of Solomon is more than an ordinary love-song" '.[61] This early tendency toward religious liberalism is acknowledged by Hopkins in a letter of June 1864, where he warns his friend E. H. Coleridge against it: 'Beware of doing what I once thought I could do, *adopt an enlightened Christianity*, I may say, horrible as it is, *be a credit to religion*. This fatal state of mind leads to infidelity, if consistently and logically developed.'[62]

IV

Hopkins was evidently imbued through Greats philosophy with the liberalism of Jowett and his acolytes. He was, for example, impatient with 'the inexplicable, mystical character' of certain accounts of cause and effect (D. VI 2, fo. 5) and anxious that his thought should not be confused with 'mysticism' (*J.* 83). Although Hopkins rejected the liberal doctrine of the Broad Church movement this did not preclude him from taking an open, *intellectually* liberal, approach to religious questions. It is, as the editors of the *Journals and Papers* observe, 'remarkable' that as late as 1865 he had read neither the *Tracts for the Times* nor the *Essays and Reviews* (*J.* 327). The titles appear consecutively in a list of 'Books to be read' (*J.* 56). The fact that Hopkins had been at Oxford for two years without reading the *Essays and Reviews* is seen by the editors to refute Addis' imputation of religious liberalism (*J.* 327). Curiously, Hopkins' similar neglect of the *Tracts* is not seen to discredit his Tractarianism. While the juxtaposition of these antipathetic works in Hopkins' reading list indicates his intellectual liberalism, an intention to examine the radical texts of both sides of the current religious debate at Oxford, the inference that the editors draw from it highlights the reluctance of his traditional commentators to associate this quality with him.[63]

[61] Quoted in Lahey, *GMH*, 19.

[62] 'To E. H. Coleridge', 1 June 1864, Letter 5, *Further Letters*, 16–17.

[63] See e.g. Bernard Bergonzi, *Gerard Manley Hopkins* (London: Macmillan, 1977), 12, and more recently, White, *Hopkins*, 112. That Hopkins read at least one of the *Essays and Reviews* is clear from the notes he took from Mark Pattison's contribution (D. VII 2).

The letter to his father in which Hopkins explains the grounds for his conversion indicates that his decision was not opposed to the rationalism encouraged by Greats at the time. While he had evaluated 'arguments for the Church of England' and 'long ago felt there were none that w[oul]d hold water', he arrived at the Catholic position by 'simple and strictly drawn arguments partly my own, partly others'.[64] This is not to say that his assent was merely *notional* in the sense that Newman gives to the term in the *Grammar of Assent*, but only to highlight that it was inextricable from intellectual conviction. Similarly it was probably the arguments of the Broad Churchmen that led him to see 'the Tractarian ground . . . broken to pieces under my feet'.[65] Another reason which he gives for his conversion to Catholicism is 'its consistency and unity',[66] the systematic quality that he champions in 'The Probable Future of Metaphysics', and which he sees to proceed from the Eucharist. It is in this principle that, after boarding for a time at the Tractarian 'Half-way House', he finds his spiritual home: 'enter these walls, one said: | He is with you in the breaking of the bread' (No. 71).

Hopkins, writing to E. H. Coleridge in June 1864, explains his conviction that the Eucharist is the fundamental proposition from which Christianity derives not only its emotional and spiritual power but its logical consistency: 'The great aid to belief and object of belief is the doctrine of the Real Presence in the Blessed Sacrament of the Altar. Religion without that is sombre, dangerous, illogical, with that it is—not to speak of its grand consistency and certainty—*loveable*. Hold that and you will gain all Catholic truth.' These attributes of logic and 'consistency' match Catholicism as a foil against the propositions of a Broad Church '*enlightened Christianity*' which he believes lead 'to infidelity, if consistently and logically developed'.[67] By writing of High-Church and Catholic theology in the same terms as he discusses liberal theology, Hopkins demonstrates his confidence in the rational coherence of his religious position and its consequent ability to meet and transcend modern forms of rationalism such as biblical criticism and Darwinism. His regard for the Eucharist is not simply an 'attitude' of High-Church

---

[64] 'To his Father', 16 Oct. 1866, Letter 47, *Further Letters*, 94, 93.
[65] Ibid. 92.   [66] Ibid. 93.   [67] Letter 5, ibid. 17.

ritualism, such as that which Geldart attributed him with, but the radical premiss of his faith and thought.

Hopkins' propensities for both religious conservatism and intellectual liberalism are dramatized in the companion poems 'Heaven-Haven (*a nun takes the veil*)' and 'I must hunt down the prize', which were written in late July 1864. The former expresses a wish to flee a hostile and unsympathetic world:

> I have desired to go
>   Where springs not fail,
> To fields where flies no sharp and sided hail
>   And a few lilies blow.
>
> And I have asked to be
>   Where no storms come,
> Where the green swell is in the havens dumb,
>   And out of the swing of the sea.   (No. 20b)

The imagery of the poem includes traditional emblems of the turbulence, uncertainties, and disappointments of human life,[68] and may be read accordingly as a conventional yearning to escape the biblical 'vale of misery'.[69] The escape envisaged is, however, not from mortal life to death, but from the secular world to an insular religious life. The poem presents two views of nature: the predominant one of strife and chance, which suggests the religious upheavals and uncertainties of the early 1860s, and its negation in the harmonious and gentle cosmology associated with the religious refuge.

While the imagery of flux suggests the foment and controversy provoked by Darwinism and biblical criticism it can be understood more concretely as representing the conception of the natural world that was promoted by such rationalist movements. Biblical criticism, by bringing into question the literal truth of the Bible, contributed to the contemporary scepticism over the account of the creation of the world in Genesis that was fostered by modern science. Lyellian geology and Darwinian biology described nature as governed by continuous processes devoid of any principle of ultimate purpose. The earth's surface is, according to Charles Lyell's uniformitarianism,

---

[68] *The Poetical Works of Gerard Manley Hopkins*, ed. Norman H. MacKenzie (Oxford: Clarendon Press, 1990), 240.   [69] Ps. 84: 6.

formed by relatively constant meteorological agents as well as by the more violent and random phenomena of volcanic activity. Darwinian biology similarly explains organic nature as proceeding from instabilities in the relations between organisms and their environment. Darwin's principle of natural selection places violence and suffering at the heart of the modern conception of nature, 'red in tooth and claw'.[70] The formulation at this time of the second law of thermodynamics, which states that all forms of energy in the universe are increasingly dissipated over time, also contributed suggestively to this view of the natural world, 'Where springs fail . . .'. The contemporary depiction of a hostile and dissolute universe promoted by these scientific developments is reflected in Hopkins' description of nature beyond the domain of the convent. In addition to the failing springs, there are storms, the vicious randomness of 'sharp and sided hail', and the menace rather than the measure implicitly attributed to 'the swing of the sea'.

A traditional, harmonious, Christian cosmology is presented by the poem as marginalized, having its only refuge within the artificial confines of an exclusively religious community. With the exception of the 'few lilies', the benign conception of nature that the poem's persona so desires is conveyed in a series of negations of the hostile external world. The defensive persona of the poem is comparable to the characterization of Hopkins that Green gave upon hearing of his conversion: 'I imagine him—perhaps uncharitably—to be one of those, like his ideal J. H. Newman, who instead of simply opening themselves to the revelation of God in the reasonable world, are fain to put themselves into an attitude—saintly, it is true, but still an attitude.'[71] Hopkins would appear to have taken the veil of the reactionary persona of 'Heaven-Haven'.

The poet's attitude to change and challenging circumstances is, however, more ambivalent than the insular stance of 'Heaven-

[70] Tennyson, 'In Memoriam', st. 56.
[71] Letter from T. H. Green to H. S. Holland, 29 Dec. 1868, in Stephen Paget (ed.), *Henry Scott Holland: Memoir and Letters* (London: John Murray, 1921), 29. Green's impression correlates with Addis' account of Hopkins at this time: 'Soon before his reception by Newman he used to invoke the Saints and became full of devotion to the Mother of Our Lord. This would astonish me, for nobody else I knew "went so far"' (quoted in Lahey, *GMH*, 19).

Haven' suggests. Its companion poem expresses a contrastingly bold resolve:

> I must hunt down the prize
>   Where my heart lists.
> Must see the eagle's bulk, render'd in mists,
>   Hang of a treble size.
>
> Must see the waters roll
>   Where the seas set
> Towards wastes where round the ice-blocks tilt and fret
>   Not so far from the pole.   (No. 21)

It can be assumed that as the poem does not specify the nature of 'the prize' to be sought it is a similar object to that which is desired in 'Heaven-Haven', namely, a sense of spiritual well-being and security, of being at home in the world. However, while this goal is identified in the first poem with an idealized refuge from the storms and hail of the naturalistic world, in the companion poem it is sought for eagerly at the site of their most intense and remorseless occurrence. The word 'lists' in the second line of the poem is, through its meaning of 'desires', reminiscent of the first line of 'Heaven-Haven', while its other meaning of 'combat' disqualifies the merely passive yearning of the companion poem, replacing it with an active and imperative resolve to struggle with protean nature for the heart's 'prize'. The synoptic meaning of the word here is of a desire that requires a determined battle if it is to be satisfied.

The Arctic was beginning to be explored during the middle of the nineteenth century and was an object of fascinated public attention, especially when in 1857 an expedition made the sensational discovery of the remains of Sir John Franklin's ill-fated expedition to find the North-West Passage, which had set out twelve years earlier.[72] Sir Edwin Landseer made this grim episode the 'starting point'[73] for his painting *Man Proposes, God Disposes* (1863–4) which depicts two polar bears contentedly

---

[72] Norman MacKenzie notes this historical connection and compares some of the poem's phrases to similar references in Capt. Francis M'Clintock's book on his discovery of the remains of the Franklin expedition (*Poetical Works*, ed. MacKenzie, 241).

[73] Robert Rosenblum and H. W. Janson, *Art of the Nineteenth Century* (London: Thames & Hudson, 1984), 273.

mauling the human and other remains of an Arctic expedition. The picture, which Hopkins almost certainly saw in the Royal Academy exhibition of 1864 a few days before writing 'Heaven-Haven' and its companion,[74] highlights the forbidding foreignness of the polar landscape and its aptness as an emblem for the modern depiction of nature as an inhuman and aimless flux. 'I must hunt down the prize' states a bold resolve to reclaim such territory for a more coherent view of nature than that which it ostensibly presents. This attitude is evident from Hopkins' nature observations in the diaries and journals, where he is typically drawn to seek determining laws or patterns in the most intense instances of natural flux, such as oak trees, which 'differ much' (*J.* 145),[75] sunsets, clouds, and running water.

'Heaven-Haven' and 'I must hunt down the prize' can be interpreted allegorically as presenting complementary strategies to vouchsafe the grounds of faith in an age of aggressive scientism and widespread liberalism. To make a retreat in the manner yearned for in the former poem is effectively to be compliant with the offensive forces which were invading territory that traditionally sustained Anglican belief, such as the natural theological conception of nature, which Darwinian biology had recently stood on its head. 'I must hunt down the prize' refuses such compliance and moreover states a resolve to mount its own offensive, its own colonizing activity. Hopkins' intention here appears to be to find the grounds that will enable him to reassert his religious and metaphysical values in ostensibly hostile territory. The colonizer's 'prize' here is the enlargement of what can be regarded as home territory, the province of Hopkins' Christian-idealist view of the world. He will decide to live not in a refuge defined by a series of negations, the qualifying 'no' of 'Heaven-Haven', but to uphold his central values of assent and affirmation in the face of whatever experience may confront him: 'I did say yes | O at líghtning and láshed ród' (No. 101, st. 2).

The following chapters argue that Hopkins makes a clear

---

[74] An undated diary entry made between 22 and 25 July 1864 indicates that Hopkins was acquainted with the Royal Academy exhibition for this year (*J.* 31). The autograph MS of the poem was written during the last week of July (*J.* 33; *Poetical Works*, ed. MacKenzie, 241).   [75] See Ch. 8, Sect. V.

choice in favour of the liberal stance of 'I must hunt down the prize', preferring to develop his faith through the creation of a new system meant to withstand contemporary threats to belief than to retreat to an outmoded and reactionary Christianity. If we accept the rather caricatured terms in which Arnold Toynbee presents this opposition in his manuscript preface to T. H. Green's *Two Lay Sermons* then Hopkins' position aligns him with the liberals rather than with Newman: 'Cardinal Newman . . . urged men to take refuge from the all corroding force of reason in the authority of the Church. Mr. Green on the contrary had absolute confidence in reason as the creator, and not the destroyer, of man's spiritual life.'[76] Hopkins' obituary in the Jesuit year-book includes a poignant reminiscence by a friend from St Bruno's which testifies to the abiding liberal legacy of Greats philosophy for him:

I have rarely known anyone who sacrificed so much in undertaking the yoke of religion. If I had known him outside, I should have said that his love of speculation and originality of thought would make it almost impossible for him to submit his intellect to authority, and I take it as a great mark of his personal holiness and of the love God had for him, that he willingly carried the Cross (for in his case it was no light one) that every good religious has to carry after Jesus Christ.[77]

Hopkins shares the belief of liberals such as Jowett and Green that however remote the grounds for faith may seem to be in the modern age they are consistent with intellectual integrity, and are ultimately revealed through the mind's pursuit of truth, wherever it may lead. 'I must hunt down the prize' answers the languid 'desire' for escape of 'Heaven-Haven' and all the empty negations this involves, with an affirmative and imperative 'Must'.

V

The imperative of 'I must hunt down the prize' is epistemic: 'Must see the eagle's bulk, render'd in mists, | Hang of a treble

---

[76] Toynbee, Balliol, T. H. Green Papers, MS II. 1(d). A catalogue of the Green Papers is given in Geoffrey Thomas, *The Moral Philosophy of T. H. Green* (Oxford: Clarendon Press, 1987), 376–86.

[77] Quoted in 'Father Gerard Hopkins', *Letters and Notices*, 20/99 (Mar. 1890), 175–6.

size'. Hopkins is concerned here with the grounds of perception, the problem of whether our ideas are simply created by
the mind or have an objective reality. The 'eagle's bulk' is either
a real object obfuscated by the polar mists or an illusion, a trick
of light and mist akin to the 'Brocken spectre' which provides
the focus for Coleridge's meditation on this fundamental problem of knowledge in the poem 'Constancy to an Ideal Object'.[78]
The dilemma is stated in a poem that dates from a few weeks
after the composition of 'I must hunt down the prize':

> It was a hard thing to undo this knot.
> The rainbow shines, but only in the thought
> Of him that looks. Yet not in that alone,
> For who makes rainbows by invention?   (No. 24)

Hopkins does not have any doubts about the objective existence of the external world and our capacity for perceiving it.
What disturbs him in the early poem cited above is that he
is unable to establish the grounds for this metaphysical faith.
His need for a theoretical basis for knowledge is addressed by
Greats philosophy and explored by him in his early essays. He
writes of the need for a 'new Realism' to oppose 'the prevalent
philosophy of . . . flux' (*J.* 120). Hopkins wishes to combat positivism and materialism by establishing the existence of fixed
forms, an impulse that has its counterpart in the heightened
awareness of the natural flux that he shares with his contemporaries. He both insists that natural 'type[s] or species' are
like 'the roots of [musical] chords . . . mathematically fixed' (*J.*
120) and delights in 'Áll things counter, original, spare, strange'
(No. 121). He accordingly sets himself the delicate task of reconciling the two principles in a synthesis that diminishes neither
one for the sake of the other. In the midst of the Darwinian
assault upon essentialism he seeks a new affirmation of form that
acknowledges and is able to incorporate the fluidity of nature,
a paradoxical requirement that 'I must hunt down the prize'
expresses with the metaphor of the Arctic Ocean: 'Must see
the waters roll | Where the seas set'.[79]

---

[78] See ll. 25–32. The phenomenon, which is of a greatly enlarged image that
occurs as the low setting sun casts the perceiver's shadow onto a body of mist,
highlights the problem of the ultimate status of the 'Ideal Object', the mental idea
of a thing.

[79] Or: 'Must see the green seas roll | Where waters set' (No. 21 (b)).

Hopkins' use of the rainbow as the focus for his epistemological speculations in 'It was a hard thing to undo this knot'
can be traced to Wordsworth.[80] This example, together with the
other phenomena of sunlight and water vapour invoked in 'I
must hunt down the prize', places Hopkins' approach to the
problem of perception within the romantic tradition of Wordsworth and Coleridge. What makes Hopkins' brand of romanticism especially interesting, however, is the fact that it does not
develop primarily from the English literary tradition initiated
by Coleridge's appropriations of Kant, Schelling, and Fichte,[81]
and which became progressively more dilute and domesticated
as the century proceeded, but through a fresh (though no less
idiosyncratic) infusion of German idealism that entered the
arena of English ideas from the middle of the century, largely
through the efforts of Benjamin Jowett. By the mid-1860s the
Regius Professor of Greek and some of his former students had
developed interesting and important new readings of Kant and
Hegel. Principal amongst this group was Hopkins' tutor T. H.
Green, who effectively detonated the 'Anglo-Hegelian' or 'British Idealist' movement that dominated English philosophy during the final quarter of the nineteenth century and well into
the present century.[82]

Pattison, writing once again in the *Suggestions on Academical
Organisation* of 1868, remarks of Greats that 'The horizon of
the examination is as wide as that of philosophical literature.'[83]
Indeed his frequently made observation that 'a limitless field'[84]
of philosophy forms the ambit of the Greats examination is
reflected in Hopkins' essays, where the range of thought discussed encompasses not only Plato and Aristotle, but also the
Pre-Socratics, the Sophists, the Stoics, Descartes, Hobbes, Locke,
Hume, Kant, Hegel, Hamilton, Mill, and Comte. Unconstrained
by a rigid curriculum and encouraged by the broad examination
outline given by the 1850 statute, Oxford lecturers and tutors

[80] See Stephen Prickett, *Coleridge and Wordsworth: The Poetry of Growth* (Cambridge: Cambridge University Press, 1970), ch. 1.
[81] This legacy is discussed by Patricia Ball, *The Science of Aspects: The Changing Role
of Fact in the Work of Coleridge, Ruskin and Hopkins* (London: Athlone Press, 1971),
ch. 3.
[82] Anthony Manser, *Bradley's Logic* (Oxford: Basil Blackwell, 1983), 2–3, 16–17.
See also Pattison, *Memoirs* (London: Macmillan, 1885), 167.
[83] Pattison, *Suggestions*, 291.   [84] Ibid. 272.

were able to broaden the general field of study in Greats philosophy whilst at the same time directing it towards current philosophical concerns, so that in the examination 'the classical books offered by the candidate afford[ed] rather the excuse, than the material'.[85] An important implication of the nebulous scope of the philosophy examination is pointed out anonymously by a person whom the *Month* for July 1869 assures us is 'at present Tutor of one of the most distinguished Colleges':[86] 'But it is obvious that when questions on philosophy are so large and vague as are often now put in the schools, there is a probability that they will often be suggested to examiners by the books, other than Plato and Aristotle, which they have been reading'. The perceived consequence of this is that 'an examinee will think it worth his while to read any philosophical writings within his reach, which he either knows to be in vogue among Oxford graduates, or suspects may be in vogue among them, because at present much read in the learned world'.[87] A more positive testimony to the prominence of modern thought in Greats is given by Pattison, who maintains that 'The best [examination] papers', a class to which Hopkins' paper belongs, are 'abounding with all the ideas with which modern society, and its best current literature, are charged'. Indeed he goes so far as to make the following bold declaration:

I do not believe that there exists at this moment in Europe any public institution for education, where what are called 'the results of modern thought', on all political and speculative subjects (the philosophy of religion, perhaps, alone excepted), are so entirely at home, as they are in our honour examinations in the school of 'Literae Humaniores'— the examination, be it observed, not as prescribed by statute, but as actually worked.[88]

What are referred to in the above passage as 'the results of modern thought' can be characterized by a broad opposition of the type that Hopkins makes in 'The Probable Future of Metaphysics' as positivistic 'materialism' and the 'new Realism'. Fyffe reports in 1869 that the 'general tendencies of thought among . . . the men engaged in study and tuition' at Oxford are

[85] Ibid. 291.   [86] 'Oxford Studies—Mr. Pattison and Dr. Gillow', 106.
[87] Ibid. 107.   [88] Pattison, *Suggestions*, 291–2.

'Positivism' and 'the more theoretical philosophy which connects itself with the names of Kant and Hegel'.[89]

Positivism was most strongly represented at Oxford by J. S.
Mill's *A System of Logic*, the single most read and discussed work
of modern philosophy amongst Greats students in the 1860s.
It 'forced its way', says Jowett, 'because it was the best and most
available treatise' on logic,[90] and consequently became a *de facto*
text. Furthermore, given that the approach to texts in Greats
philosophy was not prescribed by a curriculum and their contemporary relevance was often emphasized, it is not surprising
to find that the significance of Mill's book extended beyond its
use in teaching logic. R. L. Nettleship, who was, like Hopkins,
tutored by T. H. Green, is well placed as a source for the present
discussion. In his 'Memoir' of Green he recalls that 'the writings
of J. S. Mill, especially his *Logic*, were largely read, and either
by direct assimilation, or through the discussion and criticism
which they occasioned, were probably the most powerful element in the intellectual leaven of the place'.[91] Mill's positivism
was the object of both 'assimilation' and 'criticism', providing
a normative standard against which philosophical positions at
Oxford were defined and gauged. The use of German idealism
to criticize this orthodoxy was endemic to Oxford and most
focused at Balliol.

VI

The influence of German idealism was felt at Oxford earlier
in the century through the Tractarians' reading of Coleridge
and Carlyle. It was available around the middle of the century through H. L. Mansel, whom Pattison credits with having
'first introduced Kant into Oxford',[92] and who as Waynflete Professor of Moral and Metaphysical Philosophy until 1867 is likely
to have lectured to Hopkins.[93] Furthermore, as Anthony Manser

[89] Fyffe, 'Study and Opinion', 191.
[90] Quoted in Diderik Roll-Hansen, *The Academy 1869–79: Victorian Intellectuals in Revolt* (Copenhagen: Rosenkilde & Bagger, 1958), 50.
[91] Nettleship's 'Memoir' in Green, *Works*, iii. p. lxx.
[92] Pattison, *Memoirs*, 166.
[93] Hopkins was, as the following chapters demonstrate, especially interested in Moral and Metaphysical Philosophy and would have been encouraged by Jowett

notes, a satire that Mansel wrote on the 1850 Royal Commission indicates the currency that German idealist ideas had for an Oxford audience as early as the 1850s:

> Ye who scan
> The Universe of Being, and reveal
> How Werden, eldest born of Seyn and Nichts,
> Gave birth to Daseyn, whence in long succession
> The world of Thought and Substance. Ye who fathom
> The hidden myths of Scripture and essence
> Of Worship, Function of Psychology,—
> I summon you, appear.
> > *Enter* Chorus of Professors.
> > > Strophe *or* Twist.
> Professors we,
> From over the sea,
> From the land where Professors in plenty be;
> And we thrive and flourish, as well we may,
> In the land that produced one Kant with a K
> > And many Cants with a C.
> Where Hegel taught, to his profit and fame,
> That something and nothing were one and the same;
> The absolute difference never a jot being
> 'Twixt having and not having, being and not being,
> But wisely declined to extend his notion
> To the finite relations of thalers and groschen . . .[94]

'Oxford is', as Edwin Hatch observes in 1858, 'very slow in embodying its thoughts in print'.[95] Mansel's poem reminds us that 'often in Oxford, the oral tradition may be in advance of the written'.[96]

---

and Green, who shared Mansel's broad sympathy for German idealism, to attend the Waynflete Professor's lectures. The professorial lectures for each term were advertised together irrespective of the college from which they originated, so that, for instance, notice of lectures for Hilary term 1867 by, amongst others, Jowett of Balliol and Mansel of Magdalen, share the same bill (Papers Relating to the University 1867, Bodleian Library, Oxford. G. A. Oxon. C. 83, Item 5). Another poster (ibid., Item 16) announces that the Waynflete lectures for this term were on Socrates, and on Aristotle's *Ethics*, which Higgins ('Hopkins and "The Jowler"', 164) notes, Hopkins studied at this time.   [94] Quoted in Manser, 9–10.

[95] Hatch, review of 'Ethics', 371.

[96] Manser, *Bradley's Logic*, 10. See Mansel, *Letters, Lectures, and Reviews, Including The Phrontisterion*, ed. Henry W. Chandler (London: John Murray, 1873), which testifies to the prevalence of Kantian ideas in Mansel's Oxford lectures from 1850 to the time that Hopkins was at Oxford.

Greats examination papers in 1863 and 1869 each included a question which cited an extract from Kant, while others from the intervening years refer to the Kantian distinction between analytic and synthetic judgements and require an explanation of the term 'transcendental'.[97] The Taylorean Professor of Modern European Languages and translator of Kant, Friedrich Max Müller, established general courses in 1865 on modern German literature, which included some philosophical material,[98] and a class in February 1866 to read Kant's *Critique of Pure Reason* in German.[99] These circumstances are, however, peripheral to the German-inspired philosophical movement which arose at Balliol: 'when the most progressive of the younger Oxonian thinkers were turning towards . . . [Comte and Mill] as safe and fruitful guides in the interpretation of life, Jowett and his pupils were impregnating Balliol, and, through Balliol, the mind of Oxford and the nation, with German idealism'.[100]

Anthony Quinton writes that 'the only really effective presentation of Hegel's ideas must have been in the personal teaching of Jowett'.[101] Writing to a friend in 1870 Jowett describes himself as ever vigilant against the dangers of those types of thought that are opposed to idealism: 'I always feel the danger of utilitarianism or materialism lowering the character of education and of life'.[102] According to Edward Caird, his student and eventual successor as Master of Balliol, Jowett was in 'the earlier part of his life . . . eager to direct students to new sources of thought opened by the German philosophy and theology'.[103]

---

[97] G. R. G. Mure, 'Oxford and Philosophy', *Philosophy*, 12 (1937), 297, 298. The tendency towards direct engagement with German idealist philosophy became formally established in the revised examination statutes of 1872 in which portions of Kant's *Critique of Pure Reason* and *Critique of Practical Reason* and the entire *Groundwork of the Metaphysics of Morals* were prescribed for the Honours school of Literae Humaniores. Candidates could present these texts in German, or in English translation.

[98] Papers Relating to the Proceedings of the University 1865, Bodl. G. A. Oxon. C. 81, Item 43; Papers Relating to the University, 1864, Bodl. G. A. Oxon. C. 80, Item 175.

[99] Papers Relating to the University, 1866, Bodl. G. A. Oxon. C. 82, Item 38.

[100] William S. Knickerbocker, *Creative Oxford: Its Influence in Victorian Literature* (Syracuse, NY: Syracuse University Press, 1925), 126.

[101] A. Quinton, *Absolute Idealism* (London: Oxford University Press, 1972), 21.

[102] 'To R. B. D. Morier' [1870], in Evelyn Abbott and Lewis Campbell (eds.), *Letters of Benjamin Jowett, M.A.* (London: John Murray, 1899), 182.

[103] 'Professor Jowett', *International Journal of Ethics*, 8 (Oct. 1897), 45.

The importance of German idealism both to his own thought, an enthusiasm which waned during the 1870s, and for Greats studies at Balliol is acknowledged in a letter written in 1885 to a patron who had donated busts of Hegel and Kant to the college library: 'The two philosophers look at one another, and perhaps may find themselves at home, for they have been more read in Balliol College than probably anywhere else in England. Though not an Hegelian I think that I have gained more from Hegel than from any other philosopher.'[104]

Jowett had been to Germany with Arthur Stanley in 1844, where they consulted Hegel's chief disciple J. E. Erdmann as to 'the best manner of approaching' his master's work. The travellers also studied Kant's *Critique of Pure Reason* together in German.[105] Jowett attempted a translation of either Hegel's smaller or greater *Logic* (his biographers do not specify which), with his colleague Temple, a project which was abandoned when the latter left Balliol in 1848.[106] Commentators, from his original biographers to Quinton, 'assert that he was the first person to give any real currency in England to Hegelian philosophy'.[107]

Manser suggests that Jowett's trip to Germany and enthusiasm for Hegel should be understood in the context of the Tractarian controversy of the 1840s, arguing that the reason why this foreign and forbidding philosophy was embraced so enthusiastically by him and by 'many . . . who became professional philosophers in the [following] thirty years' was the foundation that it offered for Christian belief, 'one that was not liable to lead to atheism or to Rome'.[108] The decline of the Oxford Movement and the ascendency of positivism and Darwinian evolution meant that by the 1860s atheism was perceived by Jowett and his peers as the greater threat to the religious well-being of Oxford youth. It was due to the desire to protect religion from such factors that, Quinton maintains, Hegelianism emerged in England at this time, some thirty years after the philosopher's death.[109] This provided a receptive environment for the publica-

---

[104] Abbott and Campbell, *Life and Letters*, ii. 250.   [105] Ibid. i. 90.
[106] Ibid. i. 129. He also met Schelling and read his *System of Nature* (ibid. i. 98, 160).   [107] Hinchliff, *Benjamin Jowett*, 80.
[108] Manser, *Bradley's Logic*, 11.
[109] The other main consideration prompting British Hegelianism, according to Quinton (*Absolute Idealism*, 5) 'was the need for a politics of social responsibility'.

tion in 1865 of J. H. Stirling's *The Secret of Hegel.* The construction that Stirling places upon German philosophy in his book
is typical of the early British idealists: 'Kant and Hegel . . . have
no object but to restore Faith'.[110] Fyffe characterizes the opposing schools of thought at Oxford by their attitude to religion:

It is not hard to see how very different will be the character and tendencies of this [German-inspired] philosophy from those of Positivism.
The metaphysical and theological speculation which the latter dis-
carded as so much moonshine now appears as not only real but of
the very highest necessary truth. Those who are of this way of thinking, while paying all due honour to the sciences of observation, will
maintain that the spirit of man is one thing and the natural world
another; and, denying that the methods of physical science can ex-
haust all that there is to be known about man, will turn with interest
to theology as the highest of all studies, and endeavour in the service
of truth to reconcile religion and philosophy.[111]

The influence upon Fyffe of his teacher T. H. Green is evident
here. Although Green was the first fellow of the university not
to take holy orders, he nevertheless belongs with those whom
the above extract distinguishes by their commitment to religion.
This is testified to by Green's tutor and friend, C. S. Parker:

I think the deepest interest he felt was in combining intellectual with
moral and religious insight. On the intellectual side he seemed much
taken by what little we knew of Hegel's logic, embracing in one vast
syllogism the universe of thought and of existence. On the moral side
his early training had given him a high and holy ideal, with a deep
sense of man's inability to realise it otherwise than through a Divine
indwelling Spirit. Thus philosophy was to him no cold and barren
speculation, but a cherished creed, a help to noble life.[112]

Green's philosophical stance and teaching were directed against
'Comtism and materialism': 'against these', he writes in 1864,
'I have been declaiming in a humble way for the last six years'.[113]

---

[110] J. H. Stirling, *The Secret of Hegel* (London: Longmans, 1865), i. p. xii. Quinton
(*Absolute Idealism*, 9) quotes Muirhead: 'British idealism has been from the first a
philosophy of religion'. [111] Fyffe, 'Study and Opinion', 191.
[112] C. S. Parker, Letter to Nettleship, 26 Sept., 1886. Balliol, T. H. Green Papers,
MS II. 1(d). [113] Nettleship's 'Memoir' in Green, *Works*, iii. p. xli.

The corollary to this, his reworking of Kant and Hegel, is abundantly evident from his early essays on 'The Philosophy of Aristotle' and 'The Popular Philosophy in its Relation to Life'.[114]

Green lectured on Aristotle upon his return to Balliol as Senior Dean in October 1865, after a brief stint as the assistant commissioner with the Schools Enquiry Commission. Hopkins' studies of the *Nicomachean Ethics* begin at this time,[115] and it can confidently be assumed that Hopkins attended Green's lectures. An essay of his that Green signed (D. II 5; *J.* 115–17) indicates that he tutored Hopkins at this period, while a later notebook entitled 'Essays for T. H. Green Esq.' establishes that he also tutored Hopkins during Hilary term 1867.[116] But Hopkins would have seen much more of his tutor than these records indicate. Fyffe, who sat for the Finals examination in Greats in 1867, a few months after Hopkins, and like him gained a First, recalls that, 'Apart from lectures', he and his peers would see Green 'sometimes at breakfasts and in afternoon walks, but most regularly in the evening, twice a week with essays'.[117]

Jowett, according to Father Lahey, 'admits' that during the 1860s he was seeing every student at Balliol every week.[118] Lesley Higgins observes that Hopkins, as well as attending Jowett's lectures, was tutored by him for almost every term of his four year degree course.[119] Both Jowett's and Green's interest in their students extended to the pastoral concerns with their general welfare that were an important part of being an Oxford tutor at this time.[120] Indeed, both conceived of the teaching of metaphysics in an age of increasing hostility to religion as an especially important contribution to their students' well-being.

Hopkins writes in April 1867 that 'Jowett put me through a two days' examination',[121] a clear sign that the professor thought him a student worthy of his time. Jowett's abiding memory and

---

[114] Both essays were first published in the *North British Review* (a periodical that Hopkins read, *J.* 60), the former in Sept. 1866, the latter in Mar. 1868. They are reprinted in Green, *Works*, iii. 46–91, 92–125.
[115] This is recorded in the Report Book kept by the Master of Balliol, Robert Scott (Schmidt, 'Classical Studies', 182).   [116] Schmidt, ibid. 179, 180.
[117] Fyffe, Balliol, T. H. Green Papers, MS II. 1(b), Notebook 2, fo. 115.
[118] Lahey, *GMH*, 15.   [119] Higgins, 'Hopkins and the "Jowler"', 149.
[120] The duties of the college tutor as they were in the 1860s are described in Nettleship, 'Memoir', in Green, *Works*, iii. pp. lxiii–iv.
[121] 'To his Mother', 13 Apr. 1867, Letter 49, *Further Letters*, 100.

high opinion of Hopkins' scholarship is evident from the reference he gave on his behalf to University College Dublin in 1884. Hopkins' obituary in the *Month*, whilst recording that 'the recommendatory letters presented when he sought election' all 'spoke so highly of his character and attainments', singles out that contributed by Jowett 'in praise of his scholarship'.[122] There is, however, no clear evidence of Hopkins' personal attitude to Jowett. According to Geldart's autobiography, Hopkins admired Jowett's 'purity'.[123] Generally the professor appears to have been well liked and was, as Pater attests, famous amongst students in the early 1860s for 'his great originality as a writer and thinker'.[124] The following account from 1867 sums up the plethora of testimonies to Jowett's influence upon his students: 'as the foremost man of the foremost college, as possessing wide-spread personal influence, as the friend and guide of most of the ablest of the younger students, the Regius Professor of Greek might well be taken as the chief and the mouthpiece of all the fresher and younger intellects of Oxford'.[125] Judging from his initial impression, and notwithstanding the observation of a certain awkwardness which was often noted by his students, Hopkins seems to have been well disposed towards Jowett: 'when you can get him to talk he is amusing, but when the opposite, it is terribly embar[r]assing'.[126]

Jowett's student T. H. Green also earned a reputation as a dedicated and influential teacher. Nettleship testifies to 'The power which his teaching exercised upon others'.[127] Indeed he came to be largely responsible for the shape of philosophical studies at Oxford from the 1870s, much as Jowett was from the 1850s. He seems, however, to have exercised this power in spite of perceived deficiencies in personal charm and fluency of expression.[128] Fyffe testifies to the popularity of his lectures[129] and that 'he possessed in a singular degree the sympathy of

---

[122] 'Father Gerard Hopkins', *Month*, 176.
[123] Quoted in Bergonzi, *GMH*, 12.
[124] Abbott and Campbell, *Life and Letters*, i. 329.
[125] Quoted in Vaughan, 'Eng. Catholic Univ. Education', 422, from an anonymous Oxford Anglican source who is described as one of 'the best intellectual observers in England of the advance of modern thought'.
[126] 'To his Mother', 22 Apr. 1863, Letter 40, *Further Letters*, 73.
[127] Nettleship, 'Memoir', in Green, *Works*, iii, p. lxvi.
[128] Green, *Works*, iii, pp. lxiv–v.   [129] Ibid. p. lxiv.

those men whom he taught'.[130] According to this contemporary
report Green's earliest students 'all conceived a strong liking for
him'.[131] Indeed, it seems that Hopkins and Green 'always liked'
each other. Hopkins called on Green at Oxford in 1879, and
upon hearing of his death in 1882 wrote to Baillie 'I always liked
and admired poor Green. He seemed to me upright in mind
and life.'[132] Similarly Green remarks of Hopkins: 'I never had
his intimacy, but always liked him very much.'[133]

While Jowett and Green both encouraged Hopkins in the
development of his idealist thought, they did so using different
teaching methods. Jowett, unlike Green, was 'a critic of philosophy rather than a philosopher'.[134] While 'He . . . acknowledged
the debt which as a thinker he owed to German philosophy',[135]
Jowett adopted neither it nor any other doctrine as a philosophical creed. His tutorial teaching practices were, as was mentioned
earlier, fundamentally Socratic in nature, proceeding by eristic,
conversation, and complex irony. As his evidence to the Select
Committee of 16 July 1867 shows, Jowett conceived of his ped-
agogical function to be to act as a stimulus and catalyst to the
student's developing thought: 'It seems to me that it is good
teaching to stimulate his thoughts and to give him by anticipation general notions which he might be a long time in acquiring for himself.'[136] Abbott and Campbell write that 'it gave him
a real pain to see any of his friends fall, as he thought, under
the dominion of a system'.[137] Jowett came to regard Green as

---

[130] Cited by Nettleship, ibid. p. lxv.   [131] Cited by Nettleship, ibid. p. lxiv.
[132] 6 May 1882, Letter 138, *Further Letters*, 249.
[133] Paget (ed.), *Holland*, 29. Green's letter to Holland proceeds to refer to Hopkins
as 'a fine nature' (p. 30). Indeed, the latter part of the letter, which has been neglected by Hopkins commentators, casts light upon the earlier 'uncharitabl[e]' description of Hopkins as 'one of those . . . who . . . are fain to put themselves into an
attitude' (p. 29). Such remarks arose, Green writes, as 'a vent for passing irritation'.
The extent of his irritation is evidently a measure of his confidence in Hopkins'
intellectual and moral capacities: 'It vexes me to the heart to think of a fine nature
being victimised by a system which . . . I hold to be subversive of the Family and the
State, and which puts the service of an exceptional institution, or the saving of the
individual soul, in opposition to loyal service to society' (p. 30).
[134] Abbott and Campbell, *Life and Letters*, ii. 193.   [135] Ibid. i. 261.
[136] *Special Report from the Select Committee in the Oxford and Cambridge Universities
Education Bill, together with the Proceedings of the Committee, Minutes of Evidence, and
Appendix [and] Index* ([London,] n.p., 1867), 142.
[137] Abbott and Campbell, *Life and Letters*, ii. 193.

the most significant of such casualties, seeing his teaching to
be marred by a doctrinal adherence to systematic metaphysics:
'I wish', he writes to J. A. Symonds in 1880, 'that he could take
a different line in his philosophical teaching.'[138]
The modern and doctrinaire nature of Green's thought and
teaching suggests that he was a prominent example of a general
tendency amongst teachers at Oxford which the *Month* described
in 1869: 'they engraft the "views" of modern philosophers on
the student's knowledge of ancient authors'.[139] Nettleship feels
the need to defend Green against this charge in respect of his
main teaching duty in the 1860s, Aristotle's *Ethics*, asserting
that he did not use 'the book as a peg on which to hang dis-
quisitions on modern questions'. He argues that Green had
no need to make such impositions, as the broad 'theory of life'
which Aristotle presents 'was based substantially upon the same
principles as his own'.[140] This, however, testifies to the influence upon Nettleship of Green's idiosyncratic version of Aristotle rather than to Green's objectivity, for, as his early essay on
'The Philosophy of Aristotle' shows, Green clearly made use of
Aristotle in this anachronistic manner.[141]
Fyffe's 1869 article on 'Study and Opinion in Oxford' identifies the respective philosophical positions it designates by
the names Hegel and Comte with two contrasting dispositions:
'there seem to be in Oxford, corresponding to these two opposite tendencies of thought, two classes in the main, with the distinguishing mark that one cares for metaphysics and theology,
and the other does not'.[142] In relation to this dichotomy Fyffe's
fellow-student Hopkins must, as an undated note from the later
years at Oxford indicates, be grouped with that of the adherents

---

[138] 'December 28, 1880', ibid. ii. 199. G. Thomas (*Moral Philosophy*, 49) remarks
that 'the issue was more closely connected with Jowett's mistrust of the educational
value of metaphysics than with his discomfort at the (supposedly) Hegelian character of what Green was setting forth'.
[139] 'Oxford Studies—Mr. Pattison and Dr. Gillow', 104.
[140] Nettleship, 'Memoir', in Green, *Works*, iii, p. lxxi.
[141] The contemporary judgement of the essay, that it is obscure (Abbott and
Campbell, *Life and Letters*, i. 341) suggests that Green's affinity with Aristotle's
thought was not based upon anything as broad and as easily recognizable as a set
of fundamental principles that were generally identified with Aristotle.
[142] Fyffe, 'Study and Opinion', 192.

of 'German philosophy': 'And it is not only that Comte is to the English a stumbling-block and to the Germans foolishness but that, I suppose, people say of him what they do not say of their greatest enemies otherwise—that he is a quack' (*J.* 534). Partisanship, such as that of 'The Probable Future of Metaphysics', was demanded by the intellectual battle at Oxford in the late 1860s, and an evangelical fervour was generated as a consequence of it: 'at the present time there is an open acknowledgement of the hostility of the two systems of thought, and each side is thinking it time that the other should be converted'.[143]

VII

'The parallel between our own age and that of the Sophists has', Green writes, 'often been drawn.'[144] Hopkins follows Jowett, who saw Hegel as having completed the philosophical project begun by Plato,[145] and Green in drawing an analogy between the enemies of Plato, the sophists, and the enemies of contemporary idealism, the positivists. Hopkins presents Plato as the patron saint of the fight against 'atheism' (which he equates with 'materialism' and 'atomism') and its attendant 'scepticism': 'he wages a religious war ag[ain]st these two tendencies and is never happy but when he is attacking them' (D. VIII, fo. 4). His philosophy is described in 'The Position of Plato to the Greek World', which was read by Green (and possibly also to Jowett)[146] as 'the new religion of the Ideal Good' (*J.* 116).

In his notes on Plato, Hopkins contests George Grote's argument that the sophists are individual thinkers like Plato and hence cannot be seen to constitute a separate group:

---

[143] Ibid. 190.

[144] 'Popular Philosophy in its Relation to Life', Green, *Works,* iii. 93. Turner (*Greek Heritage*) and Richard Jenkyns (*The Victorians and Ancient Greece* (Oxford: Blackwell, 1980)) have each documented the Victorians' identification with the classical Greeks.

[145] 'But the nearest approach in modern philosophy to the universal science of Plato, is to be found in the Hegelian "succession of moments in the unity of the idea"' (quoted in Manser, *Bradley's Logic,* 16).

[146] It is initialled 'T.H.G.' (*J.* 117). Higgins ('Hopkins and "The Jowler"', 154) lists this essay amongst those that she believes were presented to Jowett.

Sophistic.

Grote says nothing in common, but Yes. There is a common element in Philistinism and so in Sophistry. This is the denying all objectivity to truth and to metaphysics.

This denial destroys earnestness in life. P[lato] therefore falls foul of not Protagoras himself but their spirit. (D. VIII, fo. 9ᵛ)

The sophists, like the positivists in 'The Probable Future of Metaphysics', are seen to repudiate metaphysics. Their failure to recognize reason, the λόγος, is seen by Hopkins to necessarily entail atheism: 'Any system explaining the world without introducing reason in any way is logically atheism' (D. VIII, fo. 4). It is in this context of Plato's opposition to atheistic materialism that the contemporary relevance of his philosophy becomes apparent: 'When we look back at P[lato] as a protest ag[ain]st atomism etc we see it is not the vague dream of transcendentalism we are inclined to think it' (D. VIII, fo. 9ᵛ). Hopkins conceives of Plato as a modern ally: 'I get more and more sympathetic with "the true men" as ag[ain]st the Sophistik (observe I say K—it is not the same thing as sophistical), Philistine, Doctrinaire, Utilitarian, Positive, and on the whole Negative (as Carlyle wd. put it) side, and prefer to err with Plato.'[147]

Hopkins distinguishes Plato from the sophists on the grounds not only of the philosopher's rationalism but also of his liberalism. He charges the doctrinal 'speculations' of Protagoras and Gorgias with being 'illiberal' and having 'imprisoned the mind' (D. II 4, fo. 13). The thought of the sophists is restricted by an uncritical 'assumption' of 'that knowledge wh[ich] seemed to map out the universe' (D. II 4, fo. 12). This corresponds to Green's notion of the positivistic 'popular philosophy': 'It takes certain formal conceptions ready-made . . . which . . . it employs to cast a reflex intelligibility on the general world of knowledge.'[148] In 'The Position of Plato to the Greek World' Hopkins sees both the sophists and Plato to share the 'Intellectualism' (*J.* 115) of their age, which involved 'the desire to have the intellect prepared for all positions'. However, in the case of the sophists this desire 'led to the drawing of commonplaces of argument and quickly deduced schemes of ethics, politics, etc,

---

[147] To Baillie, 12 Feb. 1868, Letter 128, *Further Letters*, 231.
[148] Green, *Works*, iii. 92.

[while] in Plato the same wish leads to methods going much more to the root, namely a complete and infallible education of the intellect, and, by means of that, the discovery of a few first principles from which systems might be properly drawn' (*J.* 116). Hopkins regards Plato as a transitional figure, who 'fused' 'the older forms' of speculation, principally those of the Pythagoreans, Heraclitus, and Parmenides, so that 'his successors . . . could satisfy the advance of philosophy': 'he refined with intelligence the atmosphere of thought for Aristotle to breathe' (*J.* 117).

Hopkins is peculiarly sympathetic to Plato's transitional historical predicament:

Plato was able to feel the sadness of complex thought running freely to different conclusions when the old unity of belief which gives meaning to every subordination of thought and action was gone. Perhaps we may say that in raising the new religion of the Ideal Good to fill the place of the old we feel less his enthusiasm for the new truth, the One, the Good, or whatever it is called, than his despair at the multiplicity of phenomena unexplained and unconnected, the inconsistency of current speculations on the side of enquiry, and the pettiness of the ideals of the poets on the side of imagination.   (*J.* 116)

The 'despair' that he attributes to Plato may, rather like Margaret's grieving in 'Spring and Fall' (No. 144), be referred to Hopkins' concern at his own situation. This surmise is strengthened by a note on the opposite page of the manuscript essay which includes a quotation from Wordsworth's 'Tintern Abbey'. That Hopkins does not acknowledge its source indicates the personal nature of his note: 'unexplained and unconnected, | —["]the heavy and the weary weight | Of all this unintelligible world["], | the inconsistency etc' (*J.* 116).[149] The emotional response that Hopkins attributes to Plato can be glossed by referring to Hopkins' life at the time and, more broadly, to his own historical 'position'. The essay was written in 1865, the year before his conversion, when what was for him a 'new religion' came to supersede irrevocably 'the old'. The experience was, as poems

---

[149] 'Lines written a few miles above Tintern Abbey', ll. 40–1. The note may well have been written after discussing the essay with Green. Fyffe, recalling ten days spent on holiday with him in 1868, notes that Green was especially impressed with 'Tintern Abbey' and apt to quote parts of it from memory (Fyffe, Balliol, T. H. Green Papers, MS II. 1(b), Notebook 2, fo. 127).

of the period testify, attended by a painful sense of dissipation: 'My prayers must meet a brazen heaven | And fail and scatter all away' (No. 67). The fragmentary consequences of Plato's and Hopkins' respective commitments to a 'new religion' furnish a radical contrast to the metaphysical wholeness of 'the old unity of belief which gives meaning to every subordination of thought and action'.[150] For Plato this 'old unity' was the ancient Greek mythology and the Presocratic speculations that Hopkins, following George Grote and Max Müller, believed were informed by it.[151] He notes in an essay on mythology that it 'was, as Grote says . . . the whole field and interest of the minds wh[ich] w[oul]d now enjoy poetry, science, history' (D. VI 5, fo. 10).[152] For Hopkins the 'old' religion suggests the synthetic culture of Anglicanism that he grew up with, which being based upon natural theology and revelation was shattered by Darwinism and biblical criticism, and so created the need for a 'new religion' able to re-establish a harmony between belief and knowledge. This need is addressed in Hopkins' systematic elaboration of the premiss of his new faith, the principle of the Eucharist. The personal qualities of courage and independence evident from his conversion, which separated him from his family, country,[153] and university, are matched by his speculative boldness and originality in developing the doctrine of 'instress' and 'inscape' in his notes on the Pre-Socratics.

The Pre-Socratics were, Hopkins writes, 'prepossessed by mythology with the idea of some unity'. This tendency has, according to Hopkins, its most important consequences in the work

---

[150] 'The writings of Plato', according to Jowett, 'belong to an age in which the power of analysis had outrun the means of knowledge; and through a spurious use of dialectic, the distinctions which had been already "won from the void and formless infinite", seemed to be rapidly returning to their original chaos' (*Dialogues of Plato* (Oxford: Oxford University Press, 1871), iii. 328).

[151] Hopkins' essay on 'The Connection of Mythology and Philosophy' (D. VI 6, published in James Finn Cotter, *Inscape: The Christology and Poetry of Gerard Manley Hopkins* (Pittsburgh: University of Pittsburgh Press, 1972), 307–9) acknowledges 'Two valuable theories of the rise of mythology . . . that of the Comparative Mythologists and that of those who like Grote on *a priori* grounds trace the state of mind in wh. mythology was thrown out' (fo.10). Max Müller's definitive *An Essay on Comparative Mythology* (1856) was reprinted in *Chips from a German Work-shop*, where Hopkins, who took notes from it on the subject of Eastern religions (D. VII 6), is likely to have read it.

[152] See George Grote, *A History of Greece*, 3rd end. (London: John Murray, 1851), i. 460.   [153] See 'To seem the stranger lies my lot . . .' (No. 154).

of 'Anaxagoras, Socrates, [and] Plato, [who] were engaged in finding the results of mind in the order... of nature. They begin with the belief that it is there' (fo. 12). Idealism is seen in the essay to 'begin ... with belief'; it is 'prepossessed ... with the idea of some unity'. Conversely, Hopkins writes in an essay 'On the Rise of Greek Prose Writing', that 'idealism ... enters mythology' and is regarded as natural to all the activities of 'the earliest uncivilized age' (D. I 5, fo. 10). The primacy that he gives to idealism over empirical realism is familiar from 'The Probable Future of Metaphysics' (*J.* 118). A similar principle is presented by Green in his essay on the 'Popular Philosophy': '[Man] is as metaphysical when he talks of body or matter as when he talks of force, of force as when he talks of mind, of mind as when he talks of God. He goes beyond sense as much when he pronounces that he can only know things individual, or phenomena, as when he claims to know substances and the universal.'[154] In closing his essay Green comments that his positivistic and utilitarian age requires 'a philosophy like that of Hegel, of which it was the professed object to find formulae adequate to the action of reason as exhibited in nature and human society, in art and religion'.[155] Such a view of philosophy is, as an 1877 article in *Mind* on 'Recent Hegelian Contributions to English Philosophy' observes, integral to the study of the history of philosophy, which since the 1850s, due largely to the influence of Hegel upon Jowett,[156] had been fundamental to Greats philosophy:

The fact that our English Hegelians write upon the history of philosophy rather than propound metaphysical theories for discussion may be an accident, but it reveals very clearly that in their eyes philosophy is not philosophy simply, but something more, that it is related to poetry, politics, history and science in a way that earlier English thinkers scarcely dreamed of. This relatedness of knowledge is coming to be a commonplace, and men far removed from Hegelian modes of thought are ready to declare that philosophy cannot be isolated as it was when Hamilton and Mill ruled over rival systems.[157]

---

[154] Green, *Works*, iii. 95.   [155] Ibid. 125.
[156] Abbott and Campbell (*Life and Letters*, i. 88) record that Jowett began lecturing on the history of philosophy soon after his return from Germany in the mid-1840s.
[157] Quoted in Manser, *Bradley's Logic*, 20.

Hopkins' early essays on Greek philosophy trace religious belief and the metaphysical principle of unity to the same original
principle of the ideal. While later historical circumstances make
the formulation of a 'new Realism' or a 'new religion' necessary,
this original unity of thought and religion provides Hopkins
with models for the metaphysic which he develops as an undergraduate. The Pre-Socratic apprehensions of 'the Idea in its freshness' (D. XII 1, fo. 2), especially that of Parmenides, provide
the spur for the final formulation of Hopkins' early thought.

The unity of belief and metaphysics is fundamental to British idealism.[158] Furthermore, as the article in *Mind* draws to our
attention, science is included amongst those areas of thought
that are brought together by metaphysics. For Hopkins also, current physical science is, as the later chapters of the present study
argue, integral to his metaphysical system. His early acquired
knowledge of the fundamental principles of mechanics[159] provided him with a basis from which he could grasp the greatly
enlarged dynamical understanding of the physical world which
was being established at the time through energy physics. He
recognized in this new science an integral approach to empirical data that provided a counter to the 'scopeless' atomism of
positivist biology and psychology.

Hopkins' thought was formed in the same academic context as that which was also decisive in shaping the ideas of
R. L. Nettleship, William Wallace,[160] and F. H. Bradley. Along
with their teacher, Green, and Edward Caird, these men constitute the principal figures of British idealism, a group which
with the benefit of hindsight can be identified with the actual
'new school of metaphysics' that Hopkins anticipates in 'The
Probable Future of Metaphysics': the 'new Realism' that 'will
undoubtedly once more maintain that the Idea is only given

[158] This term is favoured here over others such as 'Absolute Idealism' and 'Anglo-
Hegelianism' for the reason that it does not exclude the crucial Kantian element
of English idealist thought in the 1860s.

[159] See notebook B. I, on mechanics.

[160] Both Nettleship, the disciple, editor, and biographer of Green, and Wallace,
the translator of Hegel, were at Balliol with Hopkins. Nettleship wrote to Mrs
Hopkins after the death of her son that 'He and I were great friends when we were
undergraduates at Balliol' (*J.* 351). Nettleship acted as a referee for him in his
application to University College Dublin in 1884. Wallace's First is noted in a
journal entry for Dec. 1867 (*J.* 159).

... from the whole downwards to the parts'. This dictum states what Bertrand Russell describes as British idealism's 'one central logical doctrine ... "every relation is grounded in the natures of the related term". Let us call this the *axiom of internal relations.*' Quinton cites this axiom approvingly as the most adequate 'account of the theoretical core of absolute idealism'.[161] Monism, 'the theory that there is only one true substance, the absolute or reality as a whole', is an important corollary of this proposition.[162]

R. L. Nettleship, writing in support of Hopkins' application for the professorship in Greek at Newman House in 1884, recalls 'that he was one of the cleverest and most original men in the College at that time'.[163] Respected by many of the original British idealists and widely credited with originality of thought,[164] Hopkins furnishes his own monistic version of 'the new Realism' in the private doctrine of 'instress' and 'inscape' that he formulates through his reading in 1868 of Parmenides, 'the great father of Realism' (*J.* 127).

---

[161] Quinton, *Absolute Idealism*, 27.   [162] Ibid. 28.
[163] White, *Hopkins*, 361.
[164] Cf. the early Jesuit memoir by 'Plures' which records their consensus of opinion that 'His mental originality and droll extravagance would have assured him a warm and admiring home in some Oxford College' (*Dublin Review*, 167/334–5 (July–Dec. 1920), 56).

2   Induction and Understanding

I

The forms of writing by which Hopkins is best known, the poetry and the notes from his nature observations in the diaries and journals, are genres which naturally deal in concrete imagery and have accordingly helped to establish his reputation as an empiricist. Another factor contributing to this reputation has been the fact that his canonical status was established and has been largely maintained by practitioners of Anglo-American New Criticism, the central method of which, an allegedly unmediated 'close-reading' of texts, represents a particular application of British empiricism and hence a bias towards this epistemology. Viewed from such a perspective Hopkins' advocacy of forms of idealism in the undergraduate essays appears to be aberrant.

The apparent contrast between the empiricism of the nature observations and poetry and the idealism of the essays and notes has led the critic A. D. Nuttall to argue that Hopkins is 'a positivist in spite of himself'.[1] While there is, as this remark suggests, a tension in Hopkins' work between idealist and empiricist impulses, it does not correspond to a generic division, nor does it entail that the study of Hopkins' thought should be founded upon the presupposition, which is shared by Nuttall and the New Critics, that these broad philosophical attitudes cannot coexist in some form. The question of how to achieve such a synthesis, of how to reconcile empirical details and an ideal whole, is one of the radical problems that motivates Hopkins' early thought and remains a preoccupation throughout his later work. This and related philosophical questions are for Hopkins urgent and abiding concerns. They inform the Oxford essays and notes with a sense of purpose that ultimately draws them together in his personal metaphysics of 'instress' and 'inscape'.

Hopkins' early essays and notes theorize philosophical

[1] A. D. Nuttall, *A Common Sky* (London: Sussex University Press, 1974), 152.

thought in precisely the terms of personal disposition and purpose that inform his own work. These factors are seen to provide the 'spring' which impels the formation of particular philosophies: 'the most successful philosophies seem those where we know the sensitiveness or bias which is the spring; this makes them inventive, that is, constructive; unchecked analysis is wearisome and narrows and dies away into unimportance'. Logical analysis which is 'unchecked', not subject to personal discretion and direction, is pointless. Effective philosophy is for Hopkins radically personal and creative, requiring the shaping force of motive or intention. The individual 'sensitiveness or bias' provides 'the inspiration or prepossession' (D. X 4, fo. 22) for 'constructive' thought.

The philosopher to whom Hopkins is referring in introducing his principle of the 'prepossession' is Immanuel Kant, who in his argument from the origin of mathematics endeavours to establish that we 'proceed from concepts to intuition, not from intuition to concepts'.[2] Indeed, the very nature of Hopkins' principle asserts this epistemic priority of thought to experience, and announces his allegiance to idealism. In the 1868 letter to Baillie he declares that, rather than align himself with the likes of the positivists, he would 'prefer to err with Plato', a consideration which prompts him to specify further the nature of his prepossession: 'This reminds me to say that I find myself in an even prostrate admiration of Aristotle and am of the way of thinking, so far as I know him or know about him, that he is the end-all and be-all of philosophy.'[3] Aristotle provides Hopkins with a means of reconciling the ideal with the empirically real. He establishes the basic pattern of metaphysical realism by affirming that the ideal forms or essences of things can, whilst retaining the ontological priority over appearances that they inherited from the Platonic forms, nevertheless be intuited through our sensory apprehension of their qualities. There is accordingly no need to see any contradiction between the value which Hopkins gives to direct sensory experience and his abhorrence of positivism.

---

[2] Immanuel Kant, *Critique of Pure Reason*, trans. Norman Kemp Smith (London: Macmillan, 1933), A 160, B 199. All subsequent quotations are taken from this translation.   [3] Letter 128, *Further Letters*, 231.

The present chapter approaches Hopkins' epistemology through his essays on induction. By 1843, when the first edition of Mill's *A System of Logic* appeared, science was proving to be enormously productive, and, furthermore, was becoming established as the model for knowledge. It is accordingly not surprising to find positivists and idealists fighting to establish their jurisdiction over the prestigious field of scientific method, which both identified with induction. They also hoped that scientific discovery would be further facilitated by establishing a theoretical model of it. Hopkins acknowledges the symbiotic relation between the theory and practice of scientific method in an early essay on induction which dates from his first term at Oxford, Michaelmas 1863:[4]

It was when science was alive and widening that the *Novum Organum* appeared to shew the channel it must run in. Now, while science is more vigorous than ever before and asserting its claim to new ground continually, efforts are made to systematise and correct the method which works these effects. Thus method and science seem to enliven each other.   (D. I 4, fo. 8)

Hopkins not only parallels his own scientific age to that of Francis Bacon but, furthermore, believes that the modern period exceeds it in vigour. By the 1860s the issue of induction was the subject of a long-standing but still urgent controversy in which the radical opposition of idealism and empiricism was brought to the fore as each side argued for their account of 'laws and sequences and causes and developments' (*J.* 118).

II

The opposition of German-inspired idealism to contemporary positivism, which is voiced by Jowett and Green, is acknowledged reciprocally by J. S. Mill:

The German, or *à priori* view of human knowledge, and of the knowing faculties, is likely for some time longer (though it may be hoped in a diminishing degree) to predominate among those who occupy themselves with such inquiries, both here and on the Continent. But

[4] Schmidt, 'Classical Studies', 178.

the 'System of Logic' supplies what was much wanted, a text-book of the opposite doctrine—that which derives all knowledge from experience, and all moral and intellectual qualities principally from the direction given to the associations.[5]

Mill, like his opponents at Oxford, recognizes that wider concerns embracing 'all moral and intellectual qualities' are at stake in the contest over epistemology. The theory of mind with which Mill allies himself in this passage is the same as that which Green refers to as 'the popular philosophy' and traces to Hume. Mill's radical empiricism, 'which derives all knowledge from experience', involves a fundamentally Humean psychology. Hume characterizes the mind as 'a bundle or collection of different perceptions, which succeed each other with an inconceivable rapidity, and are in a perpetual flux and movement'.[6] In this essentially passive and receptive model the sequences of our sense impressions become registered as associations in the mind which form the basis for all thought. Hence the importance of what Mill refers to as 'the direction given to the associations'.

The full title of Mill's book announces that it is *A System of Logic Ratiocinative and Inductive: Being a Connected View of the Principles of Evidence and the Methods of Scientific Investigation*. The positivist principle of experience and the Humean associationist psychology are considered by Mill to be sufficient to explain the inductive leap from inferences drawn from particulars to such vast generalizations as the specific causal relations that are deemed by science to be laws of nature.

Both the Scottish philosopher William Hamilton and the Cambridge historian and philosopher of science William Whewell opposed Mill's positivistic account of induction with modified forms of Kantianism. Of the two Whewell was Mill's principal and most public antagonist. Their debate over the nature of induction can be traced through the successive editions of Whewell's *Philosophy of the Inductive Sciences* and Mill's *A System*

---

[5] Quoted from Mill's *Autobiography* (1873) by R. F. McRae, Introd., J. S. Mill, *A System of Logic*, ed. J. M. Robson, 2 vols. (London: Routledge & Kegan Paul, 1973), i, p. xxiii.

[6] D. Hume, *A Treatise of Human Nature*, ed. L. A. Selby-Bigge (Oxford: Clarendon Press, 1888), 252.

of Logic, which were first published in 1840 and 1843, respectively. The controversy is of particular interest here as it appears
to have oriented the study of logic in Hopkins' Greats course.
Hopkins would have had the 'heavily revised'[7] fifth edition of
the book (1862), throughout which can be found the accre-
tions of almost twenty years of argument with Whewell, which
often include direct quotations from his works. By its polem-
ical nature Mill's *System of Logic* inevitably provoked discussion
of arguments opposed to it, especially, it is reasonable to specu-
late, in the teaching of the Socratic Jowett and the idealist
T. H. Green.

The third edition of Whewell's *Philosophy* was published as
three books, the second of which, comprising the main exposition of his theory of scientific method, was entitled the *Novum
Organon Renovatum* (1858). The first attempt at a full description of the role of induction in science, which both Whewell
and Mill claim as the forebear of their respective theories,
was made by Francis Bacon in his *Novum Organon Scientiarum*
(1620). Just as this work aimed to revise the teachings of Aristotle's logical treatises, the so-called *Organon,* in the light of the
scientific revolution of the seventeenth century, so Whewell saw
his task to be to bring Bacon into line with such subsequent
thought as had affected scientific method, principally Kant's
'Copernican Revolution'. Thus, in opposition to Mill, who developed Bacon's experimentalism and hence saw induction in
empiricist terms of reasoning from particulars, Whewell emphasizes the mind's creative a priori activity of forming suitable conceptions by which such particulars can be accounted for. He
refers to this process as 'the Colligation of Facts', a phrase
which appears in one of Hopkins' earliest undergraduate essay
topics: 'Distinguish Induction from Example, Colligation of
facts and other Processes with which it has been Confounded'
(D. I 4).

Hopkins was evidently unfamiliar with Whewell's phrase at
the time of writing his essay. He notes the essay title in his
journal (*J.* 49), where his misspelling, 'Collegation', indicates
that the topic was written from dictation and suggests that he
had little experience of the written phrase. The title above the

---

[7] Robson, 'Textual Introduction', Mill, *System of Logic,* vol. i, p. lxxxiv.

essay itself shows that the error was repeated and subsequently corrected, perhaps by his tutor, as there is an emphatic 'i' written over the aberrant 'e' (fo. 7). The effort that follows the title mentions neither Whewell nor 'colligation'. It is incomplete, little more than a beginning to the essay that he was meant to write.

The prescribed essay topic is constructed on the Millian assumption that Whewell's idealist account of induction as 'the colligation of facts' is in fact not induction at all. Indeed, it appears to have been devised to test the students' comprehension of book III, chapter II of the *Logic*, 'Of Inductions Improperly So Called', where Mill directly explicates and confronts Whewell's version of induction. The close of Hopkins' essay shows that he had at least begun to read this section, for its first page furnishes him with both his reference to the 'very principle [of induction], which is to be able to predicate of the unknown by the known', and the example of enumerative or 'perfect induction' he cites: '[as] when we say all the planets shine by reflected light because we have observed it in Mercury, Venus and every one of them'.[8] He agrees with Mill that this 'should not be called an Induction strictly' (fo. 9). Hopkins appears to be satisfied in this essay with simply making what he describes as 'the first and most important step' in defining induction (fo. 8), which is to recognize the limitations of 'perfect' or strictly enumerative induction.

The question of induction is resumed from the point at which the early essay leaves it in an essay that dates from Hilary term 1867, 'Distinguish exactly between Deduction, Induction, Analogy, and Example' (D. IX 1). This essay addresses the radical epistemological question which impelled the Whewell–Mill debate, the question of the ultimate grounds upon which inductive certainty rests: 'But what right have we to make a proposition wider than the actual number observed?' (fo. 2). Hopkins, like Mill, identifies causality as a central issue for the theory of induction. Mill writes that the recognition of his 'Law of Causation . . . is the main pillar of inductive science'. The principle is described as 'the familiar truth . . . that invariability of succession is found by observation to obtain between every fact in

---

[8] Cf. Mill, *System of Logic*, i. 289.

nature and some other fact which has preceded it'.[9] Hopkins rejects this commonsense appeal to a principle of temporal succession, along with Mill's use of the Humean law of association to consecrate it as the relation of cause and effect:

> Let us say All double roses are barren. It being impossible to reach this proposition by simple enumeration it must be formed upon a number of observed instances. But what right have we to make a proposition wider than the actual number observed? The question brings out the real nature of the inductive process and serves to put in a right light certain notions held about it in modern times. In becoming double a rose changes its generative organs into petals and we find that we are stating identical propositions: a double rose is one with an unusual number of petals: the number of petals is increased by the conversion of the stamens etc: a rose without stamens etc is barren. If we know these facts we are stating a certain causal tie wh[ich] must hold good everywhere or, still more strongly, we are stating what are the mutual parts of a phenomenon, and wherever the phenomenon is found it will have these parts, else it is not the same phenomenon. This however has changed the inference into deduction. If we argue without this certainty it is as presuming the causal tie though unseen to exist, but it is plain that certainty can only be had either by shewing this or else by simple enumeration of all the cases. Modern induction therefore wh[ich] does not go upon simple enumeration is analogy. (fo. 2)

The 'causal tie' which bridges the inferential gap between particulars and the general terms of induction, and so provides the principle from which the nature of further examples of the phenomenon can be deduced syllogistically, is itself demonstrated to be a 'deduction'. The universal statement 'All double roses are barren' is established *analytically* from the fact that 'In becoming double a rose changes its generative organs into petals.' Induction by analogy is, like the complementary enumerative variety, regarded by Hopkins as tautologous ('we find that we are stating identical propositions'), but it is not so in the trivial sense. It represents the mind's synthetic judgement of identity between its conception of the phenomenon and the particular instances of it that may be apprehended through the evidence of the senses. The certainty of the generalization is predicated in Whewellian terms upon a mental *conception* which

[9] Ibid. 326–7.

is 'superinduced' upon the particulars. In his characteristically fair-minded way Mill quotes a long passage from Whewell on colligation which, as the following extract indicates, made available to Hopkins this principle of the mind's conception. Indeed, the passage is quoted in the chapter, 'Of Inductions Improperly So Called', which, as was mentioned earlier, was probably known to Hopkins as early as his first term at Oxford:

The particular facts, are not merely brought together, but there is a new element added to the combination by the very act of thought by which they are combined . . . The facts are known, but they are insulated and unconnected, till the discoverer supplies from his own store a principle of connexion. The pearls are there, but they will not hang together till some one provides the string.[10]

Such acts of mind are, according to Mill, merely descriptive, a matter, for example, of simply calling a double-rose 'barren' once this fact has been established experimentally: 'The conception is not furnished *by* the mind until it has been furnished *to* the mind . . .'[11] For Whewell this begs the question as to how such connections are possible in the first place, just as it does for Hopkins: 'But what right have we to make a proposition wider than the actual number observed?' The 'causal tie'[12] is for Hopkins, as for Whewell, an idea (*contra* Hume and Mill) that is known with 'certainty' only through the mind's conception of it. Hopkins states this fundamental principle in his unpublished undergraduate notes on Aristotle's *Ethics*, where, following the German-idealist-inspired commentary of Alexander Grant, he writes of 'induction[:] notice that it can give no necessity to anything, except so far as the mind impresses necessity. Grant says experience is the condition but not the cause of necessary truths' (G. I, fo. 20).[13]

---

[10] Ibid. 294. See also Whewell, *The Philosophy of the Inductive Sciences*, 2nd edn., 2 vols. (London: John W. Parker, 1847; repr. Frank Cass & Co. Ltd., 1967), ii. 36.

[11] Mill, *System of Logic*, ii. 655.

[12] Hopkins' phrase appears to be an abridged and amended reference to Mill's description of a current idealist principle: 'The notion of causation is deemed, by the schools of metaphysics most in vogue at the present moment, to imply a mysterious and most powerful tie' (Mill, ibid. i. 326). Metaphors of tying and gathering are much favoured by Whewell to describe what he believes to be the mind's act of drawing together facts in a conception.

[13] Hopkins is commenting upon *Nicomachean Ethics*, 1139[b]. Cf. Alexander Grant, ed., *The Ethics of Aristotle*, 2nd edn. (London: Longmans, Green, and Co., 1866), ii. 155.

The distinction between Mill's and Whewell's theories of induction is reducible to opposing accounts of the nature of synthetic judgements. The difference between empiricists such as Mill and Kantians such as Whewell and Grant is that the former see synthetic a posteriori judgements to be the basis of *all* our knowledge, while the latter believe that we are also capable of synthetic a priori judgements, which, while involving content drawn from our observations, derive their necessity and universality from the transcendental nature of the mind, which organizes sensory experience according to the a priori Forms of Sense and Categories of the Understanding. Causality, the focus of Hopkins' essay, is one of the most important of these categories.[14] The attributes of 'certainty' and of universality, evident in Hopkins' conviction that the 'causal tie . . . must hold good everywhere', define the Kantian a priori: 'Necessity and strict universality are . . . sure criteria of *a priori* knowledge, and are inseparable from one another'.[15] By seeing the mind's judgement, 'the causal tie', to be both necessary and universal Hopkins is asserting its synthetic a priori nature. This is 'the real nature of the inductive process' which 'serves to put in a right light certain notions held about it in modern times'; that is, by Mill and his fellow positivists.

III

Although Hopkins does not acknowledge Whewell's theory of induction explicitly, it is nevertheless likely to have been his earliest introduction to the fundamental Kantian principle of synthetic a priori judgements. The conceptions which Whewell maintains are applied to given groups of 'facts' (by which he means both empirical observations and established scientific ideas)[16] derive from our 'Fundamental Ideas', which are transcendental in nature,[17] like Kant's a priori forms and concepts. In the essay that immediately follows the late essay on induction

---

[14] See Kant, *Critique of Pure Reason*, A 189–211, B 233–56.   [15] Ibid. B 4.
[16] Whewell, *The Philosophy of the Inductive Sciences*, i. 40.
[17] For a list of these ideas, see David Oldroyd, *The Arch of Knowledge* (Sydney: New South Wales University Press, 1986), 158.

in notebook 'D. IX', 'The Tests of a Progressive Science',[18] Hopkins develops his theory of scientific method in terms that often coincide with the Whewellian theory and idiom of colligation.

Just as the discussion of reasoning by analogy in the 1867 essay on induction supplements the discussion of enumerative induction in the early essay (D. I 4), so similarly 'The Tests of a Progressive Science' expands upon the observation made in the early essay that 'method and science seem to enliven each other'. The distinctive character of modern science, the reasons why it is, as he puts it in 1863, 'more vigorous than ever before and asserting its claim to new ground continually' (D. I 4, fo. 8), can be traced to the suppleness of its methods, which are no longer circumscribed by strict traditional categories of induction and deduction, but freed by the speculative possibilities of synthetic a priori reasoning: 'A science is advancing which is giving us fresh knowledge of facts in the same way as a trade is advancing which is widening its connection' (fos. 2–3). This is most immediately apparent from his exposition of what 'may be called deductive development of science':

The other advance is the more exact or the more comprehensive and rational treatment of facts . . . A science must be exact in order to be deductive and to allow prediction. But so far this is rather the perfection than the progress of a science, for becoming deductive it has in a sense reached a stand-still. The advance of a science in this stage is to be looked for in development of method. This means the gathering of some of its facts and laws into groups which give new starting-points and postulates. The process meant is most conspicuously seen in mathematics: thus the properties of angles given in Euclid are in trigonometry thrown together into a new conception of the angle as a measure for a wide and alien field of matter. The change of view has in fact brought within our reach facts which the prior science was too cumbrous to treat of . . . (fos. 3–4)

The 'development of method' that Hopkins introduces here, which is able to deliver deduction from its purely analytical 'stand-still', is based upon the Kantian principle of the synthetic a priori judgement, the mind's capacity to form a 'new

[18] D. IX 2. It is published in *Journals and Papers of Gerard Manley Hopkins*, ed. G. Castorina (Bari: Adriatica, 1974), 181–2.

conception' out of the given facts. The parity given to 'facts and laws' and the language of colligation used in the references to 'gathering' and 'the properties' being 'thrown together into a new conception' present this fundamental Kantian principle in Whewellian hypothetico-deductivist terms.

The Kantian principle is also seen to facilitate the most spectacular advances made by inductive science. Mere enumeration or description is considered to be of little significance in comparison to a bold hypothesis which brings disparate areas of science together in a single conception, and so engenders a radically new form of knowledge:

In explaining more facts however it will make a great difference whether it be by way of supplement to the classes we already have formed or be an extension of class division over a field lying on the outskirts of the science. Thus the discovery of a new species of willow or the observation of parthenogenesis in aphides two generations longer than had before been found possible shews little progressiveness in science; on the other hand the spectral analysis by wh[ich] the chemical composition of non-terrestrial masses is made out is a development of optics wh[ich] cannot be called supplemental but a complete widening or alteration of its beat. (fo. 3)

The achievement in 'spectral analysis' to which Hopkins refers developed during the first half of the nineteenth century and was finally established in 1859. It was much publicized and the cause of great excitement in the 1860s, and served to discredit positivism, causing Comte to become notorious for a remark he had made only a few years earlier on the limits of scientific knowledge, in which he cited the chemical composition of the stars as precisely the kind of thing that could never be known.[19]

In 1814, whilst examining the prismatic decomposition of sunlight, the German optician Joseph Fraunhofer observed that certain 'dark lines' interrupt the continuous spectrum at precise points, one of which, he noted, coincides with the position of a 'bright line' of colour emitted by a candle flame. In the 1850s, with the aid of the clean gas burner which he invented, Robert Bunsen, together with his colleague Gustave Kirchhoff, studied

[19] Alfred Russel Wallace, *The Wonderful Century*, 4th edn. (London: Swan Sonnenschein, 1901), 48. See also David Knight, *The Age of Science* (Oxford: Blackwell, 1986), 83.

the prismatic decomposition of flames to which specific chemical elements had been added, and charted the resultant 'bright lines' which occur at definite points of the spectrum. In this way particular elements were assigned their own specific light resonances, and the terrestrial science of spectrum analysis was established. The correlation between the 'bright lines' exhibited in laboratory experiments and the 'dark lines' which Fraunhofer and others since him had noted of the light emitted from the sun and other bodies in space, although much discussed, was, however, not established scientifically until 1859. In that year Kirchhoff published a paper arguing that chemical masses both emitted their definitive light frequencies when hotter than their surroundings, thus producing 'bright lines', and absorbed them when cooler than their surroundings, hence the phenomenon of the 'dark lines'.

This insight, which constitutes Kirchhoff's Law, occurred along the lines of the hypothetico-deductive method, with experiments being devised in order to test what began as a hypothesis. Gathering together Fraunhofer's discoveries, Bunsen's findings, the second law of thermodynamics, and other 'facts' in the Whewellian sense, Kirchhoff established a theory which, while it meets the conditions of a 'Colligation', is in fact of greater significance. By bringing together two distinct classes of facts, belonging respectively to astronomy and the application of optics to chemistry, Kirchhoff's thesis provides a spectacular example of another of Whewell's principles: '*The Consilience of Inductions* takes place when an Induction obtained from one class of facts, coincides with an Induction, obtained from another different class.' That Whewell regards the consilience as 'a test of the truth of the Theory in which it occurs'[20] shows his faith in reasoning by analogy. The principle of the consilience provides a measure of the extent to which Kirchhoff's achievement in 'spectral analysis' marks, as Hopkins puts it, 'a complete widening or alteration of its [i.e. optics'] beat' (fo. 3).

Whether they can be described as 'deductive' or 'inductive', the greatest advances in contemporary science occurred, according to Hopkins, through the same methodological principle of

---

[20] Quoted in Oldroyd, *Arch of Knowledge*, 160. The case of spectroscopy furnishes a grand consilience which draws together optics and astronomy, Whewell's favourite sources of examples to illustrate his scientific theory.

hypothetico-deductivism. It is in such synthetic, Whewellian, terms of 'connexion', of gaining 'fresh knowledge' through the establishment of new relations, and finding 'a link or blending' between different sciences, that Hopkins theorizes the progress of science. He emphasizes the importance of 'new starting points and postulates', and 'a new conception', both of which involve the implication, essential to Whewell's theory, of the 'facts' 'being seen in a new light'; 'there is always a *new conception*, a principle of connexion and unity, supplied by the mind, and superinduced upon the particulars'.[21] It is this flexibility, the freeing up of scientific method to facilitate the broader application of synthetic a priori judgements, its 'change of view', that, as Hopkins puts it, 'has in fact brought within our reach facts which the prior science was too cumbrous to treat of' (fo. 4).

While the positivists were claiming that the scientific practice of the day validated their method and its epistemological presuppositions, Hopkins sees such successes to endorse the opposite epistemology and theory of mind. This perception is expressed most clearly in another essay which also dates from Hilary term 1867. As modern science is, Hopkins believes, evermore removing cases of apparent contingency in the physical world and finding in it organization, so the authority of materialism, and of the empiricist application of this principle to psychology and epistemology, is radically diminished:

And it is quite plain our thoughts grow and become complex and determine in this way or that by strength of their own and principles independent of the accidents under which their experience comes to individuals: if not, we should not find one man's thoughts agreeing with another's, break-downs w[oul]d be happening in our intelligibility, and generally the play of innumerable circumstances, 'every little gust of sense', as someone writes, would throw the matter of our ideas together into groups as accidental and uninformed by any law of subordination as the packs of bubbles spinning in a tea-cup. Indeed while science is always making the idea of the chance clashing of atoms more and more unnatural in the outer world, this theory applies Epicureanism to the making of the mind. (D. X 3, fo. 18)

The crucial distinction between Mill's and Kant's respective theories of perception is that for the former the order of succession (and hence of association) of our sense-impressions is

[21] Whewell, *The Philosophy of the Inductive Sciences*, ii. 77.

critical, whereas for the latter it is merely contingent. While the empiricists try to ground the objective authority of our thoughts in the world of appearances, Hopkins follows Kant's characterization of the mind as radically 'independent' of this phenomenal reality. The objectivity of our thought is accordingly established on the basis of its a priori 'strength' and 'principles'. It is as a consequence of the consistency provided by the transcendental nature of mind that we 'find one man's thoughts agreeing with another's'. Like the unspecified forms of metaphysics in 'The Probable Future of Metaphysics', which also dates from Hilary term 1867, the capacity to make synthetic a priori judgements allows Hopkins the means by which to refute Millian positivism (but not to establish what the status of such knowledge is exactly): 'It will always be possible to shew how science is atomic, not to be grasped and held together, "scopeless", without metaphysics: this alone gives meaning to laws and sequences and causes and developments' (*J.* 118).

IV

The essays on scientific method show that the interest in induction which Hopkins shares with his contemporaries can be traced to their radical speculations about the nature of mind. George Henry Lewes' *Biographical History of Philosophy* (1857), which is an important source for some of the essays considered in this chapter and the next, identifies induction and 'psychology' as the original and definitive concerns of modern philosophy. According to Lewes it was Spinoza who, by his development of the Cartesian axiom that consciousness provides the foundation for knowledge, 'brought about the first crisis in modern Philosophy'. Subsequent philosophers had to choose between 'Spinozism or Scepticism'. Either consciousness provides the dependable 'premiss' for thought and 'every clear and distinct idea is *absolutely* [and objectively] true', or consciousness is 'unstable' and thought must depend upon experience, which permits knowledge of phenomena only.[22]

This concern with psychology provides for Lewes the definitive

---

[22] G. H. Lewes, *Biographical History of Philosophy* (London: John W. Parker & Son, 1857; repr. Farnborough, England: Gregg International Publishers, 1970), 415.

and enduring preoccupation of modern philosophy before Fichte. According to his Comtean historicism the post-Kantian resurgence of ontology is superseded by his own age of positivism. However, as the mid-century controversy over the nature of induction shows, interest in the question of psychology was quickened rather than quelled by the rising tide of scientism. In addition to having been the basis for the 'First Epoch', induction itself became one of 'the questions agitated' in modern philosophy which depend for their answer upon a clear conception of the workings of the mind.

The present section introduces Hopkins' theory and experience of consciousness, and examines its importance mainly in Kantian terms, as the radical condition for the possibility of all mental representations, but also as it relates to his effort to re-establish a form of metaphysical realism. Hopkins' retreat notes on the 'First Principle and Foundation', which bear the date 'Aug. 20 1880', express a strong personal sense of self-consciousness that had evidently been with him since childhood:

> my selfbeing, my consciousness and feeling of myself, that taste of myself, of *I* and *me* above and in all things, which is more distinctive than the taste of ale or alum, more distinctive than the smell of walnutleaf or camphor, and is incommunicable by any means to another man (as when I was a child I used to ask myself: What must it be like to be someone else?). (*S.* 123)[23]

Like Kant, who theorizes consciousness as the sense of 'the "*I think*"'[24] that necessarily accompanies all our impressions and thoughts, Hopkins regards it as the fundamental (or even transcendental) condition for all mental representations: It is both 'above and in all things'. His emphatic and repetitive use of the possessive pronoun in the notes highlights the pervasive nature of his sense of self: 'I find myself with my pleasures and pains, my powers and my experiences, my deserts and guilt, my shame and sense of beauty, my dangers, hopes, fears, and all my fate, more important to myself than anything I see' (*S.* 122). Similarly in an early letter to Baillie, Hopkins feels a sense of propriety in his observations of particular natural phenomena,

---

[23] This passage is discussed further in Ch. 10, Sect. V.
[24] See *Critique of Pure Reason*, B 131–2.

which, he writes, become 'consigned to my treasury of explored beauty'.[25]

A corollary of the Kantian 'I think' is a fundamental distinction between the subject, or the mind which thinks, and the object, that which it thinks. For Kant, the production by the mind of the object as a radical notion of otherness from the subject is not formed *in* consciousness, but is necessarily at the very basis *of* consciousness, it is transcendental. The transcendental self is that which knows. The self that it knows, on the other hand, is the empirical self. This is the self regarded as an object, which brings together the simple combination of sense-data or 'intuitions' as the empirical unity of apperception. Consciousness draws together the manifold of mental representations as its correlative 'object in general', a diversity which is organized through the categories of the understanding as particular objects of thought.

While the version of consciousness presented in Hopkins' late notes on the 'Foundation' differs in important ways from the Kantian model, principally by not respecting Kant's prohibition upon knowledge of a noumenal self, vestiges of this influence are nevertheless discernible. Hopkins distinguishes in the notes between the self as a simple unit or point of consciousness, which he refers to as the 'inset', and those objects which belong to its experience, the 'outsetting'. He then proceeds to define the subject along transcendentalist lines by this relation: 'self consists in the relation the inset and the outsetting bear to one another'. The 'self' is, therefore, as in Kant, a 'point of reference for consciousness' which gathers to itself 'its objects':

whatever can with truth be called a self . . . is not a mere centre or point of reference for consciousness or action attributed to it, everything else, all that it is conscious of or acts on being its object only and outside it. Part of this world of objects, this object-world, is also part of the very self in question, as in man's case his own body, which each man not only feels in and acts with but also feels and acts on. If the centre of reference spoken of has concentric circles round it, one of these, the inmost, say, is its own, is óf it, the rest are tó it only. (*S.* 127)[26]

[25] To Baillie, 'July 10. 1863', Letter 120, *Further Letters*, 202.
[26] On Coleridge's use of the figure of concentric circles to describe Schelling's

This passage shows how Hopkins develops some of the theoretical implications of his personal sense of self-consciousness. His willingness to approach self-consciousness in such an analytic way may be taken to indicate not only that his deeply felt sense of self predisposed him to transcendentalist theories of consciousness which were available to him through Greats philosophy, but indeed that this readiness was a consequence of the earlier studies. The relation between consciousness and experience put by the above passage can be traced to the undergraduate essay on 'The Possibility of Separating ἠθική [Ethics] from πολιτικὴ ἐπιστήμη [Political Science]', where Hopkins associates a sense of self comparable to the apperception with the Kantian a priori moral principle of the Categorical Imperative:

Morality has already begun with him [i.e. 'Man'] before relations with others arise—scarcely in time but in thought. Conscience or the Imperative working outwards find[s] its first matter in the man himself: a man can compare his today with his yesterday, his aims with his results: many things follow from man being his own object. (*J.* 124)

The continuity between Hopkins' early and later thought is underlined by the metaphor of the 'concentric circles' 'working outwards', which is used in both the essay and the notes. Both the early and the late accounts of consciousness also indicate Hopkins' wish to establish the grounds for knowledge of a noumenal self. In the extract from the *Ethike* essay, he invokes a moral sense which is referred to rather indistinctly as 'Conscience or the Imperative'. While the Kantian principle is purely formal,[27] and as such only indicates the existence of a noumenal self from whence it issues, the conscience is more often associated with a moral nature or *soul*, a noumenal principle of self that is usually regarded as essential, unique, and knowable. Indeed, a sense of the uniqueness of the self is presented in the later notes as a condition of consciousness. The nature of the individual self can be known by and through this self, 'my knowledge of it, which is so intense, is from itself alone' (*S.* 123). This flies in the face of Kant, who regards such speculations

distinction of pure and empirical consciousness, see G. N. G. Orsini, *Coleridge and German Idealism* (Carbondale: Southern Illinois University Press, 1969), 210.

[27] See Ch. 4, Sect. VI.

as entirely illusory.[28] Self-consciousness is, according to Kant, the fact from which we illegitimately infer the existence and nature of soul. For Hopkins, on the other hand, the conscious sense of the uniqueness of the self, that is, of its nature as a soul, is logically prior to our sense of an objective world. There is, in other words, no question of trying to complete our knowledge of the self by drawing inferences from the fact of self-consciousness, for self-consciousness is founded upon just such a full and distinctive sense of self.

The pervasive pattern of consciousness 'working outwards' to the external world is a version of the fundamental idealist principle which maintains that the whole precedes the part. Consciousness is for Hopkins, as for Kant, the overarching context in which mental representations take their place and gain their meaning. This principle was available to Hopkins through the work of the idealists John Grote and T. H. Green, for whom it provides the foundation for the respective systems of metaphysics they were developing during the 1860s to oppose positivism. A group of notes that Hopkins took from John Grote's *Exploratio Philosophica* (1865)[29] dwell upon the book's central distinction between 'sensation', the physiological registration of 'phenomenal' stimuli, and 'feeling', its apprehension in a Kantian principle of consciousness:

An instance of what appears to me the confusion betw[een] philosophy or logic on the one side and physiology or phenomenalism on the other appears in the manner in wh[ich] the whole question of sensation has constantly been treated. 'Sensation' meaning by the term an affection or modification (however we may style it) of our senses (to use that misleading expression), nerves, and brain, is a phenomenon belonging to the domain of physiology. It is what I have above called 'communication'. 'Sensation', meaning by the term a feeling on our part, or *a portion or instance of consciousness, which, in whatever manner, grows into knowledge,* is a fact, so far as we call it one, belonging to a different order of thought, and it is philosophy or logic wh[ich] must deal with it so far as it can be dealt with.

(D. VII 7, fos. 5–6; my emphasis)[30]

[28] *Critique of Pure Reason*, B 409.
[29] D. VII 7, fos. 5–6; extracts from Grote, *Exploratio Philosophica Part I* (1865; repr. Cambridge: Cambridge University Press, 1900), chs. 1 and 2.
[30] Transcribed from Grote, ibid. 19–20.

According to Green a satisfactory and 'thorough analysis of the act of sensuous apprehension . . . was first really attempted by Kant':[31] 'a flux of sensations does not constitute knowledge. If an "observed uniformity of sensations" does, such uniformity must be relative to a uniting and discriminating subject. This result is simply a paraphrase of the barbaric enunciation of Kant, that a "synthetical unity of apperception" was the condition of an experience of things . . .'[32] The distinction that Grote and Green make between mere sensation and its apprehension within the context of consciousness is acknowledged by Hopkins in directly Kantian terms in the essay entitled 'Is the Difference between *a priori* and *a posteriori* Truth One of Degree Only or of Kind?' (D. VI 1), which probably dates from late 1866 or 1867.[33] For Kant the pure forms of sense, of which time is one and space the other, 'contain *a priori* the condition of the possibility of objects as appearances';[34] they provide the necessary condition for the simple combination of our representations in consciousness as the empirical unity of apperception. Hopkins regards the forms of sensibility in accordance with the primary importance that Kant attributes to them, as the 'two most prominent [a priori] forms'. He evidently understands their significance as the 'outer' and 'inner' senses, respectively: 'Space is the form under which we regard the outer world, time under w[hich we regard] the phenomena of our own minds, sensation, etc.' (fo. 1).

Hopkins' essay illustrates what he sees to be Kant's renewal of 'the scholastic distinction of form and matter' with the forms of sensibility: 'The transcendental philosophy has established the loss of meaning, of sanity in thought, when any attempt is made to regard space and time apart f[rom] their matter, or matter apart f[rom] these forms' (fos. 1–2). These are for Hopkins the 'most fundamental associations' (fo. 2) in the workings of the mind. Despite the ostensibly Humean terminology here Hopkins rejects empiricism in this essay on the grounds of its inadequacy in explaining space and time. According to the physiological explanation of the 'Empirics' these ideas are acquired through

[31] Green, *Works*, iii. 49.   [32] Ibid. iii. 51.
[33] Schmidt, 'Classical Studies', 180.
[34] See *Critique of Pure Reason*, A 89, B 121.

our sensory experience, space being abstracted from the motion of our eyes and the sense of touch as they trace the surfaces of things, and time through the sequential experience of our physical movement through space; hence his rhetorical question, 'why not a new form for each of the senses?' (fo. 3).[35] According to Hopkins this theory in fact presupposes both space and time and so lends support to the Kantian thesis: 'These ideas thus remain *a priori*' (fo. 2).

Whereas the 'outer sense' of space allows us to intuit appearances, time, 'the formal condition of inner sense',[36] has a broader application which is coincident with consciousness, for it draws together all our representations. In accordance with this understanding of the Kantian principle Hopkins finds the two forms of sensibility reducible to the inner sense: 'neither form has any meaning except as implying plurality at least in thought, two sensations'. He appears to understand that 'these most fundamental associations' provide the condition for the function of consciousness that Kant describes as the empirical unity of apperception.

Although time is the radical condition of thought the relations it produces are merely contingent, having only subjective validity. It is, according to Kant, only as the faculty of understanding applies its concepts to the representations ordered in time that they gain the status of objective knowledge.[37] While Hopkins concurs with the importance that Kant ascribes to the forms of sensibility he does not follow Kant in making a clear distinction between them and the categories. Instead it is argued that the concepts of unity, plurality, and totality which comprise the Kantian categories of quantity are necessarily inherent to the forms of sense:[38]

A further analysis however might be used to simplify the question. It will appear that space and time may be brought under one genus.

---

[35] Zaniello ignores the rhetorical nature of this question, and consequently misreads it as a proposal for a series of such 'new [sensory] form[s]', each being 'the equivalent of an "image" or "scape"' ('The Sources of Hopkins' Inscape', *Victorian Newsletter*, 52 (Autumn 1977), 24). [36] *Critique of Pure Reason*, A 99.
[37] See ibid. B 139.
[38] The principle for the objective use of the category of quantity is the 'Axiom of Intuition', which states that 'All intuitions are extensive magnitudes' (ibid. A 162, B 202).

They imply sameness and difference, one and more, end and continuance. It is agreed neither form has any meaning except as implying plurality at least in thought, two sensations. The common form then w[ould] be Quantity. But of course any definition of quantity is out of the question, since it has no meaning except f[rom] being illustrated in things, in matter. It seems therefore to be true that the Empirical explanations of space and time are only simplifications of their phenomena and that the *a priori* notion of quantity must be held to differ in kind f[rom] other thought.   (fo. 2)

The implication of 'plurality' can be regarded simply as the contingent sequence by which 'two sensations' are apprehended. It is clear, however, that by being apprehended in this way these sensations become registered in consciousness as part of a necessary sequence through the a priori function of the categories. This is one of the senses in which the forms 'may be brought under one genus', namely the category of 'Quantity'. It is also an implication of Hopkins' identification of Aristotelian ontology, 'the scholastic distinction of form and matter', with Kantian psychology. The very fact that we can apprehend the 'matter' of sense-data entails that it is arranged formally. According to Aristotle our knowledge is necessarily of form and it is only in so far as matter provides the medium for the manifestation of form that it can be known. In so far as Kant's theory of mind posits a subjective a priori principle of form which furnishes the condition of our knowledge of the material provided by experience, it lends itself to the analogy that Hopkins draws between it and the Aristotelian relation of form and matter. The 'two sensations' which represent the contingent 'matter' of experience can accordingly be known only in so far as they provide the occasion for form, their single 'genus', to be instanced: 'But of course any definition of quantity is out of the question, since it has no meaning except from being illustrated in things, in matter.'

The Kantian forms of sense 'imply sameness and difference, one and more, end and continuance'. The 'intuitive' 'idea of quantity' (fo. 3) which, according to Hopkins, comprises their 'common form' accordingly represents not only the Kantian inner sense and the category of quantity but a more general function of the categories, which Hopkins declares in a note to the essay 'may all be reduced to Relation' (fo. 1ᵛ). No sooner has

Hopkins introduced the Kantian faculty psychology and championed it over positivism than he collapses its careful distinctions into a principle of 'Relation'. This corresponds to T. H. Green's presentation of Kant in his lecture notes: ' "Critic["] &c., then, as theory of the conditions of experience must enquire what are [the] conditions in virtue of which perceived objects are connected. This with K[ant] takes [the] form of conditions which render application of category of relation to phenomena possible'.[39]

Hopkins, like such early British idealists as Grant, John Grote, and Green, values the principle of objectivity that the Kantian theory establishes for our knowledge, and hence the defence it provides against Humean scepticism, whilst being impatient of its prohibition upon knowledge of 'noumena'. He accordingly explores the possibility of establishing his own principle of transcendental form, versions of which are identified in the undergraduate essays with 'Relation', 'comparison', and 'unity'. Although Hopkins does not make the distinction himself it is useful to bear in mind two models of form that he develops in his speculations. One form can be described as a minimalist version of Kantianism, the other is a type of post-Kantian idealism.

It is clear from the essay on '*A posteriori* Truth' that Hopkins understands that Kantian form is imposed upon its matter without contributing a principle of content, it is an 'empty' form. The category of quantity, for example, has 'no meaning except from being illustrated in things, in matter'. The reductive principle of 'Relation' which emerges from this essay would appear to be a general capacity for making synthetic a priori judgements, for establishing instances of the form of 'unity' that define our objects. According to Kant, 'of all representations, *combination* is the only one which cannot be given through objects'.[40] While Hopkins' minimalist version of the transcendental form does not fix our mental representations as precisely and as finally as the full onslaught of the Kantian machinery of

---

[39] Green, 'Lecture on Logic', Balliol, T. H. Green Papers, MS II. 2(a), 1A 3, fo. 1. These notes are undated. C. A. Smith rather confusingly gives them the specific date of 1875 whilst allocating them to the period 1867–74 ('T. H. Green's Philosophical Manuscripts: An Annotated Catalog', *Idealistic Studies*, 9 (May 1979), 182). [40] *Critique of Pure Reason*, B 129.

consciousness, it allows him to develop a theory of mind that gives greater scope for principles of interpretation and choice.

Kant's pure synthetical apperception is a radically idealist principle which traces the possibility of thought to a realm of pure subjectivity autonomous of any empirical principle. His Transcendental Deduction derives from this principle of consciousness a priori forms which describe only the conditions for thought. Post-Kantian idealists from Fichte to T. H. Green disagree with this deduction and, returning to the Kantian premiss, argue that this model of consciousness entails a capacity to *constitute* (rather than simply regulate) thought. Hopkins presents a version of just such a deduction in one of his earliest essays, 'On the Signs of Health and Decay in the Arts' (D. I 6), where 'comparison, the apprehension of the presence of more than one thing', is seen to be 'inseparable in a higher or lower degree from thought'.

Having established that 'comparison' is synonymous with thought the 'Health and Decay' essay deduces various types of it from what is regarded as the most radical form of comparison which the mind can make, that 'of existence with non-existence'. Like Kant in the 'Transcendental Deduction', Hopkins claims for his scheme the rigour of mathematical deduction. He presents it as analogous to the 'degrees or dimensions' of algebra or geometry, which necessarily include their subordinate values, as in algebraic notation, the series a^4, a^3, a^2, and a, or in geometry, the relations between cube, plane, line, and point:

We may perhaps make four degrees or dimensions of it, of which each, as in mathematics, exists and is implied in the dimension above it; these will be those drawn from the comparison (i), of existence with non-existence, of the conception of a thing with the former absence of the conception;—this is an inseparable accident of all thought; (ii), of a thing with itself so as to see in it the continuance of law, in which is implied the comparison of continuance of law with non-continuance; instances of this kind are a straight line or circle; (iii), of two or more things together, so as to include the principles of Dualism, Plurality, Repetition, Parallelism, and Variety, Contrast, Antithesis; (iv) of finite with infinite things, which can only be done by suggestion; this is the ἀρχή of the Suggestive, the Picturesque and the Sublime. (*J.* 74)

Reflexive self-consciousness, the a priori capacity by which man is, in the words of the *Ethike* essay, 'his own object' is implicit

in the premiss to this deduction. The simple acknowledgement that something has a being for us, which derives from 'the
comparison . . . of existence with non-existence', is a recognition that it is accompanied by the Kantian 'I think', that is, that
it has been brought to the empirical unity of apperception. The
precondition for the comparison 'of the conception of a thing
with the former absence of the conception', is consciousness,
'an inseparable accident of all thought'. The conditions of self-
consciousness are seen here to themselves generate the content
of thought. The sense that the rudimentary 'thing' of cognition
has a being for us means that it is contained by the unity of
consciousness and hence that it is brought into relation with all
other mental representations. Our initial apprehension of it is
accordingly specified as it is progressively distinguished from all
other apprehensions, the classes of which are described by each
of the subsequent 'dimensions' of comparison. Our knowledge
of a thing increases, much as Hopkins maintains in 'The Tests of
a Progressive Science', accordingly as it is brought into new relations with other intuitions and conceptions of things.

The version of cognition that Hopkins presents in the 'Health
and Decay' essay bears a strong resemblance to that elaborated
by T. H. Green in his 1866 essay on 'The Philosophy of Aristotle': 'The simple judgment that a sensation is present . . .
involves the presence of a permanent something to which the
sensation is relative, which is a "universal", as being necessarily
present to all other sensations with which the given one is to
be compared and contrasted . . .'[41] Having been brought to consciousness each sensory impression is, according to Green, a
potentiality which becomes defined as it is differentiated from
all the other contents of consciousness: 'Each object, as known,
is indeed in relation to all other things . . . but the relation is
to us at first potential, not actual.'[42] The transcendentalist principle of self-consciousness, which was available to him in both
Kantian and post-Kantian versions, is the radical presupposition
of Hopkins' developing metaphysic.

[41] Green, *Works*, iii. 51.
[42] Ibid. iii. 73. This model is discussed in greater detail in Ch. 5.

3 The 'idea in the mind'

I

Hopkins, like the early British idealists who taught him, treats the study of historical philosophies as an opportunity both to address issues in contemporary thought and to define his own metaphysic. The undergraduate essays document the way in which his early acquaintance with particular philosophical systems is precociously interfused with the formation of his own system of philosophy. Consequently, while incomplete understandings and conflations of distinct ideas are a feature of particular essays, a unity of purpose can be discerned throughout them as a whole. The deformation of certain philosophical concepts which occurs as Hopkins interprets, or indeed misunderstands, them in accordance with his metaphysical 'prepossession' is nevertheless integral to the shaping of his system. He, like his intellectual mentors Jowett and Green, exemplifies Nietzsche's thinker who picks up the work of an earlier thinker, which is likened to an arrow shot by nature, in order to shoot it in another direction.[1]

Kant's thought, which can be understood as a development of both Humean scepticism and subjective idealism, lends itself to being shot in different directions. Hopkins' essay on 'Causation' (D. VI 2)[2] vacillates between aligning Kant's theory of causality with empiricism and with Cartesian ontologism. The essay, which probably dates from Michaelmas term 1866,[3] follows that of the positivist G. H. Lewes' *Biographical History of Philosophy*,[4] which focuses upon causation as a central issue for

---

[1] Gilles Deleuze, *Nietzsche and Philosophy*, trans. Hugh Tomlinson (London: Athlone Press, 1983), p. ix.

[2] This essay has been published in Tom Zaniello, 'The Sources of Hopkins' Inscape', *Victorian Newsletter*, 52 (Autumn 1977), 22–3.

[3] Schmidt, 'Classical Studies', 180.

[4] One of Hopkins' 'Further notes' to the essay discusses 'Lewes' friend who did not see that every thing must have a cause' (fo. 5). See Lewes, *History of Philosophy*, 558.

deciding upon the comparative validity of Cartesian ontologism, Humean empiricism, and Kantian 'psychology'. The final chapter of Lewes' section on Kant, an 'Examination of Kant's Fundamental Principles', begins with the ultimatum: 'If [causation] be found dependent on experience, all the *a priori* ideas must be likewise given up.'[5] It is not surprising given Lewes' philosophical position to find that the positivist account emerges triumphant from his enquiry. However, while Lewes' criterion orients his approach to the question, Hopkins' argument ultimately concludes by affirming a Kantian theory of mind.

Hopkins' introductory exposition of the various theories of causation corresponds to Lewes' emphases by allocating most space to the empiricists, less to Kant, while the ontologists receive little more than a mention. The essay begins by placing the Kantian theory with the ontological: 'the difference between the Cartesians and Kant is of no importance when either is contrasted with the Empirical explanation' (fo. 3). According to Humean empiricism the relation of cause and effect results from the mind's association of two events that are invariably experienced in a particular sequence. To explain cause 'properly you [must]', Hopkins writes in the 'Further notes' appended to the essay, 'take away the mystical idea' (fo. 5). This criterion is seen to set the empiricist theory apart from the two metaphysical approaches. The Cartesian conception of causation is described as 'one of our innate ideas, our necessary beliefs', while the essay maintains that for Kant the 'belief in causation is ... a[n a priori] form of thought and beyond this point allows no further analogies, is inexplicable' (fos. 3–4).

The passage from which these extracts are drawn is, however, superseded by a note that appears directly opposite it. This declares that the ontologists are 'marked off by their supposition of a *reale substratum* of power or force' which 'Kant w[oul]d deny as fully as the Empirics'. Consequently, 'his view comes to be in truth indistinguishable fr[om] theirs' (fo. 3ᵛ). This volte-face indicates that the note was added after the completion of the essay. The regrouping of Kant with the empiricists appears to be the unforeseen consequence of a line of argument that Hopkins embarks upon in order to defend the empiricist theory: 'Perhaps

---

[5] Lewes, *History of Philosophy*, 551.

1. Drawing by Hopkins of a figure representing a quatrefoil or a
Maltese cross

if the Positivist definition of cause and effect were made more
comprehensively the Cantian [*sic*] arguments would not be felt
so effective against it' (fo. 4). His argument progresses in such
a way, however, that in extending the empiricist notion of cause
and effect he does not refute transcendental theory but rather
incorporates it. It is in this way that he comes to make his
radical reassessment of the relation between the two schools of
thought, (and, overcoming his suspicion of the transcendental
theory, restores the 'K' to his aberrant spelling, 'Cantian').

Hopkins responds to the Kantian criticism of empiricist
theory that 'Mere sequence . . . may be actually shewn to be
insufficient' by suggesting that the associations made by the
mind can be of a different nature from that of antecedent and
consequent. He maintains that the 'Positivist theory of Causation properly stated would allow effects to coexist as well as to
follow causes' (fo. 3ᵛ). He endeavours to demonstrate this
with the example of a figure 'taken from the arts' (see fig. 1):

Suppose a white disk on a dark ground, say of a frescoed wall. On the
disk are four dark pear-shaped pieces, their points meeting at the
centre of the disk, their round ends touching the circumference, so
that they make a sort of letter X. The figure made will be a quatrefoil.
Its efficient cause is the draughtsman or architect, its material cause
the dark colour, its formal cause the four pieces because if there had
been three it w[oul]d have been a trefoil and if five a cinquefoil.

The passage continues: 'Here this point deserves notice, that
causes cannot be counted.' The 'causes' are identified here with
the visible attributes that are predicated of a thing, 'Every point
. . . in a figure is a cause, every [point] a condition' (fo. 4).

The idea put forward here of cause as a plurality of 'conditions' probably derives from Mill's *Logic*: 'The cause, then,

philosophically speaking, is the sum total of the conditions, positive and negative taken together.'[6] The 'positive' conditions in Hopkins' example are easily recognizable as the particular aspects of shape and colour by which he describes the figure. The 'negative' conditions involve the consideration of what the thing is not, those qualities which it does not have and which accordingly define it negatively: 'If the figure had five members we sh[oul]d cease to call it a quatrefoil at all, but if merely the curves of the foiling had been ever so little prolonged or rounded together it w[oul]d no longer have been *this* quatrefoil' (fo. 4).

The nature of Hopkins' example here permits him to construe the Millian notion of cause as a set of contingent 'condition[s]' so that they accord with Aristotelian ontology. From the point of view of the Millian epistemology the causes or 'condition[s]' are discrete sensory impressions, the atomistic units of sense data to which empiricist psychology believes thought can be reduced. In the example that Hopkins gives these empirical details also function as the Aristotelian 'causes', which are integral to a principle of form or essence. A note to the essay, which mentions Mill and appears alongside the conclusion to his discussion of the idea of 'conditions', states that this 'true theory [is] in fact anticipated by Aristotle, who gives such a list of causes for a statue as that their whole is the statue' (fo. 4^{v}). Three of Aristotle's four modes of causation (i.e. the 'efficient', 'material', and 'formal cause') are applied to the figure of the quatrefoil in the extract quoted above.[7] The formal cause is notably identified in the essay with the Millian 'conditions'. Far from being the 'Positivist theory of Causation properly stated', this conflation of Aristotle and Mill is another of Hopkins' efforts to establish the need for 'metaphysics' in order to 'give ... meaning to laws and sequences and causes' (*J.* 118).

Aristotle uses the word 'cause' to refer to the radical nature

[6] Mill, *System of Logic*, i. 332.

[7] They are, in other words, not to be regarded as distinct types of causes but rather as different ways of describing the principle of cause (Jonathan Lear, *Aristotle: The Desire to Understand* (Cambridge: Cambridge University Press, 1988), 27). The fourth way of referring to the cause, that is, in terms of the *telos*, or form considered as the end to which a thing is directed, its fulfilment or actualization, is not mentioned in the essay due to the peculiar ambiguity of Hopkins' example.

which determines a thing's being, 'the "why" of [a thing]'.[8]
This is the principle of form, which is the means by which
Aristotle tackles the fundamental problem of change that preoccupies ancient philosophy; the problem of how identity can
be discerned from the flux and diversity of appearances, and
hence of how knowledge is possible. For Aristotle, the form is
responsible for the identity of a thing, so that the changes the
object undergoes are explained accordingly as the process by
which the form becomes manifest. He uses two relative terms to
refer to this process. Form in its latent state exists as a potentiality (*dynamis*), and in its realized state as an actuality (*energeia*).

Because changes are continuous and gradual, things can
exist at once as modes of both potentiality and actuality. Thus,
in the example which Hopkins alludes to in the notes to his
essay, a block of marble is an actuality relative to its state prior
to being hewn from the quarry, and a potentiality relative to the
statue which the sculptor can make of it.[9] In the essay's example of the quatrefoil, however, the relation between potentiality and actuality is more complex. While the irreducible
empirical details of the figure, which function here as both its
Millian 'conditions' and Aristotelian 'formal cause', are easily
apparent, the form they comprise is fundamentally ambiguous
and must accordingly be referred to the mind of the perceiving subject. The figure may be seen as a dark quatrefoil on a
white ground or else conversely:

The eye looking at the figure on a church wall might however be
suddenly struck by the thought that not a quatrefoil but a Maltese
cross was meant, a white cross thrown up on a dark ground. At once
the sheaf of causes become the effect, the old effect, the quatrefoil,
is scattered into a number of causes. (fo. 5)

From the point of view of Aristotelian ontology the figure sub-
sists in two forms, each of which is in its actual state the potentiality of the other. The figure of the quatrefoil functions as the
potentiality, the matter or 'conditions', from which the perceiver
recognizes the figure of the Maltese cross, and vice versa.

---

[8] *Physics*, 194ᵇ19–20. The equation here is literally with 'its primary cause', which is
often translated as the 'efficient' cause. My generalizing it here is justified for reasons
that are emphasized in Lear, *Aristotle*, ch. 2 and become obvious as my discussion
progresses. The present explication of Aristotle draws heavily upon Lear's account.
[9] Cf. Green's use of this example, *Works*, iii. 75.

The figure of the quatrefoil/Maltese cross is, as Hopkins remarks, 'an indisputable case . . . of effects coexisting, being exactly timed, with their causes' (fo. 4). This is, however, not to say that it strengthens the case for the positivist theory of causation. The way in which what were initially recognized collectively as the effects of the quatrefoil are transformed into the causes of the Maltese cross raises the question as to how this change in perception could arise if the mind is, as the empiricists maintain, fundamentally passive. Hopkins can no longer claim to be stating the positivist case, nor, for that matter, the Aristotelian. The new form represented by the Maltese cross is neither another impression in which the mind passively receives the given sensory data as a different sequence of association nor a recognition of an essence that necessarily has an objective existence. It is a new conception which the mind constructs. This is acknowledged by Hopkins' description of the way in which our perception of the elements of the figures changes: 'The eye . . . [is] struck by the thought.' The senses are presented here as subordinate to the mind according to the familiar pattern by which 'the Idea is only given . . . from the whole downwards to the parts' (J. 120). Hopkins' analysis presupposes a model of mind that is able to both intuit the atomistic 'conditions' discretely and organize them independently of the contingent sequences of their intuition: 'Accordingly an effect is nothing but the way in which the mind ties together, not the sequences, but all the conditions it sees. A cause therefore is a condition of a thing considered as contrasted with the whole thing, an effect a whole as contrasted with its conditions, elements, or parts' (fo. 5). The power of the mind to determine perceptions is indicated by the Whewellian inflection of the phrase, 'the mind ties together', and more strongly by the specification that 'an effect is *nothing but*' (my emphasis) this colligating act of gathering the empirical 'conditions' into a whole. Hopkins' analysis arrives at a theory of causation that corresponds to that which T. H. Green presented in his Greats lectures:

What we can say about [Causality] is that there is nothing in a sensation taken by itself to determine its sequence on another; nothing in the time which it occurs . . . Its position is determined by relation to [the] whole system of sensations, and sensations only thus form a system in virtue of a synthetic principle present to each yet identical with none, characterising each by relation to rest. This = thought.[10]

In other words, Green traces causation to subjective conscious-ness: 'But cause pre-supposes effect, just as much as effect cause. Both [are] relative to [the] unity of thought, which = true sub-stance; i.e. subject, which creates its object'.[11]

Hopkins, like Green, casts the relation of cause and effect in terms of the one of subjective consciousness and the many of its empirical objects, much as he does in the late essay on induction, which equates the unity of 'the causal tie' with the manifold of 'the mutual parts' that comprise 'a phenomenon' (D. IX 1, fo. 2). This relation is determined by the contrasts, or comparisons, that the mind is able to make between the 'whole' and the 'conditions, elements, or parts'. The 'compar-ison' that 'the mind . . . mak[es] between the whole and the parts, the parts and the whole' is, as Hopkins specifies in his 1868 notes, 'what the sense of unity means; mere sense that such a thing is one and not two has no interest or value except accidentally' (J. 126).

The 'Causation' essay, far from establishing a Humean prin-ciple of cognition, arrives at a conception of mind as active and able independently to organize sense-data into ideas. The dis-tinction made between the discrete 'conditions' of sense data as 'the mind ties [them] together' and the 'sequences' by which it receives them corresponds to that between their necessity and contingency. The conclusion that Hopkins reaches at the end of his essay in fact agrees with the judgement that he attrib-utes to Kant and appears to dispute earlier in the essay, that 'Mere sequence . . . may be actually shewn to be insufficient' (fo. 4) in accounting for our ideas.

II

By taking 'a figure from the arts', especially such an ambigu-ous one as the quatrefoil/Maltese cross, Hopkins translates the

---

[10] Balliol, T. H. Green Papers, MS II. 2(a), 1A 3, fo. 4ᵛ.
[11] Ibid. II. 2(a), 1A 12, fo. 28ᵛ. 'Just as thought distinguishes itself from itself', and thus creates an object so it breaks every thing into two elements, as effect and cause'. Green, 'Causation', ibid. II. 2(a), 1A 6, fo. 1.

issue of causality into the terms of perception and cognition that were introduced in Chapter 2. In accordance with his preference for these more encompassing and radical issues of epistemology, he, like Green, is interested not so much in the specific functions of the categories but rather with the general capacity for making synthetic a priori judgements that they represent and which Kant regards as a necessary quality of consciousness. This is the clear implication of what is probably the 'Causation' essay's final word on Kant, which occurs at the close of the note that groups him with the empiricists: 'It would have however to be allowed that the category of causation was nothing more than one form of our power of making concepts, generalising, would it not?' (D. VI 2, fo. 3ᵛ). This is essentially the conclusion that the 1867 essay on induction (D. IX 1) reaches through its analysis of the statement 'All double roses are barren.' It also reiterates the point made by the essay on 'A priori and a posteriori Truth' that the Kantian categories, 'like the Aristotelian, repeat and overlap (and may all be reduced to Relation)' (D. VI 1, fo. 1ᵛ). This last extract picks up on Kant's borrowing of Aristotelian terminology, and suggests a parallel between principles of form in the philosophies of each.

The principles of matter which complement Hopkins' analogy of the Aristotelian form and the Kantian synthetic a priori are presented by the 'Causation' essay in its equation of the 'conditions' of the quatrefoil and the Aristotelian formal cause. It becomes clear as the argument of the essay proceeds, however, that the form yielded by these conditions is not objective, but subjective, and the conclusion to the essay accordingly completes the parallel of Kant to Aristotle through its recognition of an a priori formal principle by 'which the mind ties together' these 'conditions'. The analogy that Hopkins perceives to exist between the two philosophies is stated most clearly in the essay on 'A posteriori Truth', where the Kantian philosophy is characterized as 'laying a new stress on the scholastic distinction of form and matter'.

The indecisiveness in the 'Causation' essay as to whether Kant should be grouped with the empiricists or the ontologists follows from Hopkins' sense that these contrasting positions are reconciled in the critical philosophy, much as materialism and idealism may be said to be mediated in Aristotle's realism: 'The two streams of thought fall together in Kant' (D. VI 1, fo. 1). The thought of Aristotle and of Kant appealed to Hopkins as synthetic philosophies which have a complementary relation to one another, the former addressing the typical concern of the ancients with the objective world, with ontology, the latter focusing upon the modern preoccupation with subjective consciousness, with epistemology.

The 'scholastic distinction of form and matter' is the fundamental pattern, the 'prepossession', which draws Hopkins to the thought of Aristotle and Kant, and provides the basis for his theory of the idea and of words. The 1868 set of notes which begin 'All words mean either things or relations of things . . .' (D. XII 5) sees the subjective idea and words to parallel one another: 'the word is the expression, *uttering* of the idea in the mind'. The elements of form and matter, of concept and empirical referents, comprise two of the three 'terms' of the word that Hopkins specifies in the notes: 'A word then has three terms belonging to it, ὅροι, or moments—its prepossession of feeling; its definition, abstraction, vocal expression or other utterance; and its application, "extension", the concrete things coming under it' (*J.* 125). The first of these aspects of the word, 'its prepossession', is a principle of consciousness which will be examined later.[12] Of the other terms the conceptual form of the word, its 'definition' or 'abstraction', applies to the 'concrete' matter of experience. The main interest of the 'All words . . .' notes with words which mean things, rather than relations, is continuous with Hopkins' earlier speculations about the authority of our inductive generalizations, because in using 'a word meaning a thing' we bring a concrete particular under a general definition. This involves a synthetic act of judgement, the recognition by the mind of what the 1867 essay on induction refers to as 'a certain causal tie' which gives unity to a phenomenon and connects it to all its instances: the application of a word meaning a thing is effectively a shorthand way of 'stating what are the mutual parts of a phenomenon and wherever the phenomenon is found it will have these parts, else it is not the same phenomenon' (D. IX, fo. 2).

---

[12] See Ch. 10, Sect. III.

The need for a formal principle to guarantee the consistency of the ideas that words represent is noted in an essay on 'The Moral System of Hobbes': 'Since then all knowledge [according to Hobbes] is of or from sensation, and that our own sensation, general ideas in the Realist sense are impossible and only general names are used' (D. XI 3, fo. 9). Hobbesian 'psychology' disavows the realist doctrine of universals and leaves in its stead mere nominalism. It allows the contingent and subjective 'matter' of sense to determine our ideas. Without a formal principle which vouchsafes the necessity and universality of the ideas informing words, meaning 'disintegrates and drops towards atomism' (*J.* 119).

Hopkins maintains that only one of the three terms of the word he describes in the 'All words . . .' notes 'in propriety is the word', and furthermore that 'not even the whole field of the middle term is covered by the word'. However, as a corollary of his subsequent definition of the word as 'the expression, *uttering* of the idea in the mind'[13] he effectively readmits the third term, the 'concrete things', to his scheme in the form of the empirical 'image (of sight or sound or *scapes* of the other senses)' (*J.* 125). While these qualities of form and matter comprise a mental synthesis in 'the idea in the mind' the earlier, broader, account of its parallel term, the word, specifies the relation that Hopkins sees to draw them together as 'terms . . . ὅροι or moments'.

The synonyms that Hopkins uses to describe the relation between the two aspects of the word, its conceptual definition and its concrete referents, indicate that he sees them to bear a logical relation to one another. The Greek ὅροι corresponds

---

[13] A representationalist theory of language can be traced to Aristotle, where it provides the presupposition for the 'method' which Hopkins uses in some of the essays 'of accepting τὰ λεγόμενα ['the things said'] as implying in themselves a history of thought and recognition' (*J.* 82). The theory also appears in Locke, principally in *An Essay Concerning Human Understanding*, III. ii. 3, but also in *The Conduct of the Understanding* (*The Works of John Locke* (London: 1823; repr. Aalen: Scientia, 1963), iii. 258, 249, 257, 280). Hopkins read this book in 1864 (*J.* 17, 19, 22). He would also have come across a Lockian version of representationalism in his reading of Friedrich Max Müller's *Lectures on the Science of Language* (*J.* 35–6; see *J.* 317). Representationalism is championed by Max Müller as a means for opposing contemporary 'developmentalism' (See *Lectures on the Science of Language*, 1st ser., 2nd edn. (London: Longman, Green, Longman, & Roberts, 1862), 359).

to the English 'terms' as it is used in mathematics and logic. In mathematics it refers to 'the terms of a ratio or proportion', a meaning which in Hopkins' context emphasizes the unity which the 'terms' of the word form. In Aristotelian logic it designates the terms of a proposition.[14] The use of the word *horoi* suggests that an Aristotelian relation akin to the syllogism inheres amongst the elements of the word. The 'definition', which is referred to and listed as 'the middle term' of the word, the 'only one [that] in propriety is the word', corresponds to the Aristotelian middle term. Hopkins' 'middle term', the definition or universal, provides the criterion by which the minor term, the particular instance of the 'concrete things coming *under* it' (my emphasis), may each be identified. Particulars are in this way predicated of the major term, the name or word which represents the universal idea.

The recognition of 'form' by the mind is for Hopkins, as the example of the ambiguous figure in the essay on 'Causation' illustrates, coeval with the apprehension of the discrete 'matter' of empirical intuitions. Hopkins' other synonym for 'terms' suggests a more dynamic version of the relation that makes these terms logically inextricable from one another. The use of the word *horoi* in Aristotle's syllogistic logic links it to the meaning of the word 'moments', which belongs to another triadic logic. While the word is first used in its philosophical sense by Kant, it assumes a more central role in the distinctive objective idealism of G. W. F. Hegel.[15]

The term 'moment' is used by Hegel to refer to the respective stages of thesis, antithesis, and synthesis which in his dialectics describe the ascent toward the full realization of the universal 'Absolute Idea' or 'Spirit'. At each stage of this transitional process moments are both nullified and preserved in higher moments: 'They sink from their initially imagined *self-subsistence* to the status of *moments*, which are still *distinct* but at the same

---

[14] It is also 'sometimes spoken of as if they [i.e. the ὅρος] were propositions', or, used in the singular, it can refer specifically to the middle term of a syllogism, the definition. (s.v. ὅρος, in H. G. Liddell and R. Scott, *A Greek–English Lexicon*, 8th edn. (Oxford: Clarendon Press, 1891)).

[15] Kant describes the three modalities of judgement, namely, the Problematic, the Assertoric, and the Apodictic, as 'so many moments of thought' (*Critique of Pure Reason*, A 76, B 101).

time are sublated.'[16] Jowett often refers to this process of dialectic as 'the Hegelian vibration of moments', a phrase which Hopkins would have come across in reading his teacher's essay 'On Predestination and Free Will' and probably also through his teaching.[17] The use of the words *horoi* and 'moments' in the 1868 notes highlights Hopkins' abiding effort to formulate the integral relations he sees to exist between parts of the idea. This is the goal of his early experiments in cross-pollinating basic Aristotelian and Kantian ideas, a combination that is fundamental also to the formation of Hegel's thought.[18]

III

An essay from Trinity term 1866,[19] the topic of which required Hopkins to 'Shew Cases in which Acts of Apprehension apparently simple are largely influenced by the Imagination' (D. III 5), provides a rendition of the 'scholastic distinction of form and matter' that suggests an especially close parallel to that of the 'All words . . .' notes. Its reference to the mind's sensory material as 'images' links it to the term of 'the image' in the 'All words . . .' notes, and suggests that its fuller account of the second, formal, term can be used to supplement our understanding of its counterpart in the notes, 'the conception':

Now if we try to look at the field of the mind at any few moments we may choose, to reflect in Locke's sense on our consciousness, we shall find two elements in our thoughts: these are first images, wh[ich] are either the sensations of the things we are looking at or listening

---

[16] Hegel, *Science of Logic*, vol. i, bk. I, sect. I, ch. 1, c(2), trans. A. V. Miller (London: Allen & Unwin, 1969), 105. Hopkins may well have read this section of the *Logic* in Stirling's 1865 translation (see Ch. 5, Sect. IV).

[17] Benjamin Jowett, *The Interpretation of Scripture and other Essays* (London: Routledge, n.d.), 509. I take it that it is this essay from Jowett's Pauline commentaries of 1855 that Hopkins refers to as 'Jowett's essay on Necessity and Free Will' in the essay on 'Causation' (D. VI 2, fo. 4ᵛ). The phrase used in this essay and other references to 'moments' also occurs in the introductory essays to Jowett's Plato, e.g.: 'But perhaps the nearest approach in modern philosophy to the universal science of Plato, is to be found in the Hegelian "succession of moments in the unity of the idea"' (*Republic*, 2nd edn. (Oxford: Clarendon Press, 1881), p. clxxxii).

[18] The discussion of the significance of Hopkins' knowledge of the concept of 'moments' is resumed in Ch. 7, Sect. I.

[19] Schmidt, 'Classical Studies', 179.

THE 'IDEA IN THE MIND'   79

to or representations of past sensations or thirdly images like those of memory and which might be such, and secondly a certain order or sequence in the images—not mere sequence: mere sequence we see in remembering our dreams; but such as has the character of necessity, as we commonly explain it. And broadly there are only these two elements in thought, presentations or representations and sequence. The last is in the widest sense logic. It is in the former that imagination lies.   (fo. 17)

As well as anticipating the 'All words...' notes this passage draws together terms that are used in Hopkins' other accounts of mind. The simple sense impressions or 'images', which in the essay on 'Causation' comprise 'all the conditions [that] it [i.e. the mind] sees', are received in a contingent series that both essays describe as 'mere sequence' (D. VI 2, fo. 5). This 'matter' is distinguished from the mind's independent organization of it, 'a certain order or sequence in the images' which, like the relation of cause and effect, 'has the character of necessity'. The account of 'our thoughts' here is familiar as the one which this and the preceding chapter argue has its ultimate provenance in Kant.[20] The introspective method by which it is arrived at can be identified with most philosophy of the modern period. That Hopkins associated it here with Locke indicates that in writing this essay he was influenced by G. H. Lewes,[21] who in his *Biographical History of Philosophy* emphasizes Locke's 'rationalism' and defends him against the prevalent 'vulgar error' in which he is depicted as 'the chief of the so-called Sensational School'.[22]

The formal principle of thought is intriguingly identified in

[20] Indeed the broadly Kantian principle of constructive thought is acknowledged directly in a passage on the 'three meanings' of the word 'Imagination', which appears to be a note to the opening sentence of the essay, 'We must first try to have some definition of imagination' (fo. 16). The longest of these accounts notes that the word is used 'in the Kantian sense, and with the same force as *einbildung* and *envisager*, for the process by which a handful of attributes are held together in unity, become an idea' (fos. 15ᵛ–16ᵛ). However, while the general sense of this account of Kant and the passage from the main body of the essay express comparable theories of mind, the language in which they do so differs markedly. The reason for this may well be that the notes were added later, after Hopkins had discussed the essay with his tutor Walter Pater.

[21] Lewes, *History of Philosophy*, 434. See also ibid. 418.

[22] Ibid. 429, 439. Locke's rationalism is argued for by Richard Aaron (*John Locke*, 3rd edn. (Oxford: Clarendon Press, 1971), app. 4) and by Yolton.

the essay on 'Imagination' as 'in the widest sense logic'. Hopkins regards 'logic' in this essay in the same way as he does transcendental idealism in the essay on 'A posteriori Truth', that is, as having an essentially 'psychological' bearing. His psychologistic construal of 'logic' is probably a reflection of Greats philosophy at the time. Rogers' 1861 commentary on Education in Oxford observes that the subject of logic at Oxford was 'viewed especially from a psychological aspect'.[23] This suggests the influence upon Greats teaching of Kant, who uses the term 'logic' to designate the purely formal and a priori nature of pure reason. He writes, for instance, of the 'purely logical' 'meaning' that the categories have 'after elimination of every sensible condition',[24] and attributes the lack of progress in metaphysics to the practice of building arguments exclusively upon such purely logical concepts.

Hopkins' psychologistic notion of 'logic' may well have arisen from the fact that his understanding of Kant is mediated by his familiarity with Aristotle. This is most apparent from the essay on 'A posteriori Truth', which dates from soon after that on 'Imagination'.[25] Just as the categories, Aristotelian and Kantian alike, are equated here with a certain quality of 'Relation' (D. VI 1, fo. 1ᵛ), so in the essay on 'Imagination' Hopkins' principle of 'logic', which confounds formal logic with psychology, is similarly identified with a 'sequence . . . such as has the character of necessity'. An implication of this identification is that the mind's judgements of 'sequence' may be attributed not only with 'necessity' but also universality, the other quality that formal logic works to establish and which Kant regards as a definitive condition of synthetic a priori judgements.

Hopkins discusses psychologistic conceptions of 'logic' in another essay from notebook D. III, 'The Origin of Our Moral Ideas'. This essay defines 'logic in the truer sense' as 'everything which determines the mind to act'. It also makes the following curious comparison: 'In the general case logic without any medium determines the mind, as if there is no way into a field but by a gate, we go in by the gate' (J. 81). Just as a gate may be the only entrance to a fenced field, so here the rules of logic are seen to provide our only access to knowledge. This figure provides an analogy for the Kantian theory, in which the a priori structures of the mind, principally the categories, provide our only access to an understanding of objects. Hopkins' conception of logic marks a radical departure from that expounded in Mill's *System of Logic*,[26] and accordingly provides an index of the relation of his epistemology to the empiricist orthodoxy of his day.

The discussions of 'logic' in the essays from notebook D. III furnish a gloss for the principle of 'the conception', which is introduced, ostensibly without any explanation, in the 'All words . . .' notes. Familiarity with Hopkins' principle of 'logic', his distinction of necessary and contingent 'sequences' of thought, enables us to see that his bare allusion to 'the conception' in these private notes is in fact elaborated upon in the exposition that follows it of the mind's 'energy':

The mind has two kinds of energy, a transitional kind, when one thought or sensation follows another, which is to reason, whether actively as in deliberation, criticism, or passively, so to call it, as in reading etc; [and] (ii) an abiding kind . . . in which the mind is absorbed . . . taken up by, dwells upon, enjoys, a single thought . . . Art exacts this energy of contemplation but also the other one, and in fact they are not incompatible, for even in the successive arts as music, for full enjoyment, the synthesis of the succession should give, unlock, the contemplative enjoyment of the unity of the whole. (*J.* 125–6)

The attribution to the mind of its own kinds of 'energy' indicates that it is able to act independently of its 'matter'. The first or 'transitional' energy, 'which is to reason', is a constructive principle concerned with the sequence of particular 'thought[s]' and 'sensation[s]'. This is most obviously the case with the category of reasoning 'actively'. The second category, 'to reason . . . passively, *so to call it*, as in reading etc' (my emphasis) is passive only relative to the first. The qualification to the adverb indicates that it has only a nominal significance. The example that Hopkins gives illustrates the point, for reading, like

---

[26] Mill has been accused of psychologism, a charge which, however, John Skorupski sees to arise only with Husserl and, furthermore, to be substantively groundless (*John Stuart Mill* (London: Routledge, 1989), 164).

listening to music, requires that the mind create or discern 'the synthesis of the succession', for in this case as in other acts of perception, such as those discussed in the 'Causation' essay, the sequence in which information is received does not invariably coincide with the sequence that comprises its significance. This active capacity for synthesis produces the necessary unity of ideas, the formal 'conception', whereas 'mere sense', like the 'mere sequence' discussed in earlier essays, in itself lacks such authority.

IV

Given his concern with 'form' it is natural that Hopkins should find questions of aesthetics especially engaging. According to the 'All words . . .' notes 'Works of art . . . like words utter the idea and . . . represent . . . real things' (*J.* 126). His theory of art accordingly provides an interesting and revealing complement to the active 'transitional kind' of 'energy' with which the mind works actively to synthesize the intuitions it receives.

The early essay 'On the Signs of Health and Decay in the Arts' expresses the Kantian view that 'some scientific basis of aesthetical criticism is absolutely needed', and, furthermore, that 'at the beginning of any science of aesthetics must stand the analysis of the nature of Beauty' (*J.* 75). In trying to achieve this object Hopkins establishes a model of mind that is fundamental also to his epistemology. According to the essay 'the original cause of our sense of the beautiful . . . is comparison'. This is, as was observed in Chapter 2, traced in the essay to the nature of consciousness itself, the mind's radical 'comparison . . . of existence with non-existence'. That which is established in later essays as the mind's formal capacity for determining necessary relations amongst our sensory intuitions is introduced in this early essay by the 'four degrees or dimensions of [comparison]' that Hopkins deduces from his principle of consciousness. Of these the third and fourth belong to Art: 'the comparison . . . (iii) of two or more things together, so as to include the principles of Dualism, Plurality, Repetition, Parallelism, and Variety, Contrast, Antithesis; (iv) of finite with infinite things, which can only be done by suggestion; this is the ἀρχή of the Suggestive, the Picturesque and the Sublime' (*J.* 74). The third of these 'dimensions' is the most important for Hopkins' account. Such comparisons may be of two types: referential or purely formal.

Not surprisingly, given Hopkins' deduction of it from consciousness itself, the third category marks the coincidence of aesthetics with epistemology: 'The pleasure given by the presence of Truth in Art may... be referred to the third head' (*J.* 74). This is seen to lie 'in a (not sensuous but purely intellectual) comparison of the representation in Art with the memory of the true thing; the truer it is, the more exact the parallel between the two, the more pleasure is perceived' (*J.* 74–5). The 'memory of the true thing' clearly takes the form of an 'idea in the mind'. In the early essay, as in the later notes, art is seen to give expression to our idea of a thing. Much as the schematic 'image' of the idea, which is described in the 'All words ...' notes as 'a refined energy' and 'a word to oneself', partakes of both the particularity of sense impressions and the generality of 'the conception', so similarly the representation of the idea by the work of art takes an analogous, symbolic, form. The essay gives the example of a conventional medieval depiction of the tree, which blends the universal, in the form of 'a typical outline' of the tree's shape, with concrete detail, 'a few careful representative leaves' (*J.* 78). The former element is identified with 'idealism' and the latter with '[perceptual] realism', each of which corresponds respectively to the terms of 'form' and 'matter' that Hopkins presents in later essays as integral to acts of perception.

The datum for the mental comparison in cases of referential art, such as the picture of the tree, is provided by the mind's idea of the object. The other sort of beauty, which lacks any such specific content, expresses the purely formal relation of differentiated unity that characterizes ideas in the mind. Hopkins writes that the former 'kind of beauty however inseparable from a work of art is extrinsic and is implied in the spectator', while the latter, 'the deliberate beauty of composition, form, melody etc', is 'given ... intrinsic' (*J.* 75). This formal or 'intrinsic' type of beauty and the other referential or 'extrinsic' type correspond respectively to Kant's principles of 'free beauty' and 'dependent beauty':

The first presupposes no concept of what the object should be; the second does presuppose such a concept and, with it, an answering perfection of the object. Those of the first kind are said to be (self-subsisting) beauties of this thing or that thing; the other kind of beauty, being attached to a concept (conditioned beauty), is ascribed to Objects which come under the concept of a particular end.[27]

Kant, like Hopkins, judges beauty by its effect, and accordingly sees it to be a function of the nature of the mind that apprehends it. In Kant's system the mind responds to representations through cognition, the formation of the concept by the imagination and the understanding. This function is described by Hopkins in the 'All words . . .' notes as the formation of the idea in its aspects of the 'image' and the 'conception', which occurs through the efforts of the mind's 'first' or 'transitional' kind of energy. The form of the idea is defined by Hopkins as complex unity, and it is accordingly in terms of it that he acknowledges the universality of what can be referred to in the Kantian term as cognition: 'All thought is of course in a sense an effort a[t] unity' (*J.* 83). Cognition is for Kant the definitive characteristic of thought, 'the one and only representation which is valid for every one'.[28] He believes that beauty derives its universality and objectivity from the form of a 'cognition in general', a complex unity. Hopkins' description of his formal aesthetic categories as 'expressions of proportion . . . to our ideas' (*J.* 76) parallels the Kantian derivation of artistic form from the general form of thought. Furthermore, Hopkins' theory of formal beauty, which receives its most developed and elaborate exposition in the 'Platonic Dialogue', identifies it with a proportionate interaction of formal principles which express regularity and irregularity. While the immediate source for Hopkins of these principles was probably Ruskin,[29] their provenance can be traced to Kant's third *Critique*, where they answer to the respective requirements of the understanding and the imagination.

The form of the mental idea in both Hopkins' and Kant's theories of mind describes a differentiated unity. According to Kant the regulative rules or categories of the understanding

---

[27] *Critique of Judgement*, 229. All extracts from this work are from James Creed Meredith's translation (Oxford: Oxford University Press, 1952).
[28] Ibid. 217.   [29] Fraser, *Beauty and Belief*, 82.

work to bring to unity the manifold of our sense intuitions, a task that is mediated by the imagination. Similarly, in Hopkins' principle of 'the idea in the mind' 'the conception' marks the moment of formal unity that is facilitated by the mind's synthesizing 'energy', while the numerous 'sensation[s] from without' that constitute its matter are presented schematically in the moment of 'the image'. Kant expresses his principle of the understanding in terms of 'regularity': 'The regularity that conduces to the concept of an object is, in fact, the indispensable condition (*conditio sine qua non*) of grasping the object as a single representation and giving to the manifold its determinate form'. Correspondingly, the complementary Kantian faculty of the imagination embodies the opposite principle to law, namely, freedom. Scope for the free activity of the imagination is accordingly provided by cases of irregularity: 'Thus English taste in gardens, and fantastic taste in furniture, push the freedom of imagination to the verge of what is grotesque—the idea being that in this divorce from all constraint of rules the precise instance is being afforded where taste can exhibit its perfection in projects of the imagination to the fullest extent.'[30]

Although the contradictory requirements of the imagination and understanding are met respectively by principles of irregularity and regularity, Kant regards it as a mistake to speak of 'irregular beauty' and 'regular beauty'.[31] He maintains that, while the surfeit of one principle may make the other attractive, in judgements of taste the two are, as Hopkins maintains also, inextricable from one another. They fuse in a relation which derives its universality from the form of a cognition in general or, in the terms of Hopkins' parallel account, from the form of 'the idea in the mind'.

While in the case of knowledge the imagination is made to conform to the requirements of the understanding, in the apprehension of beauty this relation is seen by Kant to be reversed, so that 'understanding is at the service of imagination'.[32] In such instances of 'free' beauty the representation does not, according to Kant, provide us with a definite concept, but rather with an harmonious 'free play' between the imagination and the

---

[30] *Critique of Judgement*, 242.   [31] Ibid. 243.   [32] Ibid. 242.

understanding, in which the freedom required by the imagination coincides with the principle of law or regularity required by the understanding. This 'proportionate accord',[33] as Kant refers to it, is paralleled by Hopkins' principle of beauty as a formal synthesis of principles of regularity and irregularity, which, furthermore, bears a relation of 'proportion . . . to our ideas', that is, to the form of differentiated unity that defines 'the idea in the mind'.

V

That the understanding is 'at the service of the imagination' in the apprehension of 'free' beauty naturally entails, as Kant observes, that such aesthetic representations occur in a sensuous form: 'There is . . . no other way for the subjective unity of the relation in question to make itself known than by sensation.'[34] Hopkins expresses this definitive condition of the apprehension of 'free' beauty in the 'Health and Decay' essay, where he writes of 'deliberate Beauty' that it 'need neither imitate Nature nor express anything beyond the beauty appreciable not by the intellect, so to speak, but by the senses, that is in fact, *by the intellect employed upon the object of the sense alone*' (*J.* 75; my emphases).

It is in this abstract formal representation of the idea that its dialectical nature becomes most clearly apparent, as each principle of regularity and irregularity is determined only in relation to the other. This is illustrated in the 'Platonic Dialogue' by the example of the chestnut-fan: 'it is not the radiation which is the beauty of the fan, but the radiation heightened by its cessation near the stalk . . . Nor the likeness of the leaves, but their likeness as thrown up by their difference in size' (*J.* 93).[35] However, as 'The Probable Future of Metaphysics' makes

[33] Ibid. 219.   [34] Ibid. 219.

[35] The example of the chestnut-fan is often used by Ruskin to illustrate a similar hypothesis. See e.g. the discussion of 'The Law of Radiation', in *The Elements of Drawing* (*The Library Edition of The Works of John Ruskin*, ed. E. T. Cook and Alexander Wedderburn (London: George Allen, 1904), xv. 180–91, esp. 181). Another likely source for Hopkins was Owen Jones' *The Grammar of Ornament* (London: Day & Son, 1856). A drawing of the chestnut-fan is included amongst the ten

explicit, this relative principle does not result in relativism, but rather in a form which the mind experiences as final and absolute:

The new Realism will maintain that in musical strings the roots of chords, to use technical wording, are mathematically fixed and give a standard by which to fix all the notes of the appropriate scale: when points between these are sounded the ear is annoyed by a solecism, or to analyse deeper, the mind cannot grasp the notes of the scale and the intermediate sound in one conception; so also there are certain forms which have a great hold on the mind and are always reappearing and seem imperishable, such as the designs of Greek vases and lyres, the cone upon Indian shawls, the honeysuckle moulding, the fleur-de-lys, while every day we see designs both simple and elaborate which do not live and are at once forgotten; and some pictures we may long look at and never grasp or hold together, while the composition of others strikes the mind with a conception of unity which is never dislodged: and these things are inexplicable on the theory of pure chromatism or continuity—the forms have in some sense or other an absolute existence. (*J.* 120)

The mind is able to 'grasp or hold together' some pictorial compositions more easily than others. Similarly, in the example drawn from music, the mind recognizes the notes of a scale but not half-notes which intervene between them. This is so simply because of the nature of the mind's capacity for comparison and judgement: 'the mind cannot grasp the notes of the scale and the intermediate sound in one conception; so also there are certain forms which have a great hold on the mind'.

The 'arabesques, diapers etc' which Hopkins gives as instances of 'deliberate Beauty' in the 'Health and Decay' essay, and the examples of the 'certain forms' in the above passage—'the designs of Greek vases and lyres, the cone upon Indian shawls,[36] the honeysuckle moulding, the fleur-de-lys'—belong to the same category of forms as those which Kant gives as illustrations of

plates which Owen used to demonstrate 'principles [of beauty which] he believed were found in organic nature but could not be realized by the slavish copying of natural forms' (E. H. Gombrich, *The Sense of Order*, 2nd edn. (Ithaca, NY: Cornell University Press, 1979), 54.

[36] The use of this 'Paisley' pattern on shawls was 'extremely fashionable' in the 1860s (C. W. Cunnington and P. E. Cunnington, *Handbook of English Costume in the Nineteenth Century* (London: Faber, 1959), 477).

'free beauties': 'designs à la grecque, foliage for framework or on wall papers', and such natural phenomena as flowers, crustaceans, humming birds, and birds of paradise, as long as they are regarded only as forms and not according to their ends.[37] The chestnut-fan, which is discussed in the 'Platonic Dialogue', is the pre-eminent example in Hopkins' writings of those forms which are taken from nature and regarded according to the Kantian prescription without reference to their purpose. The same organic proportion of regularity and irregularity instanced by the chestnut-fan is easily recognizable, albeit in more idealized shapes, in the 'forms' that Hopkins lists.

The violent metaphor of *striking* which Hopkins uses to describe the effect of the apprehension of formal beauty ('the composition . . . strikes the mind with a conception of unity which is never dislodged') implies that the mind is stunned or immobilized in some way by the encounter. Such a static effect corresponds to what the 'All words . . .' notes specify as the mind's 'energy of contemplation' which 'Art exacts':

an abiding kind [of energy] for which I remember no name, in which the mind is absorbed (as far as that may be), taken up by, dwells upon, enjoys, a single thought: we may call it contemplation, but it includes pleasures, supposing they, however turbid, do not require a transition to another term *of another kind*, for contemplation in its absoluteness is impossible unless in a trance and it is enough for the mind to repeat the same energy on the same matter. (*J.* 125–6)

The representation of the formal idea consists of a proportionate interaction of principles of regularity and irregularity which, in being apprehended directly by the mind as an objective unity, engenders a correspondingly static type of contemplation. This state of mind is literally, in the words of 'The Probable Future of Metaphysics', a 'hold on the mind', a suspension of the mind's more typical energy, the 'transitional kind, when one thought or sensation follows another, which is to reason' (*J.* 125). The effect, by which proportion in our representations leads to their institution in the mind, is noted by Hopkins in 'Poetic Diction': 'parallelism in expression tends to beget or passes into parallelism in thought' (*J.* 85). For Kant and Hopkins

---

[37] *Critique of Judgement*, 229.

alike this communication of form leads to states of mind which both speak of as the pleasure of aesthetic apprehension.

Hopkins' second kind of energy, the 'energy of contemplation', is a quiescent state like the '*restful* contemplation'[38] which Kant associates with aesthetic judgement. This kind of energy, 'in which the mind is absorbed . . . taken up by, dwells upon, enjoys, a single thought', is consistent with the activity of aesthetic apprehension which the 'Health and Decay' essay describes as 'the intellect employed upon the object of the sense alone and not referring back or performing some wider act within itself'. The 'contemplative enjoyment' of art, in which the mind repeats 'the same energy on the same matter', clearly corresponds to that which Kant describes as the 'free play' of the understanding and the imagination:

This pleasure . . . involves an inherent causality, that, namely, of *preserving a continuance* of the state of the representation itself and the active engagement of the cognitive powers without ulterior aim. We dwell on the contemplation of the beautiful because this contemplation strengthens and reproduces itself. The case is analogous (but analogous only) to the way we linger on a charm in the representation of an object which keeps arresting the attention, the mind all the while remaining passive.[39]

Hopkins, like Kant, regards certain formal configurations of regularity and irregularity to have a peculiar aptness to the nature of the mind that apprehends them. Where Hopkins differs from Kant, however, is in his realist epistemology, according to which the apprehension of beauty furnishes the paradigm case for perception. He accordingly stresses the continuity that exists between the mind's 'two kinds of energy', seeing the aesthetic state of mind to supervene upon certain recognitions of unity made through the processes of reasoning: 'in fact they are not incompatible, for even in the successive arts as music, for full enjoyment, the synthesis of the succession should give, unlock, the contemplative enjoyment of the whole' (*J.* 126). The metaphoric 'unlock[ing]' suggests a precise alignment, as of a key to a lock, between the nature of the artistic form and the requirements (and hence, the nature) of the mind which

[38] Ibid. 258.   [39] Ibid. 222.

apprehends them. In this version of aesthetic apprehension the temporal conditions of perception are transcended, 'unlock[ed]', much as in 'The Windhover' the discretely perceived attributes listed in the first line of the sestet ('Brute beauty and valour and act, oh, air, pride, plume') 'Buckle' in a flash of synchronous meaning (No. 120). Hopkins, like Coleridge, sees all acts of perception to differ in *degree* rather than in *kind*.[40]

Chromatism, the condition of the 'succession', represents for Hopkins the general problem of time or change which in our perception, and as manifest in the objective flux of nature, necessarily removes the subject from the synchronous intuition of things-in-themselves. However, the first type of energy, 'which is to reason', is also that responsible for constructing from this flow of fragmentary impressions the idea, that is, an apt representation of the original objective instance of unity. The idea in the mind is, as the epiphany of 'The Windhover' highlights, thus removed from the time condition which was integral to the intuition of its actual object. Hopkins is accordingly assured that the peculiar form of the idea allows us to have knowledge of things-in-themselves. Ironically, it is from this Kantian notion of mind as a constructive principle which thinks in a way that is 'independent of the accidents under which . . . experience comes to individuals' (D. X 3, fo. 18) that Hopkins strains to realize such an unKantian conclusion.

For Hopkins the form of the idea is diatonic, but in a way that contains, rather than denies, the chromatic principle. While he has, as many of his commentators observe, an appropriately marked preference for the diatonic, this should not be understood as a simple antipathy to the principle of chromatism. It is 'the theory of *pure* chromatism' (*J.* 120; my emphasis) that is objected to in 'The Probable Future of Metaphysics', not chromatism *per se*, for the principle is as crucial to the composition of the ultimate diatonic form, the unity of the idea, as its antithetical principle, the trivial oneness of uniformity. It is precisely the synthesis of the subordinate principles of

[40] Coleridge's 'primary' imagination, which he 'hold[s] to be the living Power and prime Agent of all human Perception', differs from the 'secondary' or creative, imagination, 'only in *degree*, and in the *mode* of its operation'. As with Hopkins' first kind of energy, 'it struggles to idealize and to unify' (*Biographia Literaria*, ch. 13).

chromatism and diatonism, that is, the simple 'image' and the 'conception', that comprises the fixed form of differentiated unity which Hopkins champions.

Hopkins' aesthetic theory is predicated upon his account of 'the idea in the mind', the 'two terms' of which the essays on epistemology identify variously with the 'scholastic distinction of form and matter', the contingent and necessary types of 'sequence', and 'the image' and 'logic'. That the mind is able to apprehend beauty immediately suggests that there is a direct formal analogy between objects in the world and our mental idea, a pre-alignment that Hopkins will trace 'back to God beauty's self and beauty's giver' (No. 148). It suggests the incarnationalist understanding of the world expressed in the later poems, in which what Hopkins refers to in the 1868 'Notes' as 'the Idea' is seen to be expressed in the phenomena of Creation; a Hegelian development of Kant that was available to him from Green's teaching: 'Art posits the ideal as an object of sensuous intuition. So Art is analogous to Religion only lower; the highest Art is ecclesiastical.'[41]

[41] Merton, Bradley Papers, MS I-A1, Notes on T. H. Green's Lectures (1867), Lect. XXIII.

4   Moral Philosophy

I

While Hopkins attributes the mind with a radical capacity for making synthetic a priori judgements, and so vouchsafes the possibility of objectivity, of the mind's autonomy from the contingencies of sense intuitions, he does so without fixing the form of this objectivity to the bureaucratic processes of the Kantian faculty psychology. Whereas the Kantian categories define our understanding of objects with some precision, Hopkins' version of Kant provides no such means of specifying the forms of necessity and universality that determine particular judgements of 'Relation' or of differentiated 'unity'. The effect of this is to give to the individual mind a degree of choice in making its judgements. According to the essay on 'Causation' the subject's 'mind ties together . . . all the conditions it sees', yet the simple figure of the quatrefoil/Maltese cross that Hopkins uses to demonstrate this process offers a choice of two equally valid interpretations, different ways of discerning unity from 'its conditions, elements, or parts'.

The mutually exclusive nature of the possible interpretations of the figure means that some minds will necessarily respond to it by immediately perceiving a quatrefoil and others the Maltese cross. Which of the figures is recognized will depend upon the point of view from which it is approached.[1] The initial description of the figure as a quatrefoil, for example, gives the reader of Hopkins' essay a simple 'prepossession' with which to interpret the drawing adjacent to it in the manuscript essay. This variable is theorized in the 'Parmenides' notes, which suggest that the 'difference[s]' presented by the 'scape[s]' or

---

[1] Cf. Wittgenstein's duck–rabbit example, which he uses to distinguish a type of seeing in which 'what I perceive in the dawning of an aspect is not a property of the object, but an internal relation between it and other objects', *Philosophical Investigations*, trans. G. E. M. Anscombe, 2nd edn. (Oxford: Blackwell, 1958), 212.

appearances of 'the phenomenal world' are contingent upon perspective, 'Foreshortening' (*J.* 130). The mind has some scope for making choices as to how it will organize the 'offers' which the world of objects make 'to the eye to foredraw': 'The eye looking at the figure on a church wall might . . . be suddenly struck by the thought that not a quatrefoil but a Maltese cross was meant' (*J.* 129; D. VI 2, fo. 5).

Hopkins assumes that one of the two equally plausible possible construals of the figure 'was meant', in other words, that it is sanctioned by the artist's intention in composing it. His ascription of an underlying purpose is clearly a figure of speech, but none the less revealing for being used so unselfconsciously. It marks his presupposition of an 'author-function',[2] a strategy in literary criticism which works to limit the proliferation of a text's meanings by privileging one interpretation, which is identified with the artist's supposed intention, over all others. This argument is writ large in natural theology, where the record of the divine will furnished by the Bible is invoked as the final authority for the interpretation of Creation, God's Book of Nature. Hopkins' casual allusion to the figure perceived in one interpretation as 'meant' indicates his habituation to the idea of a 'transcendental signified',[3] namely God, which provides an anchor for meaning, and the attendant realist faith that all acts of perception, whatever their possibilities for interpretation, have a real and knowable object.

The essay on 'Causation' suggests that while the mind is able to make a number of interpretations of an object, not all of these involve a recognition of what is 'meant' by the object, that is, the intention which informs it and gives it purpose. In the case of art objects, such as the quatrefoil, this meaning or purpose originates with the artist's intention, while in the analogous case

---

[2] Michel Foucault, 'What is an Author?', in *Textual Strategies: Perspectives in Post-structuralist Criticism*, ed. and trans. Josué V. Harari (London: Methuen, 1979), 141–60. See also Roland Barthes, 'The Death of the Author', in Roland Barthes, *Image–Music–Text*, ed. and trans. Stephen Heath (London: Fontana, 1977), 142–8.

[3] For a discussion of the relation between the Derridean critique of logocentrism and Hopkins' work, see Michael Sprinker, '*A Counterpoint of Dissonance': The Aesthetics and Poetry of Gerard Manley Hopkins* (Baltimore: The Johns Hopkins University Press, 1980), 70–2, and J. Hillis Miller, *The Linguistic Moment* (Princeton: Princeton University Press, 1985), ch. 5, esp. 259–66.

of natural objects, such as the windhover, their significance must, according to Hopkins, be traced to their Creator. The figure described in the essay can sustain two equally convincing interpretations, while the construals of the windhover, as 'a bird' and as Christ the 'chevalier!',[4] similarly provide two registers of truth about the phenomenon perceived, the latter of which is for Hopkins ontologically more radical.

Perception is for Hopkins an act of choice, and a moral responsibility, for 'man' is 'Earth's eye'. The fallen nature of humankind, however, means that its vision is selfish and solipsistic. Fallen man, 'To his own selfbent so bound' (No. 149), is not well disposed to look beyond the self and so recognize the objective truth of a world suffused with divine significance.[5]

Hopkins places perception within the moral sphere, interlacing it with questions of free will and of character, and subsuming it within his larger theological concerns. Free will is required as the condition for being able to make interpretative choices, while the nature of such choices will be expressive of a particular character. For perceptions to have meaning as acts of devotion to God they must, according to Hopkins, be the outcome of the free will of a good character. The modern question of the freedom of the will is pursued by Hopkins along Kantian lines, while his other doctrine, of the moral nature of individual character, draws upon the *Nicomachean Ethics*.

II

The study of ethics was, due largely to the clerical control of Oxford, the main focus of philosophy studies at the university during the nineteenth century. Aristotle's *Nicomachean Ethics* and Butler's *Sermons* and *Analogy* were entrenched early in the century as prescribed reading for Greats.[6] The *Ethics* remained the central text for the course during the 1860s, while a growing

---

[4] On this identification, see *Poetical Works*, ed. MacKenzie, 383.

[5] For further discussion of the moral implications of perception for Hopkins, see Ch. 10, Sect. III.

[6] Turner, *Greek Heritage*, 324, dates the establishment of the *Ethics* in Greats with the Examination Statute of 1800. On Butler, see David Newsome, *Two Classes of Men* (New York: St Martin's Press, 1974), 73.

concern with Kantian moral philosophy came to supersede the study of Butler. Just as Aristotle was studied in relation to Butler earlier in the century,[7] so from the time that Hopkins was at Oxford Aristotelian and Kantian moral philosophy came increasingly to be viewed in the light of one another. This tendency is strongly represented in the writings of Hopkins' tutor for the *Ethics*, T. H. Green, who was himself to become an eminent moral philosopher. It is also considered by Alexander Grant in the essays to his edition of the *Ethics*, which was, as notebook G. I indicates,[8] the text that Hopkins studied. '[T]he changes in the interpretation of Aristotle are' Hatch writes in his 1858 review of Grant's edition, 'the key to the inner workings of the Oxford mind: the stages of the one are the stages of the other.'[9]

Hopkins characterizes moral acts according to the following distinction: 'There are two parts in moral action, the thing to be done and the impulse to do it' (*J.* 123). The first is a matter of judgement, the second of volition. He refers to these 'two factors' of 'All virtuous acts' as 'the objective and subjective, rightness in the end and rightness in the intention as towards the end' (D. X 3, fo. 12).

'Systems of moral philosophy may', Jowett observes, 'be divided into subjective & objective.' Hopkins almost certainly heard Jowett lecture on this text, which is taken from a lecture notebook that includes a loose sheet of paper listing the names of Hopkins and many of his class-mates.[10] The 'objective and subjective' factors which constitute moral acts have, Hopkins maintains in several of his essays, each been abstracted and treated as having a monopoly on moral value. Two opposed theories of morality have consequently arisen. Some theories, which Hopkins refers to as 'objective', emphasize the importance of

[7] Turner, *Greek Heritage*, 324.

[8] G. I, fo. 20; see the passage quoted near the end of Ch. 2, Sect. I.

[9] [Edwin Hatch], review article of 'The Ethics of Aristotle . . . By Sir Alexander Grant . . .', *North British Review*, 29 (Aug. 1858), 370–1. The writer goes on, 'we have in Sir Alexander Grant's "Essays" a thorough expression of the new school of Oxfordism, written by one of great authority in the University, a member of a distinguished coterie, and lately one of the public examiners' (p. 371).

[10] Balliol, Jowett Papers, MSS IB3, fo. 125; fo. VcA. Robin Darwall-Smith dates the original text of this notebook to 1851–3, noting that it was revised and used throughout the 1860s (Darwall-Smith, *The Jowett Papers: A Summary Catalogue* (Oxford: Balliol College, 1993), 7).

the *end* of morality, seeing merit to derive purely from the effects of our acts. The paradigmatic example of this theory for Hopkins is utilitarianism, the ethical consequence of materialism and associationist psychology, which 'makes morality lie in what attains or tends towards attaining the greatest happiness for the greatest number' (*J.* 80). Other, 'subjective', accounts of morality disregard the consequences in favour of the intention, the quality of will that motivates the act. The attribution of merit and blame in these terms presupposes that moral agents are possessed of free will. Put in modern terminology, the former class of theories can be described as consequentialist or teleological and the latter as intentionalist or deontological.

The topic of an 1867 essay required Hopkins to discuss 'The Possibility of Separating ἠθική ["ethics"] from πολιτικὴ ἐπιστήμη ["political science"]', terms which he identifies respectively with the subjective and objective theories of morality. The former is referred to in the essay as 'personal morality'. The latter is designated 'political morality', which, as his description of ancient morality as 'too simply political and objective' indicates, is for Hopkins synonymous with the consequentialist bias. The 'aim' of 'pure political ethics' is the utilitarian one of 'happiness', the 'comfort and amusement' of the mass of people in society (*J.* 122).

Hopkins' identification of the utilitarian 'political morality' with contemporary popular moral theory is stated clearly in the opening passage of the essay:

Two ambiguities entangle the question or two forms of the same. If one looks at the rise of morals in history it comes, we are told, out of the intercourse of men and not from the man; and also if one looks at the whole of morality as it exists now it will exactly cover the duties of men to each other in all their developments and deductions. If both things were quite true they would not prove that personal morality is the same as political morality, and the failure of insight of which this fallacy is an instance is being made by the Empirical and Utilitarian schools to overrun the whole field of thought. To know the growth from first to last is not to know the thing which grows and to know all the parts is not to know the whole.   (*J.* 122)

The diluvian suggestion of the metaphor that Hopkins uses to describe the spread of the 'Empirical' 'failure of insight' is reminiscent of the millenarian rhetoric which opens another essay of 1867, 'The Probable Future of Metaphysics'. The passage makes it clear that Hopkins regards the state of contemporary moral philosophy to be symptomatic of the wider ideological malaise discussed in the more general essay. Hopkins follows the approach that Green develops in his 1867 lectures of treating moral questions as inseparable from metaphysics and religion: 'Ethic[s can not be treated] without Metaphysic: you cannot discuss morals without a general idea of man's position in the Universe.'[11]

The argument in the passage cited above is familiar from the discussion of induction in Chapter 2. While idealists such as Whewell and Hopkins argue that the hypothesis is a synthetic a priori conception of a whole that is therefore greater than its parts, the empirical facts it contains, positivists such as Mill see the hypothesis to be a mere description of such parts, and accordingly account for induction only in terms of its empirical constituency. A similar 'ambiguit[y]' arises with respect to moral acts. Because the formal principle of the intention is realized and known primarily by its consequences (much as the formal hypothesis can be regarded as a description of an aggregate of particulars), its importance need not be acknowledged. Hopkins begins his essay with the suggestion that the prevalent conception of morality exploits this ambiguity by depicting moral acts only by the 'objective' factor.

The 'failure of insight' which characterizes 'the Empirical and Utilitarian schools' is identified with forms of reductionism. 'Purely material psychology', according to 'The Probable Future of Metaphysics', threatens metaphysics by explaining principles of mind and soul in reductionist terms of physiology. Parallel to this, the prevalent 'Empirical and Utilitarian schools' are charged in the *Ethike* essay with being responsible for the claim that 'personal morality' is reducible to 'political morality'. Hopkins probably has J. S. Mill in mind here. According to Mill the self is founded upon 'the social feelings of mankind', so that man by nature 'never conceives himself otherwise than as a member of a body'.[12] The consequence of this is that the sense of duty felt by the individual is seen necessarily

[11] Merton, Bradley Papers, MS I-A1, Lect. I.
[12] Quoted in Windelband, *History of Philosophy*, 666.

to represent the interest of the community, a point of view which is cited in the opening sentences of the *Ethike* essay. The will of individuals is, according to this view, subordinate and has in itself little value. Hopkins has no sympathy for such conclusions. The *Ethike* essay denies the reductionist claim of 'the Empirical and Utilitarian schools' and proceeds to argue 'that personal morality conditions political before political personal' (*J.* 122). All Hopkins' speculative writings on moral philosophy endeavour to substantiate this intentionalist claim.

III

The 1866 essay on 'The Origin of Our Moral Ideas' begins by introducing three contenders for the title. Two fall within the category of consequentialist theories. Along with utilitarianism Hopkins introduces the relativistic 'historical theory—an idea of morality or of good is evolved and receives localisation and recognition in the process of time' (*J.* 80). Just as Hopkins links utilitarianism to empiricism and materialism, so he sees the 'historical theory' to account for morality according to the larger contemporary ideology which is described in 'The Probable Future of Metaphysics' as 'the prevalent philosophy of . . . flux' (*J.* 120).[13] The other, 'subjective', theory is that 'of innate ideas or of one innate idea which attaches itself to some of the voluntary acts of the mind' (*J.* 80).

While the phrase 'innate ideas' is commonly used to refer to the inborn concepts posited by Cartesian rationalism, it represents in Hopkins' essay the possibility that the mind may have its own 'recondite principles' (*J.* 82), the nature of which is specified at the close of its argument. It is not Descartes who provides the touchstone for understanding Hopkins' 'subjective' theory here, but Aristotle, the only philosopher that the essay mentions by name and quotes from directly.

The approach that Hopkins takes to the question of 'The Origin of Our Moral Ideas' follows the method used in the

---

[13] Such an identification is, however, qualified by the fact that the earlier essay on 'The Origin of Our Moral Ideas' does not associate Hegel with the 'historical theory' (*J.* 118).

Nicomachean Ethics of beginning with τὰ λεγόμενα, 'the things said' or 'things known to *us*', generally accepted ideas about morality which upon analysis lead 'to the first principles'.[14] He advocates 'Aristotle's method of accepting τὰ λεγόμενα as implying in themselves a history of thought and recognition wider than we could anywhere else get' (*J.* 82). Hopkins begins his analysis with 'moral ideas in their composite state' in the belief that 'By this means we shall be led to the τόποι ["common elements"] the settlement of which must go before the choice of a theory of origin' (*J.* 80).

Hopkins' begins his main argument in 'The Origin of Our Moral Ideas' in accordance with the method of *ta legomena* by introducing a conception of morality about which there is, he suggests, a broad consensus: 'The analogy . . . of beauty and moral excellence may be followed to a point of divergence, since superficially at all events it is allowed to hold by all' (*J.* 80). This parallel, which originates with Plato and is adopted and modified by Aristotle, would have been fresh in Hopkins' mind from his studies of *The Republic* and the *Nicomachean Ethics*. It is, as he observes, based upon proportionate relations: 'Beauty lies in the relation of the parts of a sensuous thing to each other . . . Does then morality lie in a relation between acts or (otherwise) the parts of action?' (*J.* 80).

The familiar description of beauty, and more particularly the references to 'relation' here, suggest that Hopkins is looking to place morality in the context of the theory of mind discussed in earlier chapters. That this is indeed the case becomes clearer as he proceeds to specify the nature of the 'relation' which he believes may distinguish morality from that of beauty. The essay introduces the hypothesis that 'the relation of the conditions in a righteous act' is, in contrast to the 'arbitrary' relations of beauty, 'one of logic' (*J.* 81). The identification that Hopkins makes of 'logic' with his formal principle of mind is familiar from the discussion of the essay on 'Imagination' (D. III 5) in Chapter Three, section III. 'The Origin of Our Moral Ideas', the first essay in notebook D. III, offers to explain further how it is that he arrived at this position.

---

[14] *Nicomachean Ethics* 1095ᵇ3; 1095ᵃ31. All quotations are, unless otherwise specified, from W. D. Ross's translation (Oxford: Clarendon Press, 1925).

Hopkins' hypothesis that the relations of morality correspond
to those of logic marks what is often regarded as a distinctively
Aristotelian approach to moral phenomena. In the *Nicomachean
Ethics* Aristotle discusses the train of reasoning that he believes
connects the excellences of character or moral virtues, with the
intellectual excellences, *phronesis* or 'practical wisdom':

for the syllogisms which deal with acts to be done are things which
involve a starting-point, viz. 'since the end, i.e. what is best, is of such
and such a nature', whatever it may be (let it for the sake of argument be what we please); and this is not evident except to the good
man; for wickedness perverts us and causes us to be deceived about
the starting-points of action. Therefore it is evident that it is impossible to be practically wise without being good.[15]

The passage describes the importance of the 'starting-point', the
purpose provided by the good or bad state of character, which
is decisive for subsequent reasoning and the acts which such
thought facilitates: '[Moral] virtue makes us aim at the right
mark, and practical wisdom makes us take the right means.'[16]
These principles will be in harmony in the good state of character. By moderating and organizing our physical appetites they
provide the conditions for the fulfilment or flourishing of our
nature, which constitutes 'the good life'.[17] In the bad or vicious
state of character, in which the potentiality for the harmonious organization of desire has not been realized, the appetites
accordingly do not come under the sway of the regulative principle of the mean.[18] For such a character the appetites provide
the 'starting-point' for reason or 'cleverness', which accordingly determines ways of satisfying them without heed to the
ultimate good of the *eudaemon*, the happy or fulfilling, life.

Anthony Kenny observes that the phrase 'practical syllogism',
which has become a staple term for many commentators writing on the *Nicomachean Ethics*, is not employed by Aristotle
and may have proceeded from a mistranslation of the passage
quoted above. Nor, he argues, is the term an accurate one, for
the reasonings of *phronesis* correspond only very approximately

---

[15] Ibid. 1144^a30–5.   [16] Ibid. 1144^a7–8.
[17] See ibid. 1095^a19–20. The following discussion of Aristotle draws upon the
commentaries of Lear (chs. 4 and 5) and J. O. Urmson, *Aristotle's Ethics* (London:
Basil Blackwell, 1988).   [18] See *Ethics*, 1106^b17–23.

to the technical form of the theoretical syllogism.[19] The term
was, however, accepted by Alexander Grant, whose edition of the
Ethics (1857–8) includes a commentary that is likely to have
influenced Hopkins' discussion in 'The Origin of Our Moral
Ideas'.[20] The following is one of two renderings of the 'practical syllogism' which Grant evidently constructed from the
passage cited earlier:

> Major Premiss. Such and such an action is universally good.
> Minor Premiss. This will be an action of the kind.
> Conclusion. Performance of action.[21]

The 'starting-point', the purpose supplied by moral excellence,
provides the major premiss of Aristotle's syllogism, while the
deliberations of *phronesis* may by implication be regarded as
supplying the minor premiss. The conclusion to the syllogism
would accordingly be the performance of an action meant to
realize the moral aim.

Although Hopkins does not use the term, he appears to
adopt the idea of the 'practical syllogism'. He arrives at the
conclusion in 'The Origin of Our Moral Ideas' that 'the one,
the moral differ[s] from the other [i.e. vice] in having (in the
strict sense) a correct logical form' (*J.* 81). The 'strict sense'
of formal logic is, however, presented as a type of 'logic' in 'the
broad sense', which corresponds to the psychologistic formal
principle discussed above in Chapter 3. Hopkins establishes
the theoretical grounds in 'The Origin of Our Moral Ideas' for
linking the respective mental capacities for moral choice and
knowledge.

IV

Hopkins approaches the question of the relation of logic to
ethics through the familiar 'distinction of objective and subjective morality' (*J.* 80). He dispenses quickly with the former:
'It seems . . . easy to see that an objectively good deed is logical'

---

[19] Kenny, *Aristotle's Theory of Will* (London: Duckworth, 1979), 111–12. Kenny
proposes the phrase 'ethical reasoning' instead of 'practical syllogism'.
[20] Grant (ed.), *Ethics of Aristotle*, 2nd edn. (1866), i. 212–19.   [21] Ibid. 214.

(*J.* 81), for the result of the deed will correspond to a prescribed universal criterion of what the good end is. Hopkins
then introduces the element of intention, writing that the 'subjective excellence' of acts presupposes 'an inducement to . . .
[do] otherwise . . . a temptation' which is overcome (*J.* 81).
Moral acts are, according to intentionalism, worthy of praise
and blame because they are the result of a free will. It needs
however to be borne in mind that, while the question of the
freedom of the will has emerged as one of the foremost preoc-
cupations of modern philosophy, the ancient Greeks were not
greatly concerned with it.

Hopkins is aware that the Aristotelian ethics which he draws
upon in his essay do not share his concern with intentionalism:
'Aristotle's system allows us to look at the virtues objectively,
as laws wh[ich] command obedience, but not subjectively, in
equity as principles by wh[ich] to acquit or condemn' (M. II,
fo. 27ᵛ). He makes the similar observation that Aristotle's conception of 'goodness of character . . . is . . . not the impartial field
on which all men with quite as interesting stakes[,] the one as
the other[,] are winning merit or guilt' (D. X 3, fo. 14).

Goodness and viciousness are for Aristotle original potentialities of human nature, the realizations of which constitute
the particular natures of individuals. This entelechy is brought
about by the formative influences of upbringing and the consequent habituation to acting in one way or the other. Because
the good character is, once it is established, *naturally* good it
cannot help but act in a good way. There is for Aristotle no
question that such a character, having decided through *phronesis*
what the good action is, will not act accordingly. Similarly no
conflict of will can arise for the bad or vicious character, who
is incapable of entertaining a wish for the good. The remaining sections of the present chapter trace the modifications that
Hopkins makes to Aristotelian doctrine as he develops his own
intentionalist moral philosophy. The topic of an essay set by
T. H. Green, 'The Relation of the Aristotelian *phronesis* to the
Modern Moral Sense and *proairesis* to Free Will' (D. X 3), indicates that his Greats studies encouraged him in this project.[22]

---

[22] This is corroborated by F. H. Bradley's lecture notes from Green's 1867
lectures on moral philosophy, which begin by stating 'three great Differences

Hopkins, in his discussion of the Aristotelian comparison of moral to theoretical reasoning in 'The Origin of Our Moral Ideas', identifies what he believes to be a crucial distinction between the two types of 'logic':

In the general case logic without any medium determines the mind, as if there is no way into a field but by a gate, we go in by the gate. It only does not do so supposing there is reason the other side, making the conclusion uncertain. In other words the premises are not properly made out, or the logic is not perfect. If two lines of reasoning seem incompatible the difficulty is got rid of by closer attention, and from their composition follows a result. But in morals the logic may be perfect and action not follow. (*J.* 81)

Hopkins observes that even in those instances where logic stops short due to imperfections or may '*seem*' to allow of 'two lines of reasoning', it in fact follows a single line. Parallel to the inexorable logic of the syllogism, Aristotle's good and bad states of character determine both the resolve to act upon a particular end and, by providing the 'starting-point' for 'the syllogisms which deal with acts to be done', the means to this end. For Hopkins, however, the phenomena of morality are distinguished not by their formal affinity with the syllogism but by their tendency to disrupt such logical sequence: 'in morals the logic may be perfect and action not follow'. The good and bad states of character each involve an unambivalent will, whereas the break in the 'logic' that interests Hopkins suggests competing moral impulses, and hence the possibility of free will. Those cases in which moral reasoning is liable to be subverted by an 'inducement to . . . [do] otherwise' are theorized in the *Nicomachean Ethics* as two further, anomalous, states of character. In the case of incontinence or weakness of will one is aware of the right thing to do, but succumbs to a temptation to do otherwise, whilst in the complementary state of continence[23] the impulse to ignore the good aim is conquered.

between us & Aristotle & Plato', one of which concerns the relation perceived to exist between ethics and politics, the topic of Hopkins' 1867 *Ethike* essay, while another focuses upon the exclusively modern concern with free will, the relation of which to the Greeks is discussed by Hopkins in the essay on '*Phronesis*' (D. X 3), which also dates from 1867 (Merton, Bradley Papers, MS I-A1, Lect. I).

[23] These states are discussed in Book 7 of the *Ethics*.

Aristotle distinguishes these states of character by the respective trains of reasoning that they involve.[24] He uses the example
of a simple modal syllogism in which the major premiss asserts
a universal opinion, ' "everything sweet ought to be tasted".' The
minor premiss provides 'the particular facts': ' "this is sweet" '.
Accordingly as this train of thought yields 'a single opinion' so
the conclusion, the action of tasting the particular sweet thing,
follows as inevitably as that of the theoretical syllogism. In the
case of incontinence the major premiss forbids such tasting
of sweet things, *phronesis* having evidently judged such acts to
be detrimental to our best interests, perhaps because we are
diabetic or obese. Appetite, however, which by definition has
pleasure as its object, provides another opinion, namely, that
' "everything sweet is pleasant" '. Faced with such conflicting
impulses the incontinent moral agent will only realize the conclusion that the particular sweet thing is pleasant, not that it is
bad. The universal opinion derived from appetite 'is active' or
'present in us', and so eclipses the universal that forbids such
indulgence.

Aristotle does not approach the phenomena of continence
and incontinence from a concern with freedom of the will, but
rather through the Socratic tradition which questions whether
such a thing as incontinence can exist.[25] Incontinence occurs
when someone accedes to the promptings of appetite against
their long-term best interests, which they are directed to by
moral character and understand through *phronesis*. Aristotle
argues, however, that in such cases the rational understanding
of the good is suspended or repressed through a sort of intoxication with appetitive desire.[26] Knowledge of the good exists
in such circumstances as a potentiality. As it is not actualized,
that is, present to mind, the good cannot be acted upon.[27] The
phenomenon of incontinence does not indicate freedom of the
will but quite the reverse: the mastery of reason by appetite. Continence presents the contrary case in which reason ultimately
prevails over appetite.

Even though incontinence represents the enslavement of the
reason Hopkins' driven and anachronistic reading of Aristotle

[24] The following discussion is of the passage in the *Ethics* from 1147^{a}25–^{b}3.
[25] Ibid. 1145^{b}22–1146^{a}9.   [26] Ibid. 1147^{a}10–24.   [27] Ibid. 1146^{b}23–34.

finds in it scope for a theory of free will. In contrast to the good and bad states of character, continence and incontinence presuppose feelings of desire for both virtue and vice. They accordingly suggest to Hopkins a theory of mind in which the will has some freedom to make choices between acting upon virtuous and vicious impulses:

But in morals the logic may be perfect and action not follow. If however we use logic in the truer sense for everything which determines the mind to act, we find the phenomena of morals are those of two incompatible logics, for it is notorious in casuistry that the attraction of some sins is greater the greater the attention of the mind, and it cannot be said that this holds in the same way with every train of reasoning because the essence of right and wrong lies in our consciousness of the contradiction between them. (*J.* 81)

This passage establishes a moral psychology that is in keeping with the Christian psychomachy between goodness and sin: 'there are two (in the broad sense) logics putting stress on the mind, one belonging to virtue, one to vice'. Virtue and vice are not distilled in separate characters, as they are in Aristotle's mutually exclusive good and bad states of character, nor do they correspond to continence or incontinence, but rather to the respective elements that feature in these states. Having established that the mind is subject to conflicting stresses or pressures, thereby providing scope for free will, Hopkins proceeds to outline a few questions that arise from this psychology:

(i) does the one, the moral, differ from the other in having (in the strict sense) a correct logical form? (ii) If so, what are its universals? since not all logic touches morals. And why does it seem to differ in kind from other trains of thought? (iii) Or are the two motives alike, both receiving trains of reasoning or propositions and impressing each its own character on them? (*J.* 81)

The second of the questions provides the focus of discussion for the remainder of Hopkins' essay. According to Aristotle the moral universal is produced by character and provides both the major premiss for moral reasonings and the will to act upon them. Hopkins, however, identifies 'virtue' not with this linear model of reasoning but rather as one of the 'two . . . logics' which vie for the 'attention' of the mind. Having located the moral 'universals' belonging to 'virtue' within this arena of competing 'logics', he goes in search of its origin, 'the spring of moral ideas' (*J.* 81).

V

Hopkins addresses the issue of the moral universal by once again following the Aristotelian method of examining *ta legomena*. The contemporary doctrine of utilitarianism provides his enquiry with its main example of a popular conception: 'utilitarians say the morally good is what attains the good, that is the advantageous, and that of course the greatest such, and that, they add, for the greatest number' (*J.* 81). It provides the starting-point, 'moral ideas in their composite state', from which to deduce the nature of moral universals, 'the τόποι ["common elements"] the settlement of which must go before the choice of a theory of origin'(*J.* 80). In a parallel to the bold gesture expressed in the early poem 'I must hunt down the prize', in which the persona vows to find form in the most obfuscating and inhospitable circumstances, Hopkins endeavours to establish the presence of a subjective first principle or universal in 'the utilitarian formula', which, he writes, in itself 'requires much exception':

As it stands it only explains the objective part of morality, that is to say it fails to explain morality at all. It is plain that we require not only that a good deed should please our after judgment but that it should have pleased its subject in the same light, and as it falls from this so it falls from pure morality. (*J.* 82)

Hopkins' dissatisfaction with utilitarianism springs from its regard for the consequences which proceed from moral acts rather than the intentions that prompt them. Viewed from an Aristotelian perspective utilitarianism accounts for morality as simply a process of reasoning, and so fails to recognize the necessity of character in deciding the end to be acted upon and in providing the will to perform the act. Utilitarianism offers a 'teleological' account of motive, whereby the 'good deed' will 'please our after judgment' and so is presumably performed in anticipation of this reward. For Hopkins, however, this explanation begs a question. The utilitarian precept is merely an '*a posteriori* definition' (*J.* 81) which fails to recognize that the *conception* of the deed 'pleased its subject' and so engendered the will to perform it.

Hopkins argues for the importance of intention through two examples, both of which highlight the inadequacy of utilitarianism in relation to other commonly accepted ideas about morality. The first cites the actions of a Sister of Mercy, which result in the fulfilment of the utilitarian ideal but are not performed with this object in mind. In cases such as this, in which 'the form of the life be only a deduction from another motive[,] its morality ought', Hopkins maintains, 'to be diminished'. It is the 'mental attitude' which informs the actions, not the 'fact' that results from them, that is for Hopkins the crucial factor in morality (*J.* 82).

The second case which Hopkins discusses is of actions which arise from the right motives but are not recognized by utilitarianism to have moral worth because their consequences do not contribute directly to the sum of happiness. From the perspective provided by this school of thought 'those who act rightly—consistently of course and not by chance—without aiming at anyone's good are not moral at all'. Hopkins argues for the inadequacy of utilitarianism in this respect by appealing to a moral value that strikes a twentieth-century reader as peculiarly 'Victorian':

Children, if we can suppose any universal in the mind at all, must be thought to say Right is to do what one is bid. The obedience of children we regard as having moral worth. If the utilitarians do not, then they contradict the popular feeling, and in cases like this popular feeling is critical, because if we are to have any success in the analysis of recondite principles of the mind we must take up Aristotle's method of accepting τὰ λεγόμενα as implying in themselves a history of thought and recognition wider than we could anywhere else get.

(*J.* 82)

The example of childish obedience illustrates Hopkins' assertion that, even though it is integral to moral acts, the consequentialist criterion specified by utilitarianism is not an essential condition of morality. It also demonstrates the relation of moral duties to the type of ethical reasoning discussed earlier in this chapter, as it not only supplies a major premiss, 'Right is to do what one is bid', but suggests that it is in some sense innate, a 'universal in the mind'. In keeping with his earlier treatment of 'logic' in the essay Hopkins construes the Aristotelian idea of character, which is responsible for providing the major premiss and the will to act, psychologically.

Hopkins presupposes that *ta legomena* issue from subjective consciousness rather than, as they do in Aristotle, from understandings derived from experience. He believes that they can disclose the 'recondite principles of the mind'. His analysis of *ta legomena* implies that moral phenomena arise as the expression of a formal a priori principle within the temporal matter of experience. It is because utilitarianism does not recognize this that Hopkins believes that its explanation of moral phenomena 'fails historically both in mankind and in the individual' (*J.* 82).

By freeing utilitarianism of its consequentialist encrustations Hopkins reveals its universal, a *topos* which accordingly leads to 'the choice of a theory of origin'. He concludes that utilitarianism's popular appeal can be traced to the fact that its fundamental precept has, to borrow the phrase which Hopkins applies to aesthetic apprehension, a 'hold on the mind': 'If we aim at the happiness of the greatest number we must do it ... because the conception of the widest possible happiness fulfils an ideal in the mind' (*J.* 120, 82).

VI

An explanation of the 'recondite' 'ideal in the mind' to which Hopkins traces 'The Origin of Our Moral Ideas' provides the conclusion to his essay. Its final paragraph opens with his dictum that 'All thought is of course in a sense an effort a[t] unity' (*J.* 83), a statement which throws the foregoing discussion of morality into a new and clarifying perspective. Hopkins' moral theory effectively supplements Aristotle with Kant, transforming the Greek philosopher's theory of good character and its universal into a doctrine based upon the idea of an a priori 'universal in the mind'.

Reason, in Kant's theory of mind, not only legislates through the understanding to judge how things objectively *are*, it also legislates practically through the faculty of desire, the will, as to how things *ought to be*. It accordingly provides a definitive example of intentionalism.[28] The reason provides the form which combines with the matter of our desires in what Kant refers to as a *practical synthesis*, which leads to moral action. The moral application of the reason, which Kant refers to as the pure practical reason, determines the will *immediately* through its a priori criterion, the Categorical Imperative. This is a sense of duty which requires us to act in particular circumstances in accordance with what we feel to be morally good, and to do so not, as in utilitarianism and the ethics of Aristotle, from any consideration of the ends they may realize, but simply for the sake of this sense of duty. It is therefore of an imperative nature. It is also unconditioned, which is to say that it does not spring from hypothetical reasons for action, such as inducements in the form of rewards or punishment. It can accordingly be described as categorical.

Kant's moral law prescribes a form by which we may judge whether or not the matter of our desires, the subjective precepts or maxims by which we may act, are worthy as objective moral principles: 'Act so that the maxim of thy will can always at the same time hold good as a principle of universal legislation.'[29] The case of deliberate dishonesty provides Kant with one of his clearest examples of the application of the Categorical Imperative.[30] If the moral law is brought to bear upon the maxim that 'We should tell lies whenever it suits our purposes to do so,' the result will be a contradiction, for if all were to lie under the guise of telling the truth honesty would have no meaning.

---

[28] Kant, like Hopkins, upholds this stance by arguing against the popular consequentialist notion, common to Aristotle and utilitarianism (albeit as quite different conceptions) of happiness as the supreme moral value: 'The distinction between the *doctrine of happiness* and the *doctrine of morality* [*ethics*], in the former of which empirical principles constitute the entire foundation, while in the second they do not form the smallest part of it, is the first and most important office of the analytic of pure practical reason' (*Critique of Practical Reason*, 221: all extracts from this and Kant's other works on ethics are taken from Thomas Kingsmill Abbott's trans., 4th edn. (London: Longmans, Green, 1889)).

[29] *Critique of Practical Reason*, 141. In his 1867 lecture on Kant's moral philosophy Green renders the law: '[A]ct that your action may be a rule for every rational being' (Merton, Bradley Papers, Lect. XX).

[30] *Critique of Practical Reason*, 159; *The Fundamental Principles of the Metaphysics of Morals*, 389.

The Categorical Imperative involves a moral psychology in which the will to act, which is expressed by the maxim, is subject to rational nature, the universal of the moral law. This relation, which enables the dictates of appetite and other desires to be judged independently, constitutes 'the autonomy of the will'. The will is accordingly not constrained by appetitive desire, which places it within the deterministic chains of cause and effect that characterize phenomena, but is able to exercise an originative causality, that is, a capacity for spontaneously bringing a certain moral object into existence. Another way of making this distinction is to say that as rational beings human agents are, as Kant puts it, 'ends in themselves' not means to an end. This has a number of important implications. The one that is most clearly foreshadowed by the discussion so far is the freedom of the will, for autonomy frees us from the tyranny of appetitive desire, without precluding the complementary possibility that we may perversely choose to follow a maxim that is recognized by the moral law to be unethical. Hopkins' understanding of the relation between the will and its freedom is clearly apparent from an essay of 1867, which draws its title from the Kantian principle of 'The Autonomy of the Will':

This is a phrase of Kant's and takes its rise from the meeting of these two trains of thought: on the one hand the will of all reasoning beings is free—free that is from what he calls mechanical causation—because freedom is implied in having reason; on the other hand those who give us most signs of the freedom, that is the independence, of their wills, for instance the inflexibly honest, are for that reason the most consistent with themselves, the most clearly bound by one principle, that is the most clearly bound by law: the will then, which does not take any law from the outer world, must be a law to itself, or in Greek phrase autonomous.   (D. X 4, fo. 19)

It is the Kantian moral psychology, which allows the will to operate autonomously of empirical desire, that corresponds most directly to Hopkins' distinction in 'The Origin of Our Moral Ideas' between the 'two incompatible logics', not the Aristotelian, from which they can be derived only by abstracting the elements that come into play in cases of continence and incontinence. Hopkins' Aristotelian distinction early in 'The Origin' between the appetitive and the morally virtuous desires is specified later in the essay as a Kantian relation between the empirical 'conception' and the autonomous 'recondite' or a priori 'ideal in the mind'. This 'ideal', like the Kantian Imperative, provides the criterion by which the empirical matter of experience can be judged or formed. The autonomy of the 'ideal in the mind' is marked by the fact that its requirements are satisfied, 'fulfil[led]', by the particular 'conception of the greatest happiness'.

The a priori formal function of the 'ideal in the mind' entails 'a correct logical form' (*J.* 81) that corresponds to the Kantian version of the 'practical syllogism' rather than to the Aristotelian. The determination of the will by pure reason makes it entirely consistent with itself according to its own rule, that is to say, purely logical:

since it is *pure reason* that is here considered in its practical use, and consequently as proceeding from *à priori* principles, and not from empirical principles of determination, hence the division of the analytic of pure practical reason must resemble that of a syllogism, namely, proceeding from the universal in the *major premiss* (the moral principle), through a *minor premiss* containing a subsumption of possible actions (as good or evil) under the former, to the *conclusion*, namely, the subjective determination of the will (an interest in the possible practical good, and in the maxim founded on it).[31]

Hopkins' sense of the Kantian moral law as a parallel to the Aristotelian 'starting-point' for 'the syllogisms which deal with acts to be done' is apparent also from 'The Autonomy of the Will', where he refers to the 'absoluteness' of the Categorical Imperative, 'which gives it the character of a start or postulate' (D. X 4, fo. 20).

The 'ideal in the mind' that each such 'conception' 'fulfils' can be identified with the Kantian principle of universality, which is brought to the fore by Hopkins' rendering of the Categorical Imperative in 'The Autonomy of the Will': 'Act so that your action may belong to a universal principle' (D. X 4, fo. 20). The essay on 'The Origin of Our Moral Ideas' identifies the 'recondite' form or 'ideal in the mind' with the formal principle of 'unity': 'All thought is of course in a sense an effort a[t] unity'. The link that he makes between the moral law and the mind's capacity for synthetic a priori judgements

[31] *Critique of Practical Reason*, 219.

was available to Hopkins from Green's teaching: 'The subjective conception has for its object a moral Category, it tries to
reduce the many to One.'[32]

The moral impulse is, however, conditioned not only by
the a priori 'desire of unity', but also by the principle of non-
contradiction, for, as Hopkins notes earlier in the essay, 'the
essence of right and wrong lies in our consciousness of the
contradiction between them' (*J.* 81). This logical principle is
another way of saying that morality must adhere to universal
dicta. The formal basis by which the 'conception . . . fulfils an
ideal in the mind' is thus the same criterion of universality as
that by which Kant believes we judge the moral quality of our
maxims. Indeed, the two moral precepts that Hopkins gives in
his essay, that we should 'aim at the happiness of the greatest
number' and that for children 'Right is to do what one is bid'
(*J.* 82), both conform to this criterion. The radical aim of morality is presented as the 'perfect realization' of this universality,
'perfect consistency' (*J.* 83).

VII

While the late essay on 'The Relation of the Aristotelian *phronesis*
to the Modern Moral Sense and *proairesis* to Free Will' (D. X
3), which dates from Hilary term 1867, is not as boldly speculative as 'The Origin of Our Moral Ideas', it supplements the
earlier essay by providing a more direct and detailed exposition of the role that Aristotle and Kant play in Hopkins' moral
theory. The greater specificity of its references helps to identify
some of his sources. While, according to an early letter, Hopkins
emerges from Greats with 'an even prostrate admiration of Aristotle', his understanding of the philosopher was mediated by
the interpretations of such advocates of German idealism as
Jowett, Green, and Grant, so that his esteem for Aristotle must
be regarded accordingly as conditional upon such influences:
'I . . . am of the way of thinking, *so far as I know him or know
about him,* that he is the end-all and be-all of philosophy' (my
emphases).[33]

[32] Merton, Bradley Papers, Lect. I.
[33] 'To Baillie', 12 Feb. 1868, Letter 128, *Further Letters*, 231.

Green's 1866 essay on 'The Philosophy of Aristotle', which was written as a review of the second edition of Grant's *Ethics*, indicates the general approach to Aristotle that Green shares with Grant. One of the few direct references to Grant's book made in this long essay commends it as 'a corrective to the strange notion that Aristotle was a common-sense philosopher, uninfluenced by metaphysical "abstractions," and intelligible to those who are wholly unversed in them'.[34] Both Grant and Green treat Aristotle as a precursor of Kant and Hegel. Given that Grant's was the edition of the *Ethics* that he studied and Green was his lecturer and tutor for this text, it is not surprising to find that their common 'metaphysical' approach to Aristotle shaped Hopkins' reading of the book.

The moral psychology which Hopkins discusses in his essay is established by Aristotle in the first five chapters of Book 3 of the *Nicomachean Ethics* through a series of specific enquiries into 'the voluntary and the involuntary'[35] nature of our desires and acts. Hopkins construes this general concern in terms of the topic of his essay: '[Aristotle] here naturally discusses those questions of free will which have since become so common' (fo. 13). He then considers some of these questions, beginning with Aristotle's opinion of the Socratic relation of ignorance to vice, which is examined in the first chapter of Book 3, and proceeds to the discussions of 'whether resentment and the desires make action involuntary' (fo. 13) and whether our desire is for the actual or only the apparent good, an issue which is addressed in the fourth chapter of Book 3.

In respect of this last question Aristotle makes the assurance that the object of the good person will necessarily be truly good in nature. While the attempt to define the precise nature of the good is problematical, we can, according to Aristotle, always know what the good is for a particular situation by observing the actions of the virtuous character. Correspondingly, those who act on what appears to them to be the good but is actually

---

[34] Green, *Works*, iii. 46. This reading of Aristotle became endemic to Oxford during the 1860s and 1870s. Oscar Wilde, for example, writes as a Greats student during the mid- to late 1870s that 'what we think in Aristotle is the realism of sense, often turns out to be really the idealism of reason' (Philip E. Smith II and Michael S. Helfand, eds., *Oscar Wilde's Oxford Notebooks* (New York: Oxford University Press, 1989), 149.   [35] *Ethics*, 1111^{b}4.

not so are judged to be of bad character. Furthermore, they can
be blamed for permitting themselves to develop such characters: 'they are guilty in the first case of forming and allowing
such natures and such diseased fancies' (fo. 13).[36] Why then
would anyone knowingly make such a perverse use of this crucial chance to form one's character? Hopkins finds Aristotle's
account unsatisfactory because it fails to eliminate the possibility 'that the fault may have been from the very beginning'.[37]
He does, however, regard Aristotle's 'answer' to this problem
as 'interesting', perhaps because it suggests an 'innate' moral
principle of the type he advocates in 'The Origin of Our Moral
Ideas': 'we require man to be born with a sense for the right
as much as with eyes and seeing: those who are otherwise in
fact may be in some sense excusable but they are less than the
human nature he is treating of, they are not the subjects of
morals' (fos. 13–14).[38] Virtue, in the Greek ἀρετή, an excellence,
belongs to some and not to others:

His goodness of character then is still just what the Greek word expresses, a virtue, either in action or in capacity a perfection of the
organisation and likely to be finest in the finest, and not the impartial field on which all men with quite as interesting stakes the one as
the other are winning merit or guilt. And the same feeling perhaps
makes it more possible for him to lay down with so unsatisfactory an
answer as he finally gives the question of the will, while the history
of human thought since his time has made all sides uncompromis-
ingly ask Is it free or is it not free? and each press his own answer on
the world.   (fo. 14)

While Aristotle does not present a doctrine in which the
arena of moral decision-making is an 'impartial field', Hopkins
argues that free will does in fact apply to the virtuous. In so
doing he is almost certainly following Grant's notes to the first
five chapters of Book 3 of the *Ethics*. Grant cautions against
regarding this part of the treatise 'as a metaphysical discussion
of the question of free-will. Partly, the question had never yet

---

[36] *Ethics*, 1113^b14, 1114^a20-2. The analogy of the bad character's judgement to
that of the diseased is made at 1113^a28 and, less specifically, at 1114^a15-17.

[37] Hopkins probably follows Green in thinking that, as Geoffrey Thomas puts it,
'Aristotle emphasized too strongly the fixity of character once formed' (Thomas,
The Moral Philosophy of T. H. Green (Oxford: Clarendon Press, 1987), 37; see also
204–6).   [38] Cf. *Ethics*, 1114^b6-10.

been fully started; partly, Aristotle would have thought it foreign to an ethical treatise'.[39] This historical sense is, however,
part of a method that derives from Hegel. 'Grant's was', as W.
David Shaw observes, 'the first commentary to assimilate Aristotle's thought to the stages of historical development traced
by Hegel in his *Lectures on the Philosophy of History*'.[40] The fact
that 'the question [of free will] had never yet been fully started'
does not, according to Grant, prevent Aristotle from providing
a rudimentary form of its answer. This presupposition is clearly
apparent at several points of his notes, where Aristotle's discussion of 'the voluntary' is seen to grope towards a modern conception of the will. Grant typically sees Aristotle to 'imply' the
modern, specifically Kantian, grounds of free will: 'he implies
that the idea of freedom is contained in that of duty'.[41] Such
glosses probably brought to Hopkins' attention those 'things
[Aristotle] says [that] suggest an answer more completely
affirmative and by a new method' (fo. 14).

Hopkins' 'new method' consolidates the anachronistic tendency found in Grant's notes by applying to Aristotle's moral
psychology 'the word will with the definiteness it now wears':

If we are to take what he says here not so speculatively as he wrote
it but with the interest the question has got now, we may say that
practically he asserts the freedom of the will though in the ultimate
case he does not feel the repugnance familiar to us in surrendering
it . . . Following his order but using the word will with the definiteness
it now wears, we may speak of actions as being determined by purpose, purpose by the decision of the will of which phenomenon it is
only the later shape, the will in its decision by wishes, wish by longings
of nature, and those longings by the whole constitution of the man
and of man.   (fos. 14–15)

The account of the volitional process outlined here hinges
upon the Aristotelian idea of *proairesis*. Once the good character
has endorsed the end proffered by practical wisdom, the resultant wish provides the impetus for *phronesis* to choose the means

---

[39] Grant (ed.), *Ethics of Aristotle*, ii. 25.
[40] W. D. Shaw, *The Lucid Veil* (London: Athlone Press, 1987), 236–7.
[41] Grant (ed.), *Ethics of Aristotle*, ii. 14. Similarly: 'The tenet ὅτι ἀγαθοῦ βούλησίς
ἐστιν . . . implies much that modern systems would convey in other terms, such as
the "supremacy of conscience", the "autonomy of the will", &c' (ii. 23). Another
important example, which is quoted below, occurs on p. 16.

by which this end can be realized: 'wish relates . . . to the end', writes Aristotle, 'choice to the means'.[42] Such choice occurs through the deliberations of practical reason, and is referred to by Aristotle as a *proairesis*. Hopkins translates this word as 'purpose' and cites Aristotle's definition of it 'as longing which goes with reason or reason which goes with longing' (fo. 12).[43] While the wish 'ties together the good end and the good character', this resolve is transmitted through a series of deliberations which reach a final choice or *proairesis*, an act within the agent's power that is capable of realizing the desired object: it 'bring[s] together the wish and the accomplishment' (fo. 12).

The virtuous character is, as Hopkins observes, 'either in action or in capacity a perfection of the organisation' (fo. 14), that is, an organization of desire according to the *logos* or rational principle. This definition recognizes that the good character exists both as an actuality and as a potentiality: 'in action or in capacity'. It is in accordance with this ontology that Hopkins argues that longings become determined progressively as wish, purpose, and particular actions. Each of these stages occurs as a revelation of the nature of the good character, so that, for example, the description of 'purpose' as 'the later shape' of the will indicates that will belongs to this nature as a formal principle. This form also distinguishes wishes from longings: 'It is only because they become the matter of the wishes that these cravings are raised into meaning or interest above the blind and unimportant pains of nature, such as the sick feel' (fo. 17).

The series of determinations that culminate in the moral act have as their first term 'the whole constitution of the man and of man'. The phrase indicates that the moral 'constitution' consists of two elements. The physical appetites and desire for self-preservation, which Aristotle observes belong also to the other animals, comprise part of our generic nature. It is with such desires that the 'longings of nature' can be identified. An innate disposition for the good, the *logos* or 'rational principle', which according to Aristotle distinguishes man from other animals, is also part of the generic nature. Its actualization as a particular state of character, however, belongs to the individual, and it is this that is meant by the 'constitution of the man'.

---

[42] *Ethics*, 1111^{b}26–7.   [43] See ibid. 1139^{b}4–5.

The distinction is between the appetitive and the rational, from which issue respectively the 'matter' of 'longings' or 'cravings' and the formal principle of wishes and purposes.

Hopkins identifies the moral will with the Aristotelian formal or rational part of the soul, thereby regarding it as radically distinct from the other volitional principle of appetite. In doing so he draws an implication from Aristotle's moral psychology that is often perceived by Grant: 'But the psychology is not very explicit here, and Aristotle seems to imply, without definitely expressing it, that in the moral will there is an element contradicting the desires in a manner different from that in which one desire interferes with another'.[44] The moral psychology which Grant and Hopkins attribute to Aristotle is essentially that found in Kant, where the moral will proceeds from the reason, thereby ensuring the 'autonomy' that allows it to arbitrate freely over 'empirical' or appetitive desire. Hopkins evidently believes that a strong affinity links 'the Aristotelian *phronesis* to the Modern Moral Sense'.

This psychology is apparent from the definition of wish cited earlier: 'where an end is seen to be good . . . a wish for that good arises from the necessity of our [rational] nature'. The act of volition supervenes upon the conscious recognition of the goodness of the object before the mind; that is, it occurs as an act of reason. Hopkins' attitude to each of 'the two factors of virtue' as 'actual virtue as seen from one side' (fo. 12) serves to distribute evenly amongst these terms of *phronesis* and character the respective qualities of rationality and volition that Aristotle identifies with them. This makes of the capacity for virtue a single principle distinct from the appetitive desires. Inasmuch as the form consists of a principle of will that derives from the reason and is applied to the 'matter' of appetitive desire, Hopkins' versions of the Aristotelian 'wish' and 'purpose' are akin to the Kantian practical synthesis.

VIII

Hopkins, following the pattern of the Aristotelian entelechy, argues in the essay on *Phronesis* that will is the original moral

---

[44] Grant (ed.), *Ethics of Aristotle*, ii. 16.

principle: 'Wish . . . presupposes purpose and purpose will'
(fo. 17). He comes to define wish as 'the expression of purpose
in us with regard to things which are not present', and consequently arrives at the conclusion that 'by wish we mean the
purpose' (fo. 17). This version of Aristotelian moral psychology appears to have its source in Grant:

The process of deliberation is analytical, proceeding backwards ἐπι
τὴν ἀρχήν. It ends with the πρῶτον αἴτιον, i.e. the individual will. 'Will',
says Kant, 'is that kind of causality attributed to living agents, in so
far as they are possessed of reason, and freedom is such a property
of that causality as enables them to originate events independently of
foreign determining causes'. That each man is, as regards his own
acts, an originating cause not determined by other causes, is Aristotle's view throughout. Kant's definition throws light on this.[45]

Grant's commentary is likely to have encouraged Hopkins
to attempt a reconciliation of Aristotelian with Kantian moral
psychology not only in the essay on *Phronesis*, the topic of which
almost requires it, but also in others, such as 'The Origin of
Our Moral Ideas'. Hopkins feels compelled in the essay on
Phronesis, as in the earlier essay, to assert his syncretic moral
theory against the claims of contemporary 'objective' and de-
terminist doctrines. One of Grant's notes to the early chapters
of Book 3 of the *Ethics* refers to 'the maintainers of the doctrine of necessity'.[46] It is perhaps this phrase that prompts the
term 'Necessitarians' (fo. 17) which Hopkins uses in his essay
to refer to those who maintain that appetitive desire, which
they equate with wishes, determines the will, and so regard our
actions as subject to mechanical causation.

While 'Necessitarianism' provides a radical contrast to Aristotelian ethics, thereby suggesting the consistency of the latter
with the principle of free will, Hopkins' discussion of it extends
beyond the requirements of the essay to an outright refutation
of the doctrine. Appealing to *ta legomena* he observes that 'common speech' reveals that wishes are the conditioned form of

[45] Ibid. ii. 20. This passage is also suggestive as a source for 'The Autonomy of
the Will', which declares that 'freedom is implied in having reason', and follows
immediately from the essay on '*Phronesis*' in Notebook D. X.
[46] Grant (ed.), *Ethics of Aristotle*, ii. 14. There is also a reference to 'the metaphysical difficulty as to the whole world being bound by a law of necessity' (p. 27).

longings (fo. 15). The cravings, longings, or wants cannot, as the 'Necessitarians' maintain, condition the will, but do themselves need to be conditioned. They are simply the 'matter' which the will conditions, while the will itself is 'unconditioned . . . in other words free' (fo. 18).

Hopkins' polemic against the Necessitarians broadens the concerns of his essay to such an extent that its conclusion is largely given over to an outline of the metaphysical principle which he believes is threatened by the doctrine:

Thus desire or want presupposes wish and wish purpose and purpose is will. The true principle cannot but be that things truly exist only in their fullest organisation and highest development, not in their lowest, as the type is to be found in the full-grown man and not in the baby, in the lily in bloom and not in the lily-bulb. And it is quite plain our thoughts grow and become complex and determine in this way or that by strength of their own and principles independent of the accidents under which their experience comes to individuals: if not, we should not find one man's thoughts agreeing with another's, break-downs would be happening in our intelligibility, and generally the play of innumerable circumstances, 'every little gust of sense', as someone writes, would throw the matter of our ideas together into groups as accidental and uninformed by any law of subordination as the packs of bubbles spinning in a tea-cup. Indeed while science is always making the idea of the chance clashing of atoms more and more unnatural in the outer world, this theory applies Epicureanism to the making of the mind. To conclude then, every account of the will has to deal with wishing, and if we can shew therefore that wish presupposes will and not will wish, we shall have taken away those particular things which were said to be the complete conditions of the will and shall have left it unconditioned to the degree which was supposed before, in other words free. (fo. 18)

'The Probable Future of Metaphysics', which like the *Phronesis* essay dates from Hilary term 1867,[47] asserts that 'Realism will undoubtedly once more maintain that the Idea is only given . . . from the whole downwards to the parts' (*J.* 120). This fundamental Aristotelian tenet is also expressed at the start of the passage quoted above: 'The true principle cannot but be that things truly exist only in their fullest organisation and highest

---

[47] Schmidt, 'Classical Studies', 180–1.

development.'[48] While 'The Probable Future of Metaphysics' simply cites the Aristotelian principle, the *Phronesis* essay gives a brief but clear indication of how Hopkins develops a 'new Realism' (*J.* 120) from it. He makes realism 'new' by drawing into it modern strains of thought, principally, as the above extract evidences, German idealism and contemporary physics.

The conclusion to the essay on *Phronesis* makes the grounds of Hopkins' objection to Necessitarianism abundantly clear: he finds in it another manifestation of materialism. The Necessitarians maintain what is for Hopkins the preposterous idea that the contingent matter of empirical desire can engender its own forms. Their doctrine accounts for moral choices according to the materialist psychology which belongs also to utilitarianism, that is, as the result of a quantitative reckoning of atomistic particles of desire: 'they tell us the phenomena of willing may all be resolved into the mind balancing its different wishes' (fo. 17). This account of moral psychology parallels the positivist view of knowledge, 'the prevalent principle that knowledge . . . mounts from the part to the whole': 'The Necessitarians argu[e] . . . the other way [to Aristotle, i.e.], upwards' (*J.* 120, fo. 15).

The partisan approach to philosophy that Hopkins takes in the conclusion to his essay reflects the incipient British idealism of Jowett and Green, which classifies philosophical theories as either idealist or materialist. The conclusion to the essay on *Phronesis* reflects the sensitivity of his teachers to discerning forms of materialism in both the various branches of metaphysics and their historical systems: 'a foresight' of the kind that Hopkins describes in 'The Probable Future of Metaphysics', which occurs 'even at the first hint, when they come upon that kind of thought which runs upon the concrete and the particular, which disintegrates and drops towards atomism in some shape or other' (*J.* 119). The observation that Hopkins makes of a continuity between what he regards as the moral and the epistemological manifestations of Epicureanism is also made by Jowett and Green. 'As knowledge is reduced to sensation',

---

[48] '"Organization" implies multeity in unity, the co-existence and interjunction of physical parts under the law of life' (Grant (ed.), *Ethics of Aristotle*, ii. 8).

Jowett writes of the modern 'Epicurean philosophy', 'so virtue is reduced to feeling, happiness or good to pleasure'.[49]

Green, with whom Hopkins was likely to have discussed the essay topic on *Phronesis* before writing on it, is also concerned about those theories which extend the methods and findings of naturalistic science to account for morality:

The interest in the moral world, and the interest in the so-called world of nature, tend more and more to fusion with each other. In the Greek age of sophistry, as it is presented to us by Plato and Aristotle, the unsettlement of practical ideas resulted from the application to 'the good, the beautiful, and the just' of the Democritean theory of nature and our knowledge of it, and it was by a counter theory on the same subjects that Plato sought to achieve the reconstruction of morals and politics. In modern times it is the philosophy of nature and knowledge inherited from Bacon and Locke that appears in the numerous 'Natural Histories of Ethics' with which the world has been beset during the last century and a half; and, conversely, it was a moral interest—the desire to find room for freedom and immortality—that moved Kant to attempt a more profound analysis of knowledge. The moral philosophy which he set himself to reform is still the popular philosophy.[50]

Green compares the application to ethics of the sophists' relativistic humanism and atomist physics with the utilitarian ethics which arise with British empiricism and persist in 'the popular philosophy' of his own age, while the historical responses to each, that of Plato and (by implication) Aristotle in the former epoch, and Kant in the latter, are similarly seen to parallel each other. Hopkins' essay presents a comparable pattern of anachronistic alliances between moral 'Necessitarian[ism]' and Humean associationism on the one side, and Aristotle and Kant on the other.

The passage from Green highlights the fact that he, like Jowett, saw epistemology and moral philosophy to be not so much allied as interfused. In the lecture which concludes his 1867 series on moral philosophy Green asserts that 'Metaphysic & Moral Philos[ophy] meet in a point'.[51] He maintains that

[49] Quoted in Turner, *Greek Heritage*, 421.

[50] 'Popular Philosophy in its Relation to Life', Green, *Works*, iii. 96–7.

[51] 'Higher than both is the [Hegelian] Absolute Philos[ophy] that embraces both' (Merton, Bradley Papers, Lect. XXIII).

'A post[eriori] morality springs from materialism & if carried out logically leads to atheism & selfishness',[52] whilst conversely regarding Kant's epistemology as ethically motivated: 'it was a moral interest—the desire to find room for freedom and immortality—that moved Kant to attempt a more profound analysis of knowledge'. Green is interested in Kant as a constructive thinker whose notorious attack upon the foundation of traditional metaphysics, the claim that knowledge can be derived from purely a priori synthetic judgements, is motivated by his desire to establish metaphysics as a science.[53] The fundamental 'moral interest' that Green identifies with Kant is acknowledged in the Preface to the second *Critique*: 'Inasmuch as the reality of the concept of freedom is proved by an apodictic law of practical reason, it is the *keystone* of the whole system of pure reason, even the speculative.'[54] Kant's major works of moral theory endeavour to establish, as the title of two of them announce, a Metaphysic of Morals, 'a system of the *a priori* principles of moral action, or moral laws'.[55] Its foundation is the Categorical Imperative, the application of which is seen to entail a rational belief in the supersensible objects of freedom, God, and the immortality of the soul.[56] That which in the 'Transcendental Dialectic' of the *Critique of Pure Reason* 'was merely a *problem* ... now becomes', Kant writes in the Preface to the second *Critique*, '*assertion*, and thus the practical use of reason is connected with the elements of theoretical reason'.[57]

Green's idea of an 'interest' that informs the formation of a philosophy suggests a source for Hopkins' principle of 'the inspiration or prepossession'. Indeed, it is introduced in 'The Autonomy of the Will', which was written for Green, as an approving gloss on Kantian philosophy: 'the most successful philosophies seem those where we know the sensitiveness or bias which is the spring; this makes them inventive, that is, constructive' (D. X 4, fo. 22). Hopkins, like Green, develops a

[52] Ibid.

[53] My discussion of Kant's metaphysics draws upon Mary J. Gregor, 'Kant's Conception of a "Metaphysics of Morals"', *Philosophical Quarterly*, 10 (1960), 238–51. The essay is reprinted as ch. 1 of her *Laws of Freedom: A Study of Kant's Method of Applying the Categorical Imperative in the* Metaphysik der Sitten (Oxford: Blackwell, 1963).   [54] *Critique of Practical Reason*, 106.

[55] Gregor, 'Kant's Conception', 240.   [56] Ibid. 239.

[57] *Critique of Practical Reason*, 107.

metaphysic from a moral 'interest' or 'prepossession', and identifies Kant with 'constructive', rather than critical, philosophy.

The 'prepossession' that guides Hopkins' reception of Kantian principles of the moral and cognitive forms of reason is
evident from the essay on 'A posteriori Truth'. Hopkins makes
the erroneous observation in the last paragraph of this essay
that 'Kant considers the moral sense a form of thought besides various other categories' (D. VI 1, fo. 3). A note to this
comment specifies that Kant refers to 'the moral sense' 'Under
the name of the Categorical Imperative' and furthermore
observes that 'It is not among the Categories of the Understanding' (fo. 2^v). Apparently confused by the adjectival form of the
word 'category' in Kant's term for the moral law, Hopkins
approaches the Categorical Imperative as if it were one of the
a priori concepts of the understanding, rather than a dictate of
the pure reason. He sees it to exist 'besides various *other* categories' (my emphasis) and accordingly looks to find it 'among
the Categories'. His understanding of the Categorical Imperative here is simply of 'a form of thought' which he appears to
wish 'may', along with the categories which in a note to the
essay are 'reduced to Relation' (fo. 1^v), 'be simplified by analysis' (fo. 3). His 'prepossession' here is to locate the work of
the understanding and the moral law as aspects of the one,
formal, mental function.

The apparent confusion in Hopkins' work, and in that of
Green and other British idealists, over the distinction between
the practical and the theoretical or speculative reason can, as
Mary J. Gregor demonstrates, be traced to Kant. The practical
and the theoretical are 'one and the same reason which has to
be distinguished merely in its application'.[58] The purity of the
practical reason, the principle that its concepts arise from the
reflection of the reason on its own activities, is of paramount
importance to Kant's metaphysic of morals. The moral laws
which apply to experience must derive purely from our rationality, whereas those generalizations which we apply in acts of
knowledge are synthetic a priori judgements that necessarily
include a posteriori elements. However, as Gregor observes,
the term 'pure' in Kant's writings on moral philosophy is used

[58] *The Fundamental Principles of the Metaphysic of Morals*, 8.

inconsistently, and often means only a priori. Indeed, the 'pure' part of Kant's moral philosophy includes 'such empirical knowledge of man as is needed to obtain, from the supreme moral principle, those duties which all men have merely by virtue of their human nature'.[59]

Hopkins does not subscribe to Kant's fundamental distinction between the pure reason, from which the will issues directly, and reason as it is applied indirectly through the categories of the understanding. His simplified form of the Kantian theory of mind allows him to posit the capacity to make synthetic a priori judgements as a function of reason, rather than of the mediate forms of the understanding, thus giving it a parity with the moral will. This is most clearly apparent from the *Phronesis* essay. Hopkins' account of both ethics and epistemology in his conclusion to the essay instances the 'new stress on the scholastic distinction of form and matter' that he attributes to Kantian psychology in the essay on '*A posteriori* Truth' (D. VI 1, fo. 1), which probably also dates from Hilary term 1867.[60] In epistemology the overarching formal principle is, according to the extract, supplied by a priori principles of the mind which allow it to perceive regularity 'independent of the accidents under which . . . experience comes to individuals'. Just as the longings or cravings of appetitive desire provide 'the matter of the wishes', so ' "every little gust of sense" ' provides 'the matter of our ideas'. In each case 'matter' is the empirical principle to which reason, as the principle of knowledge and of will, contributes the form.

Jowett evidently provided a source for the parallel that Hopkins draws between the moral and the cognitive application of the reason. This is apparent from Jowett's lecture notes from the notebook mentioned earlier, IB3, which includes the loose sheet of paper which lists the names of Hopkins and his peers. A note on 'freedom . . . As obedience to a law' describes the appetitive desires by the term 'sequence' that Hopkins uses in the essays on 'Causation' (D. VI 2, fos. 4, 5) and 'Imagination' (D. III 5, fo. 17) to describe the contingent matter of sense intuitions: 'We can only be free by rising above the "sequence" of our passions by leaving room for the free agency of the wills of others.'[61] The portrayal of moral and cognitive ideas as similarly comprised of formal and material or empirical elements is also evident from Jowett's notes for a lecture entitled 'On Ideas of a First Principle of Morals', which presents the terms 'subjective & objective' as synonymous with the terms 'abstract and concrete'.[62]

The applications to which the mind's synthetic a priori form is suited are described at the close of 'The Origin of Our Moral Ideas'. The 'ideal in the mind', like the Kantian will, is a direct function of the reason, the principle of mind which Hopkins defines by its formal 'desire for unity'. The derivation of the moral principle from this conception of the mind is sketched in the last paragraph of the essay: 'This [unity] may be pursued analytically as in science or synthetically as in art or morality'. The 'important difference' between the 'arbitrary' proportions of art and the 'logical' relations of morality which Hopkins observes earlier in the essay is restated at its conclusion as a formal distinction between organic and strict or numerical unity:

In art we strive to realise not only unity, permanence of law, likeness, but also, with it, difference, variety, contrast: it is rhyme we like, not echo, and not unison but harmony. But in morality the highest consistency is the highest excellence. The reason of this seems to be that the desire of unity is prior to that of difference and whereas in art both are in our power, in moral action our utmost efforts never result in its perfect realisation, in perfect consistency. (J. 83)

Unlike art, where contrary principles can be reconciled in a differentiated unity, the moral impulse aims at the realization of the universal, 'perfect consistency'.

Hopkins, like his teachers Green and Jowett, is interested in the constructive impetus of the Kantian project and the possibilities that it opens up for establishing a new metaphysics. He takes from Kant the premiss that 'freedom is implied in having reason' (D. X 4, fo. 19). An important implication of this as it applies to Hopkins' theory of mind is that all synthetic a priori judgements, whether they be cognitive, aesthetic, or ethical, will involve freedom, and hence principles of choice and

[61] Balliol, Jowett Papers, MS IB3, fo. 83. [62] Ibid. fo. 125.

moral value.[63] Hopkins' definition of the formal 'ideal in the mind' as the 'desire for unity' makes it clear that it is at once desiderative and cognitive. The mind is predicated upon an a priori categorical imperative to form and discern instances of unity. Thought is accordingly regarded as a type of moral *act*, 'an effort a[t] unity'.

[63] In the closing passage of the essay 'On Predestination and Free Will', a passage which Hopkins makes a note to refer to (D. VI 2, fo. 4ʳ), Jowett extends free will to include all cognitive functions, and identifies this with a Christianity appropriate for the times: 'The great lesson, which Christians have to learn in the present day, is to know the world as it is; that is to say, to know themselves as they are; human life as it is; nature as it is; history as it is. Such knowledge is also a power, to fulfil the will of God and to contribute to the happiness of man. It is a resting place in speculation, and a new beginning in practice. Such knowledge is the true reconcilement of the opposition of necessity and free will' (*The Interpretation of Scripture and other Essays* (London: George Routledge & Sons, n.d.), 535).

5   Reflexive Self-Consciousness

I

The radical Kantian principles of self-consciousness and free-dom of the will provide the starting-points for Hopkins' thought, while the consequences that he derives from them, such as the synthetic a priori properties of mind by which we can make 'comparisons' but which involve no prohibition on knowledge of 'noumena', differ markedly from the Kantian deduction. The persistence in the undergraduate essays of these and other os-tensible misconstruals of Kant, which such readers of his essays as Jowett, Pater, and Green were well able to recognize and correct, suggest that his teachers condoned them as speculative develop-ments of Kantian themes. Hopkins' qualified adoption of Kant should be viewed in the context of the idealist tradition of inter-preting Kant that began in Germany in the late eighteenth and early nineteenth centuries and which was renewed in Hopkins' own day by the early British idealists who taught him and whose works he read.

Kant's principles of the 'transcendental unity of apperception' and of free will are the nodal points for the development of post-Kantian idealism. The pure synthetical apperception is a radic-ally idealist principle which traces the possibility of thought to a realm of pure subjectivity autonomous of any empirical principle. Such post-Kantians as Fichte and Hegel find in the principle of apperceptive consciousness the means by which to develop systems of metaphysics that challenge the Kantian pro-hibitions on speculative ontology. Later idealists, including the English thinkers S. T. Coleridge, Benjamin Jowett, John Grote, and T. H. Green, follow the lead of the German post-Kantians by taking Kant's principle of consciousness as a starting-point for their own anti-empiricist polemics and theorizing. Hopkins' speculative development of the Kantian principle is consistent with the fundamental role it plays in the British idealist thought that was available to him from Jowett's and Green's teaching and his reading of Grote's *Exploratio Philosophica* and Alexander Grant's edition of the *Nicomachean Ethics*.

The reworking of the Kantian principles of the transcendental apperception and free will by the German idealists engendered a renaissance in speculative ontology. Hegel's *Phenomenology of Spirit*, for example, can be described as tracing the free dialectical movements by which his conception of the subject, *Geist* or 'spirit', comes progressively to full consciousness, to the full realization, of itself. Hopkins' ontology is also established on the Kantian foundations of self-consciousness and free will. The conclusion to 'The Origin of Our Moral Ideas', having traced the main functions of mind to a fundamental a priori 'desire for unity', arrives at the crucial question, 'But why do we desire unity?': 'The first answer would be that the ideal, the one, is our only means of recognising successfully our being to ourselves, it unifies us, while vice destroys the sense of being by dissipating thought. ἔστι γὰρ ἡ κακία φθαρτικὴ ἀρχῆς, wickedness breaks up unity of principle. If this be thought mysticism further explanation may be given' (*J.* 83). Hopkins' offer to his reader to provide a 'further explanation' indicates that he was aware that his interpretation of Aristotle, whom he quotes and translates here, is unorthodox. In making this offer he is, however, not simply being defensive. Hopkins' expressly stated unwillingness to be misunderstood indicates that he felt the point he is making to be an especially important one. The explication of this passage needs to be pursued at some length not only because it is compressed and opaque, but because it marks the pivotal point in Hopkins' early thought where he draws from his theory of mind the grounds of his ontology. It can be approached first of all by examining his quotation from Aristotle and the translation and interpretation he makes of it.

The quotation from Aristotle that Hopkins makes in the passage is from Chapter 5 of Book 6 of the *Nicomachean Ethics*, which discusses practical reason. *Phronesis* is distinguished from theoretical reasoning in this chapter by its object of making 'judgements about what is to be done'. If, however, it is not to be confused with mere 'cleverness', the nature of *phronesis* needs to be further specified as belonging only to the good character. It may be recalled that, according to Aristotle, the good and bad states of character become established by performing

actions appropriate to each. Thus, because *phronesis* is in practice inextricable from good character, acting upon a virtue
such as 'temperance . . . preserves one's practical wisdom'. On
the other hand, however, 'pleasant and painful objects destroy
and pervert . . . judgements about what is to be done',[1] thereby
encouraging the formation of a bad character. This observation,
which highlights the distinction between the two types of 'judgements', is summed up in Hopkins' quotation: 'wickedness breaks
up unity of principle'.

The following passage, which is given in Ross' translation,
provides the immediate context for Hopkins' quotation. I place
Ross' version of the phrase that Hopkins quotes in italics:

For the originating causes of the things that are done consist in the
end at which they are aimed; but the man who has been ruined by
pleasure or pain forthwith fails to see any such originating cause—to
see that for the sake of this or because of this he ought to choose and
do whatever he chooses and does; for *vice is destructive of the originating
cause of action.*[2]

Hopkins' commentary which precedes his quotation of Aristotle offers an idiosyncratic version of the passage cited here,
so much so that the parallel is not obvious and can be apprehended initially only as a broad structural homology. His departures from the usual translation of the passage are, however,
all the more telling for being so pronounced. The central term
in the passage is *arche*, which Ross translates as 'the originating
cause' and Hopkins as the 'unity of principle' or the 'ideal'.
The passages from Hopkins and Aristotle both begin by describing the purpose of this principle, and then the perversion
of it by vice.

I argued in Chapter 4 that Hopkins does not endorse the Aristotelian states of character, but rather regards each instance
which requires moral action to invoke the 'two incompatible
logics' of virtue and vice and so necessitate a choice between
them. Each act thus serves to actualize either the good or the

[1] *Ethics*, 1140^{b}12; 1140^{b}14–15.
[2] Ibid. 1140^{b}15–19. It is immediately after this that Aristotle establishes his
definition of *phronesis* as 'a reasoned and true state of capacity to act with regard
to human goods'.

bad potentiality of our nature, not only in the developing, but also in the mature, character. Aristotle's theory, on the other hand, is according to Hopkins' understanding of it concerned primarily with morally unambivalent characters. Aristotle's reference in the quotation to 'the man who has been ruined by pleasure or pain' suggests that once a character has been formed it is thenceforth inaccessible to change,[3] so that its actions are in a sense purely deterministic. The phrase which Hopkins quotes, however, like the rest of the passage in which he places it, presents the phenomenon in the present tense, thereby allowing that our moral nature is in constant process, requiring affirmation and renewal if it is not to degenerate. This is the implication that Hopkins draws from the Aristotelian passage and the means by which he accounts for our constant 'desire for unity': 'the one . . . unifies us, while vice destroys the sense of being by dissipating thought'.

The difference between the respective translations made by Ross and Hopkins of '$\check{\epsilon}\sigma\tau\iota$ $\gamma\grave{\alpha}\rho$ $\dot{\eta}$ $\kappa\alpha\kappa\acute{\iota}\alpha$ $\phi\theta\alpha\rho\tau\iota\kappa\grave{\eta}$ $\dot{\alpha}\rho\chi\hat{\eta}\varsigma$' is highlighted by their versions of the final word of the phrase, which is often rendered as 'principle', 'source', or 'beginning'. *Arche* is used later in Book 6 in an important passage discussed in Chapter 4 which refers to the 'starting-point' or 'major premiss' of 'the syllogisms which deal with acts to be done'.[4] It is, in other words, 'the originating cause of action', the product of the Aristotelian good character which decides what needs to be done and provides the will to do it. The teleological emphasis of this translation is clearly in keeping with the doctrine it expounds. This is, however, not to say that Hopkins' alternative translation, 'unity of principle', does not also accommodate Aristotle's moral entelechy. The *logos*, the formal or rational principle that is expressed by the moral *arche*, is a potential for unity which becomes actualized as the organization of the

---

[3] Of course, once a character has been formed (that is, when certain acts have become habitual), the possibility remains that certain habits may eventually change, at least for some people, so that the good character may change, as for example through being broken by suffering and acquiring habits of bitterness, misanthropy, vindictiveness, and the like. This consideration, however, represents only a marginal possibility for change, whereas Hopkins, following Grant and Green, insists upon a theory that allows a much more supple principle of moral character.

[4] Grant's translation, Grant (ed.), *Ethics of Aristotle*, ii. 185. *Ethics*, 1144^{a}31. See Ch. 4, Sect. III.

virtuous character. The point at which Hopkins differs from normative interpretations of Aristotle is in his identification of virtue with a mental principle, the suggestively Kantian 'universal in the mind'. It is this interpretation of the Aristotelian notion of character, which traces it to 'an ideal in the mind', that shapes his translation of *arche* as 'unity of principle'.

Hopkins' notion of the *arche* in this passage entails a correspondingly different entelechy and conception of personal identity from those which are usually associated with Aristotle. The way in which 'the ideal, the one' actualizes our being, 'unifies us', is through a mental act of recognition. The apprehension by the mind of objective instances of 'the ideal, the one' is seen to actualize the potentiality of 'our being . . . it unifies us'. The equation that Hopkins presupposes here of 'the ideal, the one' with 'our being' marks his adoption of the radical idealist premiss that is stated by the post-Kantian *principium commune essendi et cognoscendi*[5] and by the dictum of Parmenides that provides one of the main texts for the 1868 'Notes on the History of Greek philosophy' and which Hopkins translates as: 'To be and to know or Being and thought are the same' (*J.* 129).

Although the conclusion to 'The Origin of Our Moral Ideas' offers one of Hopkins' most comprehensive accounts of the mind, there is a complete absence in it of any reference to the empirical part of thought. Such 'matter' is implicit here, but only as a potential which is actualized by the active principle of thought. There is no discussion of the *receptivity* of the mind, only references to its *spontaneity*. Thought is impelled by its a priori 'desire for unity, for an ideal', and is repeatedly referred to as an 'effort' and as a 'striv[ing]' to establish form. The knowledge gained from thought is, according to this account, of its form, 'unity'. This type of subjective idealism recalls Hegel's early reading of Kant in which, according to Robert B. Pippin's summary, he concludes 'that what counts as "object" can only be determined by a "subject," that all an object *is* is "that in the concept of which the manifold is united"'.[6]

[5] The 'common principle of being and knowing'. See S. T. Coleridge, *Biographia Literaria*, ed. James Engell and W. Jackson Bate, ch. 12, Thesis IX (London: Routledge & Kegan Paul, 1983), i. 281–3.

[6] R. B. Pippin, *Hegel's Idealism: The Satisfactions of Self-Consciousness* (Cambridge: Cambridge University Press, 1989), 34.

For Hopkins in the conclusion to 'The Origin of Our Moral Ideas', as for Hegel and other post-Kantian idealists, thought *constitutes* its objects. Such products of thought accordingly provide the subject with the medium by which it can grasp its own content, its essential nature as thought: 'the ideal, the one, is our only means of recognising successfully our being to ourselves'. Reflexive self-consciousness, 'the *sense* of being' (my emphasis), is seen to refer not to an 'empty' or unknowable formal condition of thought, as it does in Kant, but to the very principle of 'our being', a 'noumenal' self. The mind's transcendental form of 'unity' provides Hopkins with the *arche*, the *logos*, which in being actualized, 'recognis[ed]', through the 'efforts' of the mind also actualizes 'our being . . . it unifies us'.

The 1867 essay on 'The Possibility of Separating ἠθική from πολιτικὴ ἐπιστήμη' concludes its inquiries with a version of the principle of reflexive self-consciousness similar to that with which 'The Origin of Our Moral Ideas' closes: 'Conscience or the Imperative working outwards find[s] its first matter in the man himself: a man can compare his today with his yesterday, his aims with his results: many things follow from man being his own object' (*J.* 124). Hopkins identifies the principle of apperceptive consciousness here with the pure practical reason which, according to Kant, indicates that we have a noumenal being, albeit one that he believes we can have no knowledge of. By conflating the Kantian principles of the apperception and 'the Imperative' with 'Conscience', which is usually identified with 'noumenal' but knowable conceptions of the soul, Hopkins repudiates the Kantian prohibition and suggests that the nature of the self in-itself is knowable, much as it is in Aristotle and Christianity, as our moral nature.

The transcendental principle of reason that is identified at the close of the *Ethike* essay with 'Conscience or the Imperative', like the 'desire for unity' in the earlier essay, is seen to apply directly to the 'matter' of the empirical apperception, by which means it becomes instanced as an object. Such empirical 'idea[s]' thereby provide objective instances of unity in which we are able to recognize our generic 'being', 'our ideal of . . . man generally', which according to the essay has its 'absolute and substantive' basis in 'Conscience or the Imperative'. The radical 'ideal' of our 'being' has its parallel in the 'idea': 'Ideal

REFLEXIVE SELF-CONSCIOUSNESS 133

answers to idea: an idea is our thought of a thing as substantive, as one, as holding together its own parts and conditions;
an ideal is the thing thought of when it is most substantive and
succeeds in being distinctive and one and holding its parts or
conditions together in its own way' (*J.* 124). Both the 'idea' and
the 'ideal' are here, much as they are in 'The Origin of Our
Moral Ideas', synonymous with formal unity. The radical 'ideal'
of 'Conscience or the Imperative', which provides the condition
of the 'one[ness]' of our 'being', is accordingly recognizable
in the empirical 'matter' of our ideas in its form of the 'one',
a unity. Reflexive self-consciousness provides the means by which
the subject is able to 'hold . . . its parts or conditions together
in its own way', for it is only by 'man being his own object' and
thereby comparing his intentions and actions with his 'moral
ideal' that he is able to recognize, and thereby actualize, this
'ideal' nature. It is, according to Hopkins' 'subjective' morality,
only through such self-consciousness that our intentions and
acts have moral value.

Hopkins sees the moral law to be not only formal, in the
manner that Kant specifies as 'the [Categorical] Imperative',
but to necessarily imply a specific content, much as it does in
traditional metaphysical and Christian conceptions of 'Conscience'. The moral law is described earlier in the essay as encompassing a range of values which, while they may appear to be
ideologically disparate, Hopkins regards as homogeneous: 'Anyone who was possessed with the Roman sense of duty to the
father of the family or the Chinese awe for parents or patriot-
ism or universal love or sensibility to suffering or self-respect
or devotion to wife or husband would have no other way of
perfectly fulfilling those duties which personally were the prepossession unless by fulfilling all the rest' (*J.* 123).[7] The 'prepossession' of a word is described in the 1868 'All words . . .'
notes as synonymous with 'a passion or . . . enthusiasm' which
is in part contingent upon the individual's experience (*J.* 125).

---

[7] Cf. Jowett's essay 'On the Interpretation of Scripture', which Hopkins probably read (*J.* 56): 'The simple feeling of truth and right is the same to the Greek
or Hindoo as to ourselves. However great may be the diversities of human character, there is a point at which these diversities end, and unity begins to appear'
(*Essays and Reviews*, 11th edn. (London: Longman, Green, Longman, Roberts, and
Green, 1863), 499–500).

The moral 'prepossession' in this extract appears to refer to the particular moral passions by which the universal moral law is first apprehended by an individual. It marks the primary act of reflexive self-consciousness in which the universal form of the moral law is recognized by the subject as a specific object.

The 'prepossession', as well as being the first actualization of the formal moral law, is also a relative potentiality. It is the principle by which the subject may be said to *possess* the form of the moral law, as the prefix to the term specifies, *prior* to its full actualization. Hopkins believes that all the 'duties' by which the moral law is actualized comprise a unity, and that each is necessarily a condition for the complete fulfilment of all the others. The actualization of this moral nature accordingly occurs gradually as the subject, in its effort to realize its personal 'prepossession', recognizes the necessity of what are ostensibly other moral objects and realizes that they are integral to its own nature. The unity of the content of the moral law means that by pursuing its personal 'prepossession' the subject progressively constitutes its objects and through reflexive self-consciousness comes to actualize its nature fully.

The subject's 'ideal' nature, according to the version of reflexive self-consciousness elaborated at the close of the *Ethike* essay, requires its distinctive form, 'Conscience or the Imperative', to be instanced objectively if this nature is to be both known and actualized. The objects that are constituted by an individual consciousness either draw the being of the self together or dissipate it: this is an implication of the ambiguous phrase 'working outwards' which holds within it the optimistic sense that consciousness will realize itself as a greater, more inclusive, unity, or alternatively that it may, through 'unworthy' intentions and actions, dissipate its distinctive being. This highlights what Hopkins considers to be the essence of the moral law, of our 'ideal' or rational nature, for 'freedom is implied in having reason' (D. X 4, fo. 19).

II

Hopkins' main sources for such post-Kantian idealist principles as that which he presents in the conclusions to 'The Origin of

Our Moral Ideas' and the *Ethike* essay were also the principal influences upon his studies of Aristotle. Both Alexander Grant and T. H. Green find in the Aristotelian entelechy the means of developing their respective post-Kantian metaphysics from the Kantian principle of consciousness. In those cases where the term *energeia* is applied to the subjective mind it is translated in Grant's edition of the *Ethics* not as 'actuality', as it is usually rendered, but as 'consciousness'.[8] F. H. Bradley records that Green, in his 1867 lecture series on moral philosophy, was also in the habit of making this anachronistic identification: 'The Highest Actualization is the highest consciousness of thought[,] which is consciousness of itself'.[9]

Grant's idiosyncratic translation of *energeia* indicates the influence of Hegel's distinction between the 'in-itself' and the 'for-itself', which develops the respective Aristotelian principles of potentiality and actuality according to his principle of *Geist*, the 'idea' or 'spirit'.[10] The Hegelian 'in-itself' is the idea in its 'implicit' form, 'still in the original form [of an abstract concept]' or 'submerged in existence',[11] while the 'for-itself' is its fully developed objective form, as it exists, so to speak, 'before itself'.[12]

Grant illustrates the 'in-itself' with the principle of inherent form by which each creature in nature (including 'man') 'attains its own peculiar perfection' through 'obeying the law of its organization'. This form is in-itself unconscious: 'while each part of the creation realizes its proper end . . . this end exists not *for* the inanimate or unconscious creatures themselves, it only exists *in* them'.[13] Hopkins expresses this perception in the poem 'Ribblesdale', where the 'Earth', the world of nature, 'canst but only be' (No. 149). Grant identifies the 'for-itself' with human consciousness, our rational nature. Human beings are able to bring the realized natures of specific creatures to a further actuality in which they are recognized by the subject,

---

[8] For an early commentary on this controversial interpretation, see Hatch, review of 'Ethics', 392–3.

[9] Merton, Bradley Papers, MS I-A1, Lect. XI. This lecture was an Aristotle's *Ethics*. [10] Turner, *Greek Heritage*, 349.

[11] *Phenomenology of Spirit*, trans. A. V. Miller (Oxford University Press, 1977), sect. 29.

[12] Charles Taylor, *Hegel* (Cambridge: Cambridge University Press, 1975), 112.

[13] Grant (ed.), *Ethics of Aristotle*, i. 173, 174.

brought to consciousness. This corresponds to Hopkins' characterization of 'man' in 'Ribblesdale' as 'Earth's eye, tongue, or heart'. The subjectivity which distinguishes generic man from the other creatures demands, according to Grant, a correspondingly different conception of *energeia:*

It is clear that a psychical ἐνέργεια must be different from the same category exhibited in any external object. Life, the mind, the moral faculties, must have their 'existence in actuality' distinguished from their mere 'potentiality' by some special difference, not common to other existences. What is it that distinguishes vitality from the conditions of life, waking from sleeping, thought from the dormant faculties, moral action from the unevoked moral capacities? In all these contrasts there is no conception that approaches nearer towards summing up the distinction than that of 'consciousness'.[14]

The ability to bring the objective actuality of other creatures to subjective consciousness is integral to the rational nature of human beings. Furthermore, because this nature applies to its own objects, it has, Grant notes, the peculiar capacity of being 'in-and-for-itself':

But the ethical τέλος not only exists *in* man, but also *for* man; not only is the good realized in him, but it is recognized by him as such; it is the end not only of his nature, but also of his desires; it stands before his thoughts and wishes and highest consciousness as the absolute, that in which he can rest, that which is in and for itself desirable ... [The] ends of moral beings are ends subjectively, realized by and contemplated by those moral beings themselves. The final cause, then, in *Ethics*, is viewed, so to speak, from the inside.[15]

This passage presupposes the Kantian distinction between the will and empirical desire that Grant identifies elsewhere with Aristotle's moral psychology.[16] The Aristotelian 'ethical τέλος' is distinguished from our 'desires' in the way that the Kantian will, the autonomous principle of reason, is from the maxims which arise from the empirical self, and is realized accordingly as the latter term instances the former. Moral value is for Grant, as it is for Kant and Hopkins, predicated upon the subject's recognition of its moral purpose. It necessarily involves an

[14] Ibid. 193.   [15] Ibid. 174.
[16] E.g. ibid. ii. 16. See Ch. 4, Sects. VII and VIII.

REFLEXIVE SELF-CONSCIOUSNESS 137

act of reflexive self-consciousness. The subject's moral nature is actualized, the 'in-itself' of the 'ethical τέλος' becomes 'for-itself', accordingly not only as the objective form of desire corresponds to the dictates of the will but as this correspondence is recognized by the subject. This actualization occurs within consciousness, whether or not it is expressed externally in moral acts, so that the 'in-itself' effectively returns to itself as the 'in-and-for-itself': 'It springs out of the mind and ends in the mind'.[17]

The identification that Grant makes of the Kantian principle of reflexive self-consciousness with the terms of Aristotle's entelechy establishes it as the ground for a realist epistemology which allows knowledge not only of other creatures as they are in-themselves but also of ourselves. Whereas for Kant all that we can know of the formal condition of consciousness is the 'I think' that implicitly accompanies our cognitions, not the 'noumenal' self from which this principle springs, for Grant the principle of reflexive self-consciousness means that we can have knowledge of our essential nature, that the 'in-itself' can also be for us 'for-itself'. This provides the condition for our final actualization as the 'in-and-for-itself'.

The pattern described by Grant's development of the principle of reflexive self-consciousness is instanced by the subjective ontology presented at the close of 'The Origin of Our Moral Ideas', where the 'in-itself' of 'our being' becomes 'for-itself' accordingly as we 'recognis[e] . . . our being to ourselves'. The 'ideal, the one', which our mind 'realise[s]' as its object (whether it be through its purely moral manifestation, as in Grant's account, or another of the cognitive functions that Hopkins mentions), provides the 'only means' by which we can come to such self-consciousness, become 'in-and-for-itself'. This is the implication also of the doctrine sketched in the *Ethike* essay, in which the 'ideal' nature that constitutes the unity of our being, 'Conscience or the Imperative', is progressively actualized through the principle of reflexive self-consciousness. Furthermore, the reflexive type of *energeia* or 'consciousness' that Grant describes is itself the final actualization of our being, much as it is for Hopkins in 'The Origin of Our Moral Ideas',

[17] Ibid. i. 193.

where, he writes, 'it unifies us'. Hopkins states this metaphysic definitively in the 'Parmenides' notes, where the principle of 'instress' corresponds to the 'in-itself' of individual being that becomes 'in-and-for-itself' as the mind brings it to consciousness and so further actualizes its being or, in his verbal form of the coinage, 'instresses' it.[18]

T. H. Green's teaching worked in concert with Grant's commentary to provide Hopkins with the main idealist channel in which his ontology and epistemology were formed and would run. Green's views on Aristotle during the period from Michaelmas term 1865 to Hilary term 1867, during which he lectured and tutored Hopkins in the *Nicomachean Ethics*, are recorded in the essay on 'The Philosophy of Aristotle', which Hopkins may have read on its first appearance in the *North British Review* for September 1866.[19] Green places Aristotle within the tradition of Greek idealism, which, he writes, is founded upon the discovery that 'The thought which knows . . . [is] an essential factor in the object known'.[20] This dictum contains the seeds of the post-Kantian idea that thought constitutes its object, the principle that Hopkins relies upon in 'The Origin of Our Moral Ideas' and the *Ethike* essay and from which he develops his ontology of the subject.

Green sees both ancient and modern philosophy to be faced with the same problem, 'that of reducing the "sensible thing" to its primary simplicity'.[21] He accordingly embarks upon an analysis of the conditions of thought by examining the simple consciousness we have of a sensible thing. This, he writes, 'can only be expressed as the judgment, "something is here." The "here," however, is the next moment a "there"; the one sensation is

---

[18] This sense of Hopkins' coinage corresponds to Grant's principle of 'consciousness': 'It is not only life, but the sense of life' (ibid.).

[19] Hopkins was reading the *North British Review* at least as early as Apr. 1865. It is probable, given that the essay is on a central Greats text and written by a fellow of their college, that he and his peers would have read and discussed this controversial essay.

[20] Green, *Works*, iii. 47. While it can be argued that Aristotle's realism is a form of objective idealism, in the sense that he maintains that the reality that is independent of the individual mind is constituted by Mind, Green's humanist reconfiguration of this, in which the mind of the subject constitutes the object, is anachronistic.

[21] Ibid. 48. Green distinguishes parallel positivist and idealist responses to this fundamental question in each age, much as he does in 'Popular Philosophy in Relation to Life'. See Ch. 4, Sect. VIII.

superseded by another.'[22] The radical condition for the apprehension of such experience is accordingly identified with the
Kantian principle of consciousness: 'The stable element, then,
must be the conscious subject, and the primary judgment must
be not merely "this is here," but "this is here as an object to
me".'[23] Green claims to find such a conception of mind in Aristotle, who, he writes, 'was quite aware of the distinction between
sensation and the intelligent consciousness of a sensation'.[24]
This Kantian principle of reflexive self-consciousness provides
the foundation for Green's theory of mind.

Green, like other post-Kantians, regards Kant's Transcendental Deduction as a betrayal of the original idealist principle
of the transcendental unity of apperception. The principle does
not, according to Green, entail the distinction between a priori
form and a posteriori sense matter so much as its obliteration,
for each is known through reflexive self-consciousness only by
the other: 'The antithesis between thought, as that in which
we are active, and experience, as that in which we are simply
receptive, vanishes.' Thus, a simple sensation, which according to 'common-sense' empiricist opinion constitutes the most
particular and determinate of thoughts, is on the contrary the
most general, for all that can be predicated of it is the Kantian
'I think', the bare form of the 'universal' of consciousness that
attends all of our mental representations; 'pure "being,"' . . .
the emptiest of abstractions'. What little actual content such
sensation has at this stage derives not from itself but from its
relation to consciousness, so that 'thought appears as a factor
in experience even in its remotest germs'.[25] The self is similarly
brought forward by reflexive self-consciousness, as the sense of
'pure being' produced by the mind's initial encounter with 'the
"sensible thing"' provides 'the first "objectification" in which an
active principle of thought becomes conscious of itself'. This
initial datum of consciousness is construed according to the
Aristotelian entelechy as an 'empty form or mere potentiality'[26]

---

[22] See the discussion of Green and Hegel's dialectic of 'Sense-certainty' in
Sect. IV below.   [23] Green, *Works*, iii. 52. See also Chapter 2, Sect. IV.
[24] Green, *Works*, iii. 81. See also Green on the forms of space and time, pp. 71–
2. Aristotle, according to Green, 'insists that a "unity" must exist in the soul, apart
from the several senses' (ibid.).   [25] Ibid. 52.
[26] Ibid. 78.

the latent content of which is realized through reflexive self-consciousness not only as knowledge but also ontologically as the actualization of the self.

'The view of thought' which Green claims to derive from Aristotle 'exhibits the first idea equally with the first datum of experience, as the most simple and abstract possible, as having a minimum of form, *i.e.* as relatively matter.'[27] The potentiality for knowledge represented by the fundamental phenomenological datum, the sense that ' "something is" ', is realized reflexively, according to Green, as the mutual determination of the object and the subject. Green sees the reflexivity of consciousness itself to generate the content of thought spontaneously as each representation held within the apperception is opposed to, and hence distinguished from, all others:

'Substance,' as the outward thing, is but the reflex of the inward subject, and involves the same correlative opposites. It is individual or exclusive of all things but itself; otherwise it would be no object of definite knowledge. But it is not *merely* individual. If it were, it would be . . . out of relation to other things, and relations alone constitute the determinate properties in virtue of which a thing is known. As known, it is in implicit relation to all things else, on the principle that one item of knowledge ultimately qualifies every other; in other words, it involves an element in common with them, a universal. It is an individual universalised through its particular relations or qualities.[28]

Thinking, according to Green, 'does not begin with determinate attributes which it abstracts from each other, but has itself to create them'.[29]

The object, according to Green, is determined both as part of the self, as an instance of the universal 'being' of consciousness, and as that which is distinct from the self and all the other objects contained within apperception, while the subject is defined reciprocally as that which is other than its objects, but also as that in which all objects are brought into relation and determined, realized, so that the sum of such objects is also the self. The form shared by the subject and the objects it constitutes is accordingly that of differentiated unity.[30] Each

---

[27] Ibid. 65.   [28] Ibid. 70.   [29] Ibid. 53.
[30] 'The process of thought . . .', according to Green, ' "integrates" just so far as it "differentiates" ' (ibid. 63).

draws together a manifold, for 'every act of judgment' is, Green maintains, 'an act of synthesis'.[31] The 'self [in relation] to the world of experience' is both 'distinct from it, yet realised in it, as the unity of the world's manifold'.[32] The object is similarly determined accordingly as the simple unity represented by the fundamental judgement of 'being' is differentiated by being brought into relation with other cognitions: 'The difference has not taken something from it, but added something to it . . . It is no longer a bare unit, but a unity of differences, a centre of manifold relations.'[33]

Consciousness, according to Green, provides the form of unity which both subject and object instance and through which each is distinguished from all other mental representations: 'The "form" under which alone we can know the simplest thing as distinct from another, is given by the same unifying and distinguishing self, of which the whole series of forms is the realisation'.[34] The initial sense of being, that ' "something is" ', is the potentiality, a simple undifferentiated unity, which in being brought into relation with other mental representations is actualized as a complex unity. For Green, as for Grant, reflexive self-consciousness provides the conditions by which the subject constitutes its objects, and in so doing furnishes this act with a content, so that the self can have knowledge of itself and actualize its being through its objects:

If then the thing of experience turns out to be what 'thinking makes it', while, on the other hand, the motion of thought is no other than the correlative 'differentiation and integration', which constitutes the evolution of the phenomenal world, where is the obstacle to the admission that the world of experience is a world of ideas, or things as thought of, that its order is an order of thought, that in knowing it we do but realise ourselves?[35]

The sum of our knowledge of objects furnishes the objective form by which we are able to know our universal nature as rational moral beings: 'the self can only realise its universality through the experience of the world'.[36]

Green provides an idealist model of mind which, unlike

[31] Ibid. 81.   [32] Ibid. 79.   [33] Ibid. 63.
[34] Ibid. 84.   [35] Ibid. 65.   [36] Ibid. 73.

that which Hopkins knew from Grant's commentary, specifies a mechanism inherent to reflexive self-consciousness by which the mind is able to constitute its objects and hence actualize the self. Although Hopkins does not acknowledge this mechanism directly in either the conclusion to 'The Origin of Our Moral Ideas' or the *Ethike* essay, the doctrine sketched in the latter essay bears a suggestive relation to it. The moral 'prepossession', like the initial apperceptive sense of 'being' in Green, marks the initial term of consciousness, the potentiality, from which a determinate form is actualized, constituted by the mind accordingly as its necessary relations to all other terms of our (moral) being, our free-willed rational nature, are recognized. Indeed Green states such a parallel between the moral 'prepossession' of the will and the initial act of apperception clearly in his essay:

As the man is said to be the series of his acts, so that the first of these contains all in germ, because an outcome of the will of which the whole series is the realisation, so the simplest form of the intelligible world, taken not in abstraction but as a determination of a subject, is not a beginning merely, but a beginning which is potentially the end.[37]

In 'The Origin of Our Moral Ideas' the a priori agencies with which Hopkins endows the mind, 'the desire of unity' and the subordinate '[desire] of difference', recall the terms of Green's account and fulfil the functions that he sees to occur spontaneously through the conditions of reflexive self-consciousness. The idealist terms of Hopkins' developing theory of mind, his concerns with relation, comparison, and differentiated unity, mark an affinity between his thought and that of Green. For Hopkins, as for Green, the radical apperceptive sense of 'being' provides the initial term for knowledge; 'nothing is so pregnant and straightforward to the truth as simple *yes* and *is*' (*J.* 127).

Both Grant's and Green's respective accounts of reflexive self-consciousness demonstrate that, as Hopkins puts it, 'many things follow from man being his own object' (*J.* 124). The idealist model of mind that Green draws from Aristotle, like

---

[37] Ibid. 80. See also ibid. 58.

that which Grant presents in his commentary, furnishes Hopkins with an understanding of reflexive self-consciousness that allows him the means to develop his own realist metaphysic. Both Grant and Green provide Hopkins with versions of the idealist deduction from Kant's principle of the 'pure' transcendental unity of apperception, by which thought is seen to constitute its objects and thereby provide a content by which the self can both know and actualize itself. This theoretical insight is their principal contribution to Hopkins' developing thought.

III

Both Grant and Green present their idealist doctrine of reflexive self-consciousness in terms of the Aristotelian entelechy, which appears to be the Trojan horse by which the principle entered Hopkins' thought. Indeed the combined influence of Grant and Green accounts for the curious fact that many of Hopkins' essays draw together Kant and Aristotle, that Kantian readings of Aristotle and Aristotelian readings of Kant are so important to the development of his speculations. It is clear that his realist 'prepossession' made Hopkins amenable to such influences. It is also the case, as the analysis of the conclusions to 'The Origin of Our Moral Ideas' and the *Ethike* essays demonstrate, that he is not always aware of the provenance of the ideas he adopts or develops, nor indeed of the directions in which they are leading him. The drift in his thought toward a post-Kantian idealism can be discerned in his discussions of Kant and Aristotle not only in 'The Origin of Our Moral Ideas' and the *Ethike* essay but in many other of the essays that were discussed earlier, where he rejects the 'empty' conception of form that Kant arrives at through the Transcendental Deduction in favour of a more radical noumenal principle for which the Aristotelian conception of form provides the model.

For Kant the transcendental conditions of thought do not themselves constitute thought, but are pure forms which only furnish 'objectively' valid concepts as they are applied to sense intuitions, whereas in Aristotle the principle of form is identified with *logos*: it has a content. In contrast to the radically separate Kantian concepts of matter and form the Aristotelian principles correspond to the relative values of potentiality and actuality. While the Kantian forms are *imposed* upon their matter the Aristotelian forms exist *in* matter.

Hopkins is clearly aware of the distinctive nature of Kant's 'new stress on the scholastic distinction of form and matter' by which a priori forms organize sense intuitions without contributing any content to the resultant thought. He recognizes in the essay on '*A posteriori* Truth' that the Kantian principle of form is a criterion extrinsic to the matter to which it is applied. 'Space' and 'time' are described in the essay as 'the form[s] *under which* we regard' phenomena (D. VI 1, fo. 1, my emphases). He makes a similar reference in this essay to the category of quantity as having 'no meaning except from being illustrated in things, in matter' (fo. 2). The Kantian principle of form is analogous to the Aristotelian here only in so far as it allows Hopkins to establish a principle of 'objective' knowledge with which to counter Humean scepticism.

But even as he acknowledges the distinctive nature of the Kantian a priori forms Hopkins moves to eliminate them by suggesting that the Kantian categories 'like the Aristotelian, repeat and overlap (and may all be reduced to Relation)' (fo. 1ᵛ). This impulse to collapse the elaborate structure of the Kantian a priori is decisive for Hopkins' thought, and marks its affiliation with post-Kantian efforts to clear the Kantian site, to bring the transcendental philosophy back to its foundation in order to build upon it a new edifice. Hopkins, in typical post-Kantian fashion, agrees with Kant that self-consciousness necessarily implies a discriminating subject that forms specific unities 'spontaneously' from the manifold presented to it, but rejects the faculty psychology to which Kant entrusts the performance of this function. Hopkins' principles of 'comparison', 'relation', the 'desire for unity', and 'Conscience or the Imperative' all affirm the transcendental unity of consciousness but stop short of adopting the categories and the other a priori machinery of mind that Kant deduces from it.

By rejecting the terms of Kant's Transcendental Deduction—namely, the doctrine of the faculties and the prohibition upon an a priori content to thought that it entails—Hopkins is able to identify the radical Kantian principle of form, the synthetical unity of apperception, with the Aristotelian entelechy.

Transcendental form can be seen in these terms to itself constitute thought, rather than to be an 'empty' form which produces thought only as it is imposed upon sense intuitions. In the essay on *Phronesis*, for example, Hopkins draws a parallel between the Aristotelian ontology by which 'things truly exist only in their fullest organisation and highest development' and the Kantian principle that 'our thoughts grow and become complex and determine in this way or that by strength[s] of their own and principles independent of the accidents under which their experience comes to individuals' (D. X 3, fo. 18). Just as the *logos* constitutes the autonomous being of objects so correspondingly in Hopkins' idealist construal of the Kantian principle our 'independent' capacity for making synthetic a priori judgements is seen to constitute our objects. Radically distinct from the contingent matter, 'the accidents', of sense experience, our thoughts are seen to arise 'by strength[s] of their own', much as in 'The Origin of Our Moral Ideas' unity is established by the mind's 'effort' or 'striv[ing]'.

Once the form of consciousness is identified with the content of thought, as it is in Hopkins' transcendental principle of 'unity', its determinations can be described by the Aristotelian entelechy as the actualization of a potentiality. This is evident not only in the conclusion to 'The Origin of Our Moral Ideas' and in the doctrine of the *Ethike* essay but is an implication also of the analysis of perception in the essay on 'Causation'. True to Aristotle's relative notion of form, the ambiguous figure of the quatrefoil/Maltese cross provides two forms, each of which constitutes the potentiality of the other. Each figure is seen in accordance with Hopkins' transcendental principle, the mind's imperative form of 'unity', to be generated spontaneously as a particular instance of unity. The ambiguity of this example gives the decisive role in perception to the subject: 'an effect is *nothing but* the way in which the mind ties together . . . all the conditions it sees' (D. VI 2, fo. 5; my emphasis). In 'Causation', much as in 'The Origin of Our Moral Ideas', the transcendental 'desire for unity' furnishes the Aristotelian *arche*, the starting-point for perception, by which the mind is able to actualize its sense-matter spontaneously as one of several synthetic forms.

Hopkins' early thought is preoccupied with questions of how form and content, the ideal and the empirical, the one and the many, and knowing and being, can each be related to the other. 'This always recurring coexistence of contraries is', Hopkins writes, 'highly exciting to thought...' (D. VI 8, fo. 19). Such questions are recognized in the 1868 'Notes on the History of Greek Philosophy' as different ways of discussing the nature of 'the Idea'. They are seen to comprise a set of 'difficulties' which, although they originate with the Presocratic philosophers, 'generally ... exist still' (D. XII 1, fo. 2). While the speculations of the undergraduate essays find in the Kantian principle of free will and the post-Kantian developments of the principle of reflexive self-consciousness the means of addressing such issues and countering positivist and materialist theory, such principles are finally drawn together and developed into a systematic metaphysic only in the 1868 notes on the Pre-Socratics.

IV

The entity which is discussed in the 'Parmenides' notes as 'Being' or 'stress' (J. 129) starts life in the first group of the 'Notes on the History of Greek Philosophy' as 'the Idea': 'The Idea, it is to be remembered, is not the abstraction, indeed it is as much the concrete as the abstract and exists before the universal has been abstracted from the particulars and the particulars realised in the universal' (D. XII 1, fo. 1). There is an ambiguity in this normative definition of 'the Idea' (and in other references to it) in the 'Notes', as to whether the principle should be understood as belonging to individual consciousness or as a reification of this mental principle comparable to the Platonic Idea, the Aristotelian *logos*, and the Hegelian *Geist*.

To the extent that his speculations are, like those of Parmenides, founded upon the idealist identity theory of being and knowing, Hopkins is not greatly concerned with the modern distinction of the subject and the object: 'the distinction between men or subjects and the things without them is unimportant in Parmenides: the contrast is between the one and the many' (J. 130). The passage I have quoted from the first group of notes casts the problem of the one and the many in post-Kantian idealist terms of the 'concrete' and the 'universal', the 'particular' and the 'abstract'. Hopkins' conception of 'the

Idea' here highlights his responsiveness to the Hegelianism of his Greats studies, in which, as the following remark from Green's 1867 lectures on moral philosophy indicates, the incarnationalist doctrines of Christianity and Hegel are conflated: 'In Christianity we have the universal & particular identified [with one another]'.[38] This doctrine, which extends the Christian principle of the Incarnation as the all-encompassing metaphysical 'Idea', would naturally have appealed to Hopkins.

One of Hopkins' notes from Jowett's lectures on Plato establishes that he was aware of such terms and their source as early as Hilary term 1865: 'Progress from abstract to concrete (that is, in German sense—simple abstractions to connected abstractions)' (B. II, fo. 135[v]).[39] The identification of the 'concrete' with 'connected abstractions' made in Hopkins' note anticipates the formulation of 'the Idea' cited above and indicates the direction in which to look for its origin. The specific 'German' antecedent for Jowett and Hopkins here is the Hegelian principle of the 'concrete universal', which Hopkins may have known directly from reading J. H. Stirling's translation of the first section of Hegel's *Science of Logic*. The translation, along with a detailed commentary on it, is included in Stirling's two-volume study *The Secret of Hegel* (1865), a book which Green had an early enthusiasm for[40] and, as F. H. Bradley records in his 1867 notes, recommended to students.[41] Another of Hopkins' lecturers, Robert Williams, similarly recommended to his audience that they read the *Logic* and compare the Platonic with the Hegelian dialectic (D. VIII, fo. 18). The opening section of the *Science of Logic*, 'Quality', is concerned with questions of the

---

[38] Merton, Bradley Papers, MS I-A1, Lect. XXIII.

[39] The notebook containing this note bears the date 'May 23. 1862' on the verso of the front fly-leaf. Hopkins evidently began using it while at Highgate and continued with it at Oxford. Most of the notebook is taken up with notes on Thucydides and Sophocles, upon which Jowett lectured to Hopkins from Easter term 1863 to Michaelmas 1864. The notes on Plato occur only in the last ten pages. They are mainly of a general introductory nature and so suggest that they were made at the beginning of the course of Jowett's lectures on Plato which Hopkins attended from Hilary term 1865 (my source for the dates of Jowett's teaching of Hopkins is Higgins, 'Hopkins and "The Jowler"', 162–3).

[40] G. Thomas, *Moral Philosophy*, 50 n.

[41] Merton, Bradley Papers, MS Lect. XIV. Isobel Armstrong considers Stirling's book to have 'probably' been a 'source of Hopkins' knowledge of Hegel' (*Language as Living Form in Nineteenth Century Poetry* (Brighton: Harvester Press, 1982), 57).

relation of being and not-being, and of the one to the many, issues which were central to Greats studies of ancient Greek philosophy, and are especially important to Hopkins' 'Notes'.

Hegel's initial examination of simple being in the first chapter of the *Logic*, 'Being', reveals that it is an empty concept. The assertion of being which the copula expresses has no predicate and is therefore a generality which effectively affirms its opposite principle, that mere nothing *is*. What are commonly regarded as the exclusive categories of being and nothing are each seen to be entirely abstract and, as such, to have no bearing upon reality. Only through the acquisition of particular qualities can they become by degrees 'concrete'; that is, participate in reality, or, what amounts to the same thing for Hegel, be properly thinkable. Hence the abstract universals of properties or qualities make concrete that which was initially apprehended as an 'empty' universal. Hegel sees such determination to occur as a process of negation in which particular qualities have their significance only in their contrasting relations to other qualities: 'Being is Being, and Nothing is Nothing, only in their distinguishedness from each other.'[42] Determination occurs in this radical case as the negation of each of these moments by its opposite. The resulting synthesis is a higher category, 'becoming' or 'determinate being', a rudimentary version of the 'concrete universal'.

This reductive account of the first dialectic of the *Logic* is sufficient to introduce the schematic understanding of the 'concrete universal' that Hopkins was familiar with from Jowett: 'For example in the Sophist Plato begins with the abstract and goes on to the concrete, not in the lower sense of returning to outward objects, but to the Hegelian concrete or unity of abstractions'.[43] Hopkins would also have known of the principle directly from Sibree's translation of Hegel's *Philosophy of History* which he studied during Hilary term 1867, a few months before writing the 'Notes on the History of Greek Philosophy'. The terms that Hopkins uses in his 'Notes' to describe 'the Idea' are the same as those used by Hegel in his discussion of the

---

[42] *Science of Logic*, bk. I, sect. I, ch. 1, C(3), remark; trans. J. H. Stirling, *The Secret of Hegel* (London: Longman, Green, Longman, Roberts, and Green, 1865), i. 357.
[43] Jowett, *Plato*, 2nd edn., iv. 404. Similarly: 'Abstractions grow together and again become concrete in a new and higher sense' (p. 406).

early history of philosophy in the Introduction to the book: 'It was Socrates who took the first step in comprehending the union of the Concrete with the Universal.'[44]

Of the many sources from which the Hegelian idea of the 'concrete universal' was available to Greats students in the 1860s, Green must be judged the most significant for Hopkins. Green, unlike Jowett, is a systematic philosopher whose speculations during the 1860s have a central concern with the Hegelian principle. The idea of the 'concrete universal' is likely to have been presented in Green's teaching, much as it is in 'The Philosophy of Aristotle', in the full and systematic context of his theory of mind. Green was well acquainted with Hegel from Jowett's teaching, his reading,[45] and from translating the *Philosophical Propaedeutic*,[46] a series of lecture notes that Hegel used for teaching schoolboys in Nuremberg from 1808–11, which includes concise versions of most of his doctrines, including those of the *Phenomenology of Spirit* (1807) and the *Science of Logic* (1812). Indeed, as Ben Wempe observes, F. H. Bradley's notes from Green's 1867 lecture course on moral philosophy indicate that he used the *Propaedeutic* in his teaching, and may have intended the translation to provide an introduction to Hegel for his students.[47]

Green's development of the Kantian principle of apperception in 'The Philosophy of Aristotle', which he claims to find in Aristotle, can be read as a restatement of Hegel's dialectic of 'Sense-certainty' at the beginning of the *Phenomenology of Spirit*. 'Because of its concrete content', Hegel writes, 'sense-certainty immediately appears as the *richest* . . . [and] the *truest* knowledge'.[48] But for Hegel, as for Green after him, 'the essence of

---

[44] *The Philosophy of History*, trans. J. Sibree (New York: Colonial Press, 1899; repr. New York: Dover, 1956), 13. See also pp. 8–13 and 269, on 'the Greek principle' of 'Beauty' as 'a concrete unity of Spirit'. This translation was first published in 1858.
[45] Green took out 3 vols. of Hegel's *Werke* in 1861 (Ben Wempe, *Beyond Equality* (Delft: Eburon, 1986), 23).
[46] Balliol, Green Papers, unnumbered MS entitled 'Analysis of Hegel'. It was first identified in 1982. Since then Wempe (*Beyond Equality*, 62) has argued not only for its great importance for Green's thought but that it is not written in his hand. The issue is discussed further by G. Thomas (*Moral Philosophy*, 46–7), who sees the translation as 'a minor document' and suggests that it may be a 'fair copy', perhaps prepared for submission to a publisher.
[47] Wempe, *Beyond Equality*, 27, 62.   [48] *Phenomenology of Spirit*, sect. 91.

this certainty', of the mind's immediate sensible intuition of an object, is the emptiness of *'pure being'*. Nor is this certainty immediate, but rather consists of 'the two "Thises", one "This" as "I", and the other "This" as object', each of which is mediated by the other through reflexive self-consciousness: 'I have this certainty [of the "I"] *through* something else, viz. the thing; and it, similarly, is in sense-certainty *through* something else, viz. through the "I" '.[49] In all our efforts to express the specificity of particular experience through the word 'This' or its related forms of 'Here' and 'Now' we predicate no distinctive attributes of the sensible thing but simply '*utter* the universal' of being, the simple idea that something 'is': 'the universal is the true [content] of sense-certainty and language expresses this true [content] alone'.[50]

The Hegelian inflections to Green's developing thought are well marked in the following extract, which discusses the determination of particulars in Aristotle:

We are now in a position to review the senses in which, according to Aristotle, matter attaches to the individual substance ... The matter, which attaches to it as individual, does indeed determine it, but only as a matter which ceases to be matter, for, as we have seen, it is only the individuality which transforms itself into the universal, not one simple or absolute, that belongs to anything known. The matter, which consists in a presentation in a particular 'here' and 'now,' is a determination of substance only as a mode of the individuality just described, and 'sublates' itself in the same way.[51]

Green's criticism of Aristotle in his essay is that, by maintaining that 'matter' is real yet unintelligible, Aristotle does not go far enough in his idealism.[52] Green claims to be drawing out the real nature of Aristotelian metaphysics by effectively identifying Aristotle's principles of 'form' and 'matter' with the respective Hegelian principles of the 'universal' and the 'individual'. In this way sensible matter is not simply known *through* form, that is, inasmuch as it instantiates form, but is itself a principle

---

[49] Ibid. sect. 92.   [50] Ibid. sect. 97. Cf. Green, *Works*, iii. 52.
[51] Green, *Works*, iii. 73–4.
[52] 'He did not clearly see that being, as the matter or subject ... which is involved in all predication ... was the indeterminate thinking self, which becomes determinate speculatively in actual knowledge, as it does practically in the moral life' (ibid. iii. 81).

of form or thought, the 'empty' universal or 'pure being'. Green represents Aristotelian 'matter' in the above passage in terms of consciousness that are familiar from the *Phenomenology*. It is described as 'a presentation' to mind and more specifically identified with the pair of demonstratives which provide the main focus for the discussion of 'Sense-certainty', namely, 'here' and 'now'.[53]

Green's account of thought, of course, goes beyond the initial dialectic of immediate sense intuition to assert that knowledge of determinate being is possible. The argument of the passage cited above, that sensuous particularity is determinate even though it is known only as the universal, appears to take its cue from 'Perception', the dialectic which follows that of 'Sense-certainty' in the *Phenomenology*. Green's reference to the 'mode' of 'the individuality which transforms itself into the universal' presupposes that distinctions can be made within the universal yielded by our sense intuitions, for, as he puts it, the 'matter' or 'individuality' ' "sublates" itself' in the universal.

The term 'sublates', which, as his quotation marks indicate, Green self-consciously borrows, is the verb form of 'sublation', the standard English translation for Hegel's key term *Aufhebung*. Hegel uses this word to describe the transitional process in the dialectic whereby a particular stage (or moment) in the development of the idea is at once both preserved and annulled in a higher one.[54] The concept is used by Green, much as it is in the dialectic of 'Perception', to describe the way in which 'pure being', the 'sensible thing' as it is initially known to consciousness, has subsumed within it a content. However, the nature of this content is, according to Hegel, somewhat different from the sensuous particularity which the mind initially intended to find: 'the sense-element is still present, but not in the way it was supposed to be in [the position of] immediate certainty: not as the singular item that is "meant", but as a universal, or as that which will be defined as a *property*'.[55] Just as in 'Sense-certainty' the effort to specify the object before us with

---

[53] See in particular *Phenomenology of Spirit*, sects. 98–108. A fuller discussion of 'the "here" and the "now" in general', which draws upon the dialectic of 'Sense-certainty', occurs just prior to the passage extracted here (Green, *Works*, iii. 71–2).

[54] See Hegel's commentary on the verb '*To sublate*' in the *Science of Logic*, bk. I, sect. 1, ch. 1, C(3).   [55] *Phenomenology of Spirit*, sect. 113.

demonstratives such as 'This', 'Here', and 'Now' yields only the universal, so with the abstractions into which 'pure being' dirempts itself, each attribute, as the words which designate them demonstrate, is a general quality, a determinate universal.

Such universals may be seen to have their specific content in Hegel's scheme as a further consequence of the logic of reflexive self-consciousness: 'Being . . . is a universal in virtue of its having mediation or the negative within it; when it *expresses* this in its immediacy it is a *differentiated, determinate* property. As a result *many* such properties are established simultaneously, one being the negative of the other.'[56] This would appear to provide the model[57] for Green's development of reflexive self-consciousness in his account of the mind's determination of the subject and its objects. The subject and object are each distinguished within the simple intuition that ' "something is" ' through the mediation of the other. While the subject is a universal present to all intuitions, so, because 'it is related to all these particular objects as their negation', it is also an individual. Similarly the object is first apprehended by consciousness as a universal, 'pure being', which, in so far as its properties constitute the negation of all other attributes represented within consciousness, is specified as an individual. Green's version of Hegel's dialectic constitutes his dynamic conception of differentiated unity: 'As the individual self is universalised, so the universal is individualised, through its particular relations.'[58] This principle holds within it a tension between a set of abstract properties which are at once held together and exist indifferently alongside one another in the idea of a 'thing'.

It is well to be wary of trying to draw too close a parallel between Green's theory of thought in the essay on Aristotle and Hegel's dialectic of 'Perception'. R. L. Nettleship, Green's fellow idealist, editor, and biographer, offers an authoritative gloss on the relation of his teacher's thought to that of Hegel, the 'most controversial of Green's debts'.[59] He remarks in his 'Memoir' of Green upon 'the noticeable fact that, while he regarded Hegel's

---

[56] Ibid.
[57] The parallel argument in the *Science of Logic*, bk. I, sect. I, ch. 2, A, 'Determinate Being as Such', is also likely to be relevant here.
[58] Green, *Works*, iii. 70. Cf. *Phenomenology of Spirit*, 'Perception', esp. sects. 114–17 and 123–8. [59] G. Thomas, *Moral Philosophy*, 45.

system as "the last word of philosophy", he did not occupy himself with the exposition of it, but with the reconsideration of the elements in Kant of which it was the development'.[60] 'The Philosophy of Aristotle' gives credence to this judgement. The essay specifies the Kantian 'synthetical unity of apperception' as the foundation for its speculations, and appears to invoke Hegel only in so far as the opening dialectics of the *Phenomenology* (and probably the parallel dialectics of 'Determinateness' in the *Science of Logic*), point the way forward from Kantian scepticism.

Green is loath to follow the course of the Hegelian Idea in its dialectical ascent. The reason for this is the value that he, like Hopkins, puts upon the ethical 'primacy of persons',[61] a principle of individuality that is fundamental to his moral philosophy and which draws him to the Kantian principle of consciousness and to the Aristotelian conception of moral character.[62] He has little inclination to dissolve the conception of the individual moral agent within the all-encompassing Hegelian subject. Green's reworking of the Kantian principle of reflexive self-consciousness corresponds to that found in Hegel only in so far as it allows the preservation of the Cartesian conception of the human subject.

While Green's description of the way in which our consciousness of 'pure being' is determined by the mind as the object has a suggestive relation to the Hegelian dialectic of 'Perception', it shies away from the dialectical logic which in Hegel impels the determination of the Idea beyond this point and indeed beyond the boundaries of the Cartesian subject. Green employs an apt metaphor of containment to describe this process of determination: 'the mere universal is a shell to be filled up by particular attributes'.[63] The implication of this analogy is that our knowledge of the object of cognition can be made complete without the dialectic described in 'Perception' generating the long series of formal transformations that lead to the ultimate manifestation of the 'Absolute Idea'.

---

[60] Green, *Works*, iii. pp. lxxxv–lxxxvi. Similarly, Green's friend from youth and fellow idealist Edward Caird observed that he 'held . . . that *something like* Hegel's Idealism must be the result of the development of Kantian philosophy' (quoted in Wempe, *Beyond Equality*, 16; my emphasis).

[61] See G. Thomas, *Moral Philosophy*, 52–4.   [62] See ibid. 41–4.

[63] Green, *Works*, iii. 56. See also ibid. 78 and 91.

Green contains the restless impetus of the Hegelian dialectic by identifying it with the Aristotelian entelechy. F. H. Bradley notes that Green remarked of Hegel in a lecture of 1867 that 'In Aristotle, we have much the same doctrine.'[64] Green's construal of the principles of 'matter' and 'form' not only completes what he understands to be Aristotle's idealism,[65] it is also representative of the way in which he subordinates the Hegelian dialectic to the terms of the Aristotelian entelechy: 'Matter and form, then, are related to each other respectively at once as the more abstract and more concrete, and as the less and more perfectly or definitely known. The process of thought appears as one not of abstraction but of concretion.'[66] The apprehension of an object according to the conditions that Hegel identifies with the Kantian principle of reflexive self-consciousness is regarded as a potentiality, 'pure being', which is actualized in the dialectical form of differentiated unity. The potentiality represented by 'pure being' is completely realized not through the transformations of the full Hegelian dialectical ascent but as the fulfilment of a single dialectic in which each intuition of an object is, through being mediated by the subject, negated by all other possible mental representations. While Green sees the universal to be actualized accordingly as its emptiness is 'filled up', the Hegelian scheme would specify that, to extend Green's analogy, this can occur only when the content which 'fill[s]' it has undergone a series of chemical changes. Green effectively identifies the determination of being with a single dialectic, which orchestrates the original paradox of reflexive self-consciousness.

The principle of the 'concrete universal', especially Green's

---

[64] Quoted from F. H. Bradley's lecture notes (Merton, Bradley Papers, MS I-A1, Lect. XXI) by Wempe, *Beyond Equality*, 70.

[65] 'So far then as definition consists in the gradual differentiation of an indeterminate matter, this represents also the order both of thought and of the world . . . In putting the most abstract universal as "matter" . . . he merely after his manner "shoots from a pistol" a proposition, which properly carries with it a complete transmutation of his theory of knowledge, but which he himself never followed to its consequences. The same antagonism, pointing for reconciliation to a higher philosophy than Aristotle's own, appears under several other forms in his writings' (Green, *Works*, iii. 66). The 'higher philosophy' seen to be able to facilitate a 'reconciliation' of an 'antagonism' is strongly suggestive of Hegel's dialectic.

[66] Green, *Works*, iii. 63.

elaborate development of it in terms of Aristotelian metaphysics, provided Hopkins with a distinctive and dynamic model of differentiated unity. His understanding of 'the Idea' as a contained dialectical unity, which is introduced in the first group of the 'Notes', can be extrapolated from the curious comparison he makes of it to a riddle in the second group: 'With regard to the Idea beforehand and after—we may say the Idea asks us a riddle of which the question is more beautiful than the answer' (D. XII 2, fo. 2). The 'Idea beforehand and after' refers to the distinction which the first group of the 'Notes' makes between the original recognition of the Idea by the Greeks, who regard it as an abstraction or universal, and the modern positivist conception, which emphasizes the concrete nature of the Idea.

A riddle, like the Hegelian dialectic, consists of two strictly correlative terms. The question and the answer each derive their significance only through their relation to the other, that is, only by being a reciprocal term of a higher idea. Moreover, this synthesis often proceeds, in the case of both riddle and dialectic, from the most paradoxical juxtaposition of terms. The question which the riddle poses typically addresses an issue of identity and groups together a number of apparently unrelated abstracted qualities (e.g. 'What creature advances on four feet in the morning, on two at noon, and on three in the evening?'[67]), while, correspondingly, its answer provides the concrete object to which they belong ('Man'). The element of surprise necessary to the successful riddle marks the recognition of identity in ostensibly disparate or contingent terms. It illustrates the essential tension inherent to differentiated unity, in which a number of properties, each of which has an existence that is autonomous and exclusive of all others, are nevertheless drawn together as a unity. As in the definition given by the first group of notes, 'the Idea' of the riddle logically precedes the respective terms of its abstractions and their concretion, its correlative question and its answer.

[67] F. J. H. Letters, *The Life and Work of Sophocles* (London: Sheed & Ward, 1953), 205.

6   The Big Idea

In the theology and philosophy of England as well as of
Germany and also in the lighter literature of both coun-
tries there are always appearing 'fragments of the great
banquet' of Hegel.

(Jowett, *Plato*, 2nd edn., iv. 424)

I

While the conception of 'the Idea' which Hopkins adopts corresponds to the form of the Hegelian dialectic, it is not tied to
the progressive historicism that is integral to Hegel's principle.
Indeed, it is precisely this developmentalism which Hopkins
objects to in Hegel: 'the ideas of Historical Development, of
things both in thought and fact detaching and differencing
and individualising and expressing themselves . . .' (*J.* 119).[1]
His rejection in 'The Probable Future of Metaphysics' of 'the
philosophy of development in time' does, however, receive a
qualification: 'this at least must be allowed, that philosophy must
not so much speak of right and wrong in systems but must
acknowledge its history and growth to itself and see that it is
meaningless without such a history and growth' (*J.* 119–20).
Hence, he believes that 'the opposition of the two schools . . . of
thought [i.e. 'idealism and materialism'] . . . will continue to be
more intelligent as time goes on' (*J.* 119). Hopkins' concession
to developmentalism suggests the influence of Jowett, who, as
Frank Turner observes, believes that the history of thought describes a progressive clarification of the ultimate nature of truth,[2]

---

[1] Hopkins studied Hegel's *Philosophy of History* with Green at the time that
this essay was written (i.e. Hilary term 1867). On the contemporary conflation of
Darwinism and Hegelian developmentalism by Jowett and others, see Anthony
Ward, *Walter Pater: The Idea in Nature* (London: MacGibbon & Kee, 1966), 46–52.
[2] Turner, *Greek Heritage*, 418.

but not one that can be attributed necessarily to the action of a Hegelian self-positing spirit.

While Jowett's early enthusiasm for Hegel had waned by the time he wrote the long digression on the philosopher in his Introduction to the *Sophist* in the second edition of his *Plato* (1875), it nevertheless provides a useful account of the Hegelian ideas that he found most convincing. It is likely that such durable convictions were given some prominence in his teaching of Greek philosophy to Hopkins and his peers in the 1860s. Jowett's extended discussion in the essay on the *Sophist* concludes with some of the thoughts 'which arise in the mind of a student of Hegel, when, after living for a time within the charmed circle, he removes to a little distance and looks back upon what he has learnt'. Having discussed 'some of the doubts and suspicions'[3] that this student (who presumably represents Jowett) may have, he formulates a response to the question of 'how he can admire without believing, or what value he can attribute to what he knows to be erroneous'.[4] Jowett is, like Green and Hopkins, discriminating in his approach to Hegel and endorses only certain aspects of his system:

We may not be able to agree with him in assimilating the natural order of human thought with the history of philosophy, and still less in identifying both with the divine idea or nature. But we may acknowledge that the great thinker has thrown a light on many parts of human knowledge, and has solved many difficulties. We cannot receive his doctrine of opposites as the last word of philosophy, but we may still regard it as a very important contribution to logic.[5]

The extrication of Hegelian dialectical logic from its original historicist context, which as the last chapter noted is advocated by Green as well as by Jowett, provides one of the defining conditions for Hopkins' conception of 'the Idea'.

Jowett's teaching is also likely to have been a vector for the Viconian historicism found in 'The Probable Future of Metaphysics'. The dilute form of progressivism which qualifies Hopkins' dismissal of 'the philosophy of development in time' is incidental to the cyclical pattern with which he identifies the main impetus of intellectual history: 'The tide we may foresee

---

[3] Jowett, *Plato*, 2nd edn., iv. 422.   [4] Ibid. 423.   [5] Ibid. 424.

will always run and turn between idealism and materialism: this is clear from history, and historical generalisations are true if anywhere in tracing the phases of speculation' (*J.* 118). Turner observes that along with Jowett's modified form of Hegelian historicism, he 'also accepted in some unarticulated fashion elements of the Viconian concept of historical cycles': 'Although we cannot maintain that ancient and modern philosophy are one and continuous (as has been affirmed with more truth respecting ancient and modern history), for they are separated by an interval of a thousand years, yet they seem to recur in a sort of cycle, and we are surprised to find that the new is ever old, and the teaching of the past has still a meaning for us'.[6]

T. H. Green, no doubt influenced by Jowett's teaching, regards the Greek opposition between idealism and materialism to have revived in the modern conflict between German idealism and British empiricism (or 'the English epicureanism', as he often refers to it).[7] The fact that Hopkins was being taught by Green at the time of writing 'The Probable Future of Metaphysics' suggests that his reference to a tidal 'run and turn between idealism and materialism' is most directly a reflection of Green's preoccupation with the opposition. The basis of this opposition can be traced to what Hopkins considers to be the nature of the idea itself and the failure to understand it fully, which he sees to have occurred throughout history.

Green, it may be recalled, maintains that the 'great difficulty which now, as in ancient Greece, besets the entrance on the true path of philosophy, is that of reducing the "sensible thing" to its primary simplicity'.[8] The opposing doctrines of idealism and materialism can be understood as complementary ways of understanding the rudimentary idea of 'the "sensible thing"', which is, according to Green's theory, the product of reflexive self-consciousness. Either we recognize the idea as the pure or empty universal of consciousness, which we are aware of through the mediation of the sensible object, or as the concrete object of sense which is mediated by consciousness. Green credits the early Greeks with the idealist interpretation of the idea: 'the ancient philosophy . . . flew off at once from "sensible things"

---

[6] Turner, *Greek Heritage*, 418; Jowett quoted by Turner, ibid. 418–19.
[7] Green, *Works*, iii. 124. See Ch. 1, Sect. VII.   [8] Green, *Works*, iii. 48.

to pure being'.[9] The result of this 'Greek "criticism of the sensible"' is, Green writes, distant in time from 'the modern reader,
[who is] floating far down the stream of experience, and care-
less of tracing it to its source . . .'[10] Hopkins makes a similar
observation about the relation of modern positivism to early
Greek idealism: 'we in the midst of an elaborated knowledge
of the concrete, in the midst of science, have a difficulty in putting ourselves in the position of these philosophers' (D. XII,
fo. 2).

The 1868 'Notes on the History of Greek Philosophy' demonstrate Hopkins' understanding of the way in which what he
describes a few months earlier as a Viconian 'run and turn
between idealism and materialism' is a direct consequence of his
conception of the Idea as the 'concrete universal'. The opposing doctrines are described in the first group of the 'Notes' as
alternative ways of 'acknowledg[ing] the Idea' (D. XII 1, fo. 2),
much as the tidal 'run of thought' of 'idealism and materialism'
is regarded in 'The Probable Future of Metaphysics': 'different
times like a shifted light give prominence by turns to different
things' (J. 119). The notes contrast the thought of the early
Greek philosophers, who 'knew it [i.e. the Idea] almost by the
abstract alone', to that which predominates in Hopkins' own
age: 'we in the midst of an elaborated knowledge of the concrete, in the midst of science' (fos. 2, 1). Idealism and positivism
are thus located here, not only doctrinally, but also historically,
at the extremes of the Western philosophical tradition.

This view of the history of thought abridges the 'run and turn
between idealism and materialism' into a single representative
contrast. While the historical forms of idealism and materialism
highlight and champion the respective universal and concrete
moments of the Idea, its objective nature remains a dialectical
unity of the two. 'The Idea, it is to be remembered . . . is as much
the concrete as the abstract and exists' prior to the theories
that 'acknowledge' it—the positivist view of induction in which
'the universal has been abstracted from the particulars' and
the idealist view in which 'the particulars [are] realised in the
universal' (fo. 1). It is, in other words, the *perception* of the Idea
that varies historically, not the Idea itself:

[9] Ibid. 78.   [10] Ibid. 54.

It is true that if we acknowledge the Idea now at all it is likely to be a better conception, after the knowledge of the concrete, than before that came, when they [i.e. the Presocratics] knew it almost by the abstract alone—for no doubt, taking the Idea for a hand and the name for its glove left behind, then although to handle it by the concrete may leave it a dry crumpled piece of skin, abstraction may as injuriously blow it out into a graceless bladdery animation; in either case the charm is gone. But if we c[oul]d again catch the Idea in its freshness the difficulties w[oul]d be there.   (fo. 2)

Hopkins' odd analogy[11] describes graphically the distortions which result from an emphasis upon either term of the Idea at the expense of the other. Materialism dessicates the Idea by depriving it of the informing principle of the universal, while, correspondingly, an emphasis upon the formal principle that neglects the concrete results in an empty universal, a name devoid of substance; mere nominalism.

The deficiencies of each case are characterized by the lack of their complementary principle. Hence the restless historical alternation of 'idealism and materialism' occurs as the recognition of the shortcomings of one philosophy in representing the Idea causes a dialectical shift to the opposite principle. The new principle, being analogous to the old in its inadequacy as a representation of the Idea, ensures the cycle's continuance. Each term prompts not a 'higher' term (as in Hegelian historicism), but a revival of its opposite. This is illustrated by Hopkins' analysis of his own age and the inference he draws as to 'The Probable Future of Metaphysics': 'all this is a philosophy of flux opposed to Platonism and can call out nothing but Platonism against it' (*J.* 120). The process by which each 'opposing principle' (*J.* 121) dwells upon either the concrete or the universal aspect and in turn (in Hopkins' Hegelian phrase) 'call[s] out' the other is impelled by the dialectical tension that inheres within the Idea itself as its essential nature.

Early Greek philosophy is seen in the first group of the 'Notes' to represent not only the recurrent idealist strain in thought, a tendency towards 'abstraction' which complements the contemporary propensity for 'the concrete', but also the possibility of

[11] The hand offers a simple and familiar instance of organic unity: 'the fingers are to the hand or arm as many things are to one' (*S.* 98).

THE BIG IDEA 161

an original pure apprehension of the Idea itself, 'the thought in
its first blush' (fo. 1). The full and universal recognition of the
Idea would close the speculative cycle of 'idealism and materialism'; it would be the end of this history, a type of millennium.
According to the Bible the millennium will restore the world to
its Edenic prehistory.[12] The millenarian inflections of Hopkins'
account of 'The Probable Future of Metaphysics' imply that
the expected 'new Realism' could result in a resolute triumph
over materialism.[13] The final version of the 'new Realism' with
which Hopkins wishes to counter 'Purely material psychology'
and its correlative 'philosophy of flux' receives its definitive
formulation in the 'Notes on the History of Greek Philosophy'.
His doctrine of 'stress', 'instress', and 'inscape' is the result of
his endeavours to recover the original apprehension of the Idea;
to 'again catch the Idea in its freshness'.

The effort to 'catch the Idea in its freshness' is founded
upon Hopkins' idealist presupposition that 'the Idea is only
given . . . from the whole downwards to the parts' (*J.* 120):
'it . . . exists before the universal has been abstracted from the
particulars and the particulars realised in the universal' (fo. 1).
His discussion of these two ways of 'acknowledg[ing]' the Idea
brings to the fore the issue of *interpretation,* which he was familiar with from Jowett's teaching and from reading his teacher's
essay on biblical hermeneutics, 'On the Interpretation of Scripture'. Jowett, like Hopkins, posits an original pure and complete
conception of meaning, which his essay identifies with the experience of the first readers of the Scriptures. Subsequent interpretations, according to Jowett, have lost this original meaning,
'the freshness of early literature',[14] and have, like the historical
conceptions of Hopkins' Idea, 'differed with the philosophical
systems which the interpreters espoused'.[15] Jowett's hermeneutic
maintains that the Christian Idea has priority over all the historical acts of its interpretation: the whole is seen to precede
the parts. Like Hopkins' principle of the Idea, 'The book itself
remains as at the first unchanged amid the changing interpretations of it.'[16] Jowett repeatedly insists that the goal of biblical
hermeneutics is to retrieve the Christian principle in its original

---

[12] Rev. 20: 2–4.   [13] See Ch. 1, Sect. I.
[14] Jowett, *Essays and Reviews,* 401.   [15] Ibid. 406.   [16] Ibid. 408.

form, so that 'its beauty will be freshly seen'.[17] Hopkins shares
his teacher's idealist approach to hermeneutics, and a correlative rhetoric of originality and 'freshness' in expressing it.

Jowett's lectures on early philosophy parallel his exercises
in biblical hermeneutics by describing Parmenides' principle
of being as 'the first & purest of all conceptions' and 'really an
impersonal God'.[18] Hopkins' effort in the 'Notes' to 'catch the
Idea in its freshness' is a religious quest, the ur-text for which
is Parmenides: 'His great text, which he repeats with religious
conviction, is that Being is and Not-being is not' (*J.* 127). This
opening remark on Parmenides' philosophy in the notes makes
clear Hopkins' sense of the spiritual import of the philosopher's
central thesis. The primarily ontological significance of the Idea,
its nature as 'determinate being' or the 'concrete universal', is
in Hopkins referred to the source of all being in God.

Hopkins' emotional engagement with the principle of being
is also stated clearly early in the 'Parmenides' notes: 'But indeed I have often felt when I have been in this mood and felt
the depth of an instress or how fast the inscape holds a thing
that nothing is so pregnant and straightforward to the truth as
simple *yes* and *is*' (*J.* 127). This 'felt' response to Parmenides'
'great text' may indeed be judged to have recuperated 'the Idea
in its freshness'. Parmenides' central thesis arose, according to
Karl Jaspers, as a discovery, comparable to Hopkins' recognition
here, of the emotional and intellectual power of being:

Especially in the original Greek, these lines can either seem wonderfully meaningful or else startlingly empty. They bear witness to a profound emotion and yet they state only tautologies. For the first time in
the West a thinker expresses his surprise that being is, that it is impossible to think that nothing is . . . Being is and nothing is not; this, for
Parmenides, is a revelation of thinking through thinking.[19]

The 'mood' that Hopkins is in as he writes the 'Parmenides'
notes is associated by him with his observations of determinate

[17] Ibid. 455.
[18] Balliol, Jowett Papers, MS Notebook IB5, fo. 61. This notebook has been
dated to the period 1865–75 (Darwall-Smith, *Jowett Papers*, 8).
[19] Karl Jaspers, *Anaximander, Heraclitus, Parmenides, Plotinus, Lao-Tzu, Magarjuna*,
ed. Hannah Arendt, trans. Ralph Mannheim (New York: Harcourt Brace Jovanovich,
1974), 19.

instances of being, many of which are recorded in the diaries, journals, and poetry. It is a reverie produced by meditating on *being*, a state of mind which is prompted, as the notes record, by studying the Parmenidean fragments, and on other occasions, as the journals and poetry testify, by the apprehension of particular physical phenomena; 'Some candle clear burns somewhere I come by. | I muse at . . . its being . . .' (No. 133). Hopkins finds in Parmenides' 'great text, which he repeats with religious conviction' a Book of Revelation which aligns with the Book of Creation.

The 'mood' referred to in the notes appears to be expressed in more theoretical terms in 'The Probable Future of Metaphysics':

There is a particular refinement, pitch, of thought which catches all the most subtle and true influences the world has to give: this state or period is the orthodoxy of philosophy—there is just such an orthodoxy in art . . . This orthodoxy lasts but a limited time; it is like the freshness and strain of thoughts in the morning: materialism follows, the afternoon of thought, in which, just as in the afternoon poetry is lost on us if we read, so we are blunted to the more abstract and elusive speculation. (*J.* 118–19)

The parallel made between metaphysics and poetry is a salutary reminder that Hopkins regards the two as closely related modes of engagement with the world. His metaphorical use of the verb 'catches' underlines this point. The reference here to 'a particular refinement . . . of thought which catches all the most subtle and true influences the world has to give' anticipates the phrase in the 'Notes', to 'catch the Idea in its freshness', as well as the use of the verb in the poems, where it announces such definitive epistemological triumphs as that recorded in 'The Windhover', 'I caught this morning morning's minion' (No. 120), and, similarly, in another, untitled, poem: 'As kingfishers catch fire . . .' (No. 115).[20]

By associating philosophy, Parmenides' ontology, with a 'mood' and identifying poetry with 'a particular refinement, pitch, of thought' that is seen to engender 'the orthodoxy of philosophy', Hopkins implicitly contradicts the view of the

---

[20] The significance of this metaphor is discussed further in Ch. 10, Sect. II.

positivist intellectual ascendency of his time which restricts the sphere of poetry to 'feeling' and pleasure and makes rationality and truth the exclusive preserve of science. Poets are, according to J. S. Mill, 'Those who are so constituted, that emotions are the links of association by which their ideas, both sensuous and spiritual, are connected together.'[21] He accordingly believes that 'the philosophical speculations of poets are peculiarly liable' to a particular 'error . . . that of embracing as truth, not the conclusions which are recommended by the strongest evidence, but those which have the most poetical appearance . . .'[22] Parmenides' philosophical poem, especially as it was taught by Jowett,[23] provides Hopkins with the originary text in which poetry and philosophical truth are integral to one another.

The differences in genre between Hopkins' 'Notes' and his poetry mask the common experience and purpose which informs them. The project of the 'Notes' to 'again catch the Idea in its freshness' remains with Hopkins and is the object of many of the later poems. The original perception of the Idea is 'in its freshness' not only 'like the freshness and strain of thoughts in the morning', which 'The Probable Future of Metaphysics' identifies with poetry and metaphysical speculation. It is also Edenic like 'Spring'; 'A strain of the earth's sweet being in the beginning | In Eden garden' (No. 117). If, as 'Ribblesdale' asserts, 'man' is 'Earth's eye, tongue, or heart', and so responsible for bringing the 'earth's sweet being' to consciousness (for 'sweet Earth . . . canst but only be'), then the resultant idea can be identified with 'the Idea in its freshness': it can draw out that which is described in 'God's Grandeur' (which dates from a few months before 'Spring'), as 'the dearest freshness deep down things' (No. 111).

[21] 'Thoughts of Poetry and its Varieties' (1833), in Mill, *Autobiographical and Literary Essays*, ed. John M. Robson and Jack Stillinger (London: Routledge & Kegan Paul, 1981), i. 356. The essay received renewed attention during the 1860s, after its first reprint in the collection *Dissertations and Discussions* (1859; 2nd edn., 1867).

[22] 'Tennyson's Poems' (1835), in Mill, *Literary Essays*, i. 417.

[23] Jowett's lecture notes indicate that in discussing Parmenides in his lectures he began with his poetry: 'In these singular fragments we note first their poetical character' (Balliol, Jowett Papers, MS Notebook IB5, fo. 75; see also Notebook IB4, fo. 1 which also begins with a discussion of 'poetical form'). Robin Darwall-Smith dates these undated notebooks respectively to the period 1865–75 and the early 1860s (Darwall-Smith, *Jowett Papers*, 7–8).

Hopkins' hermeneutic in 'Spring' may be compared with that found in Jowett: 'The office of the interpreter is not to add another [meaning], but to recover the original one: the meaning, that is, of the words as they struck on the ears or flashed before the eyes of those who first heard and read them'.[24] Much as Jowett tries from his historical distance to recapture the original impact of the Scriptures, so Hopkins attempts to recover the original apprehension of the Creation from the latest impression of the Book of Nature, to extract 'the dearest freshness' from a modern world where 'all . . . wears man's smudge . . .' (No. 111). Nature is seen in 'Spring' to facilitate this prelapsarian vision. The sound of the thrush's song, for example, is described as *refreshing* the ear: 'thrush | Through the echoing timber does so rinse and wring | The ear, it strikes like lightnings to hear him sing' (No. 117). The apprehension of the thrush's song here, as well as of creatures in other poems such as the windhover (No. 120) and the kingfishers (No. 115), is described with the epiphanic metaphors of striking and flashing that Jowett employs in his account of the first readings of the Scriptures.

II

The 'Notes on the History of Greek Philosophy' begin by citing a remark by Walter Pater:

Great features of the old G[ree]k philosophy, Pater said, its holding certain truths, chiefly logical, out of proportion to the rest of its knowledge, as Parmenides his dialectic ab[ou]t Being and Not-being, Zeno the contradictions involved in Motion, the Megarians and Heracleitus the difficulties of identity. The explanation of this perhaps is that they argued on the Idea alone, on the thought in its first blush, unrealised.

(D. XII 1, fo. 1)

This account of Pater's opinion of early Greek thought is corroborated and supplemented by his early essay on 'Coleridge's Writings', which dates from January 1866, just before he began tutoring Hopkins.[25] The essay is written from a positivist position

---

[24] Jowett, *Essays and Reviews*, 408.
[25] Pater was Hopkins' private tutor in Easter term 1866 (*J.* 133).

and criticizes Coleridge for his attempts to renew grand metaphysical theory. Pater finds space in his essay to discuss early
Greek idealism, which he reproves for 'dwelling exclusively in
its observations on that which is general or formal, on that
which modern criticism regards as the modification of things
by the mind of the observer'.[26] His attitude to the Greeks' 'dwelling exclusively' upon the 'formal', which he, like Jowett and
Green, parallels with modern idealism, provides a gloss for
the reference in Hopkins' notes to what Pater considers to be
their disproportionate emphasis upon the 'logical'. It appears
that Pater intended his judgement that 'the old G[ree]k philosophy' held 'certain truths, chiefly logical, out of proportion
to the rest of its knowledge' to be understood as a censure.
His observation accordingly provides a point of departure for
Hopkins' thought here. It prompts his tentative identification
of Presocratic speculations with 'the thought in its first blush',
an equation which is consolidated and developed more confidently in the subsequent discussions of 'the Idea in its freshness'
and Parmenides.

The journal entry in which Hopkins records 'Pater talking
two hours against Xtianity' (*J.* 138), which dates from a month
after tutoring with him began, highlights the fundamental point
of difference between them. Pater was a student of Jowett and
a friend of Green, for both of whom Christian belief was inextricable from their idealism and their teaching of philosophy.
Pater's atheism can be understood within the context of Oxford
Greats philosophy of the 1850s and 1860s as having entailed
a radical revision, if not a forthright rejection, of the Christian
metaphysics which proceeded from Jowett's influence. Hopkins,
on the other hand, works within the Christian orientation of
Oxford idealism. The differences between them are indicated
by the underlinings in the manuscript of 'The Origin of Our
Moral Ideas' that Pater apparently added in marking the essay,
and most significantly by Hopkins' defensive anticipation of his
tutor's criticism of the doctrine of reflexive self-consciousness
sketched at the close of the essay: 'If this be thought mysticism
further explanation may be given' (*J.* 83).

While Pater's later writings show that he was strongly drawn to

[26] Walter Pater, 'Coleridge's Writings', *Westminster Review* (Jan. 1866), 118.

principles of unity, the early essay on Coleridge indicates that
he let this attraction 'fall into abeyance, for the time being'.[27]
It is ironic that Pater's comment on 'the old G[ree]k philosophy' provides the starting-point for a series of speculations that
establish Hopkins' grand theory of Being, his doctrine of 'stress'
and 'inscape', for Pater was at the time deeply unsympathetic
to such ventures: 'To suppose that what is called "ontology" is
what the speculative instinct seeks is the misconception of a
backward school of logicians.'[28] Furthermore, he was of course
especially disparaging of systems based on Christian presuppositions, dismissing one of Coleridge's efforts as 'an intellectual
novelty in the shape of a religious philosophy'.[29] The 'Notes'
can accordingly be read in part as a rejoinder to Pater's conception of early Greek idealism. Whereas Pater explains the Greek
principle of the idea as an abstract reification of the mytholo-
gical 'conception of nature as living, thinking, almost speaking
to the mind of man',[30] for Hopkins, who comes to identify the
Idea with Being, it 'is as much the concrete as the abstract' and
is apprehended 'in its freshness' by the Pre-Socratics.

While Pater was, at the time of writing his essay and teaching Hopkins, impatient of idealism and what he describes as
'the long pleading of German culture for the things "behind the
veil" ',[31] he was nevertheless a well-informed source for Hopkins'
knowledge of German idealism, which he, like Jowett and Green,
associated closely with Greek thought. 'Greek philosophy', Pater
writes in the essay on Coleridge, 'Step by step . . . works out the
substance of the Hegelian formula . . . Whatever is, is according to reason; whatever is according to reason, that is.'[32] Pater
knew German and borrowed a number of volumes of Hegel's
Werke from the Library of Queen's College in the early 1860s,
amongst them the *Lectures on the History of Philosophy*.[33]

Hopkins may well have known of the importance that Hegel

[27] See Ward, *Idea in Nature*, 77. Ch. 3 of the book discusses the question of
Hegel's influence on Pater. [28] Pater, 'Coleridge's Writings', 108.
[29] Ibid. 114. [30] Ibid. 118. [31] Ibid. 122. [32] Ibid. 118–19.
[33] He borrowed this title and others, including the *Science of Logic, Lectures on the
History of Philosophy, Lectures on Aesthetics,* and the Encyclopaedia *Logic,* from Feb. to
Apr. 1863 and Mar. to Apr. 1864. (Billie Andrew Inman, *Walter Pater's Borrowings
from the Queen's College Library, the Bodleian Library, the Brasenose College Library, and
the Taylor Institution Library, 1860–1894* (Tucson, Ariz.: University of Arizona, 1977),
4, 5, 6, and 9).

attributes to Parmenides in his *Lectures on the History of Philosophy* from Pater or from Jowett, who considered Hegel to be 'the greatest critic of philosophy who ever lived'.[34] Hegel's *Lectures* see philosophy to have effectively begun with Parmenides' principle that 'Thinking is . . . identical with its Being': 'In that this saying gives evidence of ascending into the realm of the ideal, genuine philosophizing began with Parmenides . . .' The criterion for this judgement comes, of course, from Hegel's own system, so that Parmenides' ontology is seen to mark the earliest philosophical recognition of his conception of the Idea or spirit. According to Hegel 'this beginning is . . . still dark and indefinite and does not further explain what is contained in it; but just this explanation constitutes the development of philosophy itself—which is not yet present here'.[35] Hopkins similarly regards Parmenides' philosophy to contain the full truth of the Idea. However, because he does not eschew Hegel's developmentalism Hopkins does not regard Parmenides' thought as an obscure 'dark and indefinite' beginning to philosophy but identifies it directly with 'the Idea in its freshness'.

III

Parmenides' treatise takes the form of an epic poem, consisting of a proem and two parts which respectively describe 'the unshaken heart of well-rounded truth, and the opinions of mortals, in which there is no true reliance'.[36] The first part contains Parmenides' argument about the nature of Being. From the premiss that Being *is*, and its correlative, the impossibility of the opposite principle, that Not-being *is*, Parmenides establishes that Being is unchangeable, having neither a beginning nor an

[34] Jowett, *Plato*, 2nd edn., iv. 423. It is abundantly clear from the Plato commentaries that Jowett (with whom Hopkins studied the Presocratics during Michaelmas term 1866 (Higgins, 'Hopkins and the "Jowler"', 164)) was familiar with Hegel's *History* (e.g. 2nd edn., iv. 409).

[35] Quoted by Heidegger, *Early Greek Thinking*, trans. David Farrell Krell and Frank A. Capuzzi (New York: Harper & Row, 1984), 83.

[36] G. S. Kirk, J. E. Raven, and M. Schofield, *The Presocratic Philosophers*, 2nd edn. (Cambridge: Cambridge University Press, 1983), fr. 288. All translations are, unless otherwise specified, by Kirk, Raven, and Schofield.

end, for there can be no transition between it and Not-being.[37]
Similarly, as Being cannot partake of its opposite principle in
any way, it must also be utterly consistent with itself, spatially
as well as temporally.[38] Parmenides argues that for Being to be
complete in itself, that is, to lack nothing and hence be perfect, it must be determinate. Hopkins makes the following translation from the fragment that presents this argument: Being
'lies by itself the selfsame thing abiding in the selfsame place:
so it abides, steadfast there; for strong Necessity has it in the
bonds of that bound that guards it all about. And this is why
it is not lawful to call Being without end ($\dot{a}\tau\epsilon\lambda\epsilon\acute{v}\tau\eta\tau\sigma\nu$); for Being
needs nothing and if it were so it would need all' (*J.* 128).[39]
If it were not determinate it would want something that made
it so. Hence, 'it would need all'; it would be subject to change
and hence imply a beginning and an end, and, similarly, lack-
ing that which makes it determinate, its substance could not
be entirely consistent.

'The paradox' of Parmenides' thought is, as Scott Austin
observes, 'that only perfect boundedness reveals the unbounded'.[40] It is understandable, given both the centrality of
the Incarnation to Hopkins' faith and his natural-theological
fascination with the particulars of Creation, that he finds Parmenides' conception of the necessarily determinate nature of
transcendent Being especially engaging, and devotes much of
his notes on the philosopher to discussing it. The fundamental
difference between the conceptions of the immanence of the
infinite within the finite that are found respectively in Christianity and in Parmenides and Hegel, is, as Austin observes, that
the former simply presupposes 'the coincidence of bounded
and unbounded', while the latter claim that this can be justified logically (albeit with quite different conceptions of what
this means).[41] Just as religious liberals such as Jowett and Green,
who argued that Christian dogma should be open to rational
scrutiny, were attracted to Hegel's incarnationalist philosophy,
so Parmenides' poem, the first logical argument of the Western

[37] Ibid. frs. 298, 296. [38] Ibid. fr. 297. [39] Ibid. frs. 298–9.
[40] S. Austin, *Parmenides: Being, Bounds, and Logic* (New Haven: Yale University
Press, 1986), 147.
[41] Ibid. 148. I am indebted here to Austin's discussion of 'The Bounded and the
Unbounded' (pp. 136–54).

tradition, was similarly appreciated for the scope it provides for developing rational accounts of the relation of God's nature to the finite nature of Creation and the Incarnation.

While his undergraduate studies provided Hopkins with some means by which to establish the rational grounds for his belief in an immanent divinity, it is only with the notes on Parmenides' poem that they finally cohere. This is attributable not only to the peculiar relevance to Hopkins' concerns of Parmenides' main argument, but also to the obscurity of its expression. With its often oracular and enigmatic utterances, and the fragmentary form in which it survives, Parmenides' poem allows scope for considerable freedom of interpretation, and so provides Hopkins with an important means by which to explore and clarify his own thought.

The suggestive nature of the fragments provides Hopkins with the opportunity to define his own doctrine of determinate being as much as to explicate that which Parmenides may have intended. The following passage, in which Hopkins translates one of the fragments, identifies determinate being with the 'foredrawn', one of the many coinages in the 'Parmenides' notes: 'It is the unextended, foredrawn—"Look at it, though absent, yet to the mind's eye as fast present here; for absence cannot break off Being from its hold on Being: it is not a thing to scatter here, there, and everywhere through all the world nor to come together from here and there and everywhere . . ."[42] (*J.* 128). The implication here is that if Being had infinite extension it would be dissipated or unevenly distributed, and so require its opposite principle of Not-being to provide the medium through which it would be interspersed. Hopkins' coinage highlights the essential coherence that Parmenides believes to subsist within Being as the condition of its limited, and therefore perfect, nature.

Another passage from Parmenides, which in its original context occurs a few lines after the extract on 'strong Necessity' and the 'bonds' of Being cited at the beginning of the present section, illustrates the idea of Being with the simile of a ball:

But since there is a furthest limit, it is perfected, like the bulk of a ball well-rounded on every side, equally balanced in every direction

---

[42] Cf. Kirk, Raven, and Schofield, *Presocratic Philosophers*, fr. 313.

from the centre. For it needs must not be somewhat more or somewhat less here or there. For neither is it non-existent, which would
stop it from reaching its like, nor is it existent in such a way that there
would be more being here, less there, since it is all inviolate: for
being equal to itself on every side, it lies uniformly within its limits.[43]

Hopkins neither quotes from nor translates the first part of
this passage, where Parmenides makes his analogy. He does,
however, provide an interesting commentary on it: 'He compares it like Xenophanes to a ball rounded true and may very
well mean this as an analogy merely, especially as the comparison is to the outline and surface rather than to the inner
flushness, the temper and equality of weight' (*J.* 128–9). It
is clear from the original passage that Parmenides means the
pre-eminently even form of the sphere to serve as a simile
for the perfect consistency of Being. Hopkins' comments on
the passage indicate that he believes this aspect of 'the inner
flushness, the temper and equality of weight', to be worthy of
greater emphasis.

Hopkins' attribution to Being of an evenly informing 'flushness' introduces a principle of motion that is foreign to Parmenides and which may take its cue from Aristotle's criticism
of Presocratic monism in the *Physics*: 'Again, does it follow that
Being, if one, is motionless? Why should it not move, the whole
of it within itself, as parts of it do which are unities, e.g. this
water?'[44] The informing principle of 'inner flushness' should be
understood as part of a pattern of imagery in Hopkins' poetry
and prose that identifies the motions of life with liquidity, as
in the poem 'Spring', which sums up this most vital and vivid
season in the phrase 'all this juice and all this joy' (No. 117).
The trees in the poem 'Binsey Poplars' are identified with the
capacity of water to counter fire, for they 'Quelled or quenched
in leaves the leaping sun' (No. 130). Organic growth is described in the late poem 'In honour of St. Alphonsus Rodriguez'
as a 'trickling increment' (No. 176c). Similarly, in a journal entry

[43] Ibid. fr. 299. Hopkins quotes the original of 'For neither is it . . .' to '. . . all
inviolate' as two extracts, which appear in *J.* 129.
[44] *The Works of Aristotle*, ii. *Physics*, Bk. I. 3 (186ª16–18), trans. R. Hardie and
R. K. Gaye (Oxford: Clarendon Press, 1930). Hopkins' text for the Presocratics,
Ritter and Preller, refers its readers to the section on Parmenides and Melissus
which begins at Bk. I. 2 (See H. Ritter and L. Preller, *Historia Philosophiae Graecae*
7th edn. (Gotha: Andr. Perthes, 1888), 92).

for August 1867: 'elms too I saw with more liquid in their growth than elsewhere, slimmer and falling towards one another, as in Turner's rows of trees' (*J.* 153). The actions of animals are described in such terms: 'sometimes they [i.e. some prancing lambs] rest a little space on the hind legs and the forefeet drop curling in on the breast, not so liquidly as we see it in the limbs of foals though' (*J.* 206). The human body is also identified with liquidity. In the poems the young bugler is seen to embody 'limber liquid youth' (No. 137) and Harry Ploughman is attributed with a 'liquid waist' (No. 169).

The human body is discussed in more general terms in Hopkins' sermon 'on *the Sacred Heart*', where it is characterized by two types of substance: 'the body consists of solid parts which are permanent or changed slowly and of liquid parts which move to and fro'. The principal example of the former is the heart, and of the latter, 'the liquid blood' (*S.* 101). Hopkins writes of blood in a sermon for the 'Feast of the Precious Blood' that '*it marks the motions of life* in mind and body', and accordingly identifies it explicitly with mortal being, 'Life is precious, it is in this world our being; therefore the blood' (*S.* 13). The smoothly regular liquid motion associated with external nature, with Creation, sums up human nature also: 'the beating of the heart is the truth of nature'. Blood is identified with 'the thoughts of the mind [which] that vessel [i.e. the heart] seems to harbour and the feelings of the soul to which it beats' (*S.* 103). This is true to a proportionately greater extent of mankind's paradigm, Christ, whose blood '*beat and sympathised with the feelings of his heart*, performing nobler offices than any other blood can ever do' (*S.* 14).

Hopkins observes that the blood of Christ can be 'traced from Adam's veins through Abraham's, royal David's, to Mary's' (*S.* 13). Christ's blood, as well as being continuous with all humanity through its origin in the biblical common ancestor, is according to Hopkins also the essence of God's love manifest throughout the world. The Crucifixion is described allegorically in the early poem '*Rosa Mystica*' as 'a wild flush on the flakes', the white petals of Mary's flower (No. 96). Its consequence for mankind is depicted graphically in one of the notes on the *Spiritual Exercises* in an image of the world flushed with the blood of Christ: 'Suppose God shewed us in a vision

the whole world inclosed first in a drop of water, allowing everything to be seen in its native colours; then the same in a drop
of Christ's blood, by which everything whatever was turned
scarlet, keeping nevertheless mounted in the scarlet its own
colour too . . .' (S. 194). Thus similarly, in cases of conversion,
the accession of Christ will 'Gush!—flush the man, the being
with it' (No. 101, st. 8).

It is not surprising given its strong association with the
Sacred Heart and Christ's sacrifice that the sanguine connota-
tions of the word 'flush' figure prominently in many of Hopkins'
uses of it.[45] The references to the quality of 'flushness' in the
'Parmenides' notes should be identified with the dynamic
liquidity which Hopkins sees to characterize *all* being, and
which, whether it is the pulse of human blood or that which
gives external nature its profound 'freshness', has its source in
divine grace:

> I stéady as a wáter in a wéll, to a póise, to a páne,
> But roped with, always, all the way down from the tall
>   Fells or flanks of the voel, a vein
> Of the góspel próffer, a préssure, a prínciple, Chríst's gift.
>   (No. 101, st. 4)

The steadiness of '*a* water' incorporates the motion that
Aristotle exemplifies in the *Physics* with 'this water'. It is a 'foredrawn' body of water which represents the discrete being of the
poet, an equilibrium that is constantly sustained by the 'pressure'
of grace: the 'flushness' of being.

IV

Hopkins defines 'instress', his principle of determinate being,
as 'the flush and foredrawn' (*J*. 127). The qualities of the
'inner flushness', with which Hopkins refers to Being in his
comments on Parmenides' comparison of it to a ball, and 'the
foredrawn', with which he sums up the idea of Being in the

---

[45] Indeed, this sense appears to have been uppermost in his thoughts when
he employed the word in the 'Parmenides' notes, for he uses the word 'blood' repeatedly in the notes to illustrate the epistemological efficacy of 'stress' (*J*. 127).

passage that describes its seamless continuity (*J.* 128),[46] each
constitute a moment of determinate Being, or 'instress'. The
quality of 'flushness' highlights the fluid informing principle
of Being, while 'the foredrawn' focuses upon the bounding
definition in which such force draws together as a unity. The
two aspects are represented in a journal entry from 1868 by a
phenomenon of water droplets, which furnishes a simile for
the behaviour of a sheepflock: 'It ran like the water-packets
on a leaf—that collectively, but a number of globules so
filmed over that they would not flush together is the exacter
comparison' (*J.* 187). This observation, which dates from
the same year as the 'Parmenides' notes, shares the notes'
preoccupation with the problem of the one and the many and
exemplifies the ontology by which they resolve this question.
Not only does it refer explicitly to the principle of 'flushness',
the 'pressure' which in the well analogy pervades the unity of 'a
water', but also, less directly, to another integral property of
water, the 'foredrawn' quality of the bounding meniscal film
of the globules, its viscosity.

Hopkins' principle of 'stress' is synonymous with 'Being'
(*J.* 129), and is seen to permeate or 'flush' everything. An
'instress' is an instance of such being to which belongs, as the
prefix indicates, an internal or intrinsic principle of unity, its
specificity or 'inscape'. It is in other words 'foredrawn', determinate. The aspects of 'the flush and foredrawn' correspond
to the respective 'universal' and 'concrete' terms of 'the Idea'
in the first group of the 'Notes'. The 'flush' represents the
most radical and ubiquitous of universals, 'Being', while the
'foredrawn' denotes its specificity as a differentiated unity, a
concrete particular.

Hopkins, probably following Jowett, recognizes 'An undeter-
mined Pantheist idealism' (*J.* 127) in place of the monism usually ascribed to Parmenides.[47] Whereas Parmenides maintains

[46] Cf. Kirk, Raven, and Schofield, *Presocratic Philosophers*, fr. 313.

[47] Jowett identifies the Eleatics with an 'abstract Pantheism' (*Plato*, 1st edn.,
iii. 457; 2nd edn., iv. 385). This offers a precise echo of Hegel's *Science of Logic*.
Stirling refers to 'the abstract Pantheism of the Eleatics' early in his translation of
the dialectic of 'Being' (*Science of Logic*, bk. I, sect. I, ch. 1, C(1); Stirling, *Secret of
Hegel*, i. 323). Jowett probably began his own translation of the greater Logic
during the late 1840s. John Addington Symonds, another of Jowett's students,

that the principles of the various, the particular, and the contingent are unreal and so exclusive of his monistic Being or 'the Truth', Hopkins believes that the Parmenidean fragments sustain his view that ultimate Being is comprised of numerous discrete instances. The position he adopts is a version of what Parmenides describes as the confused third 'way', in which some mortals follow both the 'Way of Truth' and that of mortal opinion, and consequently 'wander knowing nothing, two-headed'. They are 'dazed, undiscriminating hordes, who believe that to be and not to be are the same and not the same'.[48] The speech given in the proem by the goddess, Parmenides' muse, however, gives some hope that a form of this third 'way' may be an acceptable representation of reality. Having stated that ' "there is no true reliance" ' upon the opinion of mortals, the goddess qualifies this statement by suggesting that it could in fact bear a relation to Being itself: ' "But nonetheless you shall learn these things too, how what is believed would have to be assuredly, pervading all things throughout." '[49] While these lines 'are naturally interpreted as stating the condition upon which the genuine existence of the objects of mortal belief may be secured, viz. that they completely pervade all things',[50] Parmenides disagrees with the goddess's assertion that this condition can be met with in the case of mortal opinion: 'they [i.e. mortals] have made up their minds to name two forms, of which they needs must not name so much as one—that is where they have gone astray'.[51]

Hopkins regards Being in the manner that the goddess suggests as ' "pervading all things throughout" ', that is, as a principle of flushness or 'stress'. This entails both an epistemology able to justify and explain mortal opinion (which will be looked at in the following sections), and an ontology in which

records in his diary that a discussion of an essay of his on the Eleatics prompted his tutor to give him 'a lecture on Hegel' which disclosed his pantheistic religious understanding of *Geist*: 'His theory, one in which the existence of a universal God is to be seen in all things and thought. Distinct personalities are allowed by this God to exist under and independent of Him' (quoted in Horatio Brown, *John Addington Symonds, A Biography*, 2nd edn. (London: Smith, Elder, 1903), 84). This broad construal is most suggestive of Hopkins' cosmology, in which specific inscapes are seen to inhere within and instance all-pervasive 'stress' or Being.

[48] Kirk, Raven, and Schofield, *Presocratic Philosophers*, fr. 293.
[49] Ibid. fr. 288.   [50] Ibid. 255.   [51] Ibid. fr. 302.

the ultimate unity of Being can be reconciled with the manifold of Not-being:

For the phenomenal world (and the distinction between men or subjects and the things without them is unimportant in Parmenides: the contrast is between the one and the many) is the brink, limbus, lapping, run-and-mingle | of two principles which meet in the scape of everything—probably Being, under its modification or siding of particular oneness or Being, and Not-being, under its siding of the Many. The two may be called two degrees of siding in the scale of Being. Foreshortening and equivalency will explain all possible difference. The inscape will be the proportion of the mixture.   (*J.* 130)

Hopkins evidently takes the negative language that Parmenides uses to specify the nature of Being to refer to another entity, Not-being. The basis of Hopkins' dialectic is clear from his definition of 'Not-being' as a 'want of oneness' (*J.* 129), that is, as the lack of its opposite principle, 'Being'. This identification is made explicitly in the metaphor of 'the scale of Being' in which 'Being' is referred to 'under its modification or siding of particular oneness or Being, and Not-being, under its siding of the Many'. The mixture of the two accordingly becomes possible in the form of organic unity: 'The two may be called two degrees of siding in the scale of Being.' Parmenides' absolutism is made to give way to Hopkins' relativism, in which Being and Not-being become respective 'siding[s]' or 'modification[s]' of the ultimate ontological principle.

   The attribution of 'two degrees of siding' to 'the scale of Being' indicates that the metaphor refers not to a linear scale, as in 'The Probable Future of Metaphysics' (*J.* 120), but to a pair of scales. If a balance is to be established, the many of Not-being must accordingly be met with by a correspondingly 'foredrawn' 'oneness' of Being, that is, a formal principle of unity capable of drawing together the particular 'degree' of multiplicity. The metaphor of 'the scale' is used in an undergraduate essay to describe the dialectical relation between the Eleatic and Heraclitean philosophies: 'But the logical assurance of the Eleatics itself was balanced by Heracleitus whose teaching about flux is the reaction against the supremacy of principles established by reason, and substitutes for the immovable spherical One or Whole of Xenophanes the sole unity of variety, the certainty of change' (D. VI 3, fos. 7–8).[52] The word 'sub-stitutes' here suggests a parity between the two that anticipates the dialectical resolution which Hopkins establishes in his later reading of Parmenides. The balance between the 'two degrees of siding' describes the proportionate relation of organic unity which defines a specific instance of being: 'The inscape will be the proportion of the mixture' (*J.* 130).

Jowett, with whom Hopkins studied Presocratic philosophy in Michaelmas term 1866, is likely to have been an import-ant influence upon his interpretation of Parmenides here. His commentary on the discussion in the *Sophist* of not-being and being draws together Parmenidean and Hegelian dialectic:[53]

Not-being can only be included in being [according to Plato], as the denial of any particular class of being. If we are to attempt to pursue such airy phantoms at all, the Hegelian identity of being and not-being is a more apt and intelligible expression of the same mental phenomenon. For Plato has not distinguished between the being which is prior to not-being, and the being which is the negation of not-being.[54]

Hopkins, like Jowett, rather than acknowledging the principle of non-contradiction from which Parmenides develops his argu-ment, regards 'being ... [as] prior to not-being', the whole to precede the parts.

Hopkins' identification of Parmenidean monism with a 'Pantheist idealism' and more importantly, his reference to the 'religious conviction' with which Parmenides enunciates 'His great text ... that Being is and Not-being is not' (*J.* 127), indicates the theological importance for him of the doctrine of 'stress' and 'instress'. The relation between the 'sidings' of ultimate Being and Not-being made by the 'Parmenides' notes is representative of the relation he sees to exist between God and Creation. This is described by Hopkins in the later notes

[52] Cf. Hegel on Parmenides and Heraclitus in the *Science of Logic*, bk. I, sect. I, ch. 1, C(1), Remark I; trans. by Stirling, *Secret of Hegel*, i. 322.
[53] Indeed he boldly declares that 'The later dialogues of Plato contain many references to contemporary philosophy' and that 'In Plato we find, as we might expect, the germs of many thoughts which have been further developed by the genius of Spinoza and Hegel' (*Plato*, 2nd edn., iv. 387, 403). Cf. *Science of Logic*, bk. I, sect. I, ch. I, C(1), Remark 3 (Stirling, *Secret of Hegel*, i. 336–51).
[54] Jowett, *Plato*, 2nd edn., iv. 386.

on 'The Incarnation' in Parmenidean imagery as two spheres. The first represents the Creation as a ' "pomegranate" ', the *pomum possibilium* which the Trinity is able to see 'whole and in every "cleave", the actual and the possible', while the finite conditions of mortal perception mean that 'we are looking at it in all the actual cleaves, one after another', that is, as the flux of nature is revealed to us in accordance with our finite powers of perception, in temporal succession. 'This sphere is set off against the sphere of the divine being, a steady "seat or throne" of majesty. Yet that too has its cleave to us, the entrance of Christ on the world' (*S.* 171). The mediate principle of Christ highlights the nature of the relation between Creation and God, the respective 'spheres' of fluctuous 'Not-being' and the ultimate unity of 'Being':

>   ... For Christ plays in ten thousand places,
>   Lovely in limbs, and lovely in eyes not his
>   To the Father through the features of men's faces.   (No. 115)

Christ provides the ultimate principle of unity which has its reciprocal principle of the many in the 'ten thousand places' occupied by individual human beings, much as in the 'Parmenides' notes the 'ten thousand men to think and ten thousand things for them to think of' are counterbalanced by 'the truth itself, the burl' (*J.* 130) which they all acknowledge in their own way.

The play of light is one of the most fundamental images which Hopkins uses to depict the relation of Being to Not-being, of the one to the many. In the early poem '*Ad Mariam*', for example, the allegorical figure of 'May' provides the site for the play of light representative of the proliferation of natural life and activity during early summer: 'Spring's one daughter, the sweet child May . . . | With light on her face like the waves at play' (No. 94).[55] The image of the play of light on water, which is foundational for much of Hopkins' imagery and thought in the later poems, is stated originally and most forcefully in the 1868 'Notes':

The figure shewing how the Idea can be one though it exists in many is that of the sun in broken water, where the sun's face being once

---

[55] MacKenzie give the 'probable' date of this poem as May 1873 (Mackenzie (ed.), *Poetical Works*, 306).

crossed by the ripples each one carries an image down with it as its own sun; and these images are always mounting the ripples and trying to fall back into one again. We must therefore think wherever we see many things having one idea that they all are falling back or w[oul]d fall back but are held away by their conditions, and those philosophers have very truly said everything is becoming.

(D. XII 3, fos. 2–3)

Hopkins' image, in marked contrast to the Platonic depiction of the phenomenal world as mere shadows of real forms, sees multitudinous phenomena to proceed directly from the ultimate principle of being as sunlight does from the sun. The sunlight is accordingly distinguished from its source by being instantiated in the matter of the water, so that each is autonomous of all other such instances; 'they . . . are held away by their conditions'. The interaction between the principle of Being, the 'stress' of sunlight, and the principle of Not-being, the manifold nature of matter (represented here by water, the element of 'flushness'), produces conditioned, that is, distinctive, being. Similarly, it is the 'conditions' which in the 'kingfishers' poem distinguish mankind, the 'ten thousand places' and 'the features of men's faces' that 'Christ plays in', from Christ himself. Each of these conditioned forms discloses an aspect of Being, much as in the *Ethike* essay the exercise of each individual in 'fulfilling those duties which personally were the prepossession' (*J.* 123) serves to actualize the manifold potentialities which comprise the moral universal.

The closing lines of 'That Nature is a Heraclitean Fire and of the Comfort of the Resurrection' provide another important illustration of the relation that Hopkins refers to with his figure of 'the scale of Being':

> . . . world's wildfire, leave but ash:
> In a flash, at a trumpet crash,
> I am all at once what Christ is, | since he was what I am, and
> Thís Jack, jóke, poor pótsherd, | patch, matchwood, immortal diamond,
> Is immortal diamond.   (No. 174)

The rhyme of the phrase 'I am, and' with 'diamond' expresses the greatness that each mortal embodies by being not just a fragmentary part, a 'potsherd' or 'patch', but an integral part of a whole that is greater than the sum of such parts. This is

the significance of the supplementary 'and' which provides
the end rhyme to the line that links the crude black carbon of
'ash', with all the fluctuous associations it has acquired in the
process of the poem, to the other form of carbon, the 'immortal diamond'. The long and evocative catalogue of flux and dissipation which is brought into focus in the poem in the figure
of 'Manshape, that shone | Sheer off, disseveral, a star . . .' is
galvanized by this connective 'and' so that it is drawn together
as a part to its redemptive whole. Creation, 'nature's bonfire',
which is represented here by 'Man', 'its clearest selved spark',
accordingly comprises one of the two terms in the most auda-
cious of Hopkins' parallelisms—'immortal diamond, | Is immortal
diamond'—which in its combination of tautology and grandeur
is comparable to the Parmenidean premiss that, as Hopkins puts
it, 'Being is and Not-being is not' (*J.* 127). The endless play of
the light on the facets of the diamond represents the myriad
distinctive instances in which 'the grándeur of God' is actualized,
flashes and 'flame[s] out' (No. 111) in the Heraclitean fire of
Creation. The light which plays in and through it gives the ultimate moment of the 'diamond' (i.e. God or Being) its supreme
distinctiveness. The tautologous nature of the phrase brings
the copula to the fore and emphasizes it, so that, apparently
devoid of any other meaning, it highlights the recognition of
Being which belongs to all sentences: 'each sentence by its
copula *is* . . . [is] the utterance and assertion of [Being]' (*J.*
129). The nature of the diamond is such that it appears itself
to be emitting light, making it difficult to know which term
is the ultimate one, the source of 'stress' that the two express
and reflect. The 'immortal diamond' is at once God, the transcendent whole of 'Being', and the fluctuous manifold of 'Not-
being' manifest in Creation and history.

V

Hopkins sees each of our perceptions, each judgement we make
in identifying a thing, to acknowledge the ultimate principle of
Being: 'there are ten thousand men to think and ten thousand
things for them to think of but they are but names given and
taken, eye and lip service to the truth, husks and scapes of it:

the truth itself, the burl [of Being]' (*J.* 130). While the sceptical inflections of the phrases 'eye and lip service . . . husks and
scapes' make some concession to Parmenidean doctrine, it is
none the less clear that phenomenal appearances or 'scapes'
are for Hopkins the means by which the Idea is presented
to consciousness. Whereas Parmenides identifies phenomena
with mortal opinion, seeing them as arbitrary and disconnected
from reality, for Hopkins they are simply sensible appearances,
'husks and scapes' which, while not equivalent to 'the truth' of
ultimate reality, nevertheless provide access to it: i.e. the 'scapes'
signify the presence of essence or 'inscape'.

Mortal opinion is for Hopkins similar to the philosophical
attitudes of idealism and materialism described in the first
of the 'Notes', an inadequate way by which to 'acknowledge
the Idea' but one which nevertheless allows some grasp of it
and the hope of a complete recognition of the Idea itself, 'the
thought' in its objective 'fulness'. The variety of perceptions
are, like the materialist and idealist depictions of the Idea, 'the
seeing of one self-same thing'. The 'thought', the Idea or Being
itself, is identified with a 'fulness' (*J.* 130) which characterizes
organic forms such as the hand that provides the image for
'the Idea' at the close of the first group of notes. The various sensible perceptions or 'scapes' and the abstract universals and names they give rise to are simply 'husks' (*J.* 130),
a term which suggests both the dessicated form of the
Idea 'handle[d] . . . by the concrete' and the emptiness of the
'abstraction[, which] may . . . blow it out into a graceless
bladdery animation', as well as the 'glove' which represents
the name, the 'lip service' (*J.* 130), given to the Idea.[56]

The word 'scapes' is familiar from the 'All words . . .' notes,
where it refers to sense-impressions 'produced . . . unbidden . . .
from the involuntary working of nature' (*J.* 125). But we can,
according to Hopkins, do more than simply perceive appearances; we can know the ultimate nature of an object in-itself.
Hopkins often refers to our capacity to receive an 'instress' or
to 'inscape' an object. Acts of perception, of 'instressing' a thing,
reproduce the moments of 'the flush and [the] foredrawn'

---

[56] It also suggests Green's metaphor of 'the mere universal [a]s a shell to be
filled up by particular attributes' (*Works*, iii. 56). See Ch. 5, Sect. IV.

which describe the object's being. While the quality of 'flushness' ultimately unifies all Being, the word 'flush', with its suggestive and possibly etymological relation to the word 'flux',[57]
has strong implications of multiplicity. Its complementary term,
the 'foredrawn', focuses attention upon the coherence within
which particular manifolds subsist as a unity, the bounding
definition which makes a specific instress accessible to human
perception through the object's 'scapes'. The 'scapes' are accordingly the manifold appearances which the 'flush' or flux
of a thing presents to the senses.

This moment is described in some later theological notes,
using a metaphor drawn from the ocean tides, as the 'splay',
which complements the object's 'neap' or 'foredrawn condi-
tion' (S. 152). It is 'the quantitative, the time-long | display, of
the oneness of a fact' (S. 153). The function of the 'foredrawn'
in facilitating the mind's grasp of an inscape can be derived
from the description in the 'Parmenides' notes of its reflexive case: 'Not-being is here seen as want of oneness, all that
is unforedrawn, waste space which offers either nothing to the
eye to foredraw or many things foredrawing away from one
another'. The principle of the 'scapes' is evident here in the
certain 'offers . . . to the eye to foredraw' (J. 129) that the particular thing may make.

The epistemological act of 'foredrawing' brings together
a sensory manifold as a 'oneness', the simple consciousness
of an object. The condition which makes this possible is, for
Hopkins as it is for Green, reflexive self-consciousness. It is
presupposed by the equivalence that his coinages of 'instress'
and 'inscape' give to ontology and epistemology, and can be
traced to his interpretation of Parmenides' fundamental tenet
linking being and knowing. Parmenides argues that because
Being *is*, it cannot be thought otherwise than as being or existing: *'For the same thing is there both to be thought of and to be.'*[58]
Being is presented here as the central value which legitimizes
thought and distinguishes it from 'the opinions of mortals,
in which there is no true reliance'.[59] Hopkins' rendition of the

---

[57] The etymology of the word 'flush' is uncertain, according to *OED*, 2nd edn.
(1989).   [58] Kirk, Raven, and Schofield, *Presocratic Philosophers*, fr. 292.
[59] Ibid. fr. 288.

fragment, however, 'To be and to know or Being and thought are the same' (*J.* 129), suggests that there is a precise parity and reciprocity between 'Being and thought' which entails that whatever is an object for thought, even that which Parmenides dismisses as mortal opinion, must have an ontological status: it must be attributed with the universal of being.[60] This is consistent with the principle of apperception specified in the early 'Health and Decay' essay, where the mind's 'comparison . . . of existence with non-existence' is described as the radical condition and 'inseparable accident of all thought' (*J.* 74). The familiar Kantian principle of apperception provides the basis for Hopkins' interpretation of Parmenides' monistic conception of Being, in relation to which the modern 'distinction between men or subjects and the things without them is unimportant' (*J.* 130).[61]

The precise grounds for the parity which Hopkins gives to being and knowing can be drawn from his commentary on the final clause of the following extract from Parmenides (which he cites in Greek but is given here in Kirk, Raven, and Schofield's translation):

The same thing is there to be thought and is why there is thought. For you will not find thinking without what is, in all that has been said [or 'in which thinking is expressed'].[62]

---

[60] Cf. Green: 'It is just from his [i.e. Aristotle's] failure to recognise the identity of the "being as being," which is the object of his "first philosophy", with "thought as thought", that his shortcomings arise. He did not clearly see that being, as the matter of subject ὑποκείμενον which is involved in all predication, and to which the whole intelligible world is related as attribute, was the indeterminate thinking self, which becomes determinate speculatively in actual knowledge, as it does practically in the moral life' (*Works* iii. 80–1).

[61] Henry W. Challis, a fellow convert and one of Hopkins' earliest Oxford friends, was with him at Birmingham Oratory from late 1867, and is likely to have discussed Kantian philosophy with him close to the time that he wrote the 'Notes'. Hopkins writes to E. H. Coleridge at this time that 'I own . . . I have little entertainment to offer unless it is in Challis, once of Merton, a great swell and a friend of mine before the Flood' (14 Nov. 1867, Letter 25, *Further Letters*, 46). Challis reasserts a version of the fundamental Kantian argument about the basis of mathematical truth in his pamphlet, *A Letter to J. S. Mill, Esq., M.P., on the Necessity of Geometry and the Association of Ideas* (Oxford: James Parker, 1867), which Hopkins may have read after it was brought to his attention by E. W. Urquhart (24 Sept. 1866, Letter 11, *Further Letters*, 26).

[62] Kirk, Raven, and Schofield, *Presocratic Philosophers*, fr. 299.

... Ritter and Preller translate [the last phrase] 'in quo enuntiatum est sive a quo quid cogitatur', referring it to the subject. Perhaps it would be better referred to the object and Parmenides will say that the mind's grasp—νοεῖν, the foredrawing act—that this is blood or that blood is red is to be looked for in Being, the foredrawn, alone, not in the thing we named blood or the blood we worded as being red.

(*J.* 129)

It is, as Hopkins observes early in the 'Parmenides' notes, 'hard to translate them [i.e. the fragments] satisfactorily [either] in a subjective or in a wholly outward sense' (*J.* 127). This judgement is substantiated by the alternative translations offered by Kirk, Raven, and Schofield of the final phrase of the extract from Parmenides, as well as by Hopkins' cautious disagreement with Ritter and Preller's translation. The references which the respective translations make to the activities of expressing thought could be attributed to individual subjects, such as those which Parmenides mentions later in the fragment as having 'named' Being with 'all the names which mortals have laid down believing them to be true'.[63] However, the phrase follows upon a statement which predicates thought of being, and, in warranting the translation 'in which thinking is expressed', should be understood 'in a wholly outward sense' to refer to monistic Being as a purely self-subsistent object, much as it is portrayed by the metaphor of the ball, which also occurs later in this fragment.

The pivotal verb of the last clause of the passage from Parmenides, 'νοεῖν', embraces meanings of thinking or conceiving as well as, when used with words as the subject, '*to bear a certain sense*'.[64] Hopkins translates the word synoptically as 'the mind's grasp' or 'the foredrawing act'. This 'act' suggests the definitive 'effort a[t] unity' which in 'The Origin of Our Moral Ideas' is attributed to 'All thought'. It describes the way in which we draw together discrete attributes in synthetic judgements, as when we apply a 'word meaning a thing' in such statements as 'this is blood or ... blood is red' (*J.* 127). The

[63] Ibid.
[64] Liddell and Scott, *Greek–English Lexicon*, s.v. νοέω. I am grateful to Dr Neil O'Sullivan, of the Department of Classics and Ancient History at the University of Western Australia, for discussing this passage from Parmenides with me.

radical condition for making such judgements is, however, not identified here with subjective consciousness, as it is in Kantian idealism, nor with the concrete object, 'the thing we named blood or the blood we worded as being red', as it is by positivism. The 'object' to which 'it would be better referred' is 'Being, the foredrawn, alone'.

The original content of the 'foredrawing act' is universal 'Being', or 'the foredrawn, *alone*' (my emphasis), that is, the apprehension of Being prior to the accession of any determinate content. It is this 'object' that marks the radical parity of 'Being and knowing' for Hopkins and their confluence in his doctrine of 'instress' and 'inscape'. Hopkins' 'foredrawing act', like the apprehension of the sensible thing in Green's Hegelian account of perception, yields at first only the general sense that '"something is"' or 'pure Being'. The apperceptive condition for thought referred to in the 'Health and Decay' essay as the mind's initial 'comparison . . . of the conception of a thing with the former absence of the conception' (*J.* 74) is recast, through Hopkins' reading of Parmenides, as an *objective* condition of thought, '"for absence cannot break off Being from its hold on Being: it is not a thing to scatter here, there, and everywhere"' (*J.* 128).

Whereas the Kantian account of apperception maintains that the mind's acquaintance with being is limited to phenomena, that it is strictly contingent upon the structures of subjective consciousness, Hopkins follows the post-Kantian understanding of mind available to him through Green, in which reflexive self-consciousness yields a sense of 'pure being' that refers equally to the subject and the object, for each is recognized as the condition for knowing the other. 'Being' or consciousness ('thought') is the 'object' which transcends the modern distinction between the subject and the object and renders this distinction relatively 'unimportant' (*J.* 130). It is accordingly described as a 'bridge' which permits free and full communication between the subject and object. 'Being' functions as a 'stem of stress between us and things' (*J.* 127) that dissolves the Kantian distinction between phenomena and noumena. This special sense of 'Being, the foredrawn, alone' as ultimate 'object' is illustrated by the final lines of 'Hurrahing in Harvest':

These things, these things were here and but the beholder
Wánting; whích two whén they ónce méet,
The héart réars wíngs bóld and bolder
And hurls for him, O half hurls earth for him off under his
    feet... (No. 124)

The 'two' instances of being referred to here, the object and
the subject, 'once meet': they become a single being or thought,
a 'stem of stress', which radically destabilizes the discrete relations of the individual subject to its finite object, the earth, and
the infinite object of its aspirations, the pure Being of God.[65]

---

[65] See Ch. 10, Sect. II for an elaboration of this interpretation of the poem.

7   Hopkins' Mechanistic Ontology

I

The theory of the 'the idea in the mind' in the 'All words . . .'
notes is predicated upon that of 'the Idea' established in the
first and second groups of the 1868 'Notes on the History of
Greek Philosophy'. The 'two terms' which Hopkins sees to
belong to the mental idea, namely, 'the conception' and 'the
image (of sight or sound or *scapes* of the other senses)' not
only correspond to 'the abstract' and 'concrete' aspects which
in the earlier notes comprise 'the Idea' (D. XII 1, fo. 2), but
the relation between them is similarly characterized as dialectical. Hopkins uses the distinctive Hegelian term of 'moments',
which he was familiar with from his Greats studies, to describe
the relation of these terms of the idea as he sees them to inform the word.[1]

Kant and Hegel use the term 'moments' in a metaphoric
sense that they draw from mechanics. A full definition of the
word 'moment' was available to Hopkins from his study of
Sibree's edition of Hegel's *Philosophy of History* in Hilary term
1867, a few months before he uses the term in the 'All words . . .'
notes (*J.* 125). The 'Translator's Introduction' accounts for
the term's meaning through its etymology in mechanics:

The word 'moment' is, as readers of German philosophy are aware,
a veritable crux to the translator. In Mr. J. R. Morrell's very valuable
edition of Johnson's Translation of Tennemann's 'Manual of the History of Philosophy', the following explanation is given: 'This term
was borrowed from mechanics by Hegel (see his "Wissenschaft der
Logik", Vol. 3, P. 104, Ed. 1841). He employs it to denote the con-
tending forces which are mutually dependent, and whose contradiction forms an equation. Hence his formula, *Esse* = Nothing. Here *Esse*
and Nothing are momentums, giving birth to *Werden, i.e.* Existence.
Thus the momentum contributes to the same oneness of operation

---

[1] See Ch. 3, Sect. II.

in contradictory forces that we see in mechanics, amidst contrast and
diversity, in weight and distance, in the case of the balance'.[2]

J. H. Stirling, in his commentary on 'Moments of Becoming', the section of Hegel's *Logic* from which the extract on
'moments' cited in the above passage is taken, explains the
term satisfactorily by referring it to the 'process of Aufhebung'[3]
and providing a number of simple physical illustrations of this
meaning. The most significant of these is the example of the
lever, which is elaborated by Hegel (in Stirling's translation) as
follows:

A thing is sublated, resolved, only so far as it has gone into unity with
its opposite; in this closer determination, as what is reflected, it may
be fitly named Moment. Weight, and Distance from a point, are called,
with reference to the Lever, its mechanical Moments, because of the
identity of their action, notwithstanding their diversity otherwise; the
one being, as it were, the Real of a weight, and the other the Ideal or
Idëell of a line, a mere character of space.[4]

In mechanics the moment is a measure of the turning power
of a force acting along a given line about an axis. The moment
of a lever is therefore the product of the force exerted and
the length of the line from the point of force to the fulcrum. The
resultant moment is the indivisible effect of these factors;
the two terms may be seen to pass into one. It is because of this
'identity of their action' that Hegel regards each of the factors involved as moments, whereas, strictly speaking, the term
refers only to their product. Each of these factors or moments
is seen by Hegel to suggest the 'real' and the 'ideal', that is, the
qualitative distinction which typifies the respective theses and
antitheses of his triadic logic.

A number of forces will, in many cases, be active about an
axis in a single plane. These are particular moments which have
the effect of forming further, synthetic, moments. There are,
for instance, at least two moments acting in every lever. These
correspond to the forces exerted upon each of the segments

[2] J. Sibree, Introd. to Hegel, *Philosophy of History*, p. iv.
[3] Stirling, *Secret of Hegel*, ii. 76. Stirling offers '*Sublation, resolution*, [and] *elimination*' as synonyms for '*Aufhebung*' (ii. 77), while Charles Taylor translates it as
'Abrogation or suppression', *Hegel*, p. xi.
[4] *Science of Logic*, bk. I, sect. I, ch. 1, C(2); trans. Stirling, *Secret of Hegel*, i. 357.

on either side of the fulcrum. Such forces act to negate each other and, in equilibrium, become subordinated and cancelled in a new moment, which is their sum (i.e. zero).

Hopkins would have known the etymology of the word 'moment' from the Latin *momentum*, 'a movement, motion', a sense that bears a close relation to its use in mechanics, which he was evidently familiar with from his early studies in the subject:[5] 'The moment of a couple is the product of the arm's length and either force.' A proof 'that 2 couples of equal moment are equivalent' follows at this point in his early note-book on mechanics (B. I, fo. 20). A couple is, as Hopkins explains, the effect of '2 equal forces act[ing] in parallel but opposite directions' (fo. 16), so that its moment is calculated as the product of either force and the vertical distance between them. This case is even more suggestive of Hegel's dialectic than the example of the lever, for the moment of a couple can be neutralized and subsumed within a further moment through its interaction with another couple of equal but opposite moment. The resultant moment is calculated as the sum of its two moments, which in this case is zero, that is, equilibrium. 'The Moments in reference to the Lever are', as Stirling remarks, 'very illustrative.'[6] Hopkins' early knowledge of the literal sense that the word 'moment' has in mechanics would have left him well prepared to appreciate the Hegelian metaphoric sense of it which he encountered in his Greats studies at Oxford.

Hopkins' use of the word *horoi* as synonymous with 'moments' (*J.* 125) can, like his interpretation of Aristotelian virtue and vice at the close of 'The Origin of Our Moral Ideas', be understood as a consequence of the tendency within Greats philosophy to mediate the thought of the Greeks with the categories of modern, principally German idealist, thought. Jowett, for instance, observes a parallel between the respective Aristotelian and Hegelian sets of logical 'terms': 'The divisions of the

[5] While Hopkins' notebook on mechanics and trigonometry (B. I) is undated, the companion notebook on classics (B. II) bears the date 'May 23. 1862', and was clearly used by him at both Highgate and at Oxford. It may be the case, despite Dr Dyne's aversion to teaching 'Natural Philosophy' (White, *Hopkins*, 25), that B. I dates from Hopkins' last year at school. Alternatively it could have been part of his Greats studies of Euclid (see J. E. T. Rogers, *Education at Oxford* (London: Smith, Elder, & Co., 1861), 32).   [6] Stirling, *Secret of Hegel*, ii. 77.

Hegelian logic bear a superficial resemblance to the divisions of the scholastic logic. The first part answers to the term, the second to the proposition, the third to the syllogism.'[7] While Aristotle's ontology, which theorizes change as the actualization of form in matter, has a rough parallel in Hegel's dialectical process, by which the idea becomes ever more 'concrete', this parallel was accentuated for Hopkins by Grant's equation of his Hegelian principle of 'consciousness' with Aristotelian *energeia*, and by Green's teaching of Aristotle. It is, however, stated most boldly in Stirling's *Secret of Hegel*, which, like the description of the 'terms belonging to [the word]' in the 'All words . . .' notes, uses Aristotelian and German idealist terminology interchangeably:

If it be considered that the one moment has the nature of *Matter* in it, and the other that of *Form*, (one sees that the Aristotelian characterisation of the *Moments* is about the most general of all,) it will be easily understood that the one, as in the case of the Lever, is always relatively *Real*, and the other relatively *Ideal*.[8]

II

The science of mechanics and the respective ontologies of Aristotle and German idealism each provide theoretical accounts of change and process. The drawing together of all three theories, which is exemplified in the extract from Stirling, is a notable but neglected feature of early British idealist writing.[9] This alliance was facilitated by the nineteenth-century science of thermodynamics, which by the time that Stirling's book was published in the mid-1860s was not only well established but had extended its original jurisdiction over relations between heat and work to comprehend almost all physical phenomena, organic as well as inorganic.

Physics became increasingly mechanistic during the first half of the nineteenth century, as the paradigm used to describe such properties as heat, light, magnetism, and electricity changed

---

[7] Jowett, *Plato*, 2nd edn., iv. 418.   [8] Stirling, *Secret of Hegel*, ii. 77.
[9] See e.g. Jowett's extended discussion of the 'form of opposites' (*Plato*, 2nd edn., iv. 408–9).

from the model of imponderable fluids to that of matter in motion. This new physics was pioneered through the study of heat. The materialist theory favoured in the eighteenth century, which identified heat with an imponderable fluid named caloric, received a serious challenge in 1798 when Count Rumford's experiments disclosed a direct relation to exist between heat and friction, thereby indicating that heat occurs as motion in a medium engendered by the vibrations of particles of matter.

Hopkins' understanding of mechanistic physics is evident from his early references to spectroscopy in 'The Tests of a Progressive Science' and the project he embarked upon in 1886 of writing 'a sort of popular account of Light and the Ether'.[10] The undergraduate essay acknowledges that 'spectral analysis' constitutes a radical 'development of optics' (D. IX 2, fo. 3). The theory of optics that it confirms is predicated upon a mechanical model of light that Thomas Young and Augustin Fresnel developed early in the century in opposition to the dominant theory at the time, which saw light to consist of microscopic particles. Fresnel rejected this particulate model because he saw it to imply that light behaves as an imponderable fluid and hence according to unique laws which separate it from all other matter. By 1821 Fresnel had theorized light as a phenomenon of transverse waves which are propagated by the medium of a hypothetical ether that possesses the mechanical properties of an elastic solid.[11] The discovery of spectroscopy later in the century served to confirm this hypothesis by tracing the frequencies of light-waves, which register on the spectrum as distinctive 'bright-lines', to the vibrations of the molecules of specific elements.

While, as Fresnel observes, the theory of imponderables treats each physical force as a distinct substance, the mechanistic model accommodates the phenomena of transformations between physical forces, such as those of heat to work and electricity to magnetism, which were established experimentally during the first half of the nineteenth century. Progress in the study of heat and light is paralleled at this time by advances

[10] 7 Aug. 1886, Letter 35, *To Dixon*, 139.
[11] P. M. Harman, *Energy, Force, and Matter* (Cambridge: Cambridge University Press, 1982), 21.

in the sciences of mechanical work,[12] gravitation, chemistry, electricity, magnetism, and physiology, all of which converge in the 1840s with the understanding that the respective phenomena they treat of comprise different modes of the one constant and quantifiable entity, which became known as 'energy'. For any change to occur and be perceptible, there must, as Aristotle says,[13] be an underlying principle which remains constant. While in Aristotle this principle of form is qualitative, in the new mechanistic physics it is a quantitative value, 'energy', that is conserved throughout the transformations of the various physical powers. This understanding is expressed as the first law of thermodynamics, the principle of the conservation of energy.[14]

William Thomson and William Rankine invested the term 'energy' with its modern scientific meaning in the 1850s and in so doing facilitated the distinction between, as James Clerk Maxwell put it, 'the power a thing has of doing work' from 'force', 'the tendency of a body to pass from one place to another',[15] a word which Michael Faraday, James Prescott Joule, and Hermann von Helmholtz had confusingly used for the more comprehensive concept. Whilst a number of terms were introduced by scientists to represent the quantitative value underlying transformations between various dynamic principles, it was the term 'energy', a derivation from the Aristotelian *energeia*, that became the generally accepted usage. Similarly, following William Rankine's introduction of the terms in a paper of 1853, the Aristotelian distinction between 'potential' and 'actual'

---

[12] Work is defined as the product of distance and force.

[13] *Metaphysics*, 1010ᵃ15–39.

[14] From his measurements in the 1840s of the 'mechanical equivalents' of work to heat James Prescott Joule recognized what became known (through Rudolf Clausius' formulation in 1850) as the first law of thermodynamics, a special form of the energy conservation principle which maintains that work and heat are convertible, and that in such conversion processes the quantitive value of each term remains inversely proportionate to the other, that is, the underlying quantity of energy remains constant.

[15] Quoted by P. M. Heimann (i.e. P. M. Harman) in 'Conversion of Forces and the Conservation of Energy', *Centaurus*, 18 (1974), 148. John Hendry notes that the word 'energy' was first 'introduced to this context of conservation and convertibility by Thomson in a footnote to a paper on [Sadi] Carnot's theory of heat engines in 1849' (Hendry, *James Clerk Maxwell and the Theory of the Electromagnetic Field* (Bristol: Adam Hilger, 1986), 193).

energy became the accepted way of specifying the changes which this constant undergoes.[16] Thus, for example, the potential energy of a fuel is actualized through its combustion, and that of a suspended weight when it is allowed to fall.

Energy physics, by positing a fixed principle which describes all physical powers in nature, encouraged speculative theories of monism akin to that which emerges from Hopkins' 1868 meditations on Parmenides' 'Pantheist idealism' (*J.* 127). In the 1860s the grand ontological unity envisaged by the romantics earlier in the century looked as if it would be realized not in spite of mechanical science, but by its extension through the principle of energy. Thomas Kuhn argues in his essay 'Energy Conservation as Simultaneous Discovery' that a crucial factor explaining this famous case, in which various researchers arrived independently at the energy concept, is that its formulation was prompted and guided not by the Leibnizian principle of the conservation of *vis viva* or 'living force', an idea which had been available for over a century, but by the hypothesis of the German *Naturphilosophen* that, as Schelling puts it, 'magnetic, electrical, chemical, and finally even organic phenomena would be interwoven into one great association . . . [which] extends over the whole of nature'.[17]

By the time that Hopkins began his studies at Oxford the principle of the conservation of energy was widely discussed and had been applied to many phenomena other than those that have been mentioned. The special focus upon causation in Hopkins' philosophical studies at Oxford meant that he would have come across Mill's discussion of the energy principle in the section on causation in the *System of Logic*: 'It has of late become the general belief of scientific inquirers that mechanical force, electricity, magnetism, heat, light, and chemical action (to which has subsequently been added vital force) are not so much causes of one another as convertible into one another;

---

[16] Thomson had introduced the terms 'statical energy' and 'dynamical energy' a year earlier (Hendry, *Maxwell*, 194), which Helmholtz had designated respectively as 'tensional force' and 'living force'.

[17] Quoted by Kuhn in his essay, in *Critical Problems in the History of Science*, ed. Marshall Clagett (Madison: University of Wisconsin Press, 1962), 338. See also L. Pearce Williams, *Faraday: A Biography* (New York: Simon & Schuster, 1971), 62–72.

and are all of them forms of one and the same force, varying only in its outward manifestations.'[18] The eminent physicist Peter Guthrie Tait, writing in a lucid and comprehensive article on 'Energy' which Hopkins may have read in the *North British Review* for May 1864, observes that 'the general application of the principle . . . is every day enabling us to co-ordinate some newly discovered fact, and even occasionally to predict the result of a perfectly novel experimental combination'.[19] In addition to various physical phenomena the principle had by 1863 been applied to various 'problems encountered in the world of organic life: animal and vegetable heat, digestion, respiration, muscular force, nervous agency, vital power, the development of organized animal and vegetable structure from dormant, primordial germ cells, and the effects of plant and animal sensation and consciousness'.[20] More speculatively (and optimistically) Herbert Spencer and Edward Youmans also applied the energy concept at this time to human consciousness and 'social forces'.[21]

Energy physics sustained the romantic ontology of 'the one life within us and abroad'[22] by the paradoxical means of supplying it with a mechanistic content. Stephen Brush sums up this historical development: 'The first law of thermodynamics (conservation of energy), inspired in part by the philosophy of romanticism, provided an organizing principle for the science of the realist period [which followed it]'.[23] Energy physics, by adapting the Aristotelian principle of form and renewing a German idealist principle of monism, effectively reinvigorated

---

[18] Mill, *System of Logic*, 1120–1. Mill's discussion was first included in the 4th edn. of the *Logic* (1856) and then in all subsequent editions published during his lifetime (ibid. 1120–2). The paper on the energy concept that Mill contributed to Edward Youmans, *The Correlation and Conservation of Forces: a Series of Expositions* (1865) is also included in this appendix (ibid. 1127–30).

[19] P. G. Tait, 'Energy', *North British Review*, 40/80 (May 1864), 360. Hopkins' Journals note an article on Wordsworth by Shairp in the Aug. 1864 issue of the magazine (*J.* 60). Another essay by Tait, 'The Dynamical Theory of Heat', appeared in the Feb. no. of the periodical. Tait's articles formed the basis for his *Sketch of Thermodynamics*, the first edition of which was published in 1868. Hopkins could have come across this exposition, or reviews of it, at about the time that he discusses energy and stress in his notes on Greek philosophy. He discusses and quotes from Tait's book on optics in 1886 (*To Dixon*, 139–40).

[20] Erwin N. Hiebert, 'The Uses and Abuses of Thermodynamics in Religion', *Daedalus*, 95 (1966), 1052.   [21] Ibid. 1055, 1058.

[22] S. T. Coleridge, 'The Eolian Harp', l. 26.

[23] Stephen Brush, *The Temperature of History* (New York: Burt Franklin, 1978), 29.

the metaphysical concepts by which the early British idealists opposed positivism and both understood and facilitated religious belief. Jowett's metaphoric use of the new mechanistic physics in his references to 'the Hegelian vibration of moments' exemplifies this confluence.

While the researches of Darwin and his followers lent credibility to positivism, energy physics provided an understanding of the universe in which all things are unified as manifestations of a single constant power, which during the 1860s was often identified with God and used to counter the atheistic and agnostic implications of Darwinian biology. Regarded as an index of an original and indestructible power, 'energy' suggestively parallels the Aristotelian theological principle of the 'unmoved mover'.[24] T. H. Green, in one of his 1867 lectures, describes the God of the Stoics in anachronistic terms of modern mechanistic physics (and Hegelian *Geist*) as 'the Worldspirit, the energy of the world, related like motion to matter'.[25] James Prescott Joule sees the results of his pioneering work in thermodynamics to give credence to such a theological speculation: 'the grand agents of nature are, by the Creator's fiat, indestructible . . . wherever mechanical force is expended, an exact equivalent of heat is always obtained'.[26] Joule elaborates upon such implications in a lecture on the conservation principle, which, like the paper just quoted from, dates from 1847. The following extract is taken from Tait's extensive quotation of the lecture in his 1864 *North British Review* article on 'Energy':

Descending from the planetary space and firmament to the surface of our earth, we find a vast variety of phenomena connected with the conversion of living [i.e. 'actual'] force and heat into one another which speak in language which cannot be misunderstood of the wisdom and beneficence of the Great Architect of nature. The motion of air which we call *wind*, arises chiefly from the intense heat of the torrid zone compared with the temperature of the temperate and frigid zones. Here we have an instance of heat being converted into the living force of currents of air . . . When we consider our own animal frames, 'fearfully and wonderfully made,' we observe in the motion of our limbs a continual conversion of heat into living force

---

[24] See *Physics*, 258^{b}10–260^{a}19, and *Metaphysics*, 1072^{a}20–6.
[25] Merton, Bradley Papers, MS I-A1, Lect. VIII.
[26] *The Scientific Papers of James Prescott Joule*, 2 vols. (London: Physical Society of London, 1884), i. 157–8.

. . . Indeed the phenomena of nature, whether mechanical, chemical, or vital, consist almost entirely in a continual conversion of attraction through space, living force, and heat, into one another. Thus it is that order is maintained in the universe,—nothing is deranged, nothing ever lost,—but the entire machinery, complicated as it is, works smoothly and harmoniously. And though, as in the awful vision of Ezekiel, 'wheel may be in the middle of wheel', and everything may appear complicated and involved in the apparent confusion and intricacy of an almost endless variety of causes, effects, conversions, and arrangements, yet is the most perfect regularity preserved; the whole being governed by the sovereign will of God.[27]

Tait's long citation in the 1860s of Joule's speculations highlights the uses that the energy principle could have for post-Darwinian intellectuals such as Hopkins. Joule introduces the possibilities that energy physics presented for extending and renewing the arguments for natural theology, and indeed of sustaining this thesis, as Hopkins does, in spite of the Darwinian affronts to it. The profusion and complex diversity of nature that the life sciences, especially through Darwin's contributions to them, brought to the fore in the nineteenth century are reined in by the ordering principle of the energy principle. Put in Hopkins' terms, the 'chromati[sm]' of nature as it is understood by the prevalent 'philosophy of flux' is contained by a unifying 'diatonic' principle (*J.* 120).

If Hopkins did not know the passage from Joule through his reading of the *North British Review*, where it occupies several pages, he would almost certainly have been familiar with similar theological readings of the energy principle from other sources. Amongst the pioneers of the principle William Grove, Julius Mayer, and Ludvig Colding also explain it within a theological context. Contemporary commentators such as William Carpenter, Herbert Spencer, and George Barker were similarly quick to extrapolate the religious significance of energy theory.[28] The physicist John Tyndall, whom Hopkins met in the Swiss Alps in July 1868 (*J.* 182), remarks in a book published in 1869 that energy conservation 'bound nature fast in faith'.[29]

---

[27] Tait, 'Energy', 345–6.   [28] Hiebert, 'Uses and Abuses', 1052–60.
[29] Ibid. 1074. Tyndall's 'Belfast Address' of 1874, which Hopkins certainly read (*Further Letters*, 127–8), contains an extensive discussion of the principle of energy conservation.

Even if he did not come across such theological interpretations of the energy principle (which is unlikely), Hopkins' predisposition for ontological monism and natural theology would have led him to make such readings himself.

'All kinds of private metaphysics and theology have grown like weeds in the garden of thermodynamics.'[30] It is in this context that Hopkins' doctrine of 'stress' and 'instress' may be said to 'shoot long and lovely and lush' (No. 117). The present chapter argues that Hopkins formulates his monistic ontology along the lines of contemporary physics, by identifying all phenomena with the radical mechanical principle that he comes to refer to synonymously as 'stress or energy' (S. 137).

III

While Hegel's philosophy of material nature comprises an integral but subordinate part of his larger philosophy, energy physics reverses this hierarchical relation between mechanics and metaphysics by effectively establishing romantic monism in the form of a ubiquitous, constant, and convertible physical force. This suggests a reading of Hopkins' principle of 'stress' which reconciles it with the literal meaning that the term has in mechanics, where it is understood as a 'Physical strain or pressure exerted upon a material object; the strain *of* a load or weight'.[31] While for Hegel the mechanical principle of moments serves mainly as a metaphor for a larger metaphysical process, in Hopkins the allied principle of stress appears to be identified directly with his ontological monism.

The mechanistic sense of the word 'stress' is not one that commentators on Hopkins have been anxious to explore. Hopkins' terms 'stress' and 'instress' are traditionally explained with reference to either Duns Scotus or scholastic principles such as *energeia* or *actus*: 'The preference of "stress" to "act", the normal word in scholastic terminology, most likely finds its reason in the greater expressiveness of the Saxon word, "stress"

[30] Hiebert, 'Uses and Abuses', 1075.
[31] *OED*, 2nd edn. (1989), 'Stress', sb. 5.

well marking the force which keeps a thing in existence and
its strain after continued existence.'[32] While Aristotelian ontology is crucial to Hopkins' metaphysic, the scholastic and Scotist
developments of it were not seriously considered by him until
some time after the meanings of his distinctive terms were
established in the 'Parmenides' notes.[33]

Of all the commentaries on 'stress' and 'instress', Leonard
Cochran's essay 'Instress and Its Place in the Poetics of Gerard
Manley Hopkins' discusses the terms at greatest length.[34]
This account traces 'instress' through the meaning of
the word 'stress', situating it in relation to various senses of the
word listed by the *Oxford English Dictionary*. Of these the definition
of the verb, 'To lay the stress or emphasis on, emphasize (a
word or phrase in speaking); to place a stress accent upon (a
syllable)', and its correspondent noun, are judged to be
'the closest to that of Hopkins', with, however, the following
qualification: 'For Hopkins, *stress* has much more of the notion
of endurance, of existence. It connotes *emphasis . . .*'[35] He regards
'stress' as having a certain gravity. While the use that the word
'stress' has in poetics is important to Hopkins' term, some
literary critics, whose work predisposes them to regard it as
the word's primary meaning, have placed a disproportionate
emphasis upon this sense.[36] Cochran is not one of those who
restrict their discussion only to metrical stress. He notes that
Hopkins identifies 'stress' and 'instress' with 'energy' in the
'Meditation on Hell' and concludes that 'we have a further refinement of stress as dynamic existence, as being-in-struggle'.[37]

---

[32] W. A. M. Peters, *Gerard Manley Hopkins: A Critical Essay towards the Understanding of his Poetry* (London: Oxford University Press, 1948), 13.

[33] Hopkins' discovery of Scotus dates from Aug. 1872 (*J.* 221).

[34] L. Cochran, 'Instress and its Place . . .', *Hopkins Quarterly*, 6/4, (Winter 1980),
143–81.

[35] Ibid. 147. Similarly, with respect to its currency in epistemology Cochran
makes the equation ' "emphasis" or stress' (p. 146), and later: '[H]e preserves the
aspect of *stress* as an emphatic recognition (awareness) of something . . .' (p. 150).

[36] Hopkins is aware of the range of meanings that the word encompasses and
incorporates them in his coinage. It is typical of him to try to maximize the range
of references and meanings of the words he uses, and to draw them together. His
fondness for puns and his use of them and other cases of ambiguity in the poems
testify to this rich and inclusive approach to language (see J. Hillis Miller, *The
Linguistic Moment* (Princeton: Princeton University Press, 1985), 251–2). The
coalescence of metrical and physical stress in his poetry is discussed in Ch. 10,
Sects. IV–VII.   [37] Cochran, 'Instress', 159.

This 'struggle' is envisaged as 'one among *parts*', and instress is consequently defined as 'the tension which holds [the] parts together'.[38]

Although it acknowledges Hopkins' use of the words 'stress', 'strain', and 'energy', and identifies instress with 'the force or energy, the tension upholding each being',[39] Cochran's account of 'stress' and 'instress' is predicated upon effacing the mechanistic implications of this idiom. He establishes a distinction early in his argument between Hopkins' use of the word 'stress' and 'its commonly accepted meanings',[40] by which he evidently means those closest to its senses in mechanics. Cochran writes of the word's use in a line from the poem 'Brothers', 'Told tales with what heart's stress' (No. 143), that it 'is nothing more than the use of *stress* as a synonym for *strain*'.[41] Bearing in mind his later definitive identification of 'instress' with 'tension', his comment on the phrase 'Stand at stress' from 'Harry Ploughman' (No. 169) is especially interesting, for it derogates this use of the word 'stress' on the grounds that it is synonymous with 'tense': 'The word here has its customary meaning: the ploughman is simply standing at the ready, he is tense.'[42] Having stated the assumption at the beginning of his argument that 'Hopkins' coinage of instress derives from this already existing word [i.e. stress]', it would be reasonable to expect some comment on the relation between the 'customary meaning' of stress as tenseness and his later, presumably metaphoric, reference to this quality in his definition of 'instress' as a 'tension'.[43]

Cochran's argument strips the word 'tension' of its mechanical sense and uses it to describe the form of dynamic unity he identifies with 'instress'. The explanatory terms 'force' and 'energy' that he borrows from mechanics are in a similar way simply equated with the Aristotelian entelechy: 'The *force* which we have utilized as a genus in the definition [of instress] to this point is *energeia*. It is the energy of the thing itself, holding it in being and giving it *stress*, the tendency towards being.'[44] Why does Cochran borrow terms from mechanics but insist that they represent only organicist ideas? This is an important

---

[38] Ibid. 160. [39] Ibid. 165. [40] Ibid. 148. [41] Ibid. 149.
[42] Ibid. 151. [43] Ibid. 160. [44] Ibid. 167.

question, for his case highlights a tendency in much of the exegetical work on Hopkins' terms. Eleanor Ruggles, W. A. M. Peters, Alan Heuser, Donald McChesney, and James Cotter each describe stress and instress in terms of either 'energy' or 'force' but fail to acknowledge the mechanical references of their metaphors.[45] How can a metaphor have a clear meaning if its primary reference is suppressed or obscured?

The radical opposition of art (which is identified with organic unity) to mechanistic science was posited by many of the romantics, and was one of the original dogmas of modern English literary criticism as it was established by Coleridge. This tenet became in turn a central presupposition of Anglo-American New Criticism: 'Poetry is not only quite different from science but in its essence is opposed to science.'[46] The New Critics blame science, which they believe engendered scepticism and industrialism, for the cultural fragmentation and alienation that they see to characterize the modern world. T. S. Eliot traces the inception of this disintegration, 'the dissociation of sensibility', to the time of the scientific revolution in the seventeenth century.[47] Much as the English romantics and Hopkins had before them, the New Critics responded to a perceived cultural crisis by asserting a doctrine of organicism, which in this case champions the lyric poem as the epitome of integral relations between form and matter, thought and experience. The fact that Hopkins adopts a *similar* strategy in dealing with cultural fragmentation and wrote mainly lyric poetry explains in large part why he was so well received by the New Critics. While these commentators have of course been hugely important in championing Hopkins and establishing his reputation their hegemony has inevitably restricted the range of interpretations to which his work has been subjected.

It is a mark of the influence of New Criticism in shaping the discourse of Hopkins criticism that commentaries on 'stress' and 'instress' are often anxious to transform, defuse, or ignore

[45] Ibid. 168–76 provides a convenient group of extracts which illustrate these authors' use of mechanistic terminology.

[46] Allen Tate (1932), quoted in René Wellek, *A History of Modern Criticism: 1750–1950*, vi: *American Criticism, 1900–1950* (London: Jonathan Cape, 1986), 152.

[47] 'The Metaphysical Poets' (1921), repr. in *Selected Prose of T. S. Eliot*, ed. Frank Kermode (London: Faber, 1975), 59–67. See esp. pp. 64–5.

the mechanical implications of these idiosyncratic terms. Critics such as Cochran appear to operate on the assumption that any suggestion of mechanicality is anathema to the work of a lyric poet. This presupposition effectively precludes any serious consideration being given to the mechanistic implications that Hopkins' most deliberate ontological language is in fact laden with.

IV

The antithesis that the New Critics posit between mechanics and organic form is simply inappropriate to Hopkins' work. Far from identifying contemporary physical science with atomism he sees it to actively oppose such tendencies, which he traces instead to current positivist psychology: 'Indeed while science is always making the idea of the chance clashing of atoms more and more unnatural in the outer world, this theory applies Epicureanism to the making of the mind' (D. X 3, fo. 18). The prescriptive New Critical scheme fails to consider the peculiar historical context in which Hopkins' thought develops. The main model determining Hopkins' doctrine of organic unity was provided not by the English literary romantic tradition but through Oxford idealism, which, while it identifies the forces of cultural dissolution with the positivists, distinguishes this group from modern science and its methods (which the positivists claimed as the basis for their authority), and follows the example of Hegel in being well disposed towards the inorganic sciences.

Physics was, at the time that Hopkins was writing, a much more apt source of metaphors for (and indeed examples of) integral being and specific identity than biology. Ideas of organicism and vitalism no longer predominated in the life sciences as they had when romantic science was at its height earlier in the century. Rather, as Hopkins observes in 'The Probable Future of Metaphysics', biology after Darwin encouraged atomism and relativism. The shift at this time to inorganic phenomena in order to illustrate differentiated unity is well exemplified by Hopkins' poem 'The Blessed Virgin compared to the Air we Breathe', which invokes modern optics to describe the relation that he sees God to have to the many, the flux and diversity, of Creation (the relation that is presented in the 'Parmenides' notes in terms of 'Being' and 'Not-being'). The poem alludes not only to the traditional seven colours of the spectrum but also to the more numerous but definitive gradations of the spectral bright lines in which each chemical element is registered in a specific wave-length, 'The seven or seven times seven | Hued sunbeam' (No. 151), the sum of which is clear white light, representative of the all-inclusive and ultimate ontological principle of God.

Hopkins applies a mechanistic ontology of matter in motion to all being, including organic life:

To his Watch

Mortal my mate, bearing my rock-a-heart,
Warm beat with cold beat company, shall I
Earlier or you fail at our force and lie
The ruins of, rifled, once a world of art?   (No. 164)

For Hopkins 'all nature is mechanical' (*J.* 252), even the human heart, the beating of which he describes elsewhere as 'the truth of nature' (*S.* 103). Inorganic and organic phenomena have an affinity in Hopkins' ontology that allows them to keep each other 'company'. They share a 'force', a common principle which suggests the modern conception of a convertible principle of 'energy'.[48]

The wound watch is one of the examples that Hermann von Helmholtz uses in a lecture 'On the Interaction of Natural Forces' to illustrate the continuity that exists between different forms of mechanical force: 'all our machinery and apparatus generate no force, but simply yield up the power communicated to them by natural forces,—falling water, moving wind, or by the muscles of men'.[49] The force which, as Helmholtz

---

[48] The idiosyncratic cosmology that Simone Weil develops in *Gravity and Grace* (1947), trans. Emma Craufurd (London: Routledge & Kegan Paul, 1952), offers an interesting comparison with Hopkins' doctrine of stress. Like Hopkins she develops and expresses her Catholic religious beliefs by using instances and analogies drawn from mechanics and energy physics.

[49] Helmholtz, *Popular Lectures on Scientific Subjects, First Series*, trans. E. Atkinson, 2nd edn. (London: Longmans, Green, and Co., 1895), 145. The lecture was delivered in 1854. The example of the watch mechanism is often used to illustrate the principle of energy, as e.g. in W. Thomson and P. G. Tait's popular exposition 'Energy', *Good Words* (1862), 602.

observes, impels the workings of the watch is 'the tension of springs . . . which is accomplished when we wind [it] up'.[50] In discussing the watch Hopkins, like Helmholtz, focuses upon the 'force' for which it provides the vessel, rather than the mechanical artefact itself. Corresponding to the broad conceptual change from classical Newtonian mechanics to energy physics, Hopkins' version of natural theology dwells not so much upon the artifice of nature, as do the deists and Paley in their respective versions of the notorious watchmaker analogy, but upon the force which sustains it: 'all things are upheld by instress and are meaningless without it' (*J.* 127). His conception of God is identified with a principle that escapes the grasp of evolutionary biology and so allows him to be unperturbed by Darwinism.[51] It facilitates a conception of God not as the great watchmaker, whose creative role was in danger of being usurped by the principle of natural selection, but as the logically necessary and mysterious first principle which Darwin tactfully suggests 'originally breathed into a few forms or into one' the 'several powers' of life.[52] Furthermore, Hopkins, unlike Paley and Darwin, envisages a continuing role for God in history and conceives of this participation, much as Joule does, in mechanistic terms of hydrodynamic 'pressure' (No. 101, st. 4), 'stress', and 'force'.

The priority that Hopkins' ontology gives to force over the mechanisms it activates and sustains is depicted graphically at the beginning of 'The Wreck of the *Deutschland*':

> Thou hast boúnd bónes and véins in me, fástened me flésh,
> And áfter it álmost únmade, what with dréad
> Thy doing: and dost thou touch me afresh?
> Over agáin I féel thy fínger and fínd thée.   (No. 101, st. 1)

The creation of the body is described as perfunctory and contingent, a mere binding and fastening of parts that suggests Doctor Frankenstein's gruesome project in Shelley's novel, where the creature does indeed emerge 'almost unmade'.[53] Life is

---

[50] Helmholtz, *Popular Lectures*, 144.

[51] See 18 Aug. 1888, Letter 162, *To Bridges*, 281.

[52] C. Darwin, *The Origin of Species* (Harmondsworth: Penguin, 1968), 459–60.

[53] While there is no record of Hopkins having read *Frankenstein*, the myth was popular during the Victorian period (see Chris Baldick, *In Frankenstein's Shadow: Myth, Monstrosity, and Nineteenth-century Writing* (Oxford: Clarendon Press,

identified here not with the sum of the body's parts but rather with the informing principle of divine stress that articulates them. This is God's 'finger', which, as in Michelangelo's famous depiction of the creation of Adam, gives life to mere matter, and renews it through accesses of grace. The 'touch' of God's 'finger' implies a physical stress, 'a pressure, a principle, Christ's gift' (No. 101, st. 4).

V

Hopkins arrives at his dictum that 'all nature is mechanical' through a logic of analogy: 'The laps of running foam striking the sea-wall double on themselves and return in nearly the same order and shape in which they came. This is mechanical reflection and is the same as optical: indeed all nature is mechanical, but then it is not seen that mechanics contain that which is beyond mechanics' (*J.* 252). Hopkins' identification of 'mechanical' and 'optical' reflection restates an analogy between hydrodynamics and light that is foundational for modern optics. From these instances he makes an inductive leap to the generalization that 'all nature is mechanical', and, furthermore, states that mechanics is imbricated with certain unspecified transcendent values. Both Hopkins' method here and the conclusion he reaches through it are representative for romantic scientific practice in the nineteenth century.

The principle of analogy was, for those working in the romantic tradition of Davy, Faraday, and Whewell, fundamental to the methodology of scientific discovery. The metaphysical presuppositions of this tradition are clearly enunciated and developed by James Clerk Maxwell, whose work is based upon his theoretical insights into the nature and use of analogy. A devoted student of both William Hamilton and Whewell,[54] Maxwell was an astute metaphysician as well as one of the century's pre-eminent physicists. Analogy is theorized by Maxwell in an

---

1987))). Hopkins read gothic fiction, including Walpole's *The Castle of Otranto* (20 Oct. 1886, Letter 134, *To Bridges*, 228) and Stevenson's 'Dr Jekyll and Mr Hyde', which he considered to be 'the work of great genius' (28 Oct. 1886, Letter 138, *To Bridges*, 238).

[54] Hendry, *Maxwell*, 27.

early essay on the subject as a means of recognizing cases of differentiated unity: 'in an analogy one truth is discovered under two expressions'.[55] A principle of form is seen to facilitate the analogy and to represent a truth common to its various terms. Maxwell observes that the wave theory, for example, posits 'a resemblance *in form* between the laws of light and those of vibrations [in an "elastic medium"]'.[56] The example that Hopkins gives similarly invokes the formal principle of transverse waves to draw together the phenomena of 'optical' and 'mechanical reflection'.

The natural tendency of reasoning by analogy is to substantiate its foundational idealist belief in the rationality and consistency of nature, to bring all the terms it treats of into an ultimate unity.[57] This is well exemplified by natural theology, in which God is regarded a priori as a unified subject, the nature of which is understood through the analogous relation it is seen to have to Creation. Similarly, in the methodology of romantic science, it is only from such an idealist presupposition that a parallel perceived between a discovery in one branch of science and that of another can be considered, in the manner of Whewell's 'Consilience of Inductions', as an argument for their truth. According to such 'a [romantic] scientific point of view the *relation* is', as Maxwell puts it, 'that most important thing to know[;] a knowledge of the one thing leads us a long way towards a knowledge of the other'.[58]

The extension of the energy principle from its original application in thermodynamics to cover a much wider range of physical powers is a definitive case of the unifying impetus of reasoning by analogy. The paradigm shift in physics from theories of imponderable fluids to a mechanistic ontology of matter in motion is predicated upon the presupposition that all physical forces are continuous with one another and can accordingly be described by analogy with the behaviour

---

[55] L. Campbell and W. Garnett (eds.), *The Life of James Clerk Maxwell*, 2nd edn. (London: Macmillan, 1884), 348.

[56] J. C. Maxwell, *The Scientific Papers of James Clerk Maxwell*, ed. W. D. Niven (Cambridge: Cambridge University Press, 1890; repr., New York: Dover, 1965), i. 156.

[57] See Shaw, *Lucid Veil*, esp. ch. 2, and, on Hopkins and analogy, pp. 149–52.

[58] Campbell and Garnett, *Life of Maxwell*, 354.

of simple mechanistic models, such as those of various elastic media. Such models furnish links in a chain of analogies by which energy physics draws together all dynamic phenomena. Furthermore, the logic of such speculative developments tends to extend their province beyond the realm of experimentally testable hypotheses to make assertions similar to those of natural theology, with which they share a fundamental a priori belief in the formal unity and consistency of nature. The propensity is exemplified in the passage from Hopkins, in which, having stated that 'all nature is mechanical', he makes the further claim that this mechanical monism 'contain[s] that which is beyond mechanics'. This corresponds to the speculative leap to the transcendent that Joule makes when he extrapolates from his discovery of the convertibility of heat and mechanical work a Christian cosmology in which 'the grand agents of nature are, by the Creator's fiat, indestructible'.

The passage from Joule's 1847 lecture quoted in Section II of the present chapter demonstrates the way in which the formal principle of 'energy' can generate a chain of analogies which is so comprehensive in the connections it makes that it serves to renew natural theology and romantic monism. Hopkins' unfinished poem 'To his Watch' (No. 164), which draws a parallel between the realms of the organic and inorganic, illustrates this ambition of reasoning by analogy to establish an ultimate synthetic understanding of all being and highlights the way in which Hopkins achieves this through mechanistic analogy.

Hopkins' overarching and imperative effort to theorize syntheses and legitimate their truth claims is evident throughout his Oxford and Birmingham work, from the concern of the early aesthetic theory with parallelism and his theory of the mind's a priori 'desire for unity' to the grand monistic doctrine established in the 'Parmenides' notes. The possibilities that art presents of simply fabricating synthetic forms is not entirely satisfactory for Hopkins, who as early as 1864 argues for a form of art that has 'more or less a scientific ground and character' (*J.* 75). Furthermore he wishes to establish that such relations as those of 'laws and sequences and causes and developments' (*J.* 118) exist independently from the mind's capacity for making synthetic a priori judgements. Hence the focus of the 1858 'Notes' on ontology, an area of speculation that Kant had effectively outlawed from metaphysics. Hopkins, like the post-Kantians, tries to place ontology on a scientific footing, and in so doing he, like Hegel, looks to physics for examples and authority. Developments in the physical sciences from the 1830s to the 1860s lend further credibility to this strategy, so much so in fact that the mature statement of Hopkins' metaphysic is predicated upon a simple word drawn from physics which he is able to invest with an abstract conceptual meaning. The synthesis of mechanics and idealism in the Hegelian term 'moments' which Hopkins alludes to in the 'All words . . .' notes is writ large in the 'Parmenides' notes as 'stress', the most significant expression of his conviction that 'mechanics contain that which is beyond mechanics'. It is in this way that Hopkins establishes the 'scientific ground and character' for the boldly idiosyncratic mature poetry heralded by 'The Wreck of the *Deutschland*'.

8 'the flush and foredrawn'

I

The title of Maxwell's 1856 essay on analogy asks 'Are there Real Analogies in Nature?',[1] a question which he sees to have its main interest in relation to the mechanistic ontology of contemporary physics:

Now the question of the reality of analogies in nature derives most of its interest from its application to the opinion, that all the phenomena of nature, being varieties of motion, can only differ in complexity, and therefore the only way of studying nature, is to master the fundamental laws of motion first, and then examine what kinds of complication of these laws must be studied in order to obtain true views of the universe.[2]

Maxwell, like Hopkins, believes that 'the fundamental laws of motion' provide the forms which serve to represent more complex phenomena. This logic, which is the basis of Maxwell's own scientific practice,[3] is fundamental also to Hopkins' work. In the unfinished poem on Margaret Clitheroe, for example, the behaviour of the martyred saint is compared to that of water going down a plug-hole:

> The very victim would prepare.
> Like water soon to be sucked in
> Will crisp itself or settle and spin

---

[1] Hopkins' concern with the truth value of the relations perceived by the mind is shared by Maxwell. His paper on 'Analogies' begins with the conundrum of whether knowledge originates, as Hopkins puts it, 'in the eye or in the thought' (No. 24): 'the whole framework of science, up to the very pinnacle of philosophy, seems sometimes a dissected model of nature, and sometimes a natural growth on the inner surface of the mind' (Campbell and Garnett, *Life of Maxwell*, 348).

[2] Campbell and Garnett, ibid. 352.

[3] His paper 'On Faraday's Lines of Force', the second part of which, like that on 'Analogies', dates from early 1856, attributes 'physical analogy' with precisely this role of simplifying complex phenomena 'to a form in which the mind can grasp them' (Maxwell, *Scientific Papers*, i. 155–6).

So she: one sees that here and there
She mends the way she means to go.
The last thing Margaret's fingers sew
Is a shroud for Margaret Clitheroe.   (No. 108, ll. 8–14)

The most simple mechanical phenomena furnished scientists working in the 1840s, 1850s, and 1860s with the means
of representing a vast range of complex physical states. Such
models provided the formal terms by which more complex phenomena could be understood and connected by analogy. The
mechanical principle of stress furnishes Hopkins with just such
a term. This is evident from both his formal metaphysics and
the observations of nature recorded in the diaries, journals,
and poetry.

The following extract from Hopkins' journal for March 1871
instances a brief sequence of analogies in nature which, like
the passage on the sea striking the sea-wall quoted in Section
V of the previous chapter, refers explicitly to the mechanistic
ontology upon which it is founded:

I have been watching clouds this spring and evaporation, for instance
over our Lenten chocolate. It seems as if the heat by *aestus*, throes |
one after another threw films of vapour off as boiling water throws
off steam under films of water, that is bubbles. One query then is
whether these films contain gas or no. The film seems to be set with
tiny bubbles which gives it a grey and grained look. By throes perhaps
which represent the moments at which the evener stress of the heat
has overcome the resistance of the surface or of the whole liquid. It
would be reasonable then to consider the films as the shell of gas-
bubbles and the grain on them as a network of bubbles condensed
by the air as the gas rises.—Candle smoke goes by just the same laws,
the visible film being here of unconsumed substance, not hollow
bubbles[.] The throes can be perceived | like the thrills of a candle
in the socket . . . They may by a breath of air be laid again and then
shew like grey wisps on the surface—which shews their part solidity.
They seem to be drawn off the chocolate as you might take up a
napkin between your fingers that covered something, not so much
from here or there as from the whole surface at one reech . . . —
Clouds however solid they may look far off are I think wholly made
of film in the sheet or in the tuft.   (*J.* 203–4)

The phenomena of evaporation from boiling chocolate, boiling water, and the candle flame are seen to be drawn together

by 'the same laws' which result in the manifestation of a substantive 'film'. By reasoning analogically from such accessible phenomena Hopkins reaches his conclusion that clouds are 'wholly made up of film'.

The 'stress of heat', by prevailing over the liquids' physical forces of 'resistance', produces the 'films of vapour' with which all the phenomena treated of in the passage are identified. This physical 'stress' parallels the ontological principle which is referred to in 'The Wreck of the *Deutschland*' in hydrodynamical terms as 'a pressure, a principle' that informs the 'water in a well', a metaphor for the poet's selfhood (No. 101, st. 4). The causal link between these dynamic principles and the essential being of a thing corresponds to that between 'stress' and 'inscape' in Hopkins' metaphysics. 'Stress', understood in the mechanistic sense in which it is used in the extract, provides the irreducible formal term that facilitates the chain of analogy by which all instances of being are drawn together in Hopkins' monistic ontology.

The instance of the word 'stress' in the passage on the Lenten chocolate is the first to appear after its initial conceptual exposition in the 'Parmenides' notes. Nevertheless it is entirely overlooked by commentators, including Cochran, who cites the word's occurrence in a journal entry fifteen months later, in August 1872 (*J.* 221), as the first since the notes.[4] The meaning of the term here is, however, neither commonplace nor 'customary', as Cochran might regard it, but historically specific and, as I have suggested, central to Hopkins' metaphysics. The meaning and currency of the word 'stress' was extended greatly from the 1840s. That Hopkins places such a burden of significance upon this simple term is an index of the power and scope that the mechanistic ontology of energy physics had assumed by the 1860s.

William Rankine's seminal paper on energetics observes that 'The fact that the theory of motions and motive forces is the only complete physical theory, has naturally led to the adoption of *mechanical hypotheses* in the theories of other branches

---

[4] Cochran, 'Instress', 146. It may be recalled that Hopkins uses the word 'stress' in the 1866 essay on 'The Origin of Our Moral Ideas'. Its sense here is of a mental pressure, as good and bad impulses bear upon the mind: 'two . . . logics putting stress on the mind, one belonging to virtue, one to vice' (*J.* 81).

of physics'.[5] Models derived from the behaviour of elastic solid materials contributed greatly to the unification of physics during the 1840s and 1850s. Rankine's early work on heat energy and gases is predicated upon a model of molecules that are endowed with elastic properties, while William Thomson's researches in the 1840s on the relations between electricity, magnetism, and light also employ analogies with elastic solids.[6]

The pursuit of a unified physical theory at this time is concerned primarily with establishing mechanistic interpretations of Faraday's field theory, which repudiates Newton's mechanistic principle of action-at-a-distance by shifting attention from sources of force to the surrounding space, the field, in which it is propagated as curved 'lines of force'.[7] The concept of the field was originally employed by Faraday to account for the electrical induction of magnetism and subsequently applied to a wide range of electromagnetic, thermal, and optical phenomena.[8] Faraday provides two main models of the field. Writing in the 1830s he describes the electric and magnetic lines of force as a state of 'tension' in which contiguous particles of a mediating substance he called the dielectric are polarized (i.e. each is charged both negatively and positively) and arranged serially, negative charged end to positive.[9] His central concept of force received a greater primacy in the 1840s as he abandoned the mechanical imagery of the dielectric medium and instead explained his principle of continuous action by the behaviour of 'forces filling space'.[10] What are commonly perceived to be particles of matter are, according to Faraday, 'centres of force',[11]

---

[5] Quoted in Hendry, *Maxwell*, 195.   [6] Ibid. 102–6, 161–2.

[7] A representation of the lines appears when iron filings are sprinkled on a sheet of thin card placed over a magnet. See Maxwell, *Scientific Papers*, i. 451–2 and Faraday's *Electricity* (1852), iii, pl. III; these diagrams are also reproduced in P. M. Harman, *Energy, Force, and Matter* (Cambridge, Cambridge University Press, 1982), 80.

[8] The following brief discussion draws upon the chapter on Faraday in Harman, *Metaphysics and Natural Philosophy*, ch. 5.

[9] Faraday appears to have been influenced by the hypothesis of polar forces developed by Kant, Schelling, and Coleridge, which in contrast to the mechanistic ontology of matter in motion equates substance with the forces of attraction and repulsion (L. Pearce Williams, *Faraday: A Biography* (New York: Simon & Schuster, 1971), 60–80).

[10] Mary B. Hesse, *Forces and Fields* (London: Nelson, 1961), 201.

[11] Quoted by Harman, *Metaphysics and Natural Philosophy*, 85.

which, because they are integral to the plenum of force, extend throughout all matter and are penetrable. Faraday describes states of the field qualitatively, according to the mechanical analogy, as tensions, strains, and stresses, while his successors, principally Thomson and Maxwell, often use speculative mechanical models as a propaedeutic to formulating quantitative (i.e. mathematical) values for them.

Thomson established an analogy in 1842 between phenomena of heat conduction and electrostatics, which he extended in 1845 with the development of a mathematical schema that describes both conventional action-at-a-distance electrostatics and Faraday's account of electrical lines of force.[12] He reasoned that if there is any physical basis to the relations he had posited mathematically, then Faraday's electrical lines of force must exist in a medium which is, like that in which Joseph Fourier studied heat flow, possessed of the mechanical properties of an elastic solid.[13]

Maxwell's paper 'On Faraday's Lines of Force' (1855–6), in which the dynamics of an incompressible fluid provide the model from which he derives a mathematical description of electromagnetic phenomena, clearly springs from Thomson's influence.[14] The undulatory theory of light and Thomson's analogy between heat flow and electrostatic attraction are, as Maxwell's approving mention of them in the introduction to his paper indicates, the basis for the approach that he follows here. These theories, by describing the propagation of their respective forces in terms of the mechanics of an elastic solid, provided the paradigmatic cases for the mechanistic programme of explanation that developed rapidly during the 1850s and 1860s. As a consequence of the adoption of the elastic solid model a range of physical phenomena, especially those associated with field theory and its hypotheses of luminiferous and electromagnetic ethers, came to be described in terms of stresses and strains.

Thomson's early successes using an elastic solid model gen-

---

[12] Daniel M. Siegel, 'Thomson, Maxwell, and the Universal Ether', in G. N. Cantor and M. J. S. Hodge (eds.), *Conceptions of Ether* (Cambridge: Cambridge University Press, 1981), 240–1.

[13] Ibid. 241–2; Crosbie Smith, 'A New Chart for British Natural Philosophy: The Development of Energy Physics in the Nineteenth Century', *History of Science*, 16 (1978), 245.   [14] Siegel, 'Thomson, Maxwell', 242–3.

erated a great deal of interest in the mechanics of such materials, with the resultant research into them being used in both the closely related methodologies which dominated physics at the time, the theoretical approach based upon mathematical analogies, and the hypothetical, which employs mechanistic models. As a consequence of the importance given to the mechanics of elastic solids in the 1850s and 1860s the meaning of the term 'stress' was carefully specified and its application broadened. This chapter and those that follow it argue that Hopkins' use of this principle in his metaphysics represents what is probably the most extensive of all the wide-ranging applications it was put to during this time.

Rankine and Thomson each furnish normative definitions for mechanical 'stress' during the 1850s. Although Rankine is not so well known today his contemporaries gave him an equal place alongside Thomson and Rudolf Clausius as a creator of the science of thermodynamics.[15] An engineer by training and, from 1855 to his death in 1872, the Professor of Civil Engineering and Mechanics at the University of Glasgow, he was also recognized by his peers as an eminent authority in the area of general mechanics. In 1858 he published a very successful *Manual of Applied Mechanics* in which the following definition of 'stress' appears: 'The word STRESS has been adopted as a general term to comprehend various forces which are exerted between contiguous bodies, or parts of bodies, and which are distributed over the surface of contact of the masses between which they act.'[16] This account evidently received general acceptance quite quickly, for a version of it is quoted in the 1864 edition of *Webster's Dictionary*, where it is made to serve as the definition for the mechanical sense of the term: '[It is a f]orce exerted in any direction or manner between contiguous bodies or parts of bodies, and taking specific names according to its directions or mode of action, as *thrust* or *pressure, pull* or *tension, shear* or *tangential stress*.'[17] The importance given at the time to this concept of 'stress' can be gauged from the fact that

[15] Keith Hutchison, 'W. J. M. Rankine and the Rise of Thermodynamics', *British Journal for the History of Science*, 14/46 (1981), 1.

[16] W. J. M. Rankine, *A Manual of Applied Mechanics* (London: Charles Griffin, 1858), 68.

[17] *Dr. Webster's Complete Dictionary of the English Language*, rev. Chauncey A. Goodrich and Noah Porter (London: Bell & Daldy, n.d. [1864]), s.v. 'Stress'. The entry

it is one of only three senses distinguished and more precise and technical than, for example, the definition of this sense given in the *Oxford English Dictionary* (which was quoted above in Section III of the previous chapter). This can be accounted for by the use that the principle was being put to in physics, which, predicated upon a clear and exact conceptualization of the mechanical principle, appears to have informed Rankine's definition.

Rankine identifies mechanical stress with both the forces that are external to particular things ('between contiguous bodies') and internal ('between . . . parts of bodies'). However, in his broader application of this concept, where the reference to 'bodies' includes molecules, the meaning of 'stress' is restricted by his allocation of the first of these terms, that is, the external forces, to the word 'strain'. According to the *Oxford English Dictionary* (1989) the following passage from Rankine, which was written in 1855, marks the first use of the word 'stress' to signify a definite concept in modern physics:

In this paper, the word '*Strain*' will be used to denote the change of volume and figure constituting the deviation of a molecule of a solid from that condition which it preserves when free from the action of external forces; and the word '*Stress*' will be used to denote the force, or combination of forces, which such a molecule exerts in tending to recover its free condition, and which, for a state of equilibrium, is equal and opposite to the combination of external forces applied to it.[18]

This definition is also used in Thomson and Tait's *Treatise on Natural Philosophy* (1867), a systematic theoretical treatment of dynamics in which the 'abstract theory of physical phenomena'[19] envisaged by Rankine receives 'its definitive expression':[20] 'We adopt, from Rankine, the term *stress* to designate' (what

acknowledges its source as 'Rankine'. Alan Ward writes that *Webster's Dictionary* was 'more widely used' than Ogilvie's *Imperial Dictionary*, which was based upon it, and that 'there is slight evidence' that Hopkins may have used it (*J.* 500).

[18] *Miscellaneous Scientific Papers of W. J. Macquorn Rankine* (London, Charles Griffin, 1881), 120. See 'Stress' sb. 5c, *OED*, 2nd edn. (1989).

[19] Quoted in Donald Moyer, 'Energy, Dynamics, Hidden Machinery: Rankine, Thomson and Tait, Maxwell', *Studies in the History and Philosophy of Science*, 8/3 (1977), 253.   [20] Hendry, *Maxwell*, 196.

is referred to earlier in the account as) 'the forces called into play through the interior of a solid when brought into a condition of strain'.[21]

Thomson, writing in 1856, inverts Rankine's definition, 'A stress is an equilibrating application of force to a body', and notes the discrepancy between this and his colleague's specification of the term: 'It will be seen that I have deviated slightly from Mr. Rankine's definition of the word "stress," as I have applied it to the direct action experienced by a body from the matter around it, and not, as proposed by him, to the elastic reaction of the body equal and opposite to that action.'[22]

II

'Stress' refers in both Rankine's and Thomson's definitions to the tendency by which the equilibrium of a body is maintained. This is more clearly apparent from Thomson and Tait's *Treatise* and from Maxwell. For Thomson and Tait, stress is a potential energy which inheres within an 'isotropic substance' (that is, one within which two equal but opposite forces are distributed) and is actualized through the application of external pressures.[23] A poem which Maxwell wrote in 1876, 'Report on Tait's Lecture on Force:—B[ritish] A[ssociation], 1876', describes this use of the word:

> Both Action and Reaction now are gone.
>   Just ere they vanished,
> Stress joined their hands in peace, and made them one.[24]

It is clear from his other writings, most notably the paper 'On Physical Lines of Force', that Maxwell shares the conception of stress that he attributes to his colleague: 'Stress is action and reaction between the consecutive parts of a body.'[25]

The paper 'On Physical Lines of Force', published in four parts during 1861 and 1862, is a landmark in the realization

---

[21] W. Thomson and P. G. Tait, *Treatise on Natural Philosophy* (Oxford: Clarendon Press, 1867), i. 507.   [22] *OED*, 2nd edn., s.v. 'Stress' sb. 5c.
[23] Thomson and Tait, *Treatise on Natural Philosophy*, i. 527.
[24] Campbell and Garnett, *Life of Maxwell*, 418.
[25] Maxwell, *Scientific Papers*, i. 453.

of a unified mechanistic physics. Maxwell was one of those who were spurred by Thomson's findings in the 1840s to study the mechanics of elastic solids, some of the results of which inform a prodigious paper on 'The Equilibrium of Elastic Solids'[26] that he read to the Royal Society of Edinburgh in 1850, when he was 19. A later review article on Thomson which Maxwell wrote for *Nature* acknowledges that the theory put forward in his paper on 'Physical Lines' 'may be considered as a development of Thomson's idea' of an analogy between the behaviour of heat and electrical attraction.[27]

Maxwell, using a mechanical model endowed with the properties of an elastic solid to represent Faraday's field, formulated equations describing its behaviour which correspond to those that account for electromagnetic and optical phenomena. Whereas in the lecture on 'Faraday's Lines' the model used was, as Maxwell puts it, 'not even a hypothetical fluid', but 'merely a collection of imaginary properties which may be employed for establishing certain theorems in pure mathematics',[28] the later paper starts from the conviction that the lines of force are 'something real' and endeavours to account for magnetic and electrical phenomena as instances of continuous action by exploring the analogy with various states of stress in a mechanical medium: 'My object in this paper is to clear the way for speculation in this direction, by investigating the mechanical results of certain states of tension and motion in a medium, and comparing these with the observed phenomena of magnetism and electricity'.[29] This approach, Siegel observes, provides an experimentally verifiable 'explanatory mechanical theory rather than an illustrative analogy'.[30]

The success of Maxwell's paper in describing mathematically a unified theory of electromagnetics added greatly to the prestige of the elastic solids analogy, and, due also to the relative accessibility of the 'semi-popular form'[31] in which the paper

[26] Ibid. i. 30–73.
[27] Ibid. ii. 306. He also acknowledges Thomson's elastic solid model early in the 'Physical Lines' paper (i. 453).
[28] Ibid. i. 160. In the words of the 'Physical Lines' paper, the earlier paper used 'mechanical illustrations to assist the imagination, but not to account for the phenomena' (i. 452). [29] Ibid. i. 451, 452.
[30] Siegel, 'Thomson, Maxwell', 247.
[31] Campbell and Garnett, *Life of Maxwell*, 233.

appeared, contributed to the currency that the word 'stress' had in the 1860s. 'Stress' is used by Maxwell as a generic term: 'We come now to consider the magnetic influence as existing in the form of some kind of pressure or tension, or, more generally, of *stress* in the medium.'[32] He then proceeds at this point in the paper to specify some of the cases that the term encompasses:

Stress is action and reaction between the consecutive parts of a body, and consists in general of pressures or tensions different in different directions at the same point of the medium.

The necessary relations among these forces have been investigated by mathematicians; and it has been shewn that the most general type of a stress consists of a combination of three principal pressures or tensions, in directions at right angles to each other.

When two of the principle pressures are equal, the third becomes an axis of symmetry, either of greatest or least pressure, the pressures at right angles to this axis being all equal.

When the three principal pressures are equal, the pressure is equal in every direction, and there results a stress having no determinate axis of direction, of which we have an example in simple hydrostatic pressure.[33]

Newton's third law of motion provides the fundamental principle from which Maxwell's conception of stress was developed: 'we have, as another reading of the Third law, "Every action between two bodies is a stress" '.[34] The use of Newton's laws of motion by Maxwell (and also by Rankine, and Thomson and Tait) is, however, not restricted to classical mechanics but is extended through the mechanical concept of energy to all parts of physics.[35] Hopkins was acquainted with Newton's laws of motion from his early studies in mechanics. The following passage from his notes on mechanics presents Newton's first corollary to his laws:

The parallelogram of forces.

If AB [and] AC represent two forces acting at A, [th]en will AD, [the] diagonal of [the] corresponding par[allelogra]m[,] represent [th]eir resultant. The tru[th] of [th]is prop[osition] is manifest, [and] might

[32] Maxwell, *Scientific Papers*, i. 453.   [33] Ibid. i. 453–4.
[34] 'The "Encyclopaedia Britannica" ', *Nature*, 29 (15 Nov. 1883), 53. This issue also includes a letter from Hopkins (p. 55).   [35] Smith, 'A Chart', 249.

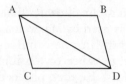

2. Parallelogram from Hopkins' notebook

be allowed to rest on experiment, for *everything wh[ich] goes on in [the] physical world around us can be shewn to corroborate it.*

(B. I, fos. 4–5; my emphasis)

While this configuration of forces describes a case of physical stress, the general application that Hopkins attributes to it is in keeping with the unifying tendency of mechanistic physics and anticipates both his dictum that 'all nature is mechanical' and his metaphysical principle of 'stress'.

While Hopkins' studies in mechanics gave him an early acquaintance with the Newtonian laws of motion, his knowledge of the wave theory of light[36] entails an understanding of their application to the theory of the luminiferous ether, which explains the undulations of light as the consequence of equal pressures of displacement and recuperation in this elastic medium. It is clear that by 1871 Hopkins was familiar with the use of the word 'stress' to refer to such undulations propagated in an elastic medium, for he characterizes the phenomenon of the boiling Lenten chocolate as a 'stress of heat' in this viscous medium, the elasticity of which is acknowledged by his references to its qualities of 'resistance' as well as of conduction.

The contexts of Newtonian physics and the mechanics of elastic solids enable a fuller appreciation of Hopkins' speculations in the journal entry on the boiling Lenten chocolate. The dynamical understanding of stress is clearly presupposed in the interaction of 'the resistance of the surface or of the whole liquid' and the 'stress of heat', which are conceived of as potential energies that are actualized through their opposition to one another. The consistency of the liquid, which left to itself is a pressure maintaining an equilibrium, is pitted against the dynamical force of the heat, which overcomes it.

[36] See Ch. 7, Sect. II.

The product of these conflicting stresses is of course the 'film', which Hopkins, reasoning by analogy, regards as the key to the phenomena of clouds, his main concern in the passage. The tentative equilibrium of vaporous water formed in the cloud can accordingly be described in purely mechanical terms as the resultant of two stresses: an equilibrium which may be said to constitute its definitive 'instress'.

The resolution of opposing forces in their resultant is instanced by the case in which two moments become subsumed in a third, which Hegel uses to describe his dialectic and which was introduced above, in Chapter 5, as characterizing Hopkins' principle of the Idea. The resultant is an equilibrium akin to the conception of stress adopted by Rankine, Thomson and Tait, and Maxwell to describe the internal distribution of forces. Hopkins' early Newtonian generalization, that 'everything w[hich] goes on in the physical world around us can be shewn to corroborate' the unity of opposing forces, appears to have been renewed by him in his later metaphysical doctrine: 'all things are upheld by instress' (*J.* 127). While Maxwell's use of the word 'stress' to designate a literally dynamic unity provides an important gloss for Hopkins' neologism, such distributions of force within a body are also described by Rankine's definition of 'internal stress'. 'Instress' may have originated as an abridgement of this phrase:

> If a body be conceived to be divided into two parts by an ideal plane traversing it in any direction, the force exerted by those two parts at the plane of division is an *internal stress*.[37]

The nature of the stresses that Hopkins sees to inhere within each instressed object, each discrete instance of being, is specified by the 'Parmenides' notes as two opposing 'principles which meet in the scape of everything—probably Being, under its modification or siding of particular oneness or Being, and Not-being, under its siding of the Many. The two may be called two degrees of siding in the scale of Being' (*J.* 130). Hopkins' metaphor of 'the scale of Being' brings forward the importance

---

[37] Rankine, *Manual of Applied Mechanics*, 82. The 'ideal plane' corresponds to the dynamical principle of the 'axes of elasticity', which he also formulated during the 1850s. Rankine uses the phrase 'to signify all directions with respect to which certain kinds of elastic forces are symmetrical' (*Miscellaneous Scientific Papers*, 119).

of 'Being' and 'Not-being' as *moments* of Being by effectively invoking the mechanical basis of the Hegelian use of this term. The beam of the scale is subject to the opposing forces occasioned by the weight in the pans on either side of its axis, two moments which are consequently reconciled in a new moment that describes the resultant balance. The ontology of organic unity is in this way described as an equilibrium, a balance or synthesis of opposing principles. Another way of putting this is to say that the opposite forces exerted by each weight place a physical stress (or, more specifically, a strain) upon the beam, and that the resultant tension, which is representative of instress, is a dynamic equilibrium.

This mechanical equilibrium corresponds to Thomson and Tait's description of the stress of an 'isotropic substance' or more broadly to the hydrostatic pressure that Maxwell identifies with Newton's third law of motion: 'Newton's stress was a hydrostatic pressure in every direction'.[38] It is the equilibrium of the well described in the fourth stanza of 'The Wreck of the *Deutschland*' which, parallel to the 'two principles' of Being and Not-being that 'meet in the scape[s] of everything' (*J.* 130), is registered in its appearance, its 'poise' (No. 101, st. 4). Hydrostatics is, as his original definition of 'instress' as 'the flush and foredrawn' (*J.* 127) indicates, the main mechanical model for Hopkins' conception of determinate being.

III

Hopkins' use of simple mechanical phenomena as analogies for complex and elevated phenomena has its most celebrated (and controversial) instances in the opening lines of 'God's Grandeur':

> The world is charged wíth the grándeur of God.
>   It will flame out, like shining from shook foil;
>   It gathers to a greatness, like the ooze of oil
> Crushed.   (No. 111)

A number of inadequate readings of the opening lines of 'God's Grandeur' have arisen from a failure to understand the

---

[38] Maxwell, *Scientific Papers*, ii. 488.

ontological significance that simple physical phenomena have for Hopkins. Yvor Winters, writing in 1962, finds the 'ooze of oil' and 'shook foil' similes 'almost grotesquely trivial as illustrations of the first line' of the poem,[39] a position which has prompted many defensive and apologetic responses from Hopkins' commentators. During the 1960s critics offered ingenious explanations for the 'ooze of oil' image in terms of, amongst other things, the hydraulic press, petroleum oil, and the oil lamp.[40] Since then the tacit acceptance by commentators of Winter's criterion that the image of a blob of oil is in itself too banal to represent the sublime grandeur of God has continued to generate elaborate and tenuous interpretations: 'olive oil . . . was among the most valuable imports into England from Italy whose oil-presses, while Hopkins was writing these sonnets, produced annually over forty million gallons of it, drop by drop . . . : of olive oil the Victorians could certainly say "It gathers to a greatness" '.[41]

This commentator is in any case right about the type of oil that the poem alludes to. The reference to 'oil | Crushed' or, as it is further specified in an earlier draft, 'Pressed', indicates a fluid vegetable oil, most probably olive oil, the 'oil of gladness' (No. 53), which has several liturgical functions. Some commentators see the image to refer to the literal nature of olive oil, an approach that is consistent with Hopkins' interest in the physics of liquids. Donald Reiman's straightforward interpretation takes the poem to refer to a viscous globule of oil that is 'crushed' by a pressure, such as that brought to bear by the tread of a foot. This provides a simile for the resilience

[39] Y. Winters, *The Function of Criticism* (London: Routledge & Kegan Paul, 1962), 125.
[40] Todd K. Bender, 'Hopkins' "God's Grandeur"', *The Explicator*, 21/7 (Mar. 1963), item 55; Michael Taylor, 'Hopkins' "God's Grandeur"', *The Explicator*, 25/8 (Apr. 1967), item 68; George E. Montag, 'Hopkins' "God's Grandeur" and "the ooze of oil crushed"', *Victorian Poetry*, 1/4 (Nov. 1963), 302–3. All such interpretations are open to the criticism that it is inappropriate, given that the poem juxtaposes the profound purity of God manifest in nature with the corruption and obfuscation of nature by man, to interpret God's grandeur as analogous to examples of the industrial exploitation of nature. A similar criticism, of Bender's suggestion that the poem refers to the hydraulic press, is made by Donald H. Reiman: 'is the relationship between man's industrial society and nature such in the sonnet that Hopkins would have wished to portray God as a great machinist?' ('Hopkins' "Ooze of oil" Rises Again', *Victorian Poetry*, 4/1 (Winter 1966), 40).
[41] N. MacKenzie, *A Reader's Guide to Gerard Manley Hopkins* (London: Thames & Hudson, 1981), 64.

of God's grandeur in the face of mankind's brutal trampling of nature and indifference to the divine will.[42] Margaret Giovannini argues that if 'attention is directed to the complex physical laws which govern the properties by which . . . oil "gathers", compelling evidence of a creative God is found'.[43] This apt interpretation can be developed further.

The 'ooze of oil' image presents the irreducible characteristics of determinate being with a clarity and directness that is not available in its more complex, organic, instances. It is not difficult to identify the essential nature by which the oil 'gathers' with the qualities of 'the flush and foredrawn' that define 'instress' in the 'Parmenides' notes. In the Roman Catholic Catechism olive oil 'signifies the fulness of grace, since oil is diffusion'. Added to this quality of 'flushness' it also has liturgical associations with strength,[44] which correspond to the other aspect of Hopkins' formula for instress, the 'foredrawn'. This quality is the oil's viscosity, which in its strict scientific sense refers to the measure of the resistance that a substance provides to motion, in this case the motion of its reciprocal term, 'the flush'. It parallels the dynamical terms of the passage on the Lenten chocolate, in which the flushness of the 'stress of heat' is tempered by the resistant 'foredrawn' quality of viscosity, the 'film'.

The 'ooze of oil', understood as an object rather than as its action, offers a refinement upon the image of determinate being in the simile describing the sheepflock: 'It ran like the water-packets on a leaf—that collectively, but a number of globules so filmed over that they would not flush together is the exacter comparison.'[45] The qualifications that Hopkins makes to his original simile, in which he strengthens the film that enforces the meniscus of the drops so that the analogy acknowledges the autonomy of each sheep, is further accentuated later in the note, where this image is supplemented by a simile that conveys a much greater sense of solidity: 'as they passed outwards they behaved as the drops would do (or a

[42] Reiman, 'Hopkins' "Ooze of oil"', 39–41.

[43] M. Giovannini, 'Hopkins' "God's Grandeur"', *The Explicator*, 24/4 (Dec. 1965), item 36.

[44] William Addis and Thomas Arnold, *A Catholic Dictionary* (London: Kegan Paul, Trench, & Co., 1884), s.v. 'Chrism'.   [45] See Ch. 6, Sect. IV.

handful of shot) in reaching the brow of a rising and running over' (*J.* 187).

The overweening quality of water's 'flushness' that Hopkins endeavours to compensate for in the passage on the sheep-flock is in the case of 'the ooze of oil' tempered by the greater viscosity of this substance; it is in other words more tightly 'foredrawn'. The definitive quality by which it 'gathers' implies not only a drawing together but also the reaching out that facilitates this action, the 'flushness' which permeates being and hence brings it 'home' to itself, ' "for Being draws-home to Being" ' (*J.* 128). The two moments of 'the ooze of oil', its 'two degrees of siding in the scale of Being', are evenly balanced and hence, in comparison to water, more representative of determinate being. Oil has in its forms of droplet or pool a 'poise' which the greater 'flushness' of water acquires only when it is contained by an extrinsic principle such as a well (No. 101, st. 4).

Particular instances of determinate being cohere as distinctive natures: an 'instress' necessarily involves a peculiar 'inscape'. This specificity is another condition of determinate being which 'the ooze of oil' image presents with an almost abstract simplicity. The nature of olive oil as a pure essence makes it an apt emblem for the 'inscapes' of specific creatures, while it is also, through its liturgical identification with the Holy Ghost, continuous with divine Being. The viscous property of oil, the capacity by which it 'gathers', is like the distinctive qualities of the creatures referred to in 'As kingfishers catch fire', enacted spontaneously by the thing itself: '*What I do is me*'. Indeed, 'the ooze of oil | Crushed' alludes to the fact that the oil is expressed by the olive, a pun[46] that further highlights its affinity with the doctrine of the 'kingfishers' poem, where distinctive being declares its nature; 'Selves—goes itself; *myself* it speaks and spells | Crying *What I do is me: for that I came*' (No. 115). In being 'Crushed' the essential oil which inheres within the olive as a potentiality is brought forth, actualized.

The word 'ooze' functions in the poem as both noun and verb, an ambiguity that suggests the paradox of the Heraclitean fire, a persistent unity (the *logos*) which is also essentially dynamic

[46] For further discussion of this point, see Ch. 10, Sect. V.

and fluctuous. This conception of the word 'ooze' suggests the image of a globule of oil moving and flushing with others, constantly gathering to a voluminous 'greatness'. The phenomenon is described in a comment on the Welsh language in one of Hopkins' letters to his mother: 'it is almost all vowels and they run off the tongue like oil by diphthongs and by triphthongs'.[47] By being run together, globules of oil, like the vowels that comprise these types of syllable, gather in a new organic whole. In the poem this unity is progressive. It 'gathers' discrete instances of being, but may also be conceived of as absolute, for 'it gathers to *a* greatness' (my emphasis). The 'ooze of oil' evokes both particular instances of determinate being and the source and sum of all being, supreme Being or God.

The principle of 'the ooze of oil' accordingly suggests the ultimate equation of the 'scale of Being', in which Being itself is identified with the sum of all instances of being, the ontological with the ontic. While 'there are', as Hopkins writes in his commentary on Parmenides, 'ten thousand men to think and ten thousand things for them to think of' they are simply 'scapes' or aspects of ultimate Being, 'the truth itself, the burl'. '[T]he phenomenal world' in its entirety, in all its 'scapes', is identified with the Parmenidean monistic conception of Being (*J.* 130).

The aptness of the phenomena of oil to this dialectical construal of Parmenidean Being is brought forward by a passage from Jean-Paul Sartre, whose ontology, although proceeding to radically divergent conclusions from those reached by Hopkins, similarly develops from Hegelian roots. Much of the final section of the last part of *Being and Nothingness*, 'Quality as a Revelation of Being', is devoted to exploring the nature of the '*visqueux*', the 'viscous' or (in Hazel Barnes' translation) the 'slimy', as an analogy for Being: 'At first, with the appearance of a fluid it manifests to us a being which is everywhere fleeing and yet everywhere similar to itself . . . which eternally is changed into itself . . . a being which is eternity and infinite temporality . . . a possible fusion of the for-itself as pure temporality and the in-itself as pure eternity.'[48] Sartre recognizes the paradoxical

[47] 'To His Mother', 1 Sept. 1874, Letter 68, *Further Letters*, 126.
[48] Trans. Hazel E. Barnes (New York, Philosophical Library, 1956), 607.

nature of the viscous, the essential and manifold tensions which inhere within it and qualify it as an eminent example of being or 'stress'. In Hopkins' poem the being for-itself, which corresponds to the 'Not-being' of flux and diversity in the notes, is represented by the droplets of oil which gather as (that is, are in a sense equivalent to) being in-itself, the ultimate principle of 'Being', 'a greatness'.

Viscid imagery is often used also in Sartre's fiction, as for example in *The Age of Reason* where the pregnant Marcelle, having just vomited in a basin, reflects upon some ... 'dabs of mucus sliding slowly towards the drain-hole ... she muttered: "It's fantastic!" She was not revolted; this was *life*, like the slimy efflorescences of spring, it was not more repulsive than the little dab of russet, odorous gum that tipped the buds.'[49] While for Hopkins the quality of viscosity is associated with the *utmost* purity of olive oil, the basic ingredient of the Chrism of Catholic ritual, Sartre associates it with what is conventionally regarded as the mucky physicality of mucus. The essential oil in the olive is analogous to the blood which Christ similarly expressed as he was 'Crushed' on the Cross. Christ's blood, unlike the blood of the rest of us, is not the genetic legacy of both parents but of the mother only. This woman's blood is, however, cleansed of its conventional associations with the abject. Christ, the Hebrew word for the Anointed, is closely linked to the olive oil of the anointing Chrism. Olive oil functions in 'God's Grandeur' as a masculinist symbol for the blood of Christ: one that transforms the suggestively feminine, abject, stigma of the wounds and flowing blood of the martyred man-God into an essence that is pure and clean, a seminal fluid, akin to the distinctively male bodily fluid which in its masculinist representations is, as Elizabeth Grosz observes,[50] privileged as pure and as somehow not polluting in the way that other bodily excrescences are seen to be. It presents a stark contrast to the sticky clinging principle of viscosity which is traditionally identified with female gendered bodies; the mucus from the pregnant

---

[49] J.-P. Sartre, *The Age of Reason*, trans. Eric Sutton (London: Hamish Hamilton, 1947), 80.
[50] E. Grosz, *Volatile Bodies: Toward a Corporeal Feminism* (Sydney, Allen & Unwin, 1994), 205–7.

woman which Sartre parallels with Mother Nature's 'slimy efflorescences of spring'.

Hopkins' later writings translate the ontology of the 'Parmenides' notes into overtly Christian terms. Thus God is seen
to include and transcend all instances of being, and accordingly to constitute the supreme case of differentiated unity: 'his
inlaw, the law of his being is unlike mine, as the Ten of Hearts
is unlike any one of the hearts in it' (S. 127). The droplets of
oil in 'God's Grandeur', like the hearts on the playing card, represent instances of being, particular inscapes, each of which
is permeated by the siding of 'Being . . . or . . . particular oneness', so that they form 'a greatness'. The properties of the oil
are identified in the poem, as in the Roman Catholic liturgy,
with the Holy Ghost. The ultimate ontological unity of 'a greatness' which the droplets of oil form is a manifestation of the
Paraclete. Creation, which according to the poem has become
subject to the moral recalcitrance of mankind, is nevertheless
constantly drawn together and renewed as 'the Holy Ghost over
the bent | World broods with warm breast and with ah! bright
wings'. The Holy Ghost is identified through this image with
the earlier allusion to 'the dearest freshness deep down things',
a phrase that similarly recalls the essential oil within the olive.

The image of 'the ooze of oil', although it is presented in
the poem as a simile, functions as synecdoche. The phenomenon is an instance, indeed, an epitome, of Being. As synecdoche for all instances of being and hence Being itself 'the
ooze of oil' not only 'gathers to a greatness', but its 'greatness'
reciprocally inheres in the very qualities of 'the flush and
foredrawn' by which it 'gathers'.

IV

The definition of 'instress' as 'the flush and foredrawn' highlights the dialectical nature of determinate being. Discrete
instances of being are, in other words, as Hopkins' coinage
suggests, essentially *in* a state of *stress* or tension. For Hegel the
essential quality of elasticity—of action and reaction, movement
and resistance, that characterizes mechanical stress and is represented by Hopkins' definition of instress—typifies ontological

unity: 'Elasticity is cohesion displaying itself in motion. It is the whole of cohesion.'[51] The mechanical phenomena invoked by Hopkins' definition of 'instress' and by the coinage itself instance what he sees to be the irreducible qualities of all being. His recorded observations of nature show that he was drawn to phenomena that strongly represent such criteria, finding in many of them the supplementary terms for his metaphysical idiom.

The tension between containment, the 'foredrawn', and the ebullient force of dispersion, 'the flush', is instanced by 'The laps of running foam striking the sea-wall', which lead Hopkins to remark that 'all nature is mechanical, but . . . that mechanics contain that which is beyond mechanics' (*J.* 252). The 'Parmenides' notes not only describe all being as synonymous with mechanical 'stress', but explain 'the phenomenal world' in its entirety with oceanic imagery as 'the brink, limbus, lapping, run-and-mingle | of two principles which meet in the scape of everything—probably Being . . . and Not-being' (*J.* 130). The 'brink' or 'limbus' indicates the function of containment which is fulfilled by the 'sea-wall' in the later journal entry on 'mechanics', and prevents the force of the 'flushness' from becoming dissipated. The 'scale of Being' metaphor which follows at this point in the 'Parmenides' notes makes explicit the consequence of the analogies for determinate being that Hopkins draws from his observations of the sea's motion, namely, a 'balance' between opposing principles. 'In watching the sea one should', Hopkins writes in a journal entry for 1872, 'be alive to the oneness which all its motion and tumult receives from its perpetual balance and falling this way and that to its level' (*J.* 225).[52] This balance is ensured by God, the 'Ground of being':

> I admire thee, master of the tides,
> Of the Yore-flood, of the year's fall;
> The recurb and the recovery of the gulf's sides,

---

[51] *Hegel's Philosophy of Nature*, 297, *Addition*, trans. Michael John Petry (London: Allen & Unwin, 1970), ii. 66.

[52] As Gerald Bruns remarks of this passage: 'what counts for Hopkins is the equilibrium of the sea's movement, not its power purely and simply but the formal intelligibility of power—the way power articulates itself through water' ('Energy and Interpretation in Hopkins', in his *Inventions: Writing, Textuality, and Understanding in Literary History* (New Haven: Yale University Press, 1982), 128).

The girth of it and the wharf of it and the wall;
Stanching, quenching ocean of a motionable mind;
Ground of being, and granite of it: past all
    Grasp God, throned behind
Death, with a sovereignty that heeds but hides, bodes but abides;
                      (No. 101, st. 32)

The two moments of Being introduced by the 'Parmenides' notes are characterized similarly in 'On Personality, Grace, and Free Will', where 'every object' is in its 'foredrawn condition' analogous to the 'neap' tide and is referred to in its 'flushness' or 'fulness' as 'the splay', an image of the unfurled state of the high tide and of the manifold scapes of an object that are revealed successively to the percipient consciousness: it is, comparable to Hegel's idea of elasticity ('cohesion displaying itself in motion'), 'the quantitative, the time-long | *display*, of the oneness of a fact' (*S.* 152, 153). Such tidal imagery is also used to describe the history of thought: 'The tide we may foresee will always run and turn between idealism and materialism' (*J.* 118), that is, between acknowledging the Idea by the respective moments of its ideal unity or the multeity of its parts, 'Being' or 'Not-being' (without, however, recognizing that it is the dialectical tension between the two that perpetuates this tidal motion, as each successively predominates and is drawn back by the resurgence of the other).

The simple 'flush and foredrawn' movement of the tides and waves can be described summarily as a 'swaying' motion. This formal principle comprehends the range of watery phenomena, drawing them together by analogy with one another, from 'the first stage' of 'the Rhone glacier' which Hopkins describes as 'like bright plucked water swaying in a pail' (*J.* 178) to the all-encompassing oceanic Being of God, 'giver of . . . | World's strand, sway of the sea' (No. 101, st. 1). As with the phenomena of the waves, where the 'flush' that impels them is at once conserved and provoked, vivified, by the containing principles of the 'limbus' and 'the sea-wall', the 'World's strand' provides the condition for the 'sway of the sea': the 'Ground of Being' provides the condition for the flux of nature. Hopkins often identifies the human body with the quality of liquidity and is, as the following account of waking from a nightmare testifies, consequently drawn to identify its being with a swaying motion: 'The feeling is terrible: the body no longer swayed as a piece by the nervous and muscular instress seems to fall in and hang like a dead weight on the chest' (*J.* 238).

Another phenomenon of liquidity that epitomizes determinate being for Hopkins is 'the burl'. The *Oxford English Dictionary* (1989) lists the word's use as a verb, 'To bubble, as a spring or fountain out of which water flows gently', and as a noun which refers to knotted strands in fabric and knots in the grain of wood.[53] Hopkins appears to abstract from these senses of the word a principle of determinate being which participates in a larger being, a unified knot-like configuration of being that is integral to the larger ocean (or fabric) of being. The configuration of the 'burl', whatever the medium it is registered in, parallels the ultimate ontological principle to which it belongs, the Parmenidean sphere of Being. Similarly, in the theological writings, the 'pomegranate' and 'sphere' imagery are used to describe the '*pomum possibilium*' of discrete instances of being, particular 'selves', each of which constitutes a ' "burl" of being' (*S.* 171, 154). The differentiated unity of the individual creature and the Creation parallel one another: the globular fleshy red seeds, representative of individual 'selves', reproduce in microcosm the form of the 'pomegranate', the ultimate principle of the '*pomum possibilium*' they compose.

Hopkins' use of the word 'burl' is most closely related to its hydrodynamic referent.[54] The concrete form of the 'burl' makes visible the dynamic principle of 'instress', 'the flush and foredrawn'. The phenomenon consists of a unity in which the 'flushness' of the water is 'foredrawn' without being artificially contained. The 'burl' is a coherent patterned form of the water which remains constant paradoxically because of the fluctive nature of its medium:[55] 'Thee, God, I come from, to thee go | All day long I like fountain flow' (No. 161). It is a

---

[53] *OED*, 2nd edn., s.v. 'Burl' sb. 1, sb. 4, and v.[2].

[54] A description of 'the greatest stack of cloud . . . I ever can recall seeing' offers a clear example of his use of the word to designate a discrete entity and convey the force and gravity of being, 'its burliness forced out everything else and loaded the eyesight' (*J.* 212).

[55] Hopkins writes for instance of 'the burly water-backs which heave after heave kept tumbling up from the broken foam and their plump heap turning open in ropes of velvet' (*J.* 200).

case of what Michel Serres calls 'homeorrhesis', a neologism 'formed from the Greek words *homos,* meaning "same," and *rhysis,* meaning "flow" '.[56] The pure and peculiar form of the water in Hopkins' image of the fountain, the 'inscape' of particular selfhood, originates in, is sustained by, and ultimately returns to, the gracious principle of Being itself. Inscape marks a particular configuration of a material medium, an instress, which has its essence only through motion: *'What I do is me'.*[57]

The energy principle provides a form that brings all physical phenomena into analogous relations to one another. The most radical and systematically understood of these phenomena, those which form the subject-matter of classical mechanics, provided the principal paradigms and idiom for this new science during the 1840s, 1850s, and 1860s. Hydrodynamic metaphors of currents and flow were endemic to the sciences of heat, electricity, and magnetism, while such phenomena were described more precisely according to the mathematized mechanics of elastic solids. This provided a universal descriptive idiom of strains, tensions, and pressures which could be applied to the entire range of physical phenomena, both terrestrial and hydrological, and were often subsumed under the generic title of 'stress'. The principle of tension by which discrete inert objects can be seen to cohere provides a suggestive (although by no means precise) parallel to the polarities of romantic science. Hopkins' restatement of the romantic principle of dynamic unity is predicated upon the principle of mechanical 'stress', which provides the fundamental term of his ontology and is elaborated in an idiom which, following from his definition of 'instress' as 'the flush and foredrawn', derives from hydrodynamics.

V

The phenomenon of the 'burl' consists of foredrawn instances of the ubiquitous media of water or air, such as 'the burl of the

[56] M. Serres, *Hermes: Literature, Science, Philosophy,* ed. Josué V. Harari and David Bell (Baltimore: Johns Hopkins University Press, 1982), 74.

[57] Cf. No. 108, ll. 8–10. Coleridge's ontological metaphor of the water eddy, which develops from his adoption of the *Naturphilosophen's* doctrine of polarities, provides an interesting parallel to Hopkins' principle of the burl that highlights

fountains of air' (No. 101, st. 16). It exemplifies the relation
of an 'instress' to universal 'stress'. An inscape is a '"burl" of
being' or instress manifest in perceptible scapes, a 'homeorrhetic' configuration of particular matter. Thus, 'Rushing
streams may be described as inscaped' (*J.* 176), and, in another
example from July 1868, the ribs of the foot of Grindelwald
glacier are seen to be 'swerved and inscaped strictly to the
motion of the mass' (*J.* 178). Or again, he writes at this time
(a matter of months after his coinage of the term 'inscape') of
the largest waterfall at Reichenbach that 'from halfway down
the whole cascade is inscaped in fretted falling vandykes in
each of which the frets or points, just like the startings of a
just-lit lucifer match, keep shooting in races, one beyond the
other, to the bottom' (*J.* 177). The scapes reveal and convey
the instress, the pattern of force in which they are held together
in an inscape. The energy of 'stress' and 'instress' is in itself an
intangible and can be discerned only as it becomes manifest in
particular 'scapes' and acts. Phenomena such as the 'burl' provide the 'scapes' of this energy in a manner that is clearly perceptible. Others require greater effort for their apprehension,
which even so may be only partially successful: 'by watching hard
the banks began to sail upstream, the scaping unfolded, the
river was all in tumult but not running, only the lateral motions
were perceived' (*J.* 200). Sometimes such phenomena, which
may be too fluctuous and fast-moving to allow their form to be
grasped clearly, become registered in a more substantive and
permanent medium. The journals testify to Hopkins' attentiveness to such phenomena, an example of which is 'the water-
runs', whereby the motion of water leaves an imprint on sand
(*J.* 205). A journal entry for September 1867 records a similar
occurrence, in which the pattern of running water is left by the
sand it has deposited: 'it had carried the sand down into the
road, throwing it *in clear expression* into [the form of] a branched
root or . . . a "treated" tree head' (*J.* 157; my emphasis).
    One of the more important qualities of liquidity that Hopkins

the formative influence upon them both of German idealism (see Edward Kessler,
Coleridge's Metaphors of Being (Princeton: Princeton University Press, 1979), ch. 1).
Gerald Bruns connects the vortex, both the physical principle and Pound's modernist idea, with Hopkins' interpretation of natural phenomena ('Energy and Interpretation', 125, 129–31).

often attributes to inscapes is a 'flowing' motion. This describes both his ontology of liquid growth and process, and the consequent facility of things to express their essential nature, to allow an understanding of it to flow to a beholder, as in the case of 'the ooze of oil | Crushed.' Such 'flow' suggests the ontological principle of coherence that the subject experiences as the 'sway' of instress, and hence the principle of the 'splay', 'the time-long | *display*, of the oneness of a fact', by which scapes and hence their organization, their inscape, are presented to the perceiver. Hopkins is accordingly able, for example, to have 'read a broad careless inscape flowing throughout [a landscape]' (*J.* 218). The word 'flowing' refers to the visible manifestation of the recondite principle of 'flushness'. The ontological 'flush' typically penetrates depths and is in its depths not immediately accessible to the senses. It describes the vitality of inscapes, their *energeia*, which gives them a clarity of definition: 'an inscape as flowing and well marked almost as the frosting on glass and slabs' (*J.* 227). While the 'inner flushness' of instress suggests a residual thing-in-itself, the 'flowing' inscape makes this essence available to human perception in the form of appearances. Like the remnants of froth which outline the form of a receding wave, 'long dribble bubble-strings which trace its set and flow' (*J.* 251), the 'flow' of spots in a painting of leopards conveys their inscape: 'Leopards shewing the flow and slow spraying of the streams of spots down from the backbone and making this flow word-in and inscape the whole animal' (*J.* 244). Similarly, another journal entry records that Hopkins:

caught that inscape in the horse that you see in the pediment especially and other basreliefs of the Parthenon . . . running on the likeness of a horse to a breaker, a wave of the sea curling over. I looked at the groin or the flank and saw how the set of the hair symmetrically flowed outwards from it to all parts of the body, so that, following that one may inscape the whole beast very simply. (*J.* 241–2)

The motion of the wind is of course in itself less visible than that of water, and Hopkins is accordingly fascinated by phenomena in which it becomes manifest, such as clouds. The journals record that on 5 July 1868 he was 'Watching from close the motion of a flag in the wind' (*J.* 169), and later bear witness to his delight in the forms they present: 'it was very

pretty to see the flags folding and rolling on the wind; the figures seemed to glide off at one end and reappear at the other'
(*J.* 249). His enthusiasm for this phenomenon is in a large
part explained by the following extract, which dates from July
1873: 'the wind ... rippled and fluttered like light linen, one
could feel the folds and braids of it—and indeed a floating
flag is like wind visible and what weeds are in a current; it gives
it thew and fires it and bloods it in' (*J.* 233). The media of
the flag and the water-weeds make the energy of the wind and
the water clearly visible: each 'fires it' just as the essential being
or stress of the creatures in the 'kingfishers' poem becomes apparent as they 'catch fire'. The revelation of patterns of stress
or energy implicit in the potentiality of the 'selves' or souls
of the '*pomum possibilium*' occurs with their embodiment. The
phrase 'bloods it in' suggests the discrete economy of the blood's
circulation in the body, which in its 'foredrawn' 'flushness' maintains life and, inasmuch as it traces a circular and surging motion, parallels the movement of eddying and burly phenomena.
It describes the recondite pattern of vital and essential motion,
the physical 'instress', of the thing. The quality of 'thew' suggests
the 'muscular instress' which it may be recalled plays a large
part in keeping 'the body ... swayed as a piece'. The tension
that belongs to the musculature is also referred to in 'Harry
Ploughman', whose various muscles, which are dwelt upon separately in the opening lines of the poem, 'Stand' in concert with
one another 'at stress' (No. 169), and in 'The Wreck of the
Deutschland' where the posture of kneeling with the head and
arms bowed forward in prayer tenses the abdominal muscles;
'the midriff astrain with leaning of, laced with fire of stress'
(No. 101, st. 2).[58]

Hopkins applies his dynamic principle of identity not only
to hydrological phenomena, but to more settled and complex
natural objects, such as trees. An example which predates the
coinage of 'inscape' offers an insight into the formation of his
principle of distinctive form in the early nature observations of
the diaries and journals. The entry for 11 July 1866 poses the
problem of the oak:

[58] This reading of the line from 'The Wreck' was suggested to me in conversation by Andrew Lynch of the Department of English, University of Western Australia.

Oaks: the organisation of this tree is difficult. Speaking generally no doubt the determining planes are concentric, a system of brief contiguous and continuous tangents, whereas those of the cedar would roughly be called horizontals and those of the beech radiating but modified by droop and by a screw-set towards jutting points. But beyond this since the normal growth of the boughs is radiating and the leaves grow some way in there is of course a system of spoke-wise clubs of green—sleeve-pieces ... (*J.* 144)

Much as he might do in beginning a drawing, Hopkins sketches 'the determining planes' which contain the form of the tree. In doing so, not only for the oak, but for the beech and the cedar also, he is seeking to identify a broad principle of specific form, which in its dynamic geometrical abstraction looks forward to the depictions of apple and other trees by the modernist painter Piet Mondrian, another deeply religious artist who is concerned, in his phrase, with the 'equilibrium of opposites'.[59]

The 'determining planes' are like the 'cleaves' of the '*pomum possibilium*' in the later notes 'On Personality, Grace and Free Will', each of which is presented through the metaphor of the pomegranate as a specific potentiality of determinate being. Aptly represented as limited to two dimensions, each 'cleave' (in the words of the 'Health and Decay' essay) 'exists and is implied in the dimension above it' (*J.* 74), that is, Being itself. The 'determining planes' of the respective trees refer to a certain scope or potentiality for the exercise and realization of specific being, a 'freedom of play', as the principle is described in the notes 'On Personality, Grace and Free Will' (*S.* 149). They represent, in other words, the familiar principle of the 'foredrawn' moment of form which defines the ambit for the vigorous principles of 'flushness', for change and variety. The form of the respective trees is not prescribed in the manner of a taxonomic class but as a broad potentiality, an 'Idea', that is realized through the course of the growth of individual specimens and the full range of their variants which comprise the concrete category of 'All things counter, original, spare, strange' (No. 121). Hopkins recognizes that the oaks 'differ much', a fact that he is evidently anxious to accommodate in

---

[59] Quoted by Robert Hughes in *The Shock of the New*, 2nd edn. (London: BBC, 1991), 203.

formulating what is referred to later as 'the law of the oak leaves' (*J.* 145, 146).

Hopkins' solution to the 'difficult' problem of the 'organisation of [the oak]' anticipates the model of form theorized in the 1868 notes. The word 'organisation' is used in the 'All words . . .' notes as a synonym for 'form' which, more specifically, 'flushes the matter' (*J.* 126). The definitive 'organisation' or 'law of the oak leaves', as it is referred to later, is conceived of as a dynamic principle of form, the 'organic articulations of the tree'. The phrase conveys the qualities of both connection amongst the parts, that is, form, and also expressiveness. Hopkins makes a similar observation of 'a budded lime against the field wall: turn, pose, and counterpoint in the twigs and buds: the *form* speaking' (*J.* 163). As in the 'kingfishers' poem, the realization of potential form occurs through definitive action that is seen to be akin to speech.[60] The form of the oak is grasped as the definitive pattern of its movement, the unfolding motion of growth which, like the glacier that also moves too slowly for the human senses to detect, is registered synchronously in its appearances. In both the passage on 'the determining planes' and the following extract on 'the law of the oak leaves', form is described in the familiar homeorrhetic pattern of the 'burl' by circular 'articulations' of matter. The fixity of 'law' is rendered here in the fluent medium of transitive verbs:[61] the particular exercise of generic potential moves along the axis of the 'determining planes':

I have now found the law of the oak leaves. It is of platter-shaped stars altogether; the leaves lie close like pages, packed, and as if drawn tightly to. But these old packs, which lie at the end of their twigs, throw out now long shoots alternately and slimly leaved, looking like bright keys. All the sprays but markedly these ones shape out and as it were embrace greater circles and the dip and toss of these make the wider and less organic articulations of the tree. (*J.* 146)

It is accordingly spring, the season of most rapid and pronounced growth, that provides the greatest opportunities for

---

[60] Cf. the discussion of the passage on the oak in Bruns, 'Energy and Interpretation', 131–3.

[61] Bruns refers in his commentary to 'the energetic language of transitive relations . . .' (ibid. 132).

grasping such form: 'End of March and beginning of April—
This is the time to study inscape in the spraying of trees, for
the swelling buds carry them to a pitch which the eye could
not else *gather*—for out of much much more, out of little not
much, out of nothing nothing: in these sprays at all events
there is a new world of inscape' (*J.* 205; my emphasis). The
transitive relations and references to circular articulations of
form found in the passages on the oak occur also in the poem
'Spring', 'When weeds, in wheels, shoot long and lovely and
lush . . .' (No. 117).[62] Once again the qualities of rapid movement, liquidity, and circular form coalesce in a manner that
suggests the figure of the 'burl'. The song of the thrush is
described in a similar vein as liquid and radiant: 'thrush |
Through the echoing timber does so rinse and wring | The
ear . . .' 'The glassy peartree leaves and blooms' in this poem
with the pressure of a fountain or burl. This description, in
which shoots of leaves and flowers push up and open out,
presents an effect similar to that of modern time-lapse photo-
graphy; a recapitulation of the tree's growth that presents its
form as fundamentally expressive and dynamic.

The principle of form exemplified by the early description
of the 'law' of the oak and other cases show that inscape is not
only inextricable from instress but seems to have developed as
a corollary of it. Instress is the universal form of determinate being, dynamic unity, which when it is embodied in perceptible matter displays certain scapes or appearances. The
articulation of such matter by instress constitutes the inscape
of the object, a particular instance of determinate being. The
parity between instress and inscape is presented early in the
'Parmenides' notes: 'I have often . . . felt the depth of an instress
or how fast the inscape holds a thing' (*J.* 127). The parallel
between the 'depth' to which instress penetrates 'a thing' and
the constraining 'hold' upon it of inscape indicates that their
relation is like that between the terms of the word in the 'All
words . . .' notes, for each presents here a respective moment of

[62] An early poem indicates the Pythagorean associations that circular articulations of energy in nature had for Hopkins: 'Let me be to Thee as the circling bird,
| Or bat with tender and air-crisping wings | That shapes in half-light his departing
rings . . .' (No. 70). For a further interpretation of these lines and of 'Spring', see
Ch. 9, Sect. II.

determinate being, 'the flush and foredrawn', that are attributed a few sentences earlier in the notes to instress alone. The
quality of 'depth' is in the 'All words . . .' notes associated with
the principle of form in art, 'the organisation' or 'the prepossession', which, like stress, 'flushes the matter': the more complex the work of art 'the deeper the form penetrates'. Depth is
an attribute of 'flushness', while the defining 'hold' of inscape
fulfils the function of the foredrawing principle. Much as with
the relation of the 'sway of the sea' to the 'World's strand', or
the 'inner flushness' of the Parmenidean ball to its 'surface', the
'depth' of instress is presupposed by the 'hold' of the inscape,
and vice versa.[63] Each of these cases reproduces the dialectic of
determinate being with which Hegel's *Science of Logic* opens.
Being or 'stress' without specific determining qualities is 'empty',
unthinkable. Nor can it exist in its essential 'flushness' or vitality if it simply spreads out equally in all directions unhindered:
the energy of stress is necessarily inextricable from a principle
which constrains and defines it, makes it finite and vigorous.

---

[63] Hence Hopkins writes in the journals of the *depth* of inscape. His observation
of 'a white shire of cloud' which 'changed beautiful changes' led him to remark
upon 'how deep the inscape in things is' (*J.* 204–5).

9 Stress, Selves, and Subjectivity

Hopkins' identification of Parmenidean monism with the physical principle of stress forms an ontology that strongly suggests
the mechanistic concept of the field that Faraday pioneered.
Instress can be represented according to the ontology of Faraday's theory as a discrete point, a knot or vortex, of energy
in the field of being, and particular stresses, such as those of
grace or the epistemological 'stem of stress' (*J.* 127), as lines
of force in this field. The field model allows Hopkins to represent being or stress not only as dynamic but also, in the manner
of Parmenidean monism, as an entirely consistent and continuous principle.

It was only in the early 1860s that Maxwell succeeded in establishing a mechanical model for an ether capable of describing
electromagnetic, thermal, and luminous phenomena and of fur-
nishing mathematical grounds for these analogies. While Faraday describes the phenomena of the field qualitatively by stresses,
strains, pressures, and tensions, Maxwell's paper 'On Physical
Lines of Force' (1861), by providing a mathematical basis for
such analogies, unifies them as instances of his generic principle
of stress. His mechanical model is developed progressively in
the four parts of his paper. The first part observes that unlike
'the most general type of a stress' (which was introduced in the
previous chapter), a given point in a line of force requires not
three but two forces to describe it: an axis of tension, which is
the consequence of the attraction exerted by the magnetic poles,
and an isotropic pressure, the resultant of equal pressures exerted at right angles to the axis, which can be resolved 'into a
simple hydrostatic pressure'.[1] The lines are manifest in a 'fluid
or mobile medium' and may, as Siegel suggests,[2] be visualized
as fine elastic tubes of liquid. '[T]he stress in the axis of a

---

[1] Maxwell, *Scientific Papers*, i. 454. [2] Siegel, 'Thomson, Maxwell', 247.

line of magnetic force is a *tension*, like that of a rope', while
the similarly even equatorial expansion that occurs when the
pressure predominates is explained with the mechanism of
'vortices or eddies' which have 'their axes in directions parallel to the lines of force'.[3] The pressure—that is, the velocity
of the vortices' rotations—represents the intensity of the field,
and the greater velocity accordingly corresponds to the effect
of the lines repelling each other, so that they tend to become
shorter.[4] The remainder of the first part of Maxwell's paper
establishes the mathematical values of stresses distributed along
the lines and consequently arrives at the conclusion that 'The
centrifugal force of these vortices produces pressures distributed in such a way that the final effect is a force identical in
direction and magnitude with that which we observe [of various electromagnetic phenomena]'.[5]

Each section of Maxwell's paper recognizes problems in the
imaginary model of the medium developed by the previous section and endeavours to solve them by further modifying it.[6] By
this means Maxwell broadens the range of phenomena that his
theory can describe mathematically. The paper has by the close
of the third part established correspondences between the equations that determine the behaviour of his elastic solid medium
and those which describe the range of electromagnetic phenomena, including electric current and electricity in its potential
form,[7] and external, electrostatic and galvanic, stresses upon
the field.[8] His model is also able to represent heat and account
for the consequent loss of usable energy through its generation.[9] Furthermore, the success of his elastic solid model in describing such phenomena leads him to compare the respective

[3] Maxwell, *Scientific Papers*, i. 455.   [4] Siegel, 'Thomson, Maxwell', 247.
[5] Maxwell, *Scientific Papers*, i. 489.
[6] E.g. the second part of the paper recognizes that the model established in the
first entails that each vortex will engender in those contiguous to it a movement
in the opposite direction. Maxwell's solution is to posit a single layer of relatively
small particles that act as 'idle wheels' (ibid. i. 468) between the vortices, which
he now specifies have a cell wall that makes them roughly spherical in shape.
[7] These phenomena are discussed in the second part of Maxwell's essay (ibid.
i. 471, 486–7) and, with the aid of a revised model, in the third section of the
paper (ibid. i. 490).
[8] Electrostatic stresses in the field result from the proximity of a charged body,
while galvanic stresses emanate from the electromotive force of a battery. See ibid.
i. 492; and Hendry, *Maxwell*, 180–2.   [9] Maxwell, *Scientific Papers*, i. 486.

numerical values which describe the elasticity of his electro-magnetic ether with that of the luminiferous media, from which he is able to infer 'that *light consists in the transverse undulations of the same medium which is the cause of electric and magnetic phenomena*'.[10]

The 'Physical Lines' paper demonstrates that mechanical stress can provide a single principle capable of representing the various active states of the medium which surrounds bodies invested with electricity, magnetism, light, and heat. This carefully developed unified model, 'published', as was noted earlier, 'in a semi-popular form', is likely to have been known to the educated reading public of the 1860s and, even as field theory was increasingly being described mathematically during this time, popular expositions of it naturally focused upon the more accessible stress analogy.[11] Indeed, as Maxwell's work highlights, the trend towards mathematical description based on analytical dynamics did not usurp the mechanistic view, but effectively presented another, formalized, development of it. Maxwell's use of this dynamical approach in his 1864 paper, 'A Dynamical Theory of the Electromagnetic Field', is especially interesting from this point of view, as it presents the general principle of stress developed in the earlier paper in the context of energy physics.

The introductory remarks to Maxwell's paper acknowledge Thomson's researches into the work values of the transmission of heat and light, which note that such radiant phenomena are conveyed through space and hence in time, not instantaneously as the action-at-a-distance hypothesis requires. Maxwell, building upon the unified theory of the 'Physical Lines' essay, observes that this time condition applies also to electromagnetic phenomena. He accordingly explains the time lapses as the consequence of the undulating movement by which such forms of energy are transmitted in the pervasive medium of the field, which is accordingly attributed with the properties of an elastic solid. Maxwell's familiar definition of stress as a summary form of Newton's third law of motion ('action and reaction between the consecutive parts of a body') is rendered in terms of energy physics:

[10] Ibid. i. 500.   [11] Campbell and Garnett, *Life of Maxwell*, 233.

The medium is therefore capable of receiving and storing up two kinds of energy, namely, the 'actual' energy depending on the motions of its parts, and 'potential' energy, consisting of the work which the medium will do in recovering from displacement in virtue of its elasticity.

The propagation of undulations consists in the continual transformation of one of these forms of energy into the other alternately, and at any instant the amount of energy in the whole medium is equally divided, so that half is energy of motion, and half is elastic resilience.[12]

While there is no direct proof that Hopkins read Maxwell's papers, they nevertheless serve to bring into clear relief the concept of a pervasive dynamic medium which was current during the 1860s and with which he was evidently familiar. The fundamental importance of this principle for Hopkins' metaphysics is apparent in part from the passages discussed in the preceding chapter, where water in particular, but also air, are seen to function as the media in which configurations of force representative of instress, such as the 'burl', become manifest. The implication here, that the medium extends throughout the spaces intervening between such configurations, is presupposed in the epistemological principle of the 'stem of stress between us and things',[13] and indeed throughout Hopkins' mature work.

II

Nature is often depicted by Hopkins in a suggestive analogy to the dynamic principle of the physical field as a plenum of activity. 'Duns Scotus's Oxford', for instance, 'Tówery city and branchy betwéen tówers', has its intervening spaces filled with energetic commotion: 'Cuckoo-echoing, bell-swarmèd, lark-charmèd, rook-racked . . .' (No. 129). Similarly in 'Spring':

[12] Maxwell, *Scientific Papers*, i. 528–9.
[13] This 'stem of stress' suggests a parallel with the lines of force which join together when two fields of force coalesce, as e.g. in the case of a pair of magnets where the south pole of one is in close proximity to the north of the other. Each of the lines of force connecting the two bodies describes an arc, a form akin to the 'bridge' which Hopkins presents as synonymous with the 'stem of stress' (*J*. 127).

...thrush
Through the echoing timber does so rinse and wring
The ear, it strikes like lightnings to hear him sing.   (No. 117)

The emphatic use of the word 'Through' at the start of the line brings forward the idea of a mediate space to be traversed. The first few words of the extract suggest that the 'thrush' itself is flying through the woods, a possibility that, while not eliminated by the lines that follow them, is effectively superseded. The thrush, like the birds and the bell described in 'Duns Scotus's Oxford', is present in the medium according to Hopkins' expressivist principle, '*What I do is me*', primarily through the distinctive sounds it produces. Much as the 'weeds, in wheels, shoot long and lovely and lush', the being of the thrush is propelled and extended through space, as its song is transmitted 'Through' the 'echoing timber' to the human ear. The arrangement of the lines is such that, following the temporal sequence of the sound travelling through space, the 'rinse and wring' of the song is associated first of all with the 'timber', and then with the ear it affects.

While the ambiguous second line of the extract from 'Spring' associates the song with the bodily form of the bird, by the time that this is resolved in the third line the suggestion of physicality has been consolidated through the identification of the medium of the air with water. The dynamic physical nature of sound is highlighted through this substantial metaphorical rendering of the acoustic medium, which serves to disclose and bring into prominence the pattern of motion effected in it by the 'rinse and wring' of the thrush's song. A similar effect of concreteness is produced by the line from the 'kingfishers' poem, 'As tumbled over rim in roundy wells | Stones ring' (No. 115), where the final word 'ring' draws together the concentric ripples of water and the analogous echoes of sound-waves which this action engenders. The pun can be traced to an early poem: 'Let me be to Thee as the circling bird, | Or bat with tender and aircrisping wings | That shapes in half-light his departing rings...' (No. 70). The 'circling' movements of the bat and bird concretely 'shape...' the centrifugal pattern of the sound-waves generated by their cries, much as the adjective 'air-crisping' does for the medium in which the sound-waves are propelled. The liquid onslaught of the skylark's song in 'The Sea and the Skylark' draws together this 'crisping' of the air and the 'crisp' of the water described in 'Margaret Clitheroe' (No. 108, ll. 9–10): 'His rash-fresh re-winded new-skeinèd score | In crisps of curl off wild winch whirl, and pour | And pelt music, till none's to spill nor spend' (No. 118).

The opposing actions of 'rinse and wring' provide a parallel to the 'echoing' movement,[14] in which sound waves instance the pattern of 'mechanical reflection' (which led Hopkins three years earlier to infer that 'all nature is mechanical'), and correspond to those of 'the flush' and the 'foredrawn'. The word 'rinse' refers to a version of the flushing motion of water, while the word 'wring' represents a contrapuntal force which is analogous in this capacity to Hopkins' 'foredrawing' principle. The tension of the song's 'rinse and wring' effect as it is communicated to the receptive ear can be understood as a *stress* in the medium. This reading is underlined by the comparison of the effect to successive strikes of 'lightnings', electrostatic discharges resulting from stresses in the air between clouds and the earth.[15] The principle of 'stress' provides the form which underlies and enables the analogy between the 'rinse and wring' movement and 'lightnings'.

The parallel between atmospheric and hydrodynamic phenomena, such as lightning and the 'rinse and wring' actions, is especially characteristic of 'The Wreck of the *Deutschland*', where the fury of the air matches that of the sea, and the one serves to describe the other, as in the reference to 'the burl of the fountains of air' (No. 101, st. 16). The blue of the ocean is met by that of the sky, the former rising to meet the latter in its tides and waves, while the sky is described correspondingly in 'Spring' as 'The descending blue . . . all in a rush . . .' (No. 117). A reference in 'The Wreck of the *Deutschland*' to the

[14] This suggests a punning reference to the way in which the 'timber' affects the *timbre* of the sound of the thrush's song as it travels from its source to the human ear.

[15] Lightning and thunder occur inseparably as the electrostatic charges between the droplets that form clouds literally 'gather to a greatness' and are discharged in the earth's atmosphere. Their expresson as these grand phenomena of light and sound naturalizes the analogy between these two modes of energy which are represented in Hopkins' poem by lightning and the thrush's song.

'beat of endragonèd seas' (No. 101, st. 27) recalls a description in the stanza immediately preceding it of the the 'Blue-beating' of the May sky.

The liquidity of the sky's blueness associates it with vigour and growth, the 'juice and . . . joy' of springtime, and more specifically with 'Mayday'. Mary's month and her emblematic colour are brought together here with her definitive function of fostering the growth of God incarnate, Christ, the type for Hopkins of all material Creation. The liquid blue sunny May sky, life-giving for organic Creation, parallels the blood that Christ derived from Mary and which he shed at the Crucifixion so that sinning mortals might receive eternal life. While Hopkins gives this ('blue') blood a biblical aristocratic provenance, tracing it from Adam to King David to Mary, it acquires its sublime character through the motion imparted to it by the Sacred Heart: '*It beat and sympathised with the feelings of his heart*' (*S.* 14). In this respect also it offers an interesting parallel to 'the jay-blue heavens . . . | Of pied and peeled May!' (No. 101, st. 26), which are described dynamically in 'Spring' as 'all in a rush'.

The May sky is, like Christ's 'blood's beating' (*S.* 14), manifest as the motion of a material medium. It is described as 'blue-beating', a phrase which can be read through Hopkins' knowledge of optics to refer to the specific rhythm of undulations in the luminiferous medium that defines this particular colour. The elastic stresses of force and resistance that characterize the blood's pulse are, as its schematic representation by the modern cardiograph draws attention to, comparable in their undulating form to light travelling through its medium. The nature of this ubiquitous medium is identified directly with Mary in the later poem, 'The Blessed Virgin compared to the Air we Breathe'.

Mary is for Hopkins the great propagator for the faith. She is presented in 'The Blessed Virgin' poem as a medium of propagation both in the bodily sense, as a mother, and in the manner of the ether in field theory. The poem allows that she 'mothers each new grace' (No. 151, l. 22) or, in the alternative analogy, that she 'transmit[s]' (l. 88) what are elsewhere described as the 'stresses' of grace. She is presented as mediating the infinite and unbearable power of the Sun, 'our daystar'

(l. 106),[16] the ultimate source of all energy in the universe which is identified here with God. The conventional gender stereotypes of amorphous female liquidity and fiery phallic power and desire are well represented in the elemental myth presented by Hopkins' poem: the airy medium of Mary, the sky which intervenes between heaven and earth, is described as 'This bath of blue' which 'slake[s] | His [i.e. God's] fire' (ll. 95–6). While Mary is identified with a dynamic physical medium that actively propagates stresses ('Wild air, world-mothering air' (l. 1)), rather than with a passive receptivity, she is nevertheless represented as a soft feminine principle whose definitive function is to be penetrated:

> ... [she] who
> This one work has to do—
> Let all God's glory through,
> God's glory which would go
> Through her and from her flow
> Off, and no way but so.   (No. 151, ll. 28–33)

Mary is presented as a familiar liquid and flowing female principle but with an important difference. She has the distinction of being literally immaculate, 'the one woman without stain' (No. 101, st. 30): she 'will not | stain light' (ll. 80–1). Neither menstruation, nor indeed any messy physicality, are necessary conditions for the possibility of reproduction here. Indeed it is precisely their lack that facilitates the generation of the ever-living and redeeming Christ. The sexuality of Mary is literally and figuratively *etherealized* by Hopkins' description of her as a physical medium.

The expanse of air that mediates heaven and earth, the sky which bears the emblematic blueness of the divine mediatrix, 'will transmit | Perfect, not alter' (ll. 88–9) the definitive wave frequencies of light that spectroscopy had recently numbered as a multiple of the traditional seven colours of the spectrum, 'The seven or seven times seven | Hued sunbeam' (ll. 87–8). While the medium does not affect the essential nature of the sun's light it does soften it and so suit it to human sight.[17]

---

[16] See 2 Pet. 1: 19.

[17] The sky, the 'one breath' of Mary, 'wild web, wondrous robe, | Mantles the guilty globe' (ll. 38–9). Cf. 'the air things wear' in No. 119, and the image at the

It allows the nature of the deity, the infinite divine light and searing fire of the Old Testament God, to be appreciated through the finite means available to human perception:

> So God was God of old:
> A mother came to mould
> Those limbs like ours which are
> What must make our daystar
> Much dearer to mankind;
> Whose glory bare would blind
> Or less would win man's mind.
> Through her we may see him
> Made sweeter, not made dim,
> And her hand leaves his light
> Sifted to suit our sight.　(ll. 103–13)

The poem recognizes that sunlight is not only transmitted through the air directly, but also, as Gillian Beer notes, by reflection. Professor Beer recognizes the importance to the poem of Tyndall's observation, first presented in 1870, that the blue colour of the sky results from the reflection of sunlight by myriad particles suspended in the air.[18]

III

'The Blessed Virgin compared to the Air we Breathe' brings to the fore Hopkins' categories of mediated and unmediated 'stresses'. The latter class is represented by the direct glare of the sun and of lightning; the former, by sunlight softened by reflection in water and from innumerable specks of dust suspended in the air. One of the most interesting and important cases of the indirect transmission of sunlight that Hopkins discusses is its reflection by particular creatures:

close of 'God's Grandeur', in which 'the Holy Ghost over the bent | World broods...' (No. 111).

[18] G. Beer, 'Helmholtz, Tyndall, Gerard Manley Hopkins: Leaps of the Prepared Imagination', in *Comparative Criticism*, 13 (Cambridge: Cambridge University Press, 1991), 117–45. The reference in the poem to God's 'light | Sifted to suit our sight' recalls a phrase from Tyndall's paper 'On the Scientific Use of the Imagination' (1870) that Gillian Beer cites in her essay, 'Pure unsifted solar light is white' (p. 134).

As kingfishers catch fire, dragonflies draw flame;
  As tumbled over rim in roundy wells
    Stones ring; like each tucked string tells, each hung bell's
Bow swung finds tongue to fling out broad its name;
Each mortal thing does one thing and the same:
  Deals out that being indoors each one dwells;
  Selves—goes itself; *myself* it speaks and spells,
Crying *What I do is me: for that I came.* (No. 115)

The phenomena of sound, with which those of light are paralleled here and which like them can be described as stresses
in their respective media,[19] provide the primary context for
understanding the first line of 'As kingfishers catch fire'. These
phenomena are each characterized by mechanical causation,[20]
the principle by which Kant describes the view of nature that
arose with Newtonian physics. Unlike human beings who, by
being possessed of free will, can act independently, external
nature consists (according to Kant's rather Humean construal
of Newton) of a series of invariable relations, which the modern scientific tradition has charted as its laws. The consequences
which follow from the bell having been rung, the stone tumbling into the well, and the plucking of a stringed instrument
can all be described by Newtonian acoustics. The lawful nature
of each of these phenomena is underlined by their being presented generically in the poem.

The physical phenomena of the octave of 'As kingfishers
catch fire' serve as analogies for 'Each mortal thing'. This parity
reflects the new perception of the relation between inorganic
and organic nature that emerged through the establishment of
the new sciences of biology and organic chemistry in the first
half of the nineteenth century. During this period the idea of
a mysterious 'vital force' which distinguishes living from non-
living things gradually fell out of favour as chemists discovered
that organic processes could be reduced to the interaction of

[19] Thomas Young proposes and defends the analogy between sound and light
in his 'Outlines of Experiments and Inquiries Respecting Sound and Light' (1800).
Gillian Beer ('Leaps of Imagination') provides a fine discussion of the later development of this analogy as it relates to Hopkins' work.
[20] Cf. Green: '[A]ll the lower animal's acts are done . . . mechanically' (Merton,
Bradley Papers, MS Notebook I-A1, Lect. XII.

inorganic chemical elements.[21] Another important factor which promoted this mechanistic view of organic nature was Darwin's principle of natural selection, according to which competition for the material requirements of life determines the preservation not only of certain physical characteristics but also of particular patterns of behaviour. Organic nature is regarded in this theory as a series of invariable chains of cause and effect which are engendered by the imperative for species survival. An instance of such mechanical causality is provided by the brilliant image with which Hopkins' poem begins: 'As kingfishers catch fire, dragonflies draw flame'. Each creature behaves instinctively: the kingfisher in hunting for its food, the dragonfly by moving reflexively to avoid its predator.

Hopkins' principle of law here is very rich and inclusive. The opening image of the poem is both a Darwinian tableau and, as it is commonly explained by Hopkins' commentators, a celebration of distinctive form or 'inscape'.[22] It presents an instance of the epiphanic flashing forth of definitive being, the pre-eminent example of which is found in 'The Windhover'. The bright flashes of colour produced by the play of sunlight on the kingfishers and the dragonflies highlights their distinctive appearances. But how can such a momentary impression, however strong, be said to be ontologically definitive?

It is clear from the rest of the poem that the flashes of 'fire' in the first line are not mere fleeting impressions but are in fact meant to be revelations of essence akin to the direct expression of purpose and identity made, for example, by the sound of a bell. This can be understood more fully by turning to a passage from 'The Probable Future of Metaphysics', where musical notes, the like of which are instanced in the poem by the bell, the stone's 'ring', and 'each tucked string', provide a metaphor for the essentialism which the 'new Realism' will assert against the current Darwinian 'philosophy of flux':

---

[21] In 1828, urea became the first organic substance to be synthesized in the laboratory.

[22] See e.g. Paul Mariani, *A Commentary on the Complete Poems of Gerard Manley Hopkins* (Ithaca, NY: Cornell University Press, 1970), 179; MacKenzie, *Reader's Guide*, 148–9; Jerome Bump, *Gerard Manley Hopkins* (Boston: Twayne Publishers, 1982), 143.

To the prevalent philosophy and science nature is a string all the differences in which are really chromatic . . . The new Realism will maintain that in musical strings the roots of chords, to use technical wording, are mathematically fixed and give a standard by which to fix all the notes of the appropriate scale . . . It may be maintainable then that species are fixed and to be fixed only at definite distances in the string and that the developing principle will only act when the precise conditions are fulfilled. To ascertain these distances and to point out how they are to be mathematically or *quasi*-mathematically expressed will be one work of this metaphysic.

(*J.* 120)

The first line of the 'kingfishers' sonnet invokes not only the essentialist law of fixed species but also the Darwinian law of self-preservation, which is connected through the principle of natural selection to the evolutionary philosophy 'of species having no absolute types' (*J.* 120). However, just as in the essay this 'developing principle' is not objected to provided it is subordinated to the essentialism of the 'new Realism', so the poem acknowledges the Darwinian struggle for survival whilst insisting that this is not the ultimate truth of nature. Hopkins is, as the early poem 'I must hunt down the prize' indicates, willing to meet what he perceives to be the enemy on its own territory. The opening line of the 'kingfishers' poem fights Heraclitean fire with 'fire'. This involves a strategy of confronting one momentous discovery in contemporary science, Darwinian biology, with another, spectroscopy.

In the first stanza's only direct reference to specific creatures their distinctiveness is not identified with sound, as in the examples drawn from inorganic nature, but with light. The principle by which the kingfishers' 'fire' and the dragonflies' 'flame' are definitive for their respective natures depends upon the new understanding of light that occurred with the establishment of spectroscopy in the late 1850s. The fundamental principle of spectroscopy consists in the fact that the light produced by each particular chemical element, either through reflection or as a direct consequence of the material's heat, has a definitive wavelength which registers at a particular point of the spectrum. It is precisely this phenomenon of reflected sunlight that yields the essence of the creatures in the first line of the 'kingfishers' poem.[23] The octave maintains that just as distinctive sounds, the fixed notes of the musical chord, mark and express the identity of such things as bells and stringed instruments,[24] so, it is implied, each degree of the spectrum marks a fixed register of being. The principle of specific identity which Hopkins develops from spectroscopy fuses empirical perception with essentialism (the 'concrete' and the 'abstract' moments of 'the Idea') and so counters atomistic positivism and the relativistic 'philosophy of flux' which developed from Darwinian biology. The poem illustrates the way in which each ontological stress is transmitted through Mary's medium of air as a literal 'stem of stress between us and things'. The energy of the external world is, as the 'All words . . .' notes suggest, convertible to the empirical 'image' in the mind, 'a refined energy accenting the nerves', and then through the mind's 'two kinds of energy' into the fully realized 'idea in the mind' itself (*J.* 125).[25]

'The world is', for Hopkins, 'charged with the grandeur of God' (No. 111). His description of the 'Charged, steepèd sky' (No. 151, l. 80) brings out the implication of 'God's Grandeur' that the medium into which this grandeur 'will flame out' is dynamic, a repository of potential energy akin to that described by Maxwell in his 1864 paper on 'the Electromagnetic Field'. The metallic glints of the kingfishers' distinctive blue plumage and the dragonflies' sheen are particular cases in which this charge is actualized, 'flame[s] out, like shining from shook foil'. One of Hopkins' letters to Bridges specifies that he meant this image to refer to lightning: 'Shaken gold-foil gives off broad glares like sheet lightning and also, and this is true of nothing else, owing to its zigzag dints and creasings and network of small many cornered facets, a sort of fork lightning too'.[26] The effect of these expressive discharges of 'fire' and 'flame' is to deliver to the beholder an instance of 'the grand-

[23] Gillian Beer observes 'that out of the white solar rays kingfishers catch fire and shining comes from shook foil' ('Leaps of Imagination', 127).

[24] For an enlightening discussion of the influence of Helmholtz's acoustical theory on Hopkins, see ibid. 119–21.

[25] On Hopkins' conception of the mind's energy, see Gerald Bruns' fine essay, 'Energy and Interpretation in Hopkins', *Inventions: Writing, Textuality, and Understanding in Literary History* (New Haven: Yale University Press, 1982), 125–42.

[26] 4 Jan. 1883, Letter 97, *To Bridges*, 169.

eur of God'. The 'shining from shook foil', like the 'ooze of oil', bears a direct relation to the 'greatness', 'the grandeur[,] of God'. It is a modest representation of the ultimate divine stress of lightning. In both cases the image of lightning, an immense electrostatic charge connecting the earth and the heavens, represents the dialectical synthesis of these domains, the realms of the infinite and the finite, the universal and the concrete.[27]

The analogous phenomena of the direct flash of lightning and the light reflected from the foil represent the unmediated and mediated types of the 'stem of stress' that Hopkins identifies respectively with God the Father and Christ. According to the Gospels, stars announced the coming of Christ, while at the Crucifixion the Father caused storms to issue from the heavens.[28] Hence, it is 'Not out of his bliss' that lightning, the 'stress that . . . storms deliver', 'Springs'. In stark contrast to this 'stress', the tender 'stroke' of Christ's love is represented by soft starlight, 'heart's light' (No. 101, st. 30):

> Not out of his bliss
> Springs the stress felt
> Nor first from heaven (and few know this)
> Swings the stroke dealt—
> Stroke and a stress that stars and storms deliver,
> That guilt is hushed by, hearts are flushed by and melt—
> But it rídes tíme like rídíng a ríver
> (And here the faithful waver, the faithless fable and miss).
>
> (No. 101, st. 6)

The fearsome infinite power of God, expressed directly in the 'electrical-horror' (st. 27) of lightning, is mediated here by the finite human form of Christ. The Son here is identified with stars, the little suns which we distinguish from the Sun, 'our daystar | . . . | Whose glory bare would', in its lightning-like intensity, 'blind' us (No. 151, ll. 106–8).

The soft light emitted by the stars provides a 'figure shewing

---

[27] The association with electrostatics is strengthened by Hugh Pendexter's thesis that Hopkins' image derives from the electroscope, in which two pieces of gold foil move apart in response to the slightest electrostatic charges ('Hopkins' "God's Grandeur"', *The Explicator*, 23/1 (Sept. 1964), item 2).

[28] Matt. 2: 2–10; Matt. 27: 51.

how the Idea can be one though it exists in many' which parallels that of 'the sun in broken water, where the sun's face being once crossed by the ripples each one carries an image down with it as its own sun' (D. XII 3, fos. 2–3). The image from the 'Notes' suggests the relation of God, the one, to those made in his image, human beings, a pattern that corresponds to the relation of the singular 'stroke' of Christ's grace to the multitude of 'stars', the little suns, with which it is identified in stanza 6 of 'The Wreck of the *Deutschland*'. A further understanding of this relation is available from stanza 5 of the poem:

> I kiss my hand
> To the stars, lovely-asunder
> Starlight, wafting him out of it . . .

The curious phrase 'lovely-asunder | Starlight' draws attention to the unity that the manifold 'stars' have through their mingled light, whilst at the same time identifying their separateness, indeed the distinctiveness of their light, with their loveliness. This insistence upon both distinctive individuation and monism, the concrete and the universal, is familiar from the theory of the 'Idea' developed in the 'Notes on the History of Greek Philosophy', where these two moments comprise a dialectical unity. Hopkins' knowledge of spectroscopy allows him to find in starlight an exemplar for his ontology, for it is only with the establishment of this science that precise distinctions between the quality of the light emitted, and hence, as he observes in 'The Tests of a Progressive Science', 'the chemical composition of non-terrestrial masses [such as stars, are] made out' (D. IX 2, fo. 3). The various registers of light from the stars are 'asunder' in the manner of the reflections of 'the sun in broken water'; 'held away by their conditions' (D. XII 3, fo. 3), that is, as a consequence of their chemical constitution.

The fifth stanza of 'The Wreck of the *Deutschland*' shares the concern of spectroscopy with the *emission* of light and clearly draws upon this science: 'Starlight, wafting him out of it . . .' Christ is to Hopkins the paradigm for the revelation of God through Creation. The peculiar light emissions of each of the stars suggest particular registers of the spectrum of being, such as those of the 'fire' of the kingfishers and the 'flame' of the dragonflies, which all combine in the principle of ultimate Being, the white light of God.[29] Stars, like the 'broken water' in the 1868 notes, reflect and so soften the direct light of 'our daystar | . . . | Whose glory bare would blind' (No. 151, ll. 106–8). The 'grandeur of God', parallel to the reflected light of the stars, 'will flame out' from particular instances of the Creation in a modest form that makes it accessible to the finite powers of human perception and understanding. This category of reflected stresses can be understood in terms of the schema presented by the 'Heraclitean Fire' sonnet (No. 174) as at once parts of the Heraclitean fire of phenomena and glints of light from the many-faceted diamond of ultimate Being.

IV

Hopkins writes in his journal entry on the action of waves striking a sea-wall that 'mechanical reflection . . . is the same as optical' (*J.* 252). This identification is presupposed in his use of the reflection of light to illustrate the mechanical causation which determines the behaviour of the creatures in the octave of 'As kingfishers catch fire'. Such imagery also appears to be used in the sestet of the poem. The image of 'Christ play[ing] in ten thousand places' recalls the thematic imagery of the play of light instanced in the first line of the poem and suggests that Christ's play is akin to the reflected sunlight on 'broken water'. Such play, however, does not occur *on* its matter, that is, by reflection, but 'in' and 'through' its matter, in the manner of such light emissions as the 'lovely-asunder starlight'. Whereas the ultimate ontological principle of the sun plays on the creatures in the first stanza, God, 'our daystar', 'plays in' human creatures, an integral and radiant part of their substance:

[29] The epistemological reflex of this, the 'stem of stress' viewed from the subject's perspective, is that the starting point of knowledge for the good person is being itself, the potentiality of white light, which is delimited through the principle of relation, so that a particular pitch of being is discriminated within the ultimate field of being.

Í say more: the just man justices;
  Keeps gráce: thát keeps all his goings graces;
Ácts in God's eye what in God's eye he is—
  Chríst. For Christ plays in ten thousand places,
Lovely in limbs, and lovely in eyes not his
  To the Father through the features of men's faces.

'[T]he just man' is presented in the poem as Christ-like, a little Son. Radiant in his individual physical being, his 'limbs' and 'eyes', he is one of the 'ten thousand places' in which 'Christ plays', like the light of each little sun; 'lovely-asunder | Starlight, wafting him out of it . . .'. The word 'plays', which is central to both the sestet's form and its content, is itself supremely playful in its punning ambiguities. It suggests both the play of light and of children, of suns and sons.

The peculiar nature of Christ, the type for the 'just man', is beautifully formulated in the poem on 'The Blessed Virgin' as 'God's infinity | Dwindled to infancy' (No. 151, ll. 18–19). The traditional metaphor of the patriarchal God is supplemented and renovated in Hopkins' imagery of the deity as a tender parent, 'Father and fondler of heart thou hast wrung' (No. 101, st. 9). Conversely the individual human being, the poet-persona of 'The Wreck of the *Deutschland*', is like the Son in the poem on 'The Blessed Virgin', identified with infancy. He is introduced as having all the vulnerability of the baby, indeed as being akin to Lacan's pre-mirror-stage infant, 'almost unmade' (st. 1). The close of the first stanza signals the resolution to this crisis through the mutual recognition of parent and child, as the child, in a definitive infantile reflex, grasps the finger that touches it: '. . . dost thou touch me afresh? | Over agáin I feel thy finger and find thee.' This reciprocal identification occurs in the play of limbs and eyes in the sestet of the 'kingfishers' poem.

'[T]hings truly exist only in their fullest organisation and highest development, not in their lowest, as the type is to be found in the full-grown man and not in the baby . . .' (D. X 4, fo. 18). While the play of Christ and 'the just man' is child-like in its exuberance and joy, its main substance and meaning emerges from a more sophisticated conception of play. In contrast to the expressive (but nevertheless mechanistic) behaviour of the rest of nature, the meaning of which exists purely in objective acts, the significance of human actions is traced in the 'kingfishers' poem to the interior life of the subject. So, while the octave makes the generalization that 'Each mortal thing . . . | Selves—goes itself' the sestet of the poem finds it necessary to 'say more' in order to account for the distinctive nature of the human moral agent.

The personal pronoun with which the sestet opens announces its thematic concern with the human subject, and, furthermore, presents the metaphysical sense of the 'I' as the subject of self-consciousness. The persona of this stanza, in marked contrast to the objects specified in the octave, introduces himself (and his kind) with a phrase that exemplifies a distinctive capacity for self-consciousness, an ability to reflect upon our individual actions and intentions: 'I say more: . . .'. The main significance of this phrase is as a declarative gesture. The colon after the phrase marks all that follows it as deliberately and self-consciously uttered, that is, as *instressed* by the persona of the poem.[30]

The opening declaration 'I say more' gives added emphasis to the statement which follows it and which provides the text for the remainder of the sestet: 'the just man justices'. The Aristotelian moral ontology is introduced as something of a tautology. The stance of the persona in relation to Aristotelian doctrine here can be read as self-conscious in its *play* on the principle of the virtuous character, the formation of which according to Aristotle results from the habitual performance of good acts and so appears to presuppose the character it is meant to produce. Of course Aristotle argues that parental and other social influences are crucial in establishing such important habits and so forming the virtuous character, whereas for Hopkins divine grace, the principle of Christ,[31] is the decisive factor. Nevertheless, the conundrum of the Aristotelian moral entelechy remains, teasing and teased out in the stanza.

The word 'plays' is at the heart of the sestet, occurring in the middle of the section which follows from and comments upon the statement of its text in the first line. It is the pivotal point of the stanza, around which revolves Hopkins' playful reworking of Aristotle's circular argument: the 'just man' is truly

---

[30] See Ch. 10, Sect. IV.
[31] Christ is described by Hopkins as the 'the first Paraclete' (*S.* 72).

himself only when he is play-acting the role of another, 'Acts in God's eye what in God's eye he is— | Christ',[32] whilst conversely 'Christ plays' the fleshly costume drama of 'the just man', 'Lovely in limbs, and lovely in eyes not his . . .' The words 'play' and 'act' are themselves used in a playfully ambiguous manner which develops and further specifies ('say[s] more' about) the Aristotelian doctrine introduced in the octave. The theatrical metaphor of play-acting attributes the actions of 'the just man' and of Christ with a self-consciousness that is entirely lacking in the involuntary acts described in the octave and by the metaphor of the play of light it invokes.

The collapse of the binary opposition of superficies and depth, of appearance and essence, consequent upon the spectroscopic understanding of light emissions alluded to in the first stanza, is presented ironically by the theatrical metaphor of the second, where 'the just man' and 'Christ' are presented as dwelling within one another. While 'God's eye' is able to directly perceive Christ within the just man, the teasing effect for the reader of trying to concretely imagine the main image of the sestet, in which the just man and Christ each apparently assumes the guise of the other, is analogous to our oscillating perceptions of such optical illusions as the quatrefoil/Maltese cross figure in the undergraduate essay on 'Causation'. The physical and the spiritual are in this way depicted as deeply interfused, as modes of the one principle. The poem playfully restates Hopkins' early anti-Manichaean dictum that 'the activities of the spirit are conveyed in those of the body as scent is conveyed in spirits of wine, remaining still inexplicably distinct' (*J.* 118).

While the dynamic of play presented by the octave is physical and mechanical, that of the sestet is, as befits Hopkins' theory of the human mind, self-conscious and ironic, playing upon the ontological ambiguity generated by the identifications with one another of Christ and 'the just man'. Human beings, according to Hopkins, enjoy a freedom of play in choosing their definitive activities. Whereas the Aristotelian ontological law that 'Each mortal thing does one thing and the same' restricts most

---

[32] The word 'Acts' here itself plays on the Scholastic principle of *actus* and the theatrical sense of the word, which anticipates the use of the word 'plays' in the subsequent line.

creatures to a rigidly defined and involuntary self-expression, the imperative moral law that Hopkins sees to define human nature is necessarily embedded in free and self-conscious mind. It is in these terms that Hopkins effectively uses Kantian moral psychology to supplement and modify Aristotelian ontology.

Another metaphor of 'play' used in the 1881 notes 'On Personality, Grace and Free Will' offers further clarification of Hopkins' later thought on moral freedom. The metaphor, like the light imagery of the octave of 'As kingfishers catch fire', is drawn from the phenomena of the physical field:

> The will is surrounded by the objects of desire as the needle by the points of the compass. It has play then in two dimensions. This is to say | it is drawn by affection towards any one, A, and this freely, and it can change its direction towards any other, as free, B, which implies the moving through an arc. It has in fact, more or less, in its affections a tendency or magnetism towards every object and the *arbitrium*, the elective will, decides which: this is the needle proper. (S. 157)

The notes distinguish between two kinds of will. The 'affective' will, which the individual possesses as a prevenient grace, is necessarily drawn to the good. As such it 'is really no freer than the understanding or the imagination'. It is the complement-ary 'elective' will or '*arbitrium*' that embodies the principle of free will, a potentiality which only 'comes into play with free-dom of field or choice of alternatives, all of which must have, though in different degrees, the quality of good' (S. 152). The stress of attraction between the affective will and its objects is comparable to magnetism, or (though it is not stated expli-citly here) to gravitation, the power by which all objects attract one another. The strongest force of attraction, which is for Hopkins distributed in all moral objects and the physical objects of nature, is of course the incarnate principle of Christ, to whom he refers in a sermon of 1879 as exerting 'a magnetic spell' (S. 23) and who is implicitly identified in the above extract with the polar magnetic forces.[33]

The affective will is the part of created nature that corres-ponds entirely to 'the law of nature, God's general will' (S. 24).

---

[33] Cf. the poem that Hopkins' father wrote on 'The Magnet', which develops the metaphor of Christ as the 'lode-stone of our race' (Manley Hopkins, *Spicilegium Poeticum* (London: The Leadenhall Press, [1892], 170–1).

The personal or elective will which chooses from amongst the range of morally acceptable objects is thus the decisive factor, 'this is the needle proper'. Whilst the balance of the needle on its pivot, a consequence of gravity, gives it a poise in relation to all points on the compass and the freedom to move 'in two dimensions', the innate properties of its substance, iron, compel its alignment with the polar magnetic forces, the vast electromagnetic field that envelops the earth in an analogous manner to the medium of the air, the 'wondrous robe' of Mary's grace discussed in 'The Blessed Virgin compared to the Air we Breathe'. The affective 'freedom of field', through which the elective will ranges and comes to settle, parallels the electro-magnetic or gravitational fields of force, the media in which the iron compass needle exists and acts.

The metaphor of the compass needle is used of the child in 'The Handsome Heart': 'With the sweetest air that said, still plied and pressed, | He swung to his first poised purport of reply' (No. 134b). This poise or 'fine function' of the 'Heart' is presented as the natural expression of the child's moral being, which is described as both 'wild and self-instressed' (No. 134a, variant),[34] a nature that is at once free and self-disciplined, and accordingly presupposes self-consciousness. The phrase renders the familiar ontological formula of the 'flush and foredrawn' into personal moral terms which have a further parallel in the respective principles of the affective and elective wills. The qualities of flushness and of wildness denote a freedom of play comparable to that of the affective will, whilst the 'foredrawn' and 'self-instressed' qualities, like the self-conscious determinations of the elective will, represent principles of law and unity. The ontological unity of the 'flush', the many, and the 'foredrawn', the one, by which Hopkins characterizes all instances of determinate being, parallels the distinctive coincidence in specifically human being of freedom, the capacity by which manifold possibilities are available to us, and the imperative moral law of our nature, which becomes manifest in the particular choices by which we exercise and realize this potential

---

[34] See MacKenzie (ed.), *Poetical Works*, 408. It is only with this edition that these lines are not presented as the definitive version. See W. H. Gardner and N. H. MacKenzie (eds.), *The Poems of Gerard Manley Hopkins*, 4th edn. (Oxford: Oxford University Press, 1970), No. 47.

freedom. Our 'wild' free-willed nature is in this way brought to self-consciousness, 'self-instressed'. The possibilities of the affective will are actualized through the decisive elective will.[35] The Kantian Categorical Imperative, which is commended in 'The Autonomy of the Will' for facilitating the coalescence of freedom and law (D. X 4, fos. 20–1),[36] provides the premiss for Hopkins' abiding theory of human subjectivity.

Hopkins' conception of the moral will as 'self-instressed', which is enacted by the persona's self-conscious statement of it throughout the sestet of the 'kingfishers' poem ('I say more: the just man justices . . .'), suggests the principle of reflexive self-consciousness established in 'The Origin of Our Moral Ideas', the a priori imperative for unity according to which 'the ideal, the one, is our only means of recognising success-fully our being to ourselves' (*J.* 83). The 1881 notes consolid-ate this doctrine:

How this freedom arises need not be treated here; but briefly it con-sists in this, that self can in every object it has see another self, per-sonal or not, and taking the whole object not in its fulness and 'splay' but in this 'neap' and foredrawn condition can treat any one thing how great or small soever as equal to any other thing how small or great soever. (*S.* 152)

The subject's identification of an 'object' as another 'self' enlists the mental functions of understanding and imagination to the service of the moral sense. It is reminiscent of the Hegelian principle of reflexive self-consciousness, which was available to Hopkins as an undergraduate through, amongst others, T. H. Green, whose early essay on Aristotle discusses the Hegelian principle by which 'the object of the philosopher's contem-plation were the world as a manifestation of spirit, and thus "another himself"'.[37]

---

[35] The 'foredrawn' quality of the elective will is formulated in 'On the Portrait of Two Beautiful Young People': 'Man lives that list, that leaning in the will | No wisdom can forecast by gauge or guess, | The selfless self of self, most strange, most still, | Fast furled and all foredrawn to No or Yes' (No. 168a, ll. 25–8).

[36] Hopkins is similarly attracted to the thought of 'Duns Scotus, who shews that freedom is compatible with necessity' (4 Jan. 1883, Letter 97, *To Bridges,* 169).

[37] Green, *Works,* iii. 90. Cf. John Grote: 'The perception, in its completeness, of an existing object of knowledge, is really a sympathy with its constitution, arising from the fact that we know *ourselves* more or less as constituted beings, and that

The moral 'object' is, like the form instanced by the 'conception' in 'The Origin of Our Moral ideas' (and indeed the 'conception' of the 'All words . . .' notes), specified as a unity. This form is what is meant by the moral 'object' being 'another self', for a 'self' is fundamentally 'foredrawn' being (S. 153).[38] Just as the gravitational pull of the moon draws the tide to its lowest point, its *neap*, so the activity of the perceiving mind actively 'foredraw[s]' the 'whole object' into a tight and necessary unity.

The subject is, according to Hopkins, free to adopt whatever attitude it wishes towards that which it identifies as another 'self'. Hopkins theorizes the case of an individual's hatred of Christianity as a rejection of an objective 'self': 'it is the attitude of mind freely taken by the man's self towards that other (so to call it) self (for bodies, principles, and so on have a oneness and a self either real and natural or else logical)' (S. 153).[39] Christianity is rejected in this case as 'other' to the subject's self. Alternatively, the subject may freely embrace another, morally good, 'self'. The subject's choice of such an object occurs accordingly as an identification with it, that is, as a recognition and hence partial realization of an aspect of its own content, its potentiality. The subject becomes conscious of this content in the Hegelian manner, by returning to the self *through* the 'other . . . self'.

This process of reflexive self-consciousness marks a particular type of '*energeia*' or (in Grant's translation) 'consciousness' of a potential self. It is, in Hopkins' distinctive term, an *instressing* of self, which may be either the recognition of a previously unacknowledged content to the self (as occurs in Hegel's developmental narrative of *Geist*), or the renewal of this recognition, a reaffirmation of an established self similar to that which occurs as the Aristotelian virtuous character acts virtuously, 'the just man justices'. The 'self' chosen by 'the just man' is, as 'God's

we can make or constitute things ourselves for purposes for which we need them. We recognise therefore in the objects, mind kindred to our own' (*Exploratio Philosophica*: *Part I*, 116).

[38] This use of the word 'self' (*Selbst*) is also found in Hegel. See e.g. *Phenomenology of Spirit*, sect. 758, part of which is cited and discussed in Ch. 10, Sect. I.

[39] Other specific objects mentioned in the essay include 'the Catholic Church, [and] a political principle' (S. 152).

eye' recognizes, Christ. Ultimately it is 'God's eyes alone' (S. 154) that can see into the human character and its potential, and through grace help it to realize its moral 'aspiration'.

The case of the morally unregenerate consciousness, such as the sinner who chooses the idea of sin as an objective 'self' (S. 153), highlights the necessity of God's intervention through grace: 'For apart from grace who supposes that, without some accession of knowledge or self interest, a heathen will arbitrarily change from disliking to liking the Christian religion?' (S. 152). Hopkins provides an account of the way in which grace affects individual psychology later in the notes, where he uses the analogy of the pomegranate to describe the full potentiality of a person's moral being. 'God's eyes alone' can see into this character, and the deity is able to 'choose countless points in the strain (or countless cleaves of the "burl") where the creature has consented, does consent, to God's will'. It is by bringing such potentialities to the individual's consciousness, presenting it with a possible 'self' which it may care to realize, that God's grace acts to change his creature's mind: 'It is into that possible world that God for the moment moves his creature out of this one [i.e. its 'actual pitch' of consent at the particular moment] or it is from that possible world that he brings his creature into this, *shewing it to itself* gracious and consenting' (S. 154, my emphases).

Grace is, as this bringing to consciousness, *instressing*, of a latent aspect of moral character indicates, equivalent to 'divine stress'. The individual moral agent, like the compass needle in Hopkins' analogy, is subject to stresses propagated within the field and, as a free consciousness, is able to affirm such stresses both by instressing them, so that the substance of the self conducts and focuses them much as the iron needle does electromagnetic stresses, and by generating its own stresses and counter-stresses in response to these stimuli. '[C]orrespondence', the reciprocity of reflexive self-consciousness, is according to the notes 'a grace and even the grace of graces'. However, while this is true of 'the momentary and constrained correspondence' in which God intervenes directly to momentarily 'shift' us 'to a better, a gracious self', 'the continued and unconstrained correspondence' by which the free individual will sustains this pitch 'is a [still] greater . . . grace' (S. 154). This is the manner in which 'the just man' of the 'kingfishers' poem 'Keeps grace . . .' (No. 115).

V

The human subject is for Hopkins an open system. Its motion and being depend, as the compass analogy serves to illustrate, upon interactions with extrinsic forces of grace or stress. The first stanza of 'The Wreck of the *Deutschland*' introduces the self as it is in itself, autonomous of the fields of force which help to sustain its being. It is in this original state radically unstable:

> Lord of living and dead;
> Thou hast bóund bónes and véins in me, fástened me flésh,
> And áfter it álmost únmade, what with dréad,
> Thy doing: and dost thou touch me afresh?
> Óver agáin I féel thy fínger and fínd thée.   (No. 101, st. 1)

According to Catholic doctrine the privation of original justice due to the Fall means that grace, although necessary to human life and to the realization of God's purpose for it, is a gift not an entitlement. The threat of dissolution, of being 'unmade', is presented here as immediate and persistent, a consequence of a selfhood predicated upon the oppositional dynamics of spirit and matter, and of created nature and original sin.

The problem of organic unity, which preoccupies so much of Hopkins' philosophical speculations, is presented in the extract above as fundamental to human physical existence. That the corporeal manifold of 'bones and veins' and 'flesh' need to be brought together with such force, 'bound' and 'fastened', is an index of the resistance that such matter presents to being 'foredrawn'. 'Spelt from Sibyl's Leaves' highlights the way in which earthly being inevitably reverts to type; the 'being' which has been 'bound' becomes 'unbound' again (No. 167, l. 5). This process is identified in the extract from 'The Wreck of the *Deutschland*' with the advent of self-consciousness, which registers as a feeling of 'dread' that threatens the force or stress of being which originally informed the body, so that it becomes 'almost unmade'. Human self-consciousness is depicted here as consciousness of original sin. It is for this reason that the consciousness which supervenes upon the creation of the body is suffused with 'dread' rather than with the joy that accompanies the spontaneous exercise of distinctive nature in other creatures. The degree of the 'dread' felt by the poet-persona is a function of his vulnerability to God's retributive and redemptive powers of 'lightning and love' (st. 9). Human subjectivity lives with the constant threat of becoming 'unmade', a threat that is averted as the reassuring stress of God's touch restores our being 'afresh': it connects it to 'the dearest freshness deep down things' which in 'God's Grandeur' (No. 111) exists despite the sinful 'selfbent' (No. 149) assertions manifest in 'man's smudge and . . . man's smell'. Even post-lapsarian human nature has a residual kernel of created nature which like external 'nature is never spent' (No. 111). God's touch is 'a pressure, a [physical] principle' (No. 101, st. 4), which, compensating for the imbalance effected by the Fall, maintains the individual's ontological equilibrium.

The relation of grace to the ontological and moral integrity of the self is further clarified in stanza 4 of 'The Wreck of the *Deutschland*'. The determinate being of the poet-persona is identified here with the unstable phenomena of trickling sands in an hourglass, and water:

> I am sóft sift
> In an hourglass—at the wall
> Fast, but mined with a motion, a drift,
> And it crowds and it combs to the fall;
> I stéady as a wáter in a wéll, to a póise, to a páne,
> But roped with, always, all the way down from the tall
> Fells or flanks of the voel, a vein
> Of the góspel próffer, a préssure, a prínciple, Chríst's gift.
>
> (No. 101, st. 4)

The 'pressure' of grace preserves the equilibrium, the 'poise', of the poet's individual being, the natural tendency of which is depicted here as degenerate. Human subjectivity is presented in the first figure of the stanza as gradually undermining itself from within. It is identified with a 'motion, a drift' toward dissolution. Indeed, the 'soft sift' invokes biblical associations with dust and death.[40] The symbol of the hourglass, which along

---

[40] *Poetical Works*, ed. MacKenzie, 324.

with the 'scythe' (st. 11) is a standard attribute of the traditional allegorical figure of Death, is regarded by Hopkins in his typical but nevertheless refreshing manner as a physical phenomenon. The being of the persona, the 'soft sift', is 'at the wall | Fast'. It is clearly contained, foredrawn, by the transparent spherical bulb of the upper chamber of the hourglass, which in its shape suggests the Parmenidean 'ball' of being and as a principle of snug containment is akin to the 'well' that in the stanza's second figure gathers the unstable 'flushness' of being into the stable unity of 'a water'. Left to its own devices, however, the 'soft sift' self forsakes this unifying principle of containment for the atomistic not-being represented by the contingent and static aggregate trapped in the underworld of the lower chamber of the hourglass. This entropic 'drift' towards disorganization and death is propelled by the pressure of postlapsarian human nature, the gravitational pull of the earthly that is opposed to the uplifting principle of grace.[41]

The self 'crowds and combs to the fall', enacting its own recapitulation of the Fall. The being of the poet 'crowds' in a contingent mass and 'combs' in the manner of the violent dispersion of a wave breaking, a trope which describes the human subject's 'ócean of a mótionable mind' (No. 101, st. 32)[42] as it pits itself against the natural (moral) limits established by the will of God, 'giver of . . . | World's strand' (st. 1). The stanza's second metaphor for human subjectivity describes the acceptance, indeed the instressing, of its fore-ordained containment as 'a water in a well'. This image celebrates the stable 'flushness' of being which Hopkins believes is available to fallen human beings through the grace of the Crucifixion, for the water in the well is 'roped with | . . . a vein | Of the góspel próffer'.

Human subjectivity is for Hopkins predicated upon the antithetical principles of original sin and a created nature open to God's will. Much as the reflections of 'the sun in broken water' described in the 1868 notes are kept by their 'conditions' from forming a single image, so the circumstances of our finitude, which centre upon original sin, alienate our being

---

[41] Cf. No. 118: 'Our make and making break, are breaking down | To man's last dust, drain fast towards man's first slime'.

[42] The identification of God with the 'foredrawn' quality of being in this stanza warrants my interpretation of the fluctuous figure of the 'ocean' here.

from that of God, its source. Conversely, just as the reflections are 'always mounting the ripples and trying to fall back into one again', the innate propensity for the good endeavours to overcome the tendencies of original sin. The human potential can, according to Hopkins, be actualized in two dynamics: an entropic one in which the subject is effectively 'unmade', and the more stable dynamic of the open system which is informed from without with grace, the 'touch' of God, 'a pressure, a principle, Christ's gift'. References to human subjectivity scattered throughout Hopkins' writings cohere through his thematic use of metaphors drawn from mechanistic physics.

The poet-persona of '(Carrion Comfort)' defies the temptation to sin: 'Not, I'll not, carrion comfort, Despair, not feast on thee' (No. 159). The consequence of surrendering to such mortal sins as despair is an ontological dissolution akin to that recounted in Hopkins' description of the nightmare, in which 'the body [is] no longer swayed as a piece by the nervous and muscular instress': 'Not untwist—slack they may be—these last strands of man | In me . . .' (No. 159). A taut rope provides one of the simplest examples of physical stress. The rope's fibres are drawn closely together as they are subjected to stress, while its 'strands' draw apart, 'untwist', in consequence of a slackening in tension.[43] Each temptation to sin is seen to present Satan with 'several strands' of being which he can 'draw upon' and manipulate, thereby inducing stresses which threaten to unravel the main stress of being that God means his human creatures to realize (*S*. 182). With the appearance of grace as a term in the correspondence of subjective self with objective 'self', the question arises as to precisely whose will, God's or the individual's, is being enacted in such gracious transactions, and hence whose identity is brought to reflexive

---

[43] On Hopkins' principle of the 'slack' see Lorraine Janzen Kooistra, '"The Proportion of the Mixture": Stress and Slack in the Perception and Poetics of Hopkins', *Hopkins Quarterly*, 17/4 (Jan. 1991), 113–25. While Kooistra identifies Hopkins' use of the idea of slackness with the principle of Not-being in the 'Parmenides' notes, and hence opposes it to 'stress', she fails to recognize the crucial mechanistic meaning of both of these terms, and consequently to integrate them into Hopkins' larger metaphysical scheme and the system of thematic imagery in which it is expressed. She notes the *OED* definition of 'slack' as 'that part of a rope, sail, etc., which is not fully strained, or which hangs loose' (p. 117) but does not connect this with Hopkins' thematic imagery of ropes and strings.

self-consciousness. Instances of good acts and intentions clearly involve a confluence of these wills. The corollary to this is that both the individual and the divine natures are in such instances the respective subjects of a single, reciprocal, act of reflexive self-consciousness.

Maxwell notes that Faraday's idea of an electromagnetic medium in a state of stress reduces the 'conception of action at a distance ... to a phenomenon of the same kind as that action at a distance which is exerted by means of the tension of ropes and the pressure of rods'.[44] The simple analogy of the rope is used by Hopkins for the same reason that it came into prominence in physics at the time, that is, to describe the perception of continuity between physical objects and the forces that act upon them. He conceives of the relation as a direct connection between human beings and divine grace, individual instresses and the ultimate source of their stress.

The dynamic equilibrium or 'instress' of virtuous being, 'steady as a water in a well, to a poise', is '*roped* with, always ... a vein | Of the góspel próffer' (No. 101, st. 4; my emphasis). Later, in 'The Soldier', which like '(Carrion Comfort)' has been dated to September 1885,[45] Hopkins writes that 'Christ ... of all can reeve a rope best' (No. 160); he can twist and secure the rope and so provide the condition by which it can enter into a state of stress. 'The Wreck of the *Deutschland*' enhances this association of grace with reeving in the rhetorical question it asks as to why God did not spare the lives of all the ship's occupants; why 'the million of rounds of thy mercy [did] not reeve even them in?' (No. 101, st. 12). This image of throwing coils of rope out into a perilous zone is reworked in the later meditation on 'The Incarnation'. The metaphor of continuous coils of a cord thrown in succession over a cliff is used to describe each generation as they enter the world in a state of original sin:[46]

The divine Persons see the whole world at once and know where to drive the nail and plant the cross. A 60-fathom coil of cord running

[44] Maxwell, *Scientific Papers*, ii. 320.
[45] *Poetical Works*, ed. MacKenzie, 454, 457.
[46] 'A coil or spiral is then a type of the Devil, who ... brought in the law of decay and consumption in inanimate nature, death in the vegetable and animal world, moral death and original sin in the world of man' (S. 198–9).

over the cliff's edge round by round, that is, say, generation by generation, 40 fathom already gone and the rest will follow, when a man
sets his foot on it and saves both what is hanging and what has not
yet stirred to run. Or seven tied by the rope on the Alps; four go
headlong, then the fifth, as strong as Samson, checks them and the
two behind do not even feel the strain. And so on.— . . . In fact, *tota
planities vel ambitus totius mundi plenus hominibus* is a graphic expression for the field in which man or humanity is seen by the divine
mind from the beginning to the end of time. (*S.* 169–70)

This passage reiterates the conviction presented in the first
stanza of 'The Wreck of the *Deutschland*' that the state of
human beings at birth is one of terror and moral urgency,
which requires the formation of character through an instressing of a fallen or a gracious 'self'. The grace of Christ's sacrifice
forestalls the impetus of original sin to hurl each new generation into the moral abyss, enhancing their being or stress and
providing heartening evidence of their potential strength, the
instress of their inchoate character, to resist sin.

The stress of grace effects a heightening of the instress to
which it is directed. In the notes on the 'First Principle and
Foundation' 'great stress' is equated with 'great perfection'
of being (*S.* 124). Hence, in 'The Handsome Heart' the poet
urges the child, already possessed of a fine 'self-instressed'
character, to 'brace sterner that strain!' (No. 134a, variant).
Personality, the individual realization of the human potentiality, which develops morally by instressing successive graces,
is a matter of degree as well as of kind, and is accordingly
described intensively as a 'pitch of being' or 'stress' (*S.* 156), a
register of the gradational ontological 'scale or range of pitch'
(*S.* 148).

The use of the word 'pitch' to designate the degree of
formal definition that individual being has achieved occurs
in a journal entry on trees in spring cited earlier: 'This is the
time to study inscape in the spraying of trees, for the swelling
buds carry them to a pitch which the eye could not else gather'
(*J.* 205).[47] The 'lovely manly mould' of the dead sailor in 'The
Loss of the *Eurydice*' is seen similarly to evidence the pitch of
stress or being which he had realized: 'he | Is strung by duty,

[47] See Ch. 8, Sect. V.

is strained to beauty' (No. 125, ll. 74, 77–8). '[P]*itch* is', Hopkins declares, 'ultimately simple positiveness' (*S*. 151). It is the intensive measure of both the cumulative stresses of grace and the subject's affirmation and instressing of them.

While most species are, in the words of 'The Probable Future of Metaphysics', 'fixed only at definite distances in the string', human beings provide a notable exception, being more like an entire chord along which the individual's pitch of stress can be shifted. In order to make his case for the 'mathematically fixed' identity of biological species and certain aesthetic forms, Hopkins reasons analogically from the example of 'musical strings' (*J*. 120), where the specific notes of the scale are easily quantified by the frequency of their vibrations, a function of their length and tension. Like the distinctive vibrations of light waves which proceed from objects and are recognized by the human eye as particular registers of colour on the spectrum, the degree of stress that characterizes the musical string similarly expresses its specific nature in a sensuous form: just 'As kingfishers catch fire, | . . . each tucked string tells . . .' Each of these and the other objects featured in the octave of the 'kingfishers' poem express their specific pitch of being or stress, asserting a 'simple positiveness': '*myself* it speaks and spells . . .' (No. 115).

Whereas most creatures, according to Hopkins, express their being as naturally and spontaneously as they reflect sunlight, human beings exercise free will in responding to each of the stresses that they are subject to, whether these be perceptions of nature or direct elevating grace. Thus the 'pressure' of stress or grace, the touch of 'God's finger' (*S*. 158), will in the case of individuals possessed of a taut instress, a developed 'pitch of being', elicit a distinctive expressive sound, a saying 'yes' or 'counter stress', while little or no response will follow when the ontological state of the particular subject is 'slack', as in the case of the 'selfbent' sinner who is impervious to grace. A rudimentary form of this Pythagoreanism is found in the early poem 'Let me be to Thee as the circling bird', where 'the root . . . of the chord' (*J*. 120) which human beings express, both by the formal recognition of speech and by action, is 'Love': 'I have found the dominant of my range and state— | Love, O my God, to call Thee Love and Love' (No. 70).

VI

The rope analogy is best suited to describing the instress of the good person, which is by definition continuous with God's will. Thus a finite length, a generational coil, of rope may be brought to stress through its continuity with the stress of God's grace, in an analogous way to the needle of the compass which aligns itself with the polar magnetic field. Both examples illustrate the assent of the individual character to divine will, a harmony of 'stress' and 'counter stress'. This is the process by which the original potential, 'the strain of creating action as received in the creature' at birth, is 'instressed', actualized (S. 137).

The realization of the opposing potential of original sin naturally takes a radically different form, and, as was noted earlier, cannot be described by the analogy of the taut rope, but rather by its slackness, the untwisted 'strands of being' disconnected from the divine stress of grace. This is, however, a negative description of a state that is itself necessarily instressed, brought to actuality by the free will of the individual, 'all foredrawn to No' (No. 168a, l. 28). The type of instress which proceeds from original sin is, as 'Ribblesdale' indicates, essentially 'selfbent' (No. 149).[48] The Devil's sin, for example, is 'an instressing of his own inscape' (S. 201). Such configurations of stress are described in 'A Meditation on Hell' by analogy with the phenomena of electromagnetism:

> the stress of God's anger which first 'prepared' or called into being fire against the Devil and his angels— . . . it was an intensification of or terrible instress upon the substance of one, Satan, first of all, casting that, with straining, in one direction (which is the being cast down to hell) and acting through that, by a subordination or hierarchy (hence 'his angels', missionaries, subalterns), on the rest, so that their obedience to him is one of slavish fear and necessity. (So, I think, as a magnetic current is heightened needles and shreds of iron rear, stare, and group themselves, *se dressent,* at the poles . . .).   (S. 137)

Whereas the reflexive self-consciousness by which the good character is instressed involves a grand gesture of assent

---

[48] Bruns ('Energy and Interpretation', 134) comments that the term implies that fallen human nature consists in 'a bound energy'.

and recognition, '*yes* and *is*', which aligns the self with God as the compass needle aligns with the polar lines of force, the instressing of the sinner's character can be described as a cramped circuit of 'current' that enslaves the being of the individual, which is represented here as in the compass analogy by a needle. However, while the even universal stress of the polar forces encourages parallelism amongst the compass needles, which are fixed as it were by their distinctive moral character, the unfixed needles (and their diminutive forms, shreds of iron) caught within the intense field of the electromagnet become arranged in a random and constrained manner. The essential stress of created being is in this case paralysed. Another description of this enthralment to Satan specifies a type of intoxication: the 'song of Lucifer's . . . an instressing of his own inscape . . . became an incantation: others were drawn in; it became a concert of voices, a concerting of selfpraise, an enchantment, a magic, by which they were dizzied, dazzled, and bewitched' (*S.* 200–1). Instead of the praise of God there is 'selfpraise', and in place of the plainchant harmonies of 'stress' and 'counter stress', there occurs 'a counterpoint of dissonance' (*S.* 201).[49]

While sin may be said to fulfil one part of our nature, namely original sin, it provides no real resolution of the 'almost unmade' state of tension that our being is, according to the first stanza of 'The Wreck of the *Deutschland*', predicated upon, but serves rather to intensify it. This consequence is introduced in the conclusion to 'The Origin of Our Moral Ideas', where, in sharp contrast to the good, 'the ideal, the one', which 'is our only means of recognising our being to ourselves . . . vice destroys the sense of being' (*J.* 83). The actualization of the potential for sin alienates the rest of our original nature: 'the strain of created action as received in the creature' and 'the strain or tendency towards God through Christ'. While the latter type of grace is in the case of the fallen angels 'broken, refracted and turned aside' in consequence of their rebellious act, the former perseveres in them, for it 'cannot cease without the creature's

---

[49] Hopkins writes of 'plain chant' that it is 'The only good and truly beautiful recitative . . . It . . . has the richness of nature; the other[, artificial, type of recitative] is a confinement of the voice' (18 Aug. 1888, *To Bridges*, 280).

ceasing to be'. The passage on the 'magnetic current' quoted above continues by comparing the ontological state of the fallen angels to that of death, the proverbial wages of human sin:

The fall from heaven was for the rebel angels what death is for man. As in man all that energy or instress with which his soul animates and otherwise acts in the body is by death thrown back upon the soul itself: so in them was that greater stock of activity with which they act, intellectually and otherwise, throughout their own world or element of spirit, which is perhaps, as I have thought, flushed by every spirit living in it. This throwing back or confinement of their energy is a dreadful constraint or imprisonment and, as intellectual action is spoken of under the figure of sight, it will in this case be an imprisonment in darkness, a being in the dark; for darkness is the phenomenon of foiled action in the sense of sight. But this constraint and this blindness or darkness will be most painful when it is the main stress or energy of the whole being that is thus balked. This is its strain or tendency towards being, towards good, towards God—being, that is | their own more or continued being, good | their own good, their natural felicity, and God | the God at least of nature, not to speak of grace. This strain must go on after their fall, because it is the strain of creating action as received in the creature and cannot cease without the creature's ceasing to be.   (S. 137)

The paradigmatic example of the fallen angels highlights the hellish ontological state into which sinners are hurled. '[I]n man all that energy or instress' is projected outward, articulating the body and determining its definitive activities: it is the means 'with which his soul animates and otherwise acts in the body'. The impetus of our 'energy or instress' is by nature to move outwards, in the manner of 'Conscience or the Imperative' in the *Ethike* essay (*J.* 124). Death is correspondingly the state in which our being is 'thrown back upon the soul itself'. The fallen angels' absolute assertion of *Non Serviam,* of their perverted self-willed *arbitrium* against the affective will, a conflict which for Hopkins defines the nature of sin, radically frustrates the realization of their created nature, the potentiality latent in their instress. Indeed, their ethereal natures are conceived of in terms that suggest the physical ether. Closer to the ontological condition of God than human beings, their nature is described not as a portion of stress, such as defines organic instress, but on the model of a perfectly diffuse force plenum (a condition of close union with God that the good character yearns for): 'their own world or element of spirit, which is perhaps, as I have thought, flushed by every spirit living in it'. The constraint of the angelic nature is accordingly all the more extreme and intensely felt.

Hopkins' conception of essential being and its frustration suggests an interesting parallel to the Freudian economy of desire: 'This throwing back or confinement of their energy is a dreadful constraint or imprisonment . . .'[50] For Hopkins it is virtue, the rational will implanted as created nature, that is fundamental to human being and can only be repressed unsuccessfully and at one's peril, whereas for Freud and his followers it is of course the irrational will. The formal parallel between these very different psychologies can be traced to two currents of thought that they appear to share. The first, by which the unstable latent or repressed nature (Freud's principle of desire and Hopkins' ebullient force of 'being, [or the] good'[51]), cannot be destroyed, suggests that the energy concept served as a paradigm for each. In presenting 'instress' or 'the main stress . . . of the whole being' as synonymous with 'energy' the above passage indicates clearly that Hopkins understood this term in its modern quantitative sense as, in Poincaré's words, a 'something which remains constant',[52] and hence regarded 'stress' in the manner of Thomson and Tait's energy physics. The other current of thought is the romantic principle of what Charles Taylor calls 'expressivism', which sees the active and objective expression of one's nature as a basic ontological activity and requirement.[53] Taylor traces this idea to Herder and argues that from this source it informed the mainstream of German romanticism, and especially Hegel's developmental doctrine of, as Hopkins puts it, 'things both in

---

[50] Cf. Bruns, 'Energy and Interpretation', 140.

[51] I.e. the 'desire for unity' (*J.* 83).

[52] Henri Poincaré, *Science and Hypothesis*, trans. W. J. G. (London: Walter Scott Publishing Co., 1905; repr. New York: Dover, 1952), 127.

[53] Helmholtz, with whose lectures Freud was familiar from both reading and attending them (Peter Gay, *Freud: A Life for our Time* (London: Dent, 1988), 34–5), provided him with a source for knowledge of the energy concept and perhaps also for expressivism. He is likely to have been acquainted with this idea through his programmatic reading of philosophy whilst at university, and in particular through his favourite philosopher at this time, the left-wing Hegelian Feuerbach (ibid. 28).

thought and fact detaching and differencing and individualising and expressing themselves' (*J.* 119).[54]

The exercise of specific nature is presented in such poems
as 'The Windhover' as a circuit of divine stress flashing between Creation and God. An analogous circuit is formed by
God's stress and the elective will's corresponding 'counter stress'.
The second and third stanzas of 'The Wreck of the *Deutschland*'
describe Hopkins' experience as the target of God's 'lightning':
'The swoon of a heart that the sweep and the hurl of thee trod
| Hárd dówn with a horror of height' (No. 101, st. 2). Hopkins'
assent to this sublime power, which he experiences as 'terror',
has the effect of unifying his being with that of God. The
'simple positiveness' of pitch consists of 'counter stresses',
affirmations of divine stresses. The gesture of assent in 'The
Wreck' is 'a fling of the heart' by which the poet 'fled . . . to
the heart of the Host', and in this way participated directly in
the lightning-like divine being, just as such creatures as the
windhover will 'flash' back to the source of their being: 'My
heart, but you were dovewinged, I can tell, | Cárrier-wítted, I
am bóld to bóast, | To flash from the flame to the flame then,
tower from the grace to the grace' (No. 101, st. 3).

In the case of the fallen, however, such joyful exercises of
nature are 'balked', short-circuited: 'all that energy . . . is . . .
thrown back upon . . . itself'. The consequences of this are
further developed in the sonnet which begins 'I wake and feel
the fell of dark, not day' (No. 155). This line introduces the
hellish state of being described in the passage quoted above:
'This throwing back or confinement of their energy is . . . an
imprisonment in darkness, a being in the dark.' For Hopkins,
'selfbeing . . . that taste of myself, of *I* and *me* [is] above and
in all things'. He rejoices in this sense of self just as he does in
the distinctiveness of such specific creatures as the windhover
which he believes disclose the nature of God. Indeed the two
are intimately linked, for through the principle of reflexive
self-consciousness scrutiny of natural phenomena provides the
condition by which he comes to recognize his own distinctive
nature: 'searching nature I taste *self* but at one tankard, that of

---

[54] See C. Taylor, *Hegel*, pt. I, ch. 1. The principle of reflexive self-consciousness
that Hopkins derives from his 'Greats' studies is a version of expressivism.

my own being' (S. 123). If, however, the self cannot be perceived through this reciprocal movement, if, for example, its
outward gestures are left unanswered, as 'cries like dead letters
sent | To dearest him that lives alas! away,' then the 'taste of
self' becomes intolerable:

> I am gall, I am heartburn. God's most deep decree
> Bitter would have me taste: my taste was me;
> Bones built in me, flesh filled, blood brimmed the curse.

A poisoned chalice takes the place of the 'one tankard'. The
creation of the body, the 'Bones built in me, flesh filled, blood
brimmed', like that in the first stanza of 'The Wreck of the
Deutschland', where God has 'bóund bónes and véins in me,
fástened me flésh', simply incarnates the 'curse' of original sin.
The condition in which Hopkins involuntarily finds himself,
whereby his essential being is deprived of grace and forced
back upon itself, is by degrees like that of the damned:

> Selfyeast of spirit a dull dough sours. I see
> The lost are like this, and their scourge to be
> As I am mine, their sweating selves; but worse.   (No. 155)

The radical instability of embodied spirit described in the
first stanza of 'The Wreck' gives it a potentiality that is liable
to become actualized in extreme forms. The destructive hellish
fire of the damned, which is synonymous with 'darkness and
chains or imprisonment', furnishes the opposite principle to
the joyous 'fire' of creatures such as the kingfishers. It is the
'imprisonment' of self bent upon itself, the destruction and
dissolution of being that substitutes the void of 'darkness' for
the ontologically definitive 'fire', 'flame', and 'flashes' of specific creatures. The jaundiced 'gall' of the self in 'I wake and
feel the fell of dark', which suggests the yellow of brimstone,
is a hideous parody of the 'góld-vermílion' of the 'embers'
which 'gall themsélves' in 'The Windhover' (No. 120).
 The perverse instressing of a sinful potential establishes a
fatal tension, an ontological short-circuit, that may erupt in
hellish fire:

Our action leaves in our minds scapes or species, the extreme 'intention' or instressing of which would be painful and the pain would be

that of fire, supposing fire to be the condition of a body (and by analogy of any substance) *texturally at stress*. The soul then can be instressed *in* the species or scape of any bodily action (whether this gives rise to a physical and quantitative extension of its substance or not) and so *towards* the species or scape of any object, as of sight, sound, taste, smell; and a high degree of such instress would in each case be the pain of fire, so that every other pain would be besides a pain of fire.   (*S.* 136–7)

This extract from 'A Meditation on Hell' leads into the long passage quoted earlier, which explains hell-fire as 'an intensification of or terrible instress upon the substance of one, Satan, first of all . . .' The 'stress of God's anger' can facilitate the fiery intensification of such perverse self-instressing, just as the stress of grace may be similarly acceded to good characters in response to their acts. In specifying the nature of fire as 'the condition of a body (and by analogy of any substance), *texturally at stress*', Hopkins clearly has in mind physical conceptions of friction between bodies, as when Tom's boot 'rips out rockfire' (No. 171), and so actualizes a potential energy. Given Hopkins' dictum that 'self can in every object it has see another self', the condition of fire, of being '*texturally at stress*', arises from instressing the object of sin, an act which draws the self into conflict with its created nature. It thus heightens rather than diminishes the precarious state into which we are born, drawn between the contrary pulls of original sin and created nature. The stress of friction occurs in the innermost being: 'our hearts grate on themselves' (No. 162) and 'selfwrung, selfstrung, sheathe-and shelterless, thóughts agaínst thoughts ín groans grínd' (No. 167).

In contrast to the stable dynamic of hydrostatic equilibrium ('I steady as a water in a well . . .'), heat is a state of instability within a substance. This disequilibrium is well exemplified by the journal entry on the Lenten chocolate. Whereas the well is foredrawn 'to a poise, to a pane' (a perfectly smooth surface), the 'stress of the heat . . . overcome[s] the resistance of the surface' of the liquid causing it to boil and so give off 'films' which have a rough 'grained' texture (*J.* 203–4). The clear implication of this dynamic conception of heat, applying it metaphorically, as Hopkins does in the 'Meditation', is that in order to contain the temptation to sin (which can like the stress of grace 'flush' the being) the moral 'substance' needs to be securely 'foredrawn', the good character needs to be well developed and defined. Ironically the logical consequence of sin, of being 'selfbent', is the complete immolation of self: 'sinners are themselves the flames of hell' (S. 242).

The destructive dark flames of hell are the antithesis to the bright flames that express realized created natures. Interestingly, while the former is destructive of individual being the latter leads to its dissolution in the infinite being of God. The emblem of this ascension, by which we aspire to the condition of pure light, 'flash from the flame to the flame', is the windhover. Like the condition of Christ on earth, and the poet's paradoxical original state of being, 'almost unmade . . . with dread', the creature *hovers* between the two realms of heaven and earth. It exemplifies the fine 'poise' of being upheld by grace, the dynamic synthesis of the universal and the concrete, the infinite and the finite. Hopkins' dialectic retains a vestigial instability: the creature's hovering can be sustained only for a limited time. At the moment of its highest pitch of being the windhover transcends this finite being: 'AND the fire that breaks from thee then, a billion | Tímes told lovelier, more dangerous' (No. 120). The pressure of stress ultimately involves the dissolution of individual being, much as does the touch of Rilke's 'terrible' angels in the first of the *Duino Elegies*: 'if one of them suddenly | pressed me against his heart, I should fade in the strength of his | stronger existence'.[55] However, in consequence of a conception of selfhood that is modelled on Christ's martyrdom, predicated upon the voluntary surrender of the self ('Give beauty back, beauty, beauty, béauty, back to God, beauty's self and beauty's giver' (No. 148, l. 35)), such integration is, in Hopkins' distinctive romantic ontology, yearned for. It constitutes the goal, the completion, of individual being:

---

[55] 'The First Elegy', ll. 2–4, Rilke, *Duino Elegies*, trans. J. B. Leishman and Stephen Spender (New York: Norton, 1939). For other comparisons of Hopkins to Rilke, see W. H. Gardner, *Gerard Manley Hopkins: A Study of Poetic Idiosyncrasy in Relation to Poetic Tradition*, 2nd edn. (London: Secker & Warburg, 1948; repr. Oxford University Press, 1961), i. 271–3, and Jeffrey B. Loomis, *Dayspring in Darkness: Sacrament in Hopkins* (Toronto: Associated University Presses, 1988), 153–4.

In a flash, at a trumpet crash,
I am all at once what Christ is, | since he was what I am, and
This jack, joke, poor potsherd, | patch, matchwood, immortal
  diamond,
Is immortal diamond.   (No. 174)

The resurrection preserves both the being and the thought of
man, 'his firedint' and 'his mark on mind', in a synthesis of the
individual with its other; that is, God. Furthermore, given that
human nature is conceived of as a profound stress or tension,
which Hopkins experiences as 'this unspeakable stress of pitch'
and is brought to an ever greater pitch by successive graces,
the longing for complete liberation in such ultimate union,
'the heaven-haven of the reward' (No. 101, st. 35), becomes
increasingly great. These observations perhaps provide a gloss
for his poignant dying words 'I am so happy, I am so happy.'[56]

[56] 'Father Gerard Hopkins', *Letters and Notices*, 20/99 (Mar. 1890), 179.

10　Stress and Breath

I

The metaphors that Hopkins uses to describe the human subject, such as the 'burl', the taut rope, and the compass needle,
illustrate the integral relation that he sees personal instress
to have to the all-encompassing field of stress. His doctrine
of stress, in which he elaborates his ontological monism as an
economy of energy, means that all physical and mental activity
occurs within this field of being and is as such both influenced
by the larger system and has implications for it. Hopkins' ontology of 'instress' is concerned with open systems of energy. His
model of the field of 'stress' or being provides him with the
means of representing the continuity which he sees to exist between the infinite being of God and the finite being of nature
and generic man.

The human subject's assent to God's will, his counter-stress
in response to divine stress, is for Hopkins a moral act which
can take a number of forms. The imagery of 'As kingfishers
catch fire' indicates two ways in which 'the just man justices'
or 'Keeps gráce'. 'Lovely in limbs', he consents to God's will
by performing Christ-like actions, whilst 'lovely in eyes' he can
perceive the divine significance of Creation, just as 'God's eye'
recognizes Christ in him (No. 115). The instressing of God's
presence in nature through perception is for Hopkins one
of the most important moral actions that human beings perform. The use of the verb 'justices' in the sestet implies not
only physical action but moral intention and cognitive judgement. Hopkins' intentionalism, established early and emphatically in his Oxford studies, means that the moral worth of actions
is predicated upon the quality of the thought and feeling that
impels them. Indeed, 'All thought' is itself presented in 'The
Origin of Our Moral Ideas' as an act of volition, 'an effort a[t]
unity' (*J.* 83).

It is not virtue or goodness that Hopkins opposes to 'vice' at the close of 'The Origin of Our Moral Ideas', but the more general principle of 'the ideal, the one'. The good intention is for him marked by this striving for unity. By identifying this desire with our created nature Hopkins naturalizes the fundamental tenet of his idealist metaphysic 'that the Idea is only given ... from the whole downwards to the parts', and conversely demonizes 'Purely material psychology' (*J.* 118) and the 'philosophy of flux', which he accordingly sees as part of a deeper malaise, a 'principle [that] traverses modern thought generally' (*J.* 120). He refers to this as the 'atomism of personality' (*J.* 121), which rather than following the objective synthetic a priori imperative by which phenomena can 'be grasped and held together' (*J.* 118) determines its understanding and relation to the world on the basis of its own arbitrary subjective criteria: 'it is an overpowering, a disproportioned sense of personality' (*J.* 120). This indicates an autistic tendency to identify only with a contingent 'self', and is by degrees akin to the 'selfbent' tendency of the sinner, 'so bound, so tied to his turn' (No. 149).[1] Such 'atomism [is] like a stiffness or sprain' (*J.* 120) which impedes the suppleness of thought and restricts the movements and gestures it can make towards the outside world.

The fundamental ontological and moral choice that human beings are faced with is, according to Hopkins, that between repudiating or fulfilling our created nature. The latter alternative consists in the individual realizing its inherent unity, and ultimately its unity with God, through the means of reflexive self-consciousness, whilst the former wars against this and is ontologically riven in the manner that was described in Chapter 9. Perception and other acts of thought express this crucial choice.

By effectively reducing the function of the Kantian Categories to his principle of relation Hopkins deprives the mind of the means of organizing sensations spontaneously in the Kantian manner. Perception presents the mind with interpretative

---

[1] Hopkins' preoccupation with the moral evil of selfishness suggests the influence of T. H. Green, whose 1867 lectures on moral philosophy are, as Bradley's notes indicate, especially concerned with it (Merton, Bradley Papers, MS I-A1). Green's focus upon selfishness is part of his effort to encourage an ethic of social responsibility and public service amongst his students, a value which became central to British idealism.

choices as to the type of configuration it can infer from the sensuous 'scapes' which an object presents, a predicament that is highlighted in the 'Causation' essay by the ambiguous figure of the quatrefoil/Maltese cross. Nature, however, in contrast to this curious example of human artifice, co-operates with good-willed human intentions by presenting 'offers ... to the eye to foredraw' (*J.* 129).

'All things', Hopkins writes, 'are charged with love, are charged with God and if we know how to touch them give off sparks and take fire, yield drops and flow, ring and tell of him' (*S.* 195). The 'shining from shook foil' and gathering drops of 'the ooze of oil' which represent for Hopkins 'the grandeur of God' (No. 111) are not simply a matter of objective fact but depend upon the active perceiving consciousness that 'know[s] how to touch them'. Indeed the very predicate of 'grandeur' implies a humble human perspective from which this loftiness (a quality that in other circumstances is perceived as 'a horror of height' (No. 101, st. 2)) is gauged and acknowledged.

The generic nature which Hopkins ascribes to 'man' as 'Earth's eye, tongue, or heart' (No. 149) requires the human subject to bring the essential being of the Creation to consciousness through his respective acts of perception, speech, and feeling, and in so doing to realize his own nature, for as the Ignatian text puts it 'Man was created to praise' (*S.* 122). Furthermore by bringing both our own created nature and that of external Creation to consciousness human beings perform a crucial role in God's recognition of his own being. Hopkins explores and explicates these interactions in a group of poems which date from 1877, 'As kingfishers catch fire', 'Hurrahing in Harvest', and 'The Windhover'.

The reflexive 'play' of individual identities in the second stanza of 'As kingfishers catch fire' yields a similarly definit-ive sense of self to that produced by the reflection of light on the creatures in the first stanza, as the divine gaze recognizes Christ, that is, himself, 'in eyes not his'. Human beings are, in other words, the crucial mediating moment for God's self-consciousness:

> ... For Christ plays in ten thousand places,
> Lovely in limbs, and lovely in eyes not his
> To the Father through the features of men's faces. (No. 115)

Christ is recognized by both the poet-persona and 'God's eye' in the natural phenomenon of other human bodies, 'Lovely in limbs, and lovely in eyes not his'. In Hegel's dialectic of the Trinity, God the Father, Universality, comes to self-consciousness of himself through his particularity, that is, as Christ: 'this God is sensuously and directly beheld as a Self, as an actual individual man; only so *is* this God self-consciousness'.[2] As self-consciousness, that is, in returning to his self through the objective mediation of Christ and thus recognizing himself in humanity, God is the Holy Spirit: he 'has realized his being as the Idea of the spirit, eternal, but alive and present in the world'.[3] This fundamental Hegelian dialectic of the Trinity does not, however, include human beings as such amongst its terms or moments. Hopkins' poem effectively alludes to a further Hegelian mode of spirit.

God, having come to self-consciousness through the particularity of Christ, needs to achieve self-consciousness of himself as the universal. This he does, according to Hegel, through the Christian church. It is to the church composed of its natural constituency of 'the just' that Hopkins refers in his poem. While his references to physical particularity recapitulate the previous mode in which God is, in Hegel's words, 'sensuously and directly beheld as a Self', the members of this community are, to be more specific, 'lovely in limbs' due to the moral actions they perform, graceful gestures towards God such as are emblematized in Mannerist painting. The 'lovely . . . eyes' and other 'features of men's faces' function similarly as means of expressing attitudes towards God, such as assent, praise, joy, and reverence; in short, their recognition of him. The 'features of men's faces' may be said to represent, in the words of the 1881 notes 'On Personality, Grace and Free Will', 'attitude[s] of mind freely taken by the man's self towards that other . . . self' (*S.* 153).[4]

By regarding 'the just man' as 'in God's eye . . . Christ', the

---

[2] *Phenomenology of Spirit*, sect. 758.

[3] Hegel, *Philosophy of Mind*, sect. 569. This and all other excerpts from the work are taken from William Wallace's translation (Oxford: Clarendon Press, 1971). 'Spirit' is defined in the *Phenomenology* (sect. 759) as 'the knowledge of oneself in the externalisation of oneself; the being that is the movement of retaining its self-identity in its otherness'.　　　　[4] This passage is discussed in Ch. 9, Sect. IV.

poem agrees with Jowett's 'rather dangerous claim'[5] that 'The highest we can imagine in man is not human but divine.'[6] Furthermore, it suggests that this moral nature, and indeed man's physical nature, provides God with the externality by which he is able to recognize himself. The doctrine of the 'kingfishers' poem all but endorses the heretical conclusion reached by Hegel's doctrine of the Trinity: 'The divine nature is the same as the human, and it is this unity that is beheld [by God in his self-consciousness]'.[7]

The 'correspondence' that occurs when we choose Christ as our objective 'self' makes him the content of our self-consciousness, and reciprocally allows God to recognize his self in us, for as independent and free self-consciousnesses we are objects adequate to the reflection of God's nature: '*Self-consciousness*', writes Hegel, '*achieves its satisfaction only in another self-consciousness.*'[8] The reciprocal relation of God and humankind found in Hopkins' writings aligns with Hegel's theology: 'God is God only so far as he knows himself: his self-knowledge is, further, a self-consciousness in man and man's knowledge *of* God, which proceeds to man's self-knowledge *in* God.'[9] This reciprocal relation between God and man corresponds suggestively to that described in a passage from the notes 'On Personality, Grace and Free Will' which Hopkins' commentators often juxtapose with the closing lines of the 'kingfishers' sonnet: 'That is Christ playing at me and me playing at Christ, only that is no play but truth; That is Christ *being me* and me being Christ' (*S.* 154). By self-consciously 'playing at' being another, each party recognizes and consequently actualizes its potential self as the other self. This idea is elaborated later in the notes, where faith is explained as the means by which we facilitate God's reflexive self-consciousness. We are, according to Hopkins, able to mediate God's reflexive self-consciousness even though his nature is for us ultimately unknowable:

faith . . . is God | in man | knowing his own truth. It is like the child of a great nobleman taught by its father and mother a compliment of

[5] Peter Hinchliff, *Benjamin Jowett and the Christian Tradition* (Oxford: Clarendon Press, 1987), 130. [6] Quoted ibid.
[7] *Phenomenology*, sect. 759. [8] Ibid. sect. 175.
[9] *Philosophy of Mind*, sect. 564.

welcome to pay to the nobleman's father on his visit to them: the child does not understand the words it says by rote, does not know their meaning, yet what they mean it means. The parents understand what they do not say, the child says what it does not understand, but both child and parents mean the welcome. (*S.* 157; my emphasis)

The nobleman's father clearly represents God the Father, while the nobleman's son corresponds to Christ.[10] The child, but one remove from Christ just as Christ is from the Father, represents humankind. The mutual confirmation of essential being through reflexive self-consciousness, a reciprocal honouring of the other, has, as Gadamer observes, one of its most 'external' and simplest instances in 'greeting customs'.[11] The value of the child's words is not their meaning but the moral intent or prepossession that informs them, the pure gesture of welcome or greeting: 'His mýstery múst be instréssed, stressed; | For I greet him the days I meet him, and bless when I understand' (No. 101, st. 5). It is through the intention that the child gives to the words that the grandfather is able to 'know their meaning', to understand them as a concrete recognition of his being.

The reciprocity of greeting is celebrated in 'Hurrahing in Harvest':

> I wálk, I líft up, Í lift úp heart, éyes,
> Down all that glory in the heavens to glean our Saviour;
> And, éyes, heárt, what looks, what lips yet gáve you á
> Rápturous love's greeting of realer, of rounder
>   replies? (No. 124)

Christ, heaven's 'eyes, heart', and 'lips', offers a full 'greeting' in answer to the uplifted 'heart' and direct gaze of the speaker (who is representative of 'Earth's eye, tongue, or heart'). The imagery here meshes with that of 'As kingfishers catch fire', where Christ looks 'through the features of men's faces' directly into 'God's eye' in open assent and acknowledgement of his being. Furthermore the felicitous implication of the phrase 'Christ plays in . . . the features of men's faces' (No. 115) suggests a tacit greeting, the meeting of smiling countenances, an

---

[10] The wife and mother suggests the figure of the Virgin Mary.

[11] H.-G. Gadamer, 'Hegel's Philosophy and Its After-effects', in id., *Reason in the Age of Science*, trans. Frederick G. Lawrence (Cambridge, Mass.: MIT Press, 1981), 32.

idea that is put more overtly in 'Hurrahing in Harvest', where the roundness of the lips that give 'love's greeting' suggests the curve of a smile. Its qualities of being both 'realer' and 'rounder' suggest the Parmenidean sphere, the ultimate monistic Being which Hopkins equates with God, and with which he believes that all instances of being can be identified as the other siding of 'the scale of Being', 'Not-being', or 'Being . . . under its siding of the Many' (*J.* 130).

II

The principle of reflexive self-consciousness provides the means which enable Hopkins to maintain the distinction between the human self and Christ whilst making what appears to be a complete identification between them: 'That is Christ *being me* and me being Christ' (*S.* 154). The recognition of otherness is a necessary condition of both Christ and the human subject being able to come to consciousness of, instress, an aspect of their nature *through* the other. Hopkins' doctrine of reflexive self-consciousness brings forward the crucial importance for him of a *medium*, a 'self' that is not the subject but an object. God for Hopkins, as for Hegel, finds his other 'self' only in another self-consciousness, that is, only in the human subject. Reciprocally, the human subject in Hopkins' scheme finds his other 'self' in Christ. This is illustrated not only by the 'kingfishers' poem and 'Hurrahing in Harvest', but also, conversely, by the sonnets of desolation. 'To have uttered a greeting in vain is', as Gadamer notes, 'an experience in which one's sense of self momentarily breaks down.'[12] This is the predicament that Hopkins describes in 'I wake and feel the fell of dark', where his expressive 'cries countless' to God are 'like dead letters sent | To dearest him that lives alas! away' (No. 155).

While 'the just man' provides the medium for God's reflexive self-consciousness, Christ and the Creation furnish the human subject with the requisite 'selves' that allow him to instress both his own nature and the divine nature. The reciprocity that defines the act of reflexive self-consciousness provides the

[12] Ibid.

pattern for more ordinary acts of perception and a criterion of their truth: 'What you look hard at seems to look hard at you, hence the true and the false instress of nature' (*J.* 204). The human percipient is able, according to Hopkins, to bring the expressive potential of nature, the way in which it 'seems to look hard at you', to *energeia* or (in Grant's translation) 'consciousness' as a manifestation of divine being. This takes the form in 'Hurrahing in Harvest' of bringing 'Down all that glory in the heavens to glean our Saviour'. Just as the reaping of a crop provides the precondition for the act of collecting the grain from the ground, so the persona of the poem looks heavenward at the clouds and brings this transcendent realm down to his level, the earth, in order to glean nourishing grains of the love and truth of divine being. The verb 'to glean' is synonymous with the Whewellian rhetorical staple of *gathering*, and similarly provides Hopkins with a metaphor for the synthetic a priori capacity by which the human mind discerns unity and significance from contingent sensuous intuitions of natural phenomena. Nature brought to consciousness in this way becomes in the poem the incarnate principle that anthropomorphically 'replies' to the poet's recognition of its ultimate being with 'a | Rápturous love's greeting' (No. 124).

The principle of law, of a mechanical causation connecting all actions in nature (such as that exemplified in the octave of the 'kingfishers' poem), entails that nature exists unconsciously: 'in itself' but not 'for itself'. The human mind provides the means of recognizing, bringing to consciousness, the ultimate significance of the Creation (our 'Earth . . . That canst but only be' (No. 149)) as the expression of God's being. Just as 'God's eye' recognizes the true nature of man, namely Christ, so the 'eyes' of 'the just man' are able to perceive the truth of the Creation, and so bring it to consciousness, complete it: 'These things, these things were here and but the beholder | Wánting' (No. 124).

Nature's want of a beholder is suggested in the 'kingfishers' poem by the urgency with which each object in nature 'fling[s] out broad its name; | . . . *myself* it speaks and spells, | Crying *What I do is me: for that I came*' (No. 115). The cries which issue from the natural world of the octave can be read not only as involuntary and exuberant but also as urgent and insistent, as

if to attract the attention of 'the just man' in a sort of epistemological courting display. While evolutionary theory accounts
for the beauties of flowers, birds, and other creatures with the
principle of sexual selection, Hopkins sees such attractions
of nature as a sort of divine wooing of free-willed human con-
sciousnesses. These self-conscious inhabitants of the distinct
world of the sestet, represented here by the persona of the poem,
are through their powers of interpretation and language able to
'say more', to supplement and complete the creatures' expressive actions, bring them to consciousness. This progress from
unconscious natural phenomena to their integral and full realization in self-consciousness, and the allegory of the sun's reflections that prefigures it, corresponds closely to Green's Hegelian
reading of Aristotle's ontology in the 1867 lectures on moral
philosophy: 'Nature is struggling to reach the divine thought;
when it [i.e. 'Nature' in its 'highest stage' as it culminates in
human 'reason'] knows the relation then it identifies itself with
the divine thought, & becomes part of it; is conscious.'[13]

The textual metaphor of 'As kingfishers catch fire', by which
'Each mortal thing . . . | . . . speaks and spells' its identity, can
be traced to the early poetic fragment 'It was a hard thing
to undo this knot'. The play of sunlight in this poem 'writes
the text' (No. 24), much as it does upon the 'kingfishers' and
'dragonflies' in the later poem. Whereas the textual metaphor is used in the early poem to put the sceptical question
as to whether what we perceive 'is in the eye or in the thought',
the later poem implies full confidence in our hermeneutic and
linguistic capacities to decipher the texts generated by nature.
'It was a hard thing . . .' was written early in Hopkins' struggle
as an undergraduate[14] to establish the epistemology which would
provide a firm ground for the confident poetic practice of such
mature works as the 'kingfishers' poem.

Hopkins' textual metaphor for identity in the octave of 'As
kingfishers catch fire' suggests that the attributes of each creature are like a letter of the respective name that it enunciates,

[13] Merton, Bradley Papers, MS I-A1, Lect. XI. At the close of lecture XX, which
is on Kant, Green recapitulates this doctrine as an anticipation of the subject of
his next lecture, which is Hegel.
[14] A draft of the poem appears in the early diaries (*J.* 34), which dates it to early
Aug. 1864.

'speaks and spells'. Recognition of the creature's nature occurs accordingly as the active human consciousness discerns the
necessary relations that connect these attributes, which are presented to the mind in the contingent sequences of sense-data,
as 'either successive or spatially distinct' (*J.* 126). The synthetic
a priori capacity of mind constructs a whole (the written name,
representative of an essentialist definition) that is greater than its
parts (the 'spelt' letters or sensible attributes).

This process of perception is represented not only in the
'kingfishers' poem and through the metaphor of gleaning in
'Hurrahing in Harvest', but also in 'The Windhover', where
a catalogue of particular impressions becomes 'caught' as a
necessary unity by the onlooker, who thereby recognizes not
simply the objective identity of the creature but the source of
all being, including his own:

> Brute beauty and valour and act, oh, air, pride, plúme, here
>   Buckle! AND the fire that breaks from thee then, a billion
> Tímes told lovelier, more dangerous, O my chevalier!   (No. 120)

The windhover, of course, not only 'spells' itself through the
sense impressions which allow it to be 'caught' as a result of
the effort or 'shéer plód' (No. 120) of the observing mind's
synthetic 'power of comparison' (*J.* 126), it also 'speaks' itself
directly in its definitive action of diving, which, as in the cases
of the kingfishers and the dragonflies, registers as the 'fire' of
reflected sunlight.

The account of perception in 'The Windhover' is, like that
of the 'Causation' essay, based upon the Aristotelian entelechy.
Just as the disintegration of the quatrefoil into its 'conditions'
occurs as the recognition of another form, the Maltese cross, so
similarly in the poem, with the acknowledgement of the various aspects of the bird ('Brute beauty and valour and act, oh,
air, pride, plume'), these conditions 'Buckle' in the recognition, the actualization, of the creature's divine 'fire', its nature
as Christ the 'chevalier!'. The word 'Buckle' at once signifies the
disintegration of the temporal attributes of 'a bird', as they collapse under the pressure of their actualization as divine 'fire',
and their preservation, their *sublation*, in a new unity ('my chevalier!'), in which they are drawn together, circumscribed, as
by a buckled belt.

The content of the reflexive self-consciousness described
in 'The Windhover' is not restricted to the creature's specific
registration of ultimate Being, as is the case with the brilliantly
coloured kingfisher, but is close to a blinding flash ('the fire
. . . a billion | Tímes told lovelier, more dangerous') in which the
perception of differences is superseded by a momentary revelation of ultimate Being.[15] The God which in constructing the
poet 'almost unmade' him in 'The Wreck of the *Deutschland*', is
present here in a vision of such intensity that it threatens to
obliterate the sensory means which facilitated it. The perception cannot, in other words, be measured by the finite human
scale. God and the poet-persona are carried along the one
lightning-like 'stem of stress' in a reciprocal movement of
reflexive self-consciousness.

This profound communication with the divine in nature and
the ontological instability that it generates in the subject is also
represented in 'Hurrahing in Harvest':

And the azurous hung hills are his wórld-wielding shoulder
Majestic—as a stallion stalwart, very-violet-sweet!—
These things, these things were here and but the beholder
Wánting; whích two whén they ónce méet,
The héart réars wíngs bóld and bolder
And hurls for him, O half hurls earth for him off under his feet.

(No. 124)

Having at once acknowledged the essential created nature
both of himself as 'the beholder' and of the natural world surrounding him, the speaker loses his finite being as the 'two . . .
meet' in an ontological 'stem of stress' that draws his innermost
being, 'The heart', up towards heaven on angelic wings. This
ascension completes the circuit which began with the poet
'Down[ing]' all that glory in the heavens'. As with the epiphany
of the windhover, this 'stem of stress' involves a huge surge of
energy, as the heart 'hurls for him', throws the speaker's being
towards union with Christ, 'O half hurls earth for him'. Para-
doxically, the moment of recognizing the transcendental signified, 'Gróund of béing, and gránite of it' (No. 101, st. 32), is
represented as disorientating, as effecting a loss of stability. It,

---

[15] The dull colours of the windhover suggest that the 'fire' is likely to be of
white light reflected off the sheen of the bird's feathers.

like the shift in perception in 'The Windhover' from seeing 'a bird' to recognizing 'my chevalier!', marks the rupturing of one mode of interpreting the world, that is, as temporal and finite, by another, the divine, which transcends time and is infinite. The imagery of the last line of 'Hurrahing in Harvest' suggests an earthquake, the world quaking with divine stress; 'the gránd-eur of God' discharged, actualized through human perception. The beholder's act of abstracting divine spirit from corporeal nature offers a formal echo of Christ's soul leaving his mortal body, which according to the Bible was marked by a huge earth-quake.[16] Such acts are relatively humble instances in which the speaker has allowed Christ to 'éaster in' him (No. 101, st. 35).

The last lines of 'Hurrahing in Harvest', like those of 'As kingfishers catch fire', work to confuse the distinction between Christ's being and that of the human subject, 'the beholder'. The objective 'things' of nature and the percipient subject are clearly differentiated in the poem up until the point where the 'two . . . once meet'. This union, which appears to dissolve the subject–object distinction, is enacted by the last lines of the poem. Much of the confusion is generated by the use of the masculine personal and possessive pronouns in the final line, all of which can be construed as referring to the beholder or to Christ: 'And hurls for him, O half hurls earth for him off under his feet.' The reader is at this point of the poem set the task of untangling the references that these possessive pro-nouns make, much as in the sestet of the 'kingfishers' poem the reader can attribute the various 'eyes' and 'limbs' to either human bodies or to the spirit of Christ which informs them.

Despite the fact that he is not referred to by name at all in the sestet it is reasonably clear that the 'him' to which 'The héart . . . half hurls earth' is the Saviour. Similarly, in what appears to be the most plausible reading of the subsequent use of the possessive pronoun in the phrase 'off under his feet' its reference changes to the beholder (or it may be to 'The heart'). A further uncertainty hovers over this phrase in so far as the 'feet' could, following the precedents in the poem of the 'lips' and 'shoulder', be attributed to Christ. 'The heart' may belong not to 'the beholder' but could rather be Christ's Sacred Heart,

---

[16] Matt. 27: 51–4.

which 'hurls for' man by delivering a powerful stress of grace through nature. The residual ambiguity of the final lines, like the intimate allocation of physical 'features' in the last lines of 'As kingfishers catch fire', where 'Christ plays . . . | Lovely in limbs, and lovely in eyes not his' (No. 115), depicts the peculiar predicament in which the being of man and God coalesces whilst remaining distinct, much as the quatrefoil and the Maltese cross do in the figure that fascinates Hopkins in his early essay on 'Causation'.

The gesture in 'Hurrahing in Harvest' of the hurling of the earth by the (beholder's) heart, which inasmuch as it only 'half hurls' does not reach its mark, has its counter in the more assured and controlled 'wórld-wíelding' action of the Saviour's shoulder. The motion of throwing, of hurling, is of course active, but so too is the reciprocating movement of catching, especially if the object is only 'half hurl[ed]', and so requires the effort of moving forward in order to meet or steady it. Indeed catching marks a kind of meeting which acknowledges the actions of another in a way that is analogous to the exchange of greetings, and is for Hopkins an important trope for human interactions with nature and God.

The first line of 'The Windhover' ('I caught this mórning morning's mínion . . .') announces that the persona has receptively 'caught' what was thrown to him. This metaphor refutes the mutually excluding logic which demands that perception occurs either 'in the eye or in the thought', that either subjective mind is subordinate to sense impressions or, vice versa, that sense intuitions are organized (or, for that matter, discredited) by mind. Sense data and subjective mind cannot, according to the binary logic of much Western philosophy, both be credited as active principles in the way that they are in Hopkins' dynamic version of objective idealism. Catching is both active and receptive, an apt figure for a model of perception in which, as the 1868 notes present it, the mind's synthetic a priori 'power of comparison' is synonymous with the 'capacity for *receiving* that synthesis' which constitutes the object (*J.* 126; my emphasis).[17]

---

[17] Cf. *J.* 118–19: 'There is a particular refinement, pitch, of thought which catches all the most subtle and true influences the world has to give: this state or period is the orthodoxy of philosophy—there is just such an orthodoxy in art'.

The idea of catching necessarily implies an object to be caught, the definitive instance of which is probably the ball. In Hopkins' use of the metaphor in the 1868 notes, the 'Idea in its freshness' which he sets out to 'catch' is identified later in the notes with Parmenides' and Xenophanes' figures of the 'ball' (*J.* 128). The object 'caught' by the poet-persona of 'The Windhover' is effectively the Parmenidean ball of Being,[18] which is identified in Hopkins' Christian ontology with that great ball of fire, the sun, 'our daystar' (No. 151, l. 106). The windhover and the kingfishers 'catch fire' in the manner of mechanical causation: sunlight hits their plumage, just as the acoustic potential of 'each . . . string tells' as it is 'tucked' by an external force. Such dynamic expressions of light and sound energy require reciprocal mental acts of synthesis from the beholder in order for their significance to be disclosed. While the instances of 'fire' and 'flame' which the kingfishers and dragon-flies 'catch' from the sun can be likened to the little suns caught as reflections in 'broken water', which are all trying to come together in a unified image of their source, the fully conscious principle of the poet-persona of 'The Windhover' is able to facilitate the apprehension of this ultimate unity, to catch an epiphanic flash of Being which in its intensity appears to be complete and unmediated. The pivotal word 'Buckle' which marks the moment of this epiphany refers to a type of *catch* in which things are held together, 'caught'. It is the completion of a circuit. The trajectory described by the object of knowledge being thrown and caught marks the epistemological 'stem of stress between us and things' (*J.* 127), by which the energy or stress of instressed bodies link like lines of force between electromagnetically charged bodies.

While reflexive self-consciousness actualizes the human subject and its natural objects in Creation, progressively defining the distinctions between them, it also draws them together through the recognition of their common being. Indeed, it is through and in this common principle, the 'stem of stress', that the subject and object are drawn together, 'once meet', in acts of perception. In such acute instances as that described in

---

[18] The 'world' or the 'earth', the whole sphere of mortal being, which is described as wielded and hurled in 'Hurrahing in Harvest', is an echo of this monistic metaphor.

'The Windhover' the stress of the individual beings not only meets in a 'stem of stress' but short-circuits back to the ultimate source of Being. The bringing together of the attributes of the creature in the recognition of determinate being is, as the pun on the word 'Buckle!' in the poem highlights, also the moment at which it collapses into original and transcendent Being.[19] Although the epiphanies of 'Hurrahing in Harvest' and 'The Windhover' present the act of reflexive self-consciousness between the human subject and God as paradoxical, it is for Hopkins nevertheless the paradigm for all morally good acts of perception. These poems describe the recognition of the ultimate 'unity' to which 'All thought' aspires.

III

The tropes that Hopkins uses to represent reflexive self-consciousness describe a range of communicative acts: the exchange of looks and of verbal greetings, the throwing and catching of an object, and the physical lines of force generated between two objects charged with electromagnetic energy. Free and open forms of communication, whether they be the unconscious expressivist gestures of natural phenomena, or self-conscious acts of assent and recognition from human beings, are for Hopkins all good in themselves and represent the contrary principle to the autistic 'selfbent' tendencies of the sinner. Language, the definitive medium of human communication, is invested with great ontological power and significance in Hopkins' metaphysic. This is registered in part by the tropes that he draws from language practices, such as the textual metaphors of 'It was a hard thing to undo this knot . . .' and 'As kingfishers catch fire', and the figure of verbal greeting customs in 'Hurrahing in Harvest' and the notes 'On Personality, Grace and Free Will'. It is significant that Hopkins' most comprehensive and dynamic metaphor for the metaphysical relations represented and instanced by these tropes, the 'stem

---

[19] See Beer, who argues that the word 'Buckle' refers at once to 'collapsing and containing'—the collapse of individual being and its containment within ultimate Being ('Leaps of the Imagination', 119).

of stress between us and things', emerges in a discussion of language. The phrase is prompted by a Parmenidean fragment that asserts a parity between knowing, saying, and being, relations which are presupposed in the language metaphors of the later poems and notes:

'Thou couldst never either know or say | what was not, there would be no coming at it'. There would be no bridge, no stem of stress between us and things to bear us out and carry the mind over: without stress we might not and could not say | Blood is red | but only | This blood is red | or | The last blood I saw was red | nor even that, for in later language not only universals would not be true but the copula would break down even in particular judgments. (*J.* 127)

One of the main reasons that Hopkins finds the Parmenidean poem so engaging is because of the radical ontological status it attributes to language, an understanding of language that he establishes in the 1868 notes in his own terms (of the 'prepossession' and 'stress') and which furnishes the basis for the innovative and audacious practices that distinguish the mature from the early poetry.

The remarkable passage quoted above, in which Hopkins effectively asserts that 'without stress we . . . could not say' anything at all, is, like so much in the 'Parmenides' notes, the culmination of a strain of his earlier speculations. His impulse here is to demonstrate the truth of being or stress according to the Aristotelian criterion of *ta legomena*, 'the things said'. For Hopkins, however, the value of the principle here is not so much the access it provides to mortal opinion (which broadly speaking is the Aristotelian approach), but rather the means it allows of reaching the contrary Parmenidean principle of Being itself.

Hopkins' earliest extant notes on language, in his diary for 1863, document his efforts to establish cases in which words participate directly in the being they signify: 'In fact I think the onomatopoetic theory has not had a fair chance. Cf. *Crack, creak, croak, crake, graculus, crackle*. These must be onomatopoetic' (*J.* 5). Most of the word-lists in the early diaries consist of such graduated scales of word-sounds which lend credence to the hypothesis of an onomatopoeic origin for language and comprise important precursors for some of the sequences of word-sounds used in the later poetry.

Hopkins plays with the idea of onomatopoeia in 'As king-fishers catch fire', where 'each hung bell's | Bow swung finds tongue to fling out broad its name' (No. 115). The definitive sounds of the bell are easily and conventionally rendered into onomatopoeic forms (e.g. 'ding-dong'), and accordingly warrant the anthropomorphic metaphor in which the bell's 'tongue' speaks 'its name'. The suggestion of the poem is, however, that the phenomenon of the bell lends itself to definition through onomatopoeia only because of its irreducibly simple nature. It can, in other words, be characterized satisfactorily by this single quality. Other, more complex, natural objects cannot express their distinctive nature in the direct auditory manner of the bell, but rather each 'speaks and spells' its identity and accordingly depends upon 'Earth's . . . tongue' in order for its 'name' to be articulated, for its essential being to be grasped and recognized. Hopkins' metaphysic is like that of the young Walter Benjamin, whose thought also supplements and develops Kant with language theory. Benjamin attributes each thing with a 'linguistic being', its own language (for, he writes, 'that which in a mental entity is communicable is its language').[20] For Benjamin, as for Hopkins, it is man who, following the prerogative and duty of naming ascribed to him in Genesis, actualizes these various languages in 'language as such' or 'the mental being of man', the form which 'communicates itself to God'.[21]

While Hopkins' early attraction to the 'onomatopoetic theory' indicates his readiness to establish an ontological status for language, he evidently found this means too reductive to do justice to the complexities of phenomena and language. It is only with the mature language theory established in the 1868 'Notes' that he fulfils the hope that he had for the onomatopoeic theory. The intimate relation that he sees to exist between words and being is described graphically in the first group of the 1868 notes, where 'the Idea' is likened to 'a hand' and its 'name' correspondingly to 'its glove left behind' (D. XII 1, fo. 2).[22] The figure of the glove is a sort of Platonic shadow of the hand. The main implication of the metaphor is

---

[20] W. Benjamin, *One-Way Street and other Writings*, trans. Edmund Jephcott and Kingsley Shorter (London: New Left Books, 1979), 109.
[21] Benjamin, ibid. 111.   [22] This passage is cited in Ch. 6, Sect. I.

that 'the Idea' can inform the name and so give it life, actualize it and make it dynamic, much as a hand fills and articulates
a glove, an object which is itself artificial and inert. The analogy that the 'Notes' make of the 'name' to a 'glove left behind'
after the living principle of the hand has been withdrawn represents the word as a material sign which bears a relation to its
signified that, while it has the potential to be quite fitting, is in
itself arbitrary and autonomous.

The characterization of the 'name' established in the first
group of the 'Notes' is sustained and developed in those that
follow them. Names, or 'words mean[ing] . . . things' (*J.* 125),
the specific linguistic form which according to Genesis God
entrusted man to formulate and apply to the Creation, are
the principal concern of the 'All words . . .' notes. In defining
this type of word the notes bring to the fore its arbitrary and
material nature as the 'definition, abstraction, vocal expression
or other utterance' (*J.* 125). Such words are referred to similarly in the 'Parmenides' notes, albeit with some concession
to Parmenides' scepticism about mortal opinion and language,
as 'but names given and taken' (*J.* 130). Indeed Parmenides'
main criticism of mortal opinion, that it names that which it
should not, highlights the arbitrary nature of linguistic signs,
a point that Hopkins acknowledges in his reference to the terms
of Parmenides' speculative cosmology as 'conventional, men's
names for things' (*J.* 130). Words are described here as 'lip service to the truth', and then in imagery which recalls the metaphor of the 'glove left behind' as 'husks and scapes of [the
truth]' (*J.* 130). Such inert and empty pieces of matter need
to be informed with being or stress if they are to fulfil their
function.

The 'appropriation of one . . . noise as a sign', 'a permanent
name', depends, according to T. H. Green, upon the apperceptive capacity to 'consciously present . . . a sensation to myself as
a permanent object'.[23] Hopkins' mature theory of language follows a similar line of argument. His observation that 'All words
mean either things or relations of things[,] . . . wholes or parts'
(*J.* 125) is consistent with the idealist theory of language that
Green presents in 'The Philosophy of Aristotle': 'We do not talk

[23] Green, *Works*, iii. 50.

of sensations, but of things, which our language assumes to
be permanent, while sensations are transitory. As permanent
we name them. If the permanence or generality corresponding to the name is not to be found in an outward thing, whence
is it?'[24] The answer for Green is of course subjective human
consciousness: 'This permanent relation, however, could not
have been so observed as to give occasion to the employment of
the name, unless the sensations themselves had been retained
by us as permanent objects of consciousness . . .'[25] Green's teaching is the most likely source for Hopkins' understanding of
how such generalizations as 'Blood is red', and the 'particular
judgments' which derive from them and are routinely made
in language acts, can be sustained: 'Mere intuition would enable me to say "this is here", "this is here" and so on[,] but
not "this stone is here" . . . [it] would not enable me to hold
this and this together. That I do hold them together is evident from [the] use *of words* . . . This, in fact, is self-conscious
thought . . .'[26]

The 'All words . . .' notes are concerned with words and works
of art, things which, unlike 'the Idea' and 'Being' or 'stress'
discussed elsewhere in the 'Notes', have significance only for
subjective consciousness. The apperceptive principle by which
the arbitrary material word, the 'utterance', is able to function
is specified in the 'All words . . .' notes as its 'prepossession of
feeling' (*J.* 125). The noun 'feeling' is used here in the special
sense that John Grote establishes in his *Exploratio Philosophica,*
and which is specified in a passage that Hopkins copied from
the book as 'a portion or instance of consciousness, which
. . . grows into knowledge' (D. VII 7, fo. 5). Hopkins' principle
of the 'prepossession' is in part a recapitulation of the mind's
initial apprehension of the particular as the Hegelian 'empty'
or 'pure' being, which Green describes as the simple sense
that ' "something is" ' and Hopkins refers to in the 'Parmenides'

---

[24] Ibid. 49.   [25] Ibid. 50.
[26] Balliol, T. H. Green Papers, MS II. 2(a), 1A, 'Lecture[s] on Logic', 12, fo. 16.
Isobel Armstrong also argues for the influence of Green upon Hopkins' language
theory in the 'Parmenides' notes (Armstrong, *Victorian Poetry: Poetry, Poetics and
Politics* (London: Routledge, 1993), 422–3). Professor Armstrong follows W. David
Shaw (*Lucid Veil*, 101–4) in using Green's critique of Hume in his Introd. to
Hume's Treatise on Human Nature (1874) as her main source for Green's thought
here.

notes as 'Being, the foredrawn, alone' (*J.* 129). It can, how-ever, be described more precisely as a particular inflection of consciousness:

> To every word meaning a thing and not a relation belongs a passion or prepossession or enthusiasm which it has the power of suggesting or producing but not always or in everyone. This *not always* refers to its evolution in the man and secondly in man historically.
>
> The latter element may be called for convenience the preposses-sion of a word. It is in fact the form, but there are reasons for being cautious in using form here, and it bears a valuable analogy to the soul, one however which is not complete, because all names but proper names are general while the soul is individual. (*J.* 125)

The 'prepossession of a word' is like the moral 'prepossession' in the *Ethike* essay a personal principle which provides the means by which a universal is acknowledged and realized. It is contin-gent upon historical experience, 'its evolution in the man and secondly in man historically' (*J.* 125), in a manner that paral-lels the determination of the moral prepossession by histor-ical and cultural factors as, for example, 'the Roman sense of duty to the father of the family or the Chinese awe for parents'. Just as 'those duties which personally were the prepossession' (*J.* 123) acknowledge and actualize 'the [moral] Imperative', 'the whole duty of man', so the 'prepossession' of the notes gives us a purchase on the universal principle of Being.

Objects in nature are in-themselves prepossessed with being, while the being with which humans are prepossessed is dis-tinguished by being self-reflexive, present to consciousness a priori as its radical condition. The specific 'prepossession' that belongs to words and works of art is a confluence of these two principles. It marks the reciprocal communication and deter-mination of being between the subject and object that Hopkins refers to in the 'Parmenides' notes as the 'stem of stress be-tween us and things' (*J.* 127). Analogous to the soul and syn-onymous with 'organisation', the prepossession is an ideal principle of 'form' which requires the mind's synthetic 'power of comparison' in order for it to be 'conveyed'. The other con-dition which permits the conveyance of the prepossession is that the object of contemplation has an actual objective exist-ence, that it be 'real': 'Works of art of course like words utter the idea and in representing real things convey the prepossession with more or less success' (*J.* 126).

The prepossession of a word is the schematic form which represents something 'real' that has been brought to subjective consciousness.[27] It marks a specific inflection of Being which becomes registered in a particular word meaning a thing, just as in nature each thing 'speaks and spells' itself and is brought to consciousness by the beholder and 'foredrawn' as an instance of determinate being or unity, a 'name'. The prepossession of the word is a finite moment of the ineffable and infinite *logos*, the Word which means Being itself. It accordingly presents a direct parallel to such creatures as the kingfishers and dragonflies which, prepossessed with a specific being, mark a particular register of ultimate, all-inclusive, Being. It is this prepossession of Being, or stress, that gives authority to 'words mean[ing] . . . things' and allows us to make generalizations such as 'Blood is red.'

The recognition of the prepossession of being, the stress, which words (and indeed 'anything, as a work of art'), convey is for Hopkins a morally good act that supervenes upon 'the act of contemplation as contemplating that which really is expressed in the object' (*J.* 126). The failure to contemplate the 'real' nature of the object can produce another, narcissistic, form of prepossession which relates purely to the subject's consciousness, the contingent associations of the word or work of art's 'evolution in the man'. '[S]ome minds', Hopkins writes in the notes, 'prefer that the prepossession they are to receive should be conveyed by the least organic, [the least] expressive, by the most suggestive, way' (*J.* 126). While the contemplation of that which is 'expressive' of an objective principle of determinate being draws the mind outwards in acknowledgement of it, contemplation of the merely 'suggestive' encourages the subject to indulge in its own arbitrary and solipsistic associations:[28] 'By this means the prepossession and the definition, uttering,

[27] Hence, its contingency upon historical considerations and the fact that it does not occur 'in everyone' (*J.* 125).

[28] This principle of the 'suggestive' can be traced to the early essay 'On the Signs of Health and Decay in the Arts', where a 'health[y]' art, which combines empirically real and ideal elements, is contrasted with an art that indulges what it

are distinguished and unwound'. The entropic metaphor of un-winding, an important ontological trope in Hopkins' writings,[29] connects this 'disengaged and unconditioned prepossession' (*J.* 126) with what he refers to elsewhere as the 'weariness or slackening' (*J.* 119) that materialism effects in thought. This forsaking of a coherent 'organic' apprehension of being is for Hopkins another alienating consequence of a 'disproportioned sense of personality' (*J.* 120), the 'selfbent' tendency of the sinner. It is a dwelling upon the self which foreshadows Hopkins' later description of Satan's sin as 'an instressing of his own inscape' (*S.* 201).

The final paragraph of the notes identifies the 'preference for the disengaged and unconditioned prepossession' with a mind that is also attracted to the machinery of rhetoric ('the two axes on which rhetoric turns', *J.* 126). The person who enjoys words and works of art for the effect they have on his mind naturally values the means by which they can be manipulated to act on the minds of others. Those who prefer the decadent type of prepossession and are attracted to rhetoric favour a perverse and degraded use of words which denies language's responsibility 'of acknowledging Being' (*J.* 129). This prepossession, like rhetoric, is an emptying out of language's function to communicate objective truth, to make authentic gestures of 'simple *yes* and *is*'.

IV

> The spoken word, it might be said, is the ecstasy of the creature, it is exposure, rashness, powerlessness before God; the written word is the composure of the creature, dignity, superiority, omnipotence over the objects of the world.[30]

---

considers to be a decadent taste: 'the love of the picturesque, the suggestive, when developed to the exclusion of the purely beautiful is a sure sign of decay and weakness' (*J.* 79).

[29] See e.g. 'Spelt from Sibyl's Leaves', No. 167, ll. 10–11.

[30] Walter Benjamin, *The Origin of German Tragic Drama*, trans. John Osborne (London: New Left Books, 1977), 201.

The 'word is', for Hopkins, 'the expression, *uttering* of the idea in the mind' (*J.* 125). Words provide the material medium for the 'idea', clothing and objectifying it as, in the terms of Hopkins' analogy, the glove does the hand. 'Only. . . as uttered', T. H. Green writes, 'can thought know or act upon itself.'[31] In Hopkins' scheme 'every word meaning a thing' embodies the soul-like prepossession, the mutual principle of being which connects a subject and its object. Each time that such a word is used it discloses being in the manner of reflexive self-consciousness, bringing it to consciousness, actualizing it, as a specific 'idea'. The material signifier of the word is accordingly able to function like a glove, providing the means by which the real world can 'be grasped and held together' (*J.* 118) by human consciousness. Much as in 'Ribblesdale', where 'man', in his capacity as 'Earth's . . . tongue' (No. 149), brings the being of the Earth (for 'sweet Earth . . . canst but only be') to utterance and consciousness, so similarly our words draw out and 'acknow-ledg[e]' the 'truth in thought . . . Being' (*J.* 129).

The 'prepossession', as Hopkins introduces his great onto-logical metaphor, 'flushes the matter' of the signifier just as it does the material work of art (*J.* 126). Words are not only upheld by stress but are reciprocally the medium in which stress is revealed, just as the flag makes manifest the form of the wind and water-weeds reveal the current of the stream: 'a floating flag is like wind visible and what weeds are in a current; it gives it thew and fires it and bloods it in' (*J.* 233).[32] The cloth or other material of the glove, like that of the flag, 'foredraw[s]' and so discloses the flushness of being, just as the matter of the word, its 'vocal expression or other utterance' (*J.* 125), does the more abstract prepossession of being. This analogy between the ubiquitous 'flushness' of air and that of being, which Hopkins elaborates in his figure of the 'burl' and in 'The Blessed Virgin compared to the Air we Breathe', is fundamental also to his theory of language and his practice of poetry.

Hopkins' definition of the word as the '*uttering*' (*J.* 125)

---

[31] 'Popular Philosophy in its Relation to Life', Green, *Works*, iii. 95. This essay was first published in the *North British Review* for Mar. 1868.

[32] See Ch. 8, Sect. V.

emphasizes its physicality, not only as materiality but also as *act*.[33] The spoken word is distinguished from its written counterpart by the life-giving principle of air which informs and impels it:

> This air, which, by life's law,
> My lung must draw and draw
> Now but to breathe its praise ...   (No. 151, ll. 13–15)

The 'praise' which Hopkins 'breathe[s]' here is his poem 'The Blessed Virgin compared to the Air we Breathe'. The ubiquitous ontological principle of the air informs and enlivens the spoken word just as it does the human being. The breath is the physical counterpart to the ideal principle of the 'prepossession of feeling', and they respectively represent the concrete and abstract moments of being that are brought together in Hopkins' coinage of instress.[34] The prepossession, like breath, *pneuma*, 'bears a valuable analogy to the soul' (*J.* 125). The physical act of utterance, according to Hopkins, gives breath, being, to the dead matter or atoms of arbitrary word-signs, much as in Genesis God, through the agency of the Holy Ghost, forms the 'living being' of man by breathing life into dust.[35]

The act of 'breath[ing] ... praise', which Hopkins identifies directly with speech and poetry in 'The Blessed Virgin compared to the Air we Breathe', has one of its most literal and illuminating instances in the closing line of 'God's Grandeur': 'the Holy Ghost óver the bent | World broods with warm breast and with ah! bright wings' (No. 111). The exclamatory 'ah!' here is a simple exhalation of breath, a pure gesture of wonder and admiration.[36] It is also a direct recognition, indeed a physical instressing, of the distinctive being of the Holy Ghost, whose 'name' is, as Hopkins observes, 'Spirit or Breath'. The Paraclete

---

[33] Speech is something that we *do*. This understanding of utterance is evident from Hopkins' use of it as a metaphor for the respective activities that define 'Each' of all the other 'mortal thing[s]' in Creation: '*myself* it speaks and spells, | Crying *What I do is me: for that I came*' (No. 115).

[34] Cf. D. X 4, fo. 22, where 'the inspiration' is presented as synonymous with the 'prepossession'.

[35] (Gen. 2: 7). For another approach to the issue of breath in Hopkins' work, see Paul Mariani, 'The Sound of Oneself Breathing', in Alison Sulloway, ed. *Critical Essays on Gerard Manley Hopkins* (Boston: G. K. Hall & Co., 1990), 53–9.

[36] Cf. its use in 'The Windhover' (No. 120, l. 13).

is being in its moment of 'flushness': 'The Holy Ghost then is, as I may say, a spirit of multitude and can spread and scatter his being and breath and be where Christ, being but one and like but one, cannot' (*S.* 98).[37]

Hopkins' mature poetry is full of exclamations of 'ah!' and 'O', words which make sense only through the intonation they receive as they are spoken, enacted, and so almost require us to comply with his frequently made request that his poetry be read aloud.[38] These simple acts of the exhalation of breath, unencumbered by a precise meaning or complex articulation, are the epitome of Hopkins' mature poetry. They embody the principle of faith outlined in the notes 'On Personality, Grace and Free Will', in which language functions primarily as an act, a gesture toward God: 'The parents understand what they do not say, the child says what it does not understand, but both child and parents mean the welcome' (*S.* 157). The praise which is for Hopkins the ultimate purpose of human speech and poetry is a giving back of breath that replicates and extends the motions of divine spirit in the world:

as the breath is drawn from the boundless air into the lungs and from the lungs again is breathed out and melts into the boundless air so the Spirit of God was poured out from the infinite God upon Christ's human nature and by Christ, who said: Receive the Holy Ghost: as my Father sent me so I send you |, was breathed into his Apostles and by degrees into the millions of his Church, till the new heavens and new earth will at last be filled with it. (*S.* 98)

Christ's words are the breath of Spirit which is in turn breathed into the apostles and the church, so that the world is gradually re-created as a dynamic plenum akin to the Edenic world described in the poem 'Spring' (No. 117). For this to occur, however, human beings must, Hopkins maintains, reciprocate the gracious inspirations which they receive from the Holy Spirit. In the case of the highest form of grace, elevating grace, 'man can respond . . . by no play whatever, by bare acknowledgment

---

[37] The spirit of God dwells within man, just as the Idea is seen in the 1868 notes to inform the word, in the manner of the hand in the glove: 'God rests in man as in a place, a *locus*, bed, vessel, expressly made to receive him as a jewel in a case hollowed to fit it, as the hand in the glove'. Hopkins goes on to compare the informing principle of divine being to the wind: 'This too best brings out the nature of the man himself, as the lettering on a sail or device upon a flag are best seen when it fills' (*S.* 195).   [38] See below, Sects. VI–VII.

only, the counter stress which God alone can feel'. This is
described by Hopkins using a metaphor of respiration as 'the
aspiration in answer to his inspiration' (S. 158).

This answering of God's grace is dramatized in the two parts
of 'The Leaden Echo and the Golden Echo' (No. 148). The
exclamatory 'O' is used frequently in both parts of the poem
in its appeals for a solution to the mortal predicament of
decaying physical beauty. The first part of the poem demands
that the exclamation be intoned as an expression of pain and
'despair' rather than of hope, and it finds its leaden echo in
the words 'no' and 'none'; 'O there's none; no no no there's
none' (l. 14). The answer to this 'nothing' and not-being is
the monistic 'One' of Being or God, and resurrection through
Christ. The 'O' of the first part of the poem has its golden
echo in the astonished and joyful intonation of the simple
exclamatory syllable in the phrase 'it is an ever-lástingness of,
O it is an áll youth!' (l. 29). Indeed the typographical 'O' and
the shape of the lips it requires for its utterance,[39] a circular
form representative of the Parmenidean sphere, itself suggests
the monistic 'One', 'an ever-lastingness of . . . O'.

The poem implores the reader to sacrifice her or his incarnate being: 'Give beauty back, beauty, beauty, béauty, back to God
beauty's self and beauty's giver' (l. 35). The resigned but joyful
exclamations of 'O' and 'Ah!' are the sighs which the poem
urges us to send heavenward in surrendering mortal beauty:

> Winning ways, airs ínnocent, maiden manners, sweet looks,
>   loose locks, long locks, lovelocks, gaygear, going gallant,
>   girlgrace—
> Resign them, sign them, seal them, send them, mótion them
>   with breath,
> And with sighs soaring, sóaring síghs, deliver
> Them . . .   (No. 148, ll. 31–4)

The human beauties catalogued here are properties to be
returned to God, 'beauty's self and beauty's giver'.[40] The way

---

[39] Eric Griffiths makes this observation about the shape of the lips required to
pronounce the letter 'O', which he describes as 'the prime, calling word of poetry'
(*The Printed Voice of Victorian Poetry* (Oxford: Clarendon Press, 1989), 264).

[40] Indeed they are like not only postal letters but the letters of the alphabet, the
human equivalent of those that each creature in the 'kingfishers' poem 'speaks
and spells' as its attributes.

to 'Resign' such beauties is first of all to 'sign them', not only in the manner of signing a letter, a contract, or an authorization, but more fundamentally in the demonstrative sense of signalling the direction in which they are to be sent, as in the mannerist gesture of a figure pointing heavenward. This is the sign made by aspirant sighs, which the notes 'On Personality, Grace and Free Will' identify with prayer, a 'sigh or aspiration or stirring of the spirit towards God' (S. 155). The signed and sealed letters of resignation are only sent, 'motion[ed]', accordingly as their written words are infused 'with breath', *uttered*, and then delivered in the more prolonged exhalation of 'sighs soaring, soaring sighs . . .' These balanced phrases present the intimate collocation of pain and transcendence which the Crucifixion of Christ makes foundational for Roman Catholic ideology: it is the paradox of the aspirant sigh, the synonymous 'sigh or aspiration' which is embodied in the poem's ambiguous exclamations 'O' and 'ah'.

The Crucifixion is the ultimate act of giving being back to God in which all other such acts are seen by Hopkins to participate. The death of the tall nun in 'The Wreck of the *Deutschland*' parallels this act and signals the way in which praise and other speech 'contribute[s] to that sacrifice'. The nun's last utterance, '"O Chríst, Chríst, come quíckly"' (No. 101, st. 24), is itself like death, a final exhalation of breath, an act of *expiration* which, as the etymology of this word from the Latin *spiritus* indicates, has long served classical and Christian cultures as the emblem for the soul leaving the body. The inhalation of air, with which our being in the world begins, has its counterpart in its exhalation, which ultimately marks our physical death; 'But man—we, scaffold of score brittle bones; | Who breathe, from groundlong babyhood to hoary | Age gasp; whose breath is our *memento mori*' (No. 178). The 'world-mothering air' is at once the providential 'nursing element' (No. 151, ll. 1, 10) that sustains our existence and that which, as another poem reminds us, fuels the 'Heraclitean Fire' of change and mortality with oxygen, which all animal life burns.[41] The

---

[41] Our exhalations of carbon dioxide can accordingly be recognized, along with charcoal and diamond, as a type of the carbon 'ash' referred to in 'That Nature is a Heraclitean Fire' (No. 174).

inspiration of divine grace is answered not only by the *aspiration* of 'sighs soaring' but ultimately by *expiration,* the 'death' which is made to rhyme with God's 'breath' in the parallel invocations of the Holy Ghost and Christ in stanza 25 of 'The Wreck of the *Deutschland'*: 'Breathe, arch and original Breath. | ... | Breathe, body of lovely Death' (No. 101).

V

Hopkins, evidently building upon the account in Genesis of the creation of Adam, uses imagery of air and breath thematically to describe and develop his ontology of the human subject. Fresh air, like clean water, is a sustaining clear and pure medium that Hopkins identifies with Being in its moment of 'flushness'. It is described in 'The Blessed Virgin compared to the Air We Breathe' as 'more than meat and drink' (No. 151, l. 11). The taking of breath is presented by the poem as a sacrament, a parallel to the Eucharist, which according to Catholic dogma makes Christ integral to individual human beings. Just as Christ received life from Mary's flesh, so through the physical medium of the air the life-giving principle of Christ's grace is able to 'flush' individual being; 'Men here may draw like breath | More Christ and baffle death' (ll. 66–7). Such grace informs all the person's being much as oxygen does through the lungs and the circulation of the blood. It reaches the heart of the creature's being. This makes of us signifiers of real meaning,[42] one of the 'things' referred to in 'God's Grandeur' in which the 'dearest freshness' dwells 'deep down' (No. 111). Indeed, by allowing his being to be informed with grace, just as breath informs the utterance of a word, the good person follows the example of Christ (who 'take[s spirit or breath] fresh and fresh' (No. 151, l. 56)) and so replicates the Word itself.

If, as Hopkins maintains, the ontology of human subjectivity parallels that of the word, with both being treated as types of

---

[42] The Eucharist, which Hopkins' doctrine of breath effectively extends, consecrates the traditional metaphysical–realist conception of meaning, for it asserts that the appearance of bread and wine signify meaning or truth, the actual body and blood of Christ.

matter that are upheld by breath, then the act of smelling provides a trope for self-consciousness. In the notes on the 'First
Principle and Foundation' Hopkins renders his personal sense
of subjectivity in terms that translate the Kantian unity of apperception into essentialist terms of smell and taste:

my selfbeing, my consciousness and feeling of myself, that taste of
myself, of *I* and *me* above and in all things, which is more distinctive
than the taste of ale or alum, more distinctive than the smell of wal-
nutleaf or camphor, and is incommunicable by any means to another
man . . . Nothing else in nature comes near this unspeakable stress of
pitch . . . this selfbeing of my own.   (*S.* 123)

The sense of self is, like the qualities of smell, both pervasive
and 'incommunicable', even 'unspeakable'. The distinctive
smells that Hopkins alludes to here are however pure and clean,
the vapours released by natural essences. Each such smell is
the very breath of its substance,[43] which Hopkins regards metaphorically as a corollary of spiritual fervour, 'the shewing the
stir of life, of a life not shared by all other things . . . the being
ready to pass, by evaporation, into a wholly spiritual condition'
(*S.* 208). Such odours parallel the purity of the Catholic ritualistic chrism, the 'oil of gladness' (No. 53). 'Chrism', which
means literally 'anything smeared on', is a mixture of the pure
essence of olive oil with balm, which according to the Roman
Catholic Catechism signifies the incorruption and 'good odour
of Christ'.[44]

The 'freshness' of being is described in the poem 'Spring',
where the season is presented as the recapitulation of the pure
prelapsarian state of the world:

What is all this juice and all this joy?
   A strain of the earth's sweet being in the beginning
In Eden garden.—Have, get, before it cloy,
Before it cloud, Christ, lord and sour with sinning . . .   (No. 117)

The Fall introduces the principle of change and mortality; the
wages of sin being death. The pure unchanging original state

[43] Cf. No. 119: 'Cómforting smell bréathed at very entering, | Fetched fresh . . . off
some sweet wood'.
[44] Addis and Arnold, *Catholic Dictionary*, s.v. 'Chrism', 152.

is *soured*, the 'freshness' made rancid, thereby acquiring the various stenches that signify our mortality. The grubby world of fallen humanity is described at greater length in 'God's Grandeur':

> ... all is seared with trade; bleared, smeared with toil;
> And wears man's smudge and shares man's smell ...   (No. 111)

Sin is for Hopkins characterized by an overweening sense of self, which is represented here by man's imposition upon the world of his 'smudge' and 'smell'. The sinner is depicted as polluting the original 'freshness',[45] filling it with his human and personal smell. Breathing in these conditions becomes a narcissistic activity of savouring the smell of self, of instressing one's own being rather than the clean air shared by all being, or the 'good odour of Christ' that promises salvation. Such sin holds within it the seeds of the utter alienation from all other being that Hopkins identifies with Hell, where sinners dwell only with themselves: 'their impurity comes up before them[;] they loved it once and breathed it, now it revolts them, it is to them like vomit and like dung' (*S.* 242). The miasma in which the sinner surrounds her- or himself and pollutes the world makes it all the more difficult to breathe, to be literally and figuratively inspired with, the 'good odour of Christ', the 'dearest freshness' of Being itself.

The binary opposition of freshness and filth which structures the ideology of 'God's Grandeur' can be traced to the first group of the 1868 notes, in which 'the Idea in its freshness' is juxtaposed with the 'positivists', 'those who are quite grimed with the concrete'. In handling 'the Idea' the positivists fail to recognize the fresh moist quality of flushness that informs it and so 'leave it a dry crumpled piece of skin'. While the idealist propensity for 'abstraction may as injuriously blow it out into a graceless bladdery animation' (D. XII 1, fo. 2), the doctrine that Hopkins develops from Parmenides emphasizes the informing and upholding principle of being, which it presents as synonymous with meaning: 'all things are upheld by instress and are meaningless without it' (*J.* 127). The scapes

---

[45] Cf. No. 119: 'Lóvely the woods, wáters, méadows, combes, vales, | All the air things wear that build this world of Wales; | Ónly the inmate does not correspond'.

here refer to an underlying principle of being or meaning, while the dessicated skin by which positivism recognizes the form of the Idea makes only the merest reference to substance, to an informing principle of meaning.

The simple superficies designated by the 'smudge' and the purely sensory intuition of smell in 'God's Grandeur' can be read as allegorical representations of the positivist criteria for knowledge. Positivism is for Hopkins effectively a down-payment on Baudrillard's anti-epistemology of simulacra. This is an implication of grimy humanity in the poem, where appearances are *only* obfuscating, offering no indication of a deep ideal principle of meaning. Appearances or 'scapes', the outward signs of intrinsic meaning, are blurred here; 'seared . . . bleared, smeared . . . smudge . . . smell'. However, while even such distorted appearances may nevertheless suggest the promise of meaning, the final term of Hopkins' protean series of words allows no possibility of such redemption. Smells are formless, they have no fixity or definition beyond our barely communicable subjective impressions. They are completely 'chromatic', or continuous and relativistic, and cannot be recuperated for rationalism. Smell is antithetical to the modern rationalist metaphor of vision, 'the figure of sight' in which, as Hopkins observes, 'intellectual action is spoken of' (*S.* 137). Smells are invasive and entropic, the pungent signifier of that which is out of control, of our animality and our mortality. While the pure and fresh odour of personal being discussed in the notes on the 'First Principle and Foundation' entails a death that is really a resurrection, an evaporation of finite being within the infinity of God, the wilful personal smell of the sinner is terminal.

The positivist 'grim[ing] with the concrete' is for Hopkins like sin, a failure to acknowledge the fulness of Being. The failure of positivism to recognize an upholding principle of instress means that both its objects and the words it applies to them are, judged by Hopkins' criterion, 'meaningless'. Its conception of the word resembles the empty matter of the glove, a mere nominalistic skin, the likes of which are instanced by the words of the poem: 'seared . . . bleared, smeared . . . smudge . . . smell'. Such mutating fluctuous sounds are often used in

Hopkins' poetry to refer to dissipation. This is clear from their predominance in 'Spelt from Sibyl's Leaves' (No. 167),[46] and in such lines as the following, from 'That Nature is a Heraclitean Fire', where a 'chromatic' series of word-sounds represents the process of dessication: 'Squandering ooze to squeezed dough, crúst, dust; stánches, stárches . . .' (No. 174). Such sequences exemplify the relativistic conception of language familiar to us from de Saussure and which Hopkins, like the early Walter Benjamin,[47] opposes with an idealist conception of 'pure' language or 'linguistic being'.

Hopkins traces all meaning to the *logos*, the transcendental signified of the 'Word'. The principle which underwrites meaning is for Hopkins a pure essence, namely Being, which like the oil in the olive can be *expressed*. In other words, essence can be uttered: 'each word', Hopkins writes in the 'Parmenides' notes, 'is one way of acknowledging Being' (*J.* 129). Hopkins' implicit pun on *expression* in 'God's Grandeur' is gruesomely brought to the fore by an unfinished poem that was written at the same time or shortly before it. While an early draft of 'God's Grandeur' refers to the 'ooze of oil | Pressed', the fragments on Margaret Clitheroe[48] focus upon a saint who was '*Pressed to death*' and who heroically uses this forced expiration of breath to affirm Christ's being and her devotion to him: 'When she felt the kill-weights crush | She told His name times-over three; | *I suffer this* she said *for Thee*' (No. 108, ll. 4, 55–7). Breath is, like olive oil, a traditional symbol for the Holy Ghost. It represents pure or essential being. The breath, the very being, of Margaret Clitheroe is through her torture translated into words that are voluntarily given to God.

---

[46] See below, Sect. VII.

[47] See Benjamin, 'On Language as Such and on the Language of Man' (1916), in *One-Way Street*, 107–23, and Benjamin, 'On the Task of the Translator' (1923) in *Illuminations*, ed. Hannah Arendt, trans. Harry Zohn (New York, 1968, repr. New York: Schocken, 1969), 69–82.

[48] The early draft ('F') of 'God's Grandeur' is not given a date by MacKenzie, although it probably predates the version that has been commonly accepted as definitive, which was complete at the end of Feb. 1877 (*Poetical Works*, ed. MacKenzie, 361). The fragments on Margaret Clitheroe date from late 1876 or early 1877 (ibid. 358).

VI

Hopkins' is a Trinitarian metaphysics of Being, Thought, and Word. Insistently reiterating and developing St John's principle of Christ as *logos*, the realization of God's 'Word', Hopkins' theory and poetic practice of 'utterance' make words material and mediate: incarnate. The distinctiveness of Christ which is so celebrated in Hopkins' poetry, as in much Western art since the Renaissance, is not so much his divinity as his corporeality. This value marks Hopkins' departure from the classical idealism of Parmenides and Plato, a difference that is highlighted in his commentary on Parmenides' cosmology near the end of his notes. Hopkins, having approached Parmenides' poem through the 'religious conviction' of its 'great text' (*J.* 127), finds it 'remarkable that he [i.e. Parmenides[49]] himself speaks of these [i.e. his cosmological principles of fire and earth] as conventional, men's names for things, and one of them, body, as wrongly given' (*J.* 130). What Hopkins finds 'remarkable' here is the idea of a cosmology without incarnation, the principle by which he effectively salvages 'Not-being' earlier in the notes.

God is the paradigm for Hopkins' understanding of utterance as act: 'God's utterance of himself in himself is God the Word, outside himself is this world' (*S.* 129). The act of utterance here represents the incarnate and objective form of *logos* manifest as Christ and Creation. This idea is elaborated upon in the poem on Margaret Clitheroe. Like 'The Wreck of the *Deutschland*', which was completed about six months before it,[50] this poem presents what are effectively fragments of a manifesto for his mature practice of poetry. Hopkins refers to the Trinity in this poem as 'The Utterer, Utterèd, Uttering' (No. 108, l. 25). The first term refers to the Father, and the second to Christ. The act of the 'Uttering' itself is the Holy Ghost. It is the actual breath which informs the word, the

[49] It does not seem likely, given the sparse paraphrase of Parmenides in the quotation from the *Metaphysics* (986^a34–9887^a1; quoted in Ritter and Preller, *Philosophiae Graecae*, 2nd edn., 110, with fr. 49) that immediately precedes Hopkins' comment here, that he is referring to Aristotle.

[50] Hopkins probably finished working on 'The Wreck' during May or June of 1876 (26 June 1876, Letter 75, *Further Letters*, 138).

'chromatic' principle of the 'flushness' of being which 'delights in multitude' (*S.* 98). God the Father is the principle of unity, or ultimate Being which 'foredraws' the 'flushness' of the Spirit, while Christ, the Word made flesh, is the emblem of the 'flush and foredrawn' itself, the type for determinate being or 'instress'.

While the Word existed, according to the Gospel of St John, 'in the beginning',[51] before the Creation, yet, as Hopkins' colleagues Addis and Arnold observe, 'As the spoken word is distinct from him who utters it, so was the Word distinct from God the Father.'[52] It is precisely the utterance of the Word that marks the distinction of Christ's being from that of the Father. The 'Utterèd' of the poem on Margaret Clitheroe is aptly endowed with the extra emphasis of a stress mark, a subtle suggestion of the marks of the Crucifixion, 'the márk . . . of mán's máke' which Christ 'scores . . . in scarlet himself on his own bespoken' (No. 101, st. 22). The context of interpretation provided by the poem on Margaret Clitheroe draws out the pun on the word 'bespoken' here so that as well as being a reference to the doctrine of predestination it encompasses its meaning of speech or exclamation.[53] The 'mark' 'scores' the utterance of the Word in the manner of the notation of metrical stress, making it emphatic, impassioned, and so suggesting, as the stress mark on the word 'Utterèd' does also, the Son's passionate stress of utterance on the Cross: 'My God, my God, why hast thou forsaken me?'[54] The act and materiality of speech make it analogous to the Word made flesh. This understanding of the word, which can be traced to the ostensibly secular terms of the 1868 notes on philosophy, is the basis of Hopkins' mature practice and theory of poetry.

The utterance of the word for Hopkins marks the incarnation of the idea: 'For the word is the expression, *uttering* of the idea in the mind'. The relation between the divine Word

[51] John 1: 1.
[52] Addis and Arnold, *Catholic Dictionary*, s.v. 'Trinity', 816. Addis was one of Hopkins' best friends from their student days together at Oxford. They remained close until Addis left the church in 1888 (See Lahey, *Gerard Manley Hopkins*, 18–19). Hopkins worked with both Addis and Arnold at University College, Dublin.
[53] For another discussion of Hopkins' use of this word, see Armstrong, *Language*, 435.   [54] Mark 15: 34.

and the 'word meaning a thing' (*J.* 125) of human language
is elaborated upon in 'The Wreck of the *Deutschland*':

> Jésu, héart's líght,
> Jésu, máid's són,
> Whát was the féast fóllowed the níght
>   Thou hadst glóry of thís nún?—
> Féast of the óne wóman withóut stáin.
> For so conceivèd, so to conceive thee is done;
>   But here was heart-throe, birth of a brain,
> Wórd, that héard and képt thee and úttered thee outright.
>
> (No. 101, st. 30)

For a word to be 'uttered . . . outright' suggests a rapid exclamatory exhalation, a greater stress of emphasis than is usual in
ordinary speech. It is a compression of breath which accordingly gives it a greater force, a compression that has its parallel
in the temporal compression of the various epiphanic flashes
of the poems, and its type in Christ, 'God's infinity | Dwindled
to infancy' (No. 151, ll. 18–19). The stress of outright utterance in the extract applies not simply to a word but to the
being of Christ. It is an instressing of his being that occurs
synecdochically as a stress of utterance, the extra breath required by the long *e* of the 'thee' by which Christ is addressed
here.

While 'the Idea' is in the 1868 Notes described as a riddle,
Hopkins' Parmenidean dictum 'To be and to know or Being
and thought are the same' (*J.* 129) is translated into Christian
terms in the extract from 'The Wreck' through the use of a
pun, a play on the idea of conception. The mental conception of Christ in the mind of the nun, the 'birth of a brain', is
paralleled with, and indeed seen to participate in, the physical conception of Christ by Mary. Both conceptions are drawn
together as the single principle of the 'Word' with which the
final line of the stanza begins. The octave is, as its first two
lines establish, addressed to Christ, and the 'Word' is the title
by which he is addressed in the last line. It is, however, also the
expression of the nun's idea, for the 'Word' follows immediately from the phrase 'birth of a brain'. The mental 'conception' is introduced in the 'All words . . .' notes as a moment
of 'the idea in the mind', for which of course 'the word is the
expression, *uttering*'. The 'Word' has a capital letter not only

because it refers to Christ but also because it is the first word in a line of poetry, and so can accordingly be stripped of this convention and viewed as a simple word representing the nun's thought, just as the incarnation allows God to be apprehended as an ordinary man ('he was what I am' (No. 174)). The synthesis of the Word with the human word yields the mediate figure of Christ. The physical conception, in which the Spirit assumes a human guise, and the mental conception, 'the idea in the mind' of the Christ-like nun, both have their expression, their incarnation, in the one utterance of the 'Word'. 'Being and thought are', indeed, 'the same' here.

The 'Word', in which the nun's thought and the actual being of Christ converge, determines the similarly ambiguous meaning of its correspondent term, the accommodatingly ungendered personal pronoun 'thee'[55] that is 'heard and kept . . . and uttered'. These terms represent the diremption of the 'Word' into its moments of subject and object which provide the condition for its full recognition of itself. The medium of the 'Word' is the principle which Christ recognizes in the nun and the nun recognizes in Christ. The pattern in which a moment of the idea or 'Word' is receptively 'heard' and then 'kept' (or 'caught'), instressed by consciousness, before being actively 'uttered . . . outright' in recognition of the principle that was originally 'heard', describes the greeting protocol discussed in Section I of the present chapter. Through its diremption here, the 'Word' both hears and utters itself; the nun hears, keeps, and then utters, the being of Christ, who reciprocally hears, keeps, and utters the being in Christ of the nun. The radical ambiguity of the last line of the stanza is, like that of the sestet of the 'kingfishers' poem and the last lines of 'Hurrahing in Harvest', indicative of a mutual act of reflexive self-consciousness.

The instressing of the 'Word' described by stanza 30 of 'The Wreck', the process by which it is 'heard . . . and uttered', corresponds to the way that this poem and its successors should, according to Hopkins, be read: 'take breath and read it with the ears'.[56] By 'tak[ing] breath' and uttering it, the poem is

---

[55] This archaic pronoun is also, significantly, not given a capital letter, as it is when it is used to refer to Christ in such poems as 'Let me be to Thee . . .' (No. 70) and 'The Half-way House' (No. 71).

[56] 22 Apr. 1879, Letter 59, *To Bridges*, 79.

read 'as if the paper were declaiming it at you'; it assumes an autonomous being.[57] It is only when the reader renders it in this material and active state that a word or indeed a poem can be properly 'read'; recognized, or 'caught' and 'kept', as an instance of being. The investment of stress gives words, and ultimately poems, a determinate being, so that they parallel natural objects. This analogy is made conversely in Hopkins' many descriptions of natural phenomena using tropes drawn from language practices. Trees as they grow are referred to as expressing and articulating, 'speaking' (*J.* 163), their form,[58] while each creature 'speaks and spells' its nature. The force of breath which impels utterance is understood by Hopkins as an important instance of his ontological principle of stress, the universal 'flushness' of Being.

VII

It is the task of the philosopher to restore, by representation, the primacy of the symbolic character of the word, in which the idea is given self-consciousness, and that is the opposite of all outwardly-directed communication.[59]

The theory of language developed in the 1868 notes, the tropes of greeting and other verbal addresses in his theological writings and poetry, and the expressivist metaphors used in the nature observations, all testify to Hopkins' belief that language is a natural rather than an artificial phenomenon, that it bears a direct relation to Being. His literal understanding of utterance as the issue of breath, as a physical pressure or stress, makes it representative for the emphatic affirmation and assertion of 'simple *yes* and *is*' which he believes is 'so pregnant and straightforward to the truth' (*J.* 127). The stress of breath in utterance is accentuated in metrical stress, and further intensified and brought to the fore by Hopkins' principle of 'Sprung Rhythm'. The dwelling upon and concentration of stress that sprung rhythm requires means that it is for

---

[57] 21 May 1878, Letter 40, *To Bridges*, 51–2. [58] See Ch. 8, Sect. V.
[59] Benjamin, *Origin of German Tragic Drama*, 36.

Hopkins 'the most natural of things'.[60] Hopkins' theory instates
stress as poetry's centre of gravity:[61]

Sprung Rhythm . . . is measured by feet of from one to four syllables,
regularly, and for particular effects any number of weak or slack syllables may be used. It has one stress, which falls on the only syllable,
if there is only one, or, if there are more, then scanning . . . on the
first . . . And hence Sprung Rhythm differs from Running Rhythm
[i.e. conventional metrical verse] in having or being only one nominal rhythm, a mixed or 'logaoedic' one, instead of three, but on
the other hand in having twice the flexibility of foot, so that any two
stresses may either follow one another running or be divided by one,
two, or three slack syllables . . . In Sprung Rhythm . . . the feet are
assumed to be equally long or strong and their seeming inequality
is made up by pause or stressing.[62]

Hopkins makes a single stress the measure of each metrical
foot and the principle which upholds it. The stress effectively
'flushes the matter' of its syllables (or indeed the letters of
its syllable), 'foredraw[ing]' its manifold to the organic unity
of the metrical foot:

Only let this be observed in the reading, that, where more than one
syllable goes to a beat, then if the beating syllable is of its nature
strong, the stress laid on it must be stronger the greater the number
of syllables belonging to it, the voice treading and dwelling: but if
on the contrary it is by nature light, then the greater the number of
syllables belonging to it the less is the stress to be laid on it, the voice
passing flyingly over all the syllables of the foot and in some manner
distributing among them all the stress of the one beat.[63]

[60] [Author's Preface on Rhythm], *Poetical Works*, ed. MacKenzie, 117. See also 18
Oct. 1882, Letter 90, *To Bridges*, 156.
[61] This is precisely Hopkins' approach in the undergraduate essay 'On the
True Idea and Excellence of Sculpture', which, following Lessing, argues that the
nature of stone, literally its centre of gravity, determines its most appropriate use
in depicting attitudes of 'repose', and earthbound, rather than airy, figures (*Journals
and Papers*, ed. Castorina, 176–7).
[62] [Author's Preface on Rhythm], *Poetical Works*, ed. MacKenzie, 116.
[63] 'Author's Note on the Rhythm in "The Wreck of the *Deutschland*"', *Poetical
Works*, ed. MacKenzie, 118. Furthermore, Hopkins' theory makes the larger unity
of the stanza (and by extension the complete poem) dependent upon stress, for
'the scanning runs on without break from the beginning, say, of a stanza to the
end and all the stanza is one long strain, though written in lines asunder' ([Author's
Preface on Rhythm], ibid. 116).

In his theory of sprung rhythm, much as in his ontology, the principle of stress counteracts that of the 'slack', the unity of 'Being' encompasses and articulates the many of 'Not-being'.

Hopkins writes of sprung rhythm that 'it is the nearest to the rhythm of prose, that is[,] the native and natural rhythm of speech', and that it is prevalent in such popular cultural forms as jingles, 'Nursery Rhymes, Weather Saws, and Refrains'.[64] His theory appears to be a development of the romantic ideology established by Wordsworth in the 'Preface' to the *Lyrical Ballads*, which asserts 'the strict affinity of metrical language with that of prose' and that poetry should draw empirically upon 'language really spoken by men'.[65] Like Wordsworth, Hopkins claims to be reforming prosody by championing the use of common and 'natural' principles of language: 'what I do in the *Deutschland* etc is to enfranchise them [i.e. instances of sprung rhythm] as a regular and permanent principle of scansion'.[66] His doctrine is, however, based upon a critique of Wordsworth, which he makes in the undergraduate essay on 'Poetic Diction'.[67]

The essay opens with a statement of the doctrine it will contest: 'Wordsworth's view was that poetic diction scarcely differed or ought to differ from that of prose: he said "The most interesting parts of the best poems will be found to be strictly the language of prose when prose is well written"' (*J*. 84). Hopkins, drawing upon his reading of G. E. Lessing's *Laocoon*,[68] argues that Wordsworth fails to acknowledge the importance that the formal structures of poetry have in shaping their distinctive language and thought. Lessing is accordingly used by Hopkins to 'modify what Wordsworth says[:] An emphasis of structure stronger than the common construction of sentences gives asks for an emphasis of expression stronger than that of common speech or writing, and that for an emphasis of thought stronger than that of common thought.' Even

[64]   21 Aug. 1877, Letter 37, *To Bridges*, 46. See also *To Dixon*, 14 (5 Oct. 1878, Letter 3).

[65]   Wordsworth, *Lyrical Ballads*, 2nd edn. (1805), repr. in *Wordsworth's Literary Criticism*, ed. W. J. B. Owen (London: Routledge & Kegan Paul, 1974), 76.

[66]   21 Aug. 1877, Letter 37, *To Bridges*, 45.

[67]   The essay probably dates from 1865 (*J*. 84; Schmidt, 'Classical Studies', 179).

[68]   The *Laocoon* was translated by W. Ross in 1836, and then by E. C. Beasley in 1853, the edn. that Hopkins used.

though it may, as Wordsworth says, be possible to trace the words of 'the best poems' to ordinary prose and common speech, Hopkins maintains that the form of poetry acts upon such matter to draw from it a greater 'emphasis of expression' and 'emphasis of thought' (*J.* 85). This inclusive principle of 'emphasis' anticipates the 'stress' of Hopkins' later theory and practice of sprung rhythm, 'the most . . . emphatic of all possible rhythms'.[69]

Hopkins' doctrine of sprung rhythm effectively radicalizes Wordsworth's tenets about the use of common language and prose rhythms in poetry. It removes this discourse from Wordsworth's empiricist and social approach to language into the Parmenidean sphere of ontology. The 'common' principle which poetry derives from ordinary speech acts and prose is for Hopkins being or stress, an energy which the formal structures of poetry focus and intensify:[70]

Sprung rhythm gives back to poetry its true soul and self. As poetry is emphatically speech, speech purged of dross like gold in the furnace, so it must have emphatically the essential elements of speech. Now emphasis itself, stress, is one of these: sprung rhythm makes verse stressy; it purges it to an emphasis as much brighter, livelier, more lustrous than the regular but commonplace emphasis of common rhythm as poetry in general is brighter than common speech. But this it does by a return from that regular emphasis towards, not up to[,] the more picturesque irregular emphasis of talk—without however becoming itself lawlessly irregular.[71]

[69] 21 Aug. 1877, Letter 37, *To Bridges*, 46.
[70] The other undergraduate essay which Hopkins bases upon his reading of Lessing, 'On the True Idea and Excellence of Sculpture' (D. V 1), which, like 'Poetic Diction', dates from 1865, prescribes that 'The true artist will accept and even strengthen his conditions, because Art shews that perfection is only in this way attainable, and that man's faculties deliver their strongest blows thus concentrated'. The strong blows of sprung rhythm in Hopkins are produced similarly according to this formulation, by heightening not just the metrical conditions of poetry, but more radically the stress of speech. Hopkins' approach to sculpture in the early essay is effectively transposed and applied to poetry in his later theory: 'If we take its conditions one by one, the convergence of the logical results of each of them will point to a centre which we may conclude to be the true nature of sculpture' (*Journals and Papers*, ed. Castorina, 174, 176). This centre is, in Hopkins' conception of poetry, sprung rhythm.
[71] To Everard Hopkins, 5 Nov. 1885, in Anthony Bischoff, SJ, 'Hopkins's Letters to his Brother', *Times Literary Supplement*, 8 Dec. 1972, p. 1511.

Sprung rhythm presents stress in its most pure and abstract form, a suggestive parallel to the stress of Parmenidean Being. The 'true soul and self' of poetry is disclosed here, much as the stress of Being is in 'The Windhover', through a process of refining a commonplace phenomenon. The imagery of 'speech purged of dross like gold[,] ... purge[d] ... to an emphasis as much brighter, livelier, more lustrous', parallels the pattern in the poem by which the 'blue-bleak embers ... | Fall, gáll them- sélves, and gásh góld-vermílion' (No. 120). Each yields a bril- liant effect of reflected light. Sprung rhythm, the 'soul' of poetry, emerges from the 'husks and scapes' (*J.* 130) of phe- nomenal language. It is resurrected from the 'mortal trash' or 'ash' of the semiotic 'Heraclitean fire' like the 'flash' of Being in its hard crystalline form of the diamond (No. 174).

The stress of sprung rhythm is a form of the energy of being, which like that of 'God's Grandeur' 'will flame out, like shin- ing from shook foil' (No. 111). Sprung rhythm, according to Hopkins' metaphor, gives stress a property that is analogous to shining by reflected light, a quality of being 'lustrous'. Its stress of utterance shines by the reflected being or stress of the speaker, the kinetic energy of breath that is invested in it and which returns to the speaker in the energy of sound as we 'take breath and read it with the ears'. This process of reflec- tion, according to Hopkins, marks the difference between poetry and common prose: 'For instance the line "she had come from a cruise training seamen" read without stress and declaim is mere Lloyd's Shipping Intelligence; properly read it is quite a different thing. Stress is the life of it'.[72]

Hopkins' example here, a line from 'The Loss of the *Eurydice*', demonstrates the priority he gives to the formal principle of stress over the semantic content of poetry. Here is another example:

> Earnest, earthless, equal, attuneable, | vaulty, voluminous, ...
>   stupendous
> Evening strains to be tíme's vást, | womb-of-all, home-of-all,
>   hearse-of-all night.   (No. 167)

Lines such as these, with which 'Spelt from Sibyl's Leaves' begins, remain obscure well beyond a first reading of them.

---

[72] 21 May 1878, Letter 40, *To Bridges*, 52.

Hopkins' is not an instrumentalist theory of language, but an idealist one akin to that of the early Walter Benjamin, who like Hopkins argues in the traditions of post-Kantianism that 'mental being communicates itself *in* language and not *through* language'.[73] Words are not for Hopkins transparent signs representing things, but themselves material objects. W. B. Yeats has commented that 'His meaning is like some faint sound that strains the ear, comes out of words, passes to and fro between them, goes back into words.'[74] This perception of precise 'meaning' in Hopkins' poetry as a whisper or ghost that emerges from and returns to the reified structures of the words themselves, barely distracting from their materiality, is incisive. The specific meanings of Hopkins' language are indeed often only a 'faint sound' next to the substance and stridency of the metrical stresses. The determinate meaning of such poems as 'The Leaden Echo and the Golden Echo' and 'Spelt from Sibyl's Leaves' emerges tentatively from the solid and powerful utterances which assert the fundamental materiality of the words, their ultimate nature as ciphers for ubiquitous Being. Meaning itself is sacrificed, given back to God.

Sprung rhythm makes Hopkins' words analogous to 'The dense and the driven Passion' (No. 101, st. 7) of the Word.[75] Much of his poetry, like the words of Christ in his Passion, appears to be impelled by the body, most apparently through the exhalation of breath: 'Is out with it! Oh, | We lash with the best or worst | Word last! . . .' (st. 8). It gives primacy to the Kristevan 'semiotic' of bodily pulsations, as it is registered in stress, rhythm, and alliteration, over the 'symbolic', the prescribed meanings of conventional linguistic signs.[76] This vestigial pre-linguistic element to language is, as the earlier

[73] Benjamin, *One-Way Street*, 108.

[74] From the 'Introduction' to *The Oxford Book of Modern Verse* (Oxford: Clarendon Press, 1936), repr. in Gerald Roberts (ed.), *Gerard Manley Hopkins: the Critical Heritage* (London: Routledge & Kegan Paul, 1987), 345.

[75] Hopkins urges Bridges in reading 'Spelt from Sibyl's Leaves' to '*above all* remember what applies to all my verse, that it is, as living art should be, made for performance and that its performance is not reading with the eye but loud, leisurely, poetical (not rhetorical) recitation, with long rests, long dwells on the rhyme and other marked syllables, and so on' (11 Dec. 1886, Letter 143, *To Bridges*, 246; my emphasis).

[76] See Julia Kristeva, *Desire in Language: A Semiotic Approach to Literature and Art*, trans. Thomas Gora, Alice Jardine, and Leo S. Roudiez (Oxford: Blackwell, 1981).

discussion of the simple utterances 'ah' and 'O' argue, fundamental to Hopkins' understanding of the moral significance of
speech acts. The figure representing mankind in Hopkins'
allegory of faith in 'On Personality, Grace and Free Will', the
child, is effectively pre-linguistic; the words he speaks being
sounds that he imitates from his parents but does not understand. The faithful 'just man' effectively 'plays' with language.
He enjoys it as he does the creation, with spontaneous good-
will, as an end in itself rather than instrumentally, as a means
to an end. This simple and joyous 'play' of the 'semiotic' directly acknowledges the 'flushness' of Being, of God as oceanic
maternal principle, the nurturing 'fondler of heart thou hast
wrung' who is 'Beyond saying sweet'. It is the complement to
the fully self-conscious linguistic recognition of divine authority,
the deliberate utterance of assent to the 'foredrawn' principle
of law, the phallogocentric order of the 'Father' (st. 9): 'I did
say yes | O at lightning and lashed rod; | Thou heardst me truer
than tongue confess' (st. 2).

Hopkins' mature poetry, like the poetry of Parmenides, is
devoted to Being. His conception of being as 'stress', however,
draws together the ideal (Parmenides' 'Being') with the bodily
and contingent conditions of existence ('Not-being'), both of
which he sees to converge in speech acts. The duty of 'man' to
be 'Earth's . . . tongue' (No. 149) involves not only the content
of our utterances, but also their irreducible form as stress, the
'simple' recognition and assertion that they make of '*yes* and
is'. The stress of utterance brought to the fore by sprung rhythm
is one of Hopkins' gestures of recognizing Being, an acknowledgement of a principle greater than its specific instances, which
provide the particular content of poetry. Being is, as Hopkins
maintains throughout his writings on metaphysics and theology, the whole to which all its parts are subordinate. The recognition of the larger principle of Being is accordingly given
priority over the communication of particular meaning. This
idealist perspective determines Green's theory of the origin of
language. The priority that his psychology gives to the original
sense in consciousness of an object in general, ' "this is here
as an object to me" ',[77] is seen by Green in some unpublished

[77] Green, *Works*, iii. 52.

lecture notes from the 1860s to be corroborated by recent
findings in language theory: 'This coincides with [the] philological discovery that language begins with words which are
not definitely either substantives or verbs, but sounds expressing consciousness of phenomena, which phen[omena] may be
substantiated, i.e. fixed by thought as permanent centres upon
which other sensations are to gather, or referred to substances
as their acts.'[78] This theory suggests that such exclamations as
'ah!' and 'O' are the ur-words from which all language develops.
Green's theory of the relational determination of meaning, by
which, from the general apperceptive sense of consciousness,
the 'individual thing . . . is capable of infinite determination, as
in the motion of knowledge it is brought into new relations',[79]
is effectively enacted in Hopkins' poetry. The relation between
particular words within this system and their source in Being is
introduced in the 'Parmenides' notes as that between 'names
given and taken, eye and lip service to the truth', and 'the truth
itself, the burl' (*J.* 130). The logical field of meaning is divided
amongst particular words: 'With swíft, slów; sweet, sóur; adázzle,
dím; | He fathers-forth whose beauty is pást chánge' (No. 121).
These binary oppositions each represent the entire spectrum of
their respective categories of movement, taste, and light, all of
which are contained within the ultimate category of Being itself,
from which they are generated. They present an orderly division
within the general sense or *stress*,[80] the prepossession of being
or consciousness, with which all knowledge begins.

While the relational language system functions in 'Pied
Beauty' as a taxonomy of Being that organizes the natural flux,
it is identified in 'Spelt from Sibyl's Leaves' with the disintegration of meaning:

---

[78] Balliol, T. H. Green Papers, MS 1A, No. 12 (loose insert, 1 fo.). The dates
are uncertain, but the inclusion in this notebook of another loose note made
on Schools Commission notepaper suggests a date of composition soon after his
return from this job to Oxford in 1865.   [79] Green, *Works*, iii. 60.

[80] The play of words in Hopkins is like the play of light in the 'kingfishers' poem
or the analogy of the sunlight on water in the 'Notes' (D. XII 3), determined by
his idealism and the Pythagorean rhetoric that often accompanies it. He aims for
play in the regulated sense of playing music. Hence in the early word-lists onomatopoeic words are arranged in a manner that is analogous to a musical scale
(and hence also to the taxonomic arrangement of biological 'species' [*J.* 120])
and referred to explicitly as different 'tone[s]' of a shared meaning (*J.* 11).

... Lét life, wáned, ah lét life wínd
Off hér once skéined stained véined varíety upon, áll on twó
  spools; párt, pen, páck
Now her áll in twó flocks, twó folds—bláck, white; | ríght, wrong;
  réckon but, réck but, mind
But thése two; wáre of a wórld where bút these twó tell, éach off
  the óther; of aráck
Where, selfwrung, selfstrung, sheathe- and shelterless, | thóughts
  agaínst thoughts ín groans grínd.   (No. 167)

The binary 'flocks' which diminish the variety of nature celebrated in 'Pied Beauty' work wilfully against one another here;
the 'twó tell, éach off the óther'. Breath, which in Hopkins'
scheme incarnates thought, and 'flushes' and unifies difference, is pained here, issued in 'groans' which define and assert themselves only as they 'grind' against one another. This
destructive process, whilst it ostensibly works to distinguish
particular meanings within the field of being, effectively pre-
cipitates a heat death in which the stark binary oppositions
represented by 'black, white', and indeed 'right, wrong', are
worn down to a meaningless entropic grey. In lines like this,
however, the stress is made all the more strong and insistent,
so that the diatonic generic meaning of all utterances predominates over the 'chromatic' meanings generated by words
as they wear away, deconstruct, their meanings. That which to
a modern reader can be identified with a relativistic Saussurean
conception of language is subordinated to an idealist doctrine
in which language represents pure being.

Green's theory of language, like Jowett's biblical hermeneutics, depends upon the 'theological' presupposition of a
'primal word', which J. Hillis Miller identifies with Hopkins'
early word-lists.[81] While the early poem 'Let me be to Thee'
finds its 'dominant' chord 'in a common word', 'Love, O my
God, to call Thee Love and Love' (No. 70), his later theory of
the Word and of sprung rhythm is based upon a conception of
a primal word that draws together these aspects of the word as
utterance and act, distilling their fundamental participation in
Being through the principles of breath and stress. Poetry is the
medium which facilitates the revelation of the primal word in
ordinary language: 'Poetry is speech framed for contemplation

---

[81] Miller, *Linguistic Moment*, 261–2.

of the mind by the way of hearing or speech framed to be heard for its own sake and interest even over and above its interest of meaning[,] . . . at least the grammatical, historical, and logical meaning' (*J.* 289).[82] It facilitates a 'contemplation' of the very being of speech, the 'contemplation . . . [of] that which really is expressed in the object' (*J.* 126) of speech itself, just as Hopkins' attentiveness to particulars in nature, most notably in the case of the windhover, yields a perception of the ultimate principle of Being to which they belong.

While exclamations such as 'ah!' and 'O' are epitomes of Hopkins' poetry which suggest Green's primal word of consciousness, its paradigm is the nun's cry in 'The Wreck of the *Deutschland*', ' "O Chríst, Chríst, come quíckly" ' (No. 101, st. 24). The quotation marks that contain these words, like the italicization of Margaret Clitheroe's dying words (No. 108, l. 57), effectively function as *de facto* stress marks, a cue to the reader to endow them with an additional stress of utterance as direct and actual speech, indeed speech that was originally informed with a peculiarly desperate urgency akin to that of Christ's passion. Drawn directly from a press report of the wreck in *The Times*, these words exemplify Hopkins' definition of sprung rhythm as 'in fact the *native rhythm* of the words used bodily imported into verse'.[83] This transposition of real speech is the type for Hopkins' verse: it is flushed with the stress of being, appeals to its source in God, and offers its being (a revivification of the nun's last breath) to Christ.

Our utterances go out into the world, like the cry of the tall nun, informed by our being and impelled by our will. Utterances, like other acts, gain their moral significance for Hopkins from the intentions which inform them. This is clearly demonstrated by his allegory of faith, in which the child means the

[82] Michael Sprinker and Gerald Bruns fruitfully explore some of the implications of Hopkins' definition of poetry as 'the inscape of speech' (*J.* 289), the former with regard to his interest in musical composition (*Counterpoint of Dissonance*, 73–6), the latter by focusing in particular on its relation to the energy concept: 'verse becomes something like an energy field in which written words behave like charged bodies: they are not ponderous particles acted upon merely by forces from without but particles that change from within' (Bruns, 'Energy and Interpretation', 135).

[83] 21 Aug. 1877, Letter 37, *To Bridges*, 46. *The Times* of 11 Dec. 1875 reports that 'the chief sister . . . called loudly and often "O Christ, come quickly!" ' On this and other reports, see White, *Hopkins*, 254–5.

words that he utters even though he does not understand their meaning. It is also fundamental to his poetic practice of sprung rhythm. Hopkins, discussing the poetry of the Elizabethan poet Robert Greene in a letter to Bridges in 1882, refers to the crucial importance of employing sprung rhythm 'consciously'. Intention is for Hopkins fundamental to sprung rhythm: 'In a matter like this a thing does not exist, is not *done* unless it is wittingly and willingly done; to recognise the form you are employing and to mean it is everything'. Walt Whitman's poetry is judged by this criterion to have only the appearance of sprung rhythm: 'If he does not mean it then he does not do it.'[84] Hopkins' objection to Whitman is rendered in terms of the intentionalism of the undergraduate essays. It is a moral criticism of someone who he describes earlier in his letter as 'a very great scoundrel'.[85]

If, as Pater famously declares, '*All art constantly aspires towards the condition of music*',[86] then specific content must be judged inessential to art. The plainchant rhythms of Hopkins' sprung rhythm exemplify his tutor's dictum, and leave him open to charges of formalism: 'His innovations . . .', T. S. Eliot writes, 'sometimes come near to being purely *verbal*, in that a whole poem will give us *more* of the same thing, an accumulation, rather than a real development of thought or feeling.'[87] The stresses of sprung rhythm, like the modes which 'instress' the harmony in the plainchant music of which Hopkins is so fond, provide a repetitive assertion and reiteration of Being.

The doctrine of 'The Two Vocations',[88] which emphasizes the apparent conflicts between Hopkins' work as a priest and as a poet, is entrenched in Hopkins studies. He should not, however, be confused with Joyce's young Stephen Dedalus and characterized as torn between a romantic calling to poetry, to becoming a Coleridgean priest of the eternal imagination, and a religious vocation with the Jesuits. Hopkins recognizes no contradiction in declaring in a brief letter to Bridges in early

[84] 18 Oct. 1882, Letter 90, *To Bridges*, 156.   [85] Ibid. 155.

[86] 'The School of Giorgione', originally published in *Fortnightly Review*, Oct. 1877, repr. in *The Renaissance*, ed. Kenneth Clark (London: Collins, 1961), 129.

[87] From T. S. Eliot, *After Strange Gods* (London: Faber & Faber, 1934), repr. in Roberts (ed.), *Critical Heritage*, 285.

[88] This is the title of the introductory chapter to W. H. Gardner's hugely influential study *Gerard Manley Hopkins, 1844–1889: A Study of Poetic Idiosyncrasy in Relation to Poetic Tradition*, and signals an integral part of its approach to the poet's work.

August 1868 that he has both burnt his early verses because, as he puts it, 'I saw they wd. interfere with my state and vocation', and invented a new prosody, a 'peculiar beat', which he has 'introduced into [his poem on] St. Dorothea'. This new 'development', which he declares proudly 'is mine',[89] is, as Gardner notes,[90] sprung rhythm. Hopkins (like his twentieth century readers) makes a radical distinction between his early poetry and the later poetic practice which he introduces here, 'the echo of a new rhythm' which he would have 'haunting' his ear until it is granted substantive form in 'The Wreck of the Deutschland' in 1875.[91]

The revised version of 'St. Dorothea' that Hopkins mentions was necessarily written at some time prior to the date of his letter, although, judging from his evident enthusiasm for it, probably not very much before. There would be at most only a few months separating the writing of the 'Parmenides' notes and the inception of Hopkins' new poetic practice. This 'peculiar beat' follows not from the early poetry, which he burnt, but from his metaphysical doctrine of the 'Parmenides' notes; it is the incipient form of a poetry that is consistent with his conviction that 'The truth in thought is Being, stress, and each word is one way of acknowledging Being . . .' (*J.* 129). Hopkins' undergraduate essays in philosophy testify to his early and strong 'prepossession' of unity, his romantic predisposition for synthesizing the apparently disparate, a tendency which has its ultimate expression in the monistic doctrine of stress and instress in the 1868 notes, where he works to reconcile physics and metaphysics, the material and the ideal. It is not surprising to find him later in 1868 experimenting with a new poetic principle of 'stress' that will extend the terms of his syncretic metaphysic of Being to the practice and theory of his poetry.

'The Wreck of the *Deutschland*', while written at the suggestion of one of his superiors,[92] is the avant-garde for an eccentric body of poetry that was not composed for publication: 'I cannot think of altering anything. Why shd. I? I do not write for the public.'[93] Hopkins, like William Blake before him,

---

[89] 7 Aug. 1868, Letter 22, *To Bridges*, 24.
[90] Gardner, *GMH: A Study*, i. 38.   [91] 5 Aug. 1878, Letter 3, *To Dixon*, 14.
[92] Ibid.
[93] He continues, addressing Bridges, 'You are my public and I hope to convert you' (*To Bridges*, 46). The word 'convert' would have been an especially charged

manages to establish a private and idiosyncratic system of thought and, despite the lack of a public audience, to confidently maintain a highly independent, indeed aberrant, practice of poetry. It has long been recognized that the individuality of Blake's poetry springs from his peculiarly personal system of thought. The same is true also of Hopkins. The distinctiveness of Hopkins' poetry can be accounted for not by the normative understandings of Roman Catholic doctrines that he shared with his peers, but by focusing upon his departures from such norms in the metaphysic that he develops as an undergraduate, and which is formulated finally in his notes on Greek philosophy early in 1868: his instressing of the metaphysical grounds of his belief in preparation for his new life in the Society of Jesus.[94]

While Hopkins became used during his novitiate to the control and surveillance of his correspondence by his superiors,[95] and so may have thought of letters as a semi-public genre, his poetry remained intensely private. Not only did he 'not write for the public', but, as his instructions for reading the poetry indicate, he did not even envisage that they would be read aloud by one person to another, but only by himself and a couple of his friends, each to himself. The reading of his poetry is, like praying or the medieval monastic practice of 'chewing' the words of the Bible,[96] an ostensibly solitary activity. Hopkins' mature poems are a series of personal gestures 'sen[t] . . . soaring' to Being, which, having been accidentally delivered to a secular century, oddly continue to be 'motion[ed] . . . with breath'.

one for Hopkins. Its use here suggests the close connection that he sees to exist between his religious beliefs and his poetry. He hopes that his verse may win his friend over to his poetic practice, and indeed to his Church.

[94] Hopkins' doctrine of 'stress', 'instress', and 'inscape' also provides the 'pre-possession' for Hopkins' later reading of Duns Scotus, determining his later attraction to, and understanding of, the medieval theologian.

[95] 7 Aug. 1868, Letter 22, *To Bridges*, 24.

[96] Medieval clergy are said to have moved their lips whilst silently reading the Bible to themselves. M. T. Clanchy cites St Anselm's invocation to '"Taste the goodness of your redeemer. . . chew the honeycomb of his words, suck their flavour which is sweeter than honey, swallow their wholsome [*sic*] sweetness. Chew by thinking, suck by understanding, swallow by loving and rejoicing." Reading was a physical exertion, demanding the use not only of the eyes, but of tongue, mouth and throat' (*From Memory to Written Record: England 1066–1307* (London: Edward Arnold, 1979), 217).

Bibliography

AARON, RICHARD I., *John Locke*, 3rd edn. (Oxford: Clarendon Press, 1971).

ABBOTT, EVELYN, and CAMPBELL, LEWIS (eds.), *The Life and Letters of Benjamin Jowett: Master of Balliol College, Oxford*, 2nd edn. 2 vols. (London: John Murray, 1897).

—— —— *Letters of Benjamin Jowett: M. A.* (London: John Murray, 1899).

ADDIS, WILLIAM, and ARNOLD, THOMAS, *A Catholic Dictionary* (London: Kegan Paul, Trench, & Co., 1884).

ALLSOPP, MICHAEL, 'Hopkins at Oxford 1863–1867: His Formal Studies', *Hopkins Quarterly*, 4/3–4 (1977–8), 161–76.

ARISTOTLE, *The Works of Aristotle*, ix, *Nicomachean Ethics*, trans. W. D. Ross (Oxford: Clarendon Press, 1925).

—— *The Works of Aristotle*, ii. *Physics*, trans. R. P. Hardie and R. K. Gaye (Oxford: Clarendon Press, 1930).

ARMSTRONG, ISOBEL, *Language as Living Form in Nineteenth Century Poetry* (Brighton: Harvester Press, 1982).

—— *Victorian Poetry: Poetry, Poetics and Politics* (London: Routledge, 1993).

AUSTIN, SCOTT, *Parmenides: Being, Bounds, and Logic* (New Haven: Yale University Press, 1986).

BAIN, ALEXANDER, *The Senses and the Intellect*, 3rd edn. (London: Longmans, Green, & Co., 1868).

Balliol College, Oxford. Gerard Manley Hopkins Papers, MS Notebook D. II.

—— Benjamin Jowett Papers, MS Notebooks IB3, IB4, IB5.

—— T. H. Green Papers, MS Notebooks 1A, 1B, two unnumbered MSS. Notebooks, transcriptions by Charlotte B. Green of recollections of T. H. Green (Thomas, II, i(a) and (d)).

BALL, PATRICIA, *The Science of Aspects: The Changing Role of Fact in the Work of Coleridge, Ruskin and Hopkins* (London: Athlone Press, 1971).

BEER, GILLIAN, 'Helmholtz, Tyndall, Gerard Manley Hopkins: Leaps of the Prepared Imagination', *Comparative Criticism*, 13 (Cambridge: Cambridge University Press, 1991), 117–45.

BENDER, TODD K., *Gerard Manley Hopkins: The Classical Background and Critical Reception of his Work* (Baltimore: Johns Hopkins University Press, 1966).

—— 'Hopkins' "God's Grandeur"', *The Explicator*, 21/7 (Mar. 1963), item 55.

BENJAMIN, WALTER, *Illuminations*, ed. Hannah Arendt, trans. Harry Zohn (New York: Schocken, 1969).

—— *The Origin of German Tragic Drama*, trans. John Osborne (London: New Left Books, 1977).

—— *One-Way Street and other Writings*, trans. Edmund Jephcott and Kingsley Shorter (London: New Left Books, 1979).

BENNETT, JONATHAN, *Kant's Analytic* (Cambridge: Cambridge University Press, 1966).

BERGONZI, BERNARD, *Gerard Manley Hopkins* (London: Macmillan, 1977).

BERKSON, WILLIAM, *Fields of Force: The Development of a World View from Faraday to Einstein* (London: Routledge & Kegan Paul, 1974).

BISCHOFF, ANTHONY, 'Hopkins' Letters to his Brother', *Times Literary Supplement*. 8 Dec. 1972, pp. 1511–2.

—— 'The Manuscripts of Gerard Manley Hopkins', *Thought*, 26/23 (Winter 1951/2), 551–80.

BROWN, HORATIO R. F., *John Addington Symonds: a Biography, Compiled from his Papers and Correspondence*, 2nd edn. (London: Smith, Elder, 1903).

BRUNS, GERALD L., 'Energy and Interpretation in Hopkins', in his *Inventions: Writing, Textuality, and Understanding in Literary History* (New Haven: Yale University Press, 1982).

BRUSH, STEPHEN G., *The Temperature of History: Phases of Science and Culture in the Nineteenth Century* (New York: Burt Franklin & Co., 1978).

BUMP, JEROME, *Gerard Manley Hopkins* (Boston: Twayne Publishers, 1982).

CAIRD, EDWARD, 'Professor Jowett', *International Journal of Ethics*, 8 (Oct. 1897), 40–7.

CAMPBELL, LEWIS, and GARNETT, WILLIAM, *The Life of James Clerk Maxwell*, 2nd edn. (London: Macmillan, 1884).

Campion Hall, Oxford, Gerard Manley Hopkins Papers, MS Notebooks B. I–II; D. I; D. III–XII; G. I; M. II; G. IA.

CHALLIS, H. W., *A Letter to J. S. Mill, Esq., M.P., on the Necessity of Geometry and the Association of Ideas* (Oxford: James Parker, 1867).

CHUBB, PERCIVAL, 'The Significance of Thomas Hill Green's Philosophical and Religious Teaching', *Journal of Speculative Philosophy*, 22 (Jan., Apr., 1888), 1–21.

CLANCHY, M. T., *From Memory to Written Record: England 1066–1307* (London: Edward Arnold, 1979).

COCHRAN, LEONARD, 'Instress and its Place in the Poetics of Gerard Manley Hopkins', *Hopkins Quarterly*, 6/4 (Winter 1980), 143–81.

COLEMAN, WILLIAM, *Biology in the Nineteenth Century: Problems of Form, Function and Transformation* (New York: John Wiley, 1971).

COLERIDGE, S. T., *Biographia Literaria, or Biographical Sketches of My Literary Life and Opinions*, ed. James Engell and W. Jackson Bate, 2 vols. (London: Routledge & Kegan Paul, 1983).

—— *The Poems of Samuel Taylor Coleridge*, ed. Derwent and Sara Coleridge (London: Edward Moxon, 1854).

[CONINGTON, JOHN], '[Review article of] Report of Her Majesty's Commissioners appointed to Inquire into ... the University ... of Oxford ...', *North British Review*, 18 (Nov. 1852), 1–38.

COTTER, JAMES FINN, *Inscape: The Christology and Poetry of Gerard Manley Hopkins* (Pittsburgh: University of Pittsburgh Press, 1972).

CROW, MICHAEL, 'Science a Century Ago', in Frederick J. Crosson (ed.), *Science and Contemporary Society* (Notre Dame: University of Notre Dame Press, 1967), 105–26.

CUNNINGTON, C. W., and CUNNINGTON, P. E., *Handbook of English Costume in the Nineteenth Century* (London: Faber, 1959).

DARWALL-SMITH, ROBIN, *The Jowett Papers: A Summary Catalogue* (Oxford: The Masters and Fellows of Balliol College, 1993).

DARWIN, CHARLES, *The Origin of Species* (Harmondsworth: Penguin, 1968).

DELEUZE, GILLES, *Nietzsche and Philosophy*, trans. Hugh Tomlinson (London: Athlone Press, 1983).

—— *Kant's Critical Philosophy: The Doctrine of the Faculties*, trans. Hugh Tomlinson and Barbara Habberjam (London: Athlone Press, 1984).

ELIOT, THOMAS STEARNS, *Selected Prose of T. S. Eliot*, ed. Frank Kermode (London: Faber, 1975).

ELLIS, IEUAN, *Seven Against Christ* (Leiden: E. J. Brill, 1980).

ENGELS, FREDERICK, *Dialectics of Nature*, trans. Clement Dutt, 2nd edn. (Moscow: Progress Publishers, 1954).

'Father Gerard Hopkins', *Letters and Notices*, 20/99 (Mar. 1890), 173–9.

FLUGEL, J. C., *A Hundred Years of Psychology: 1833–1933* (London: Duckworth, 1933).

FOUCAULT, MICHEL, 'What is an Author?', in *Textual Strategies: Prespectives in Post-structuralist Criticism*, ed. and trans. Josué V. Harari (London: Methuen, 1979).

FRASER, HILARY, *Beauty and Belief: Aesthetics and Religion in Victorian Literature* (Cambridge: Cambridge University Press, 1986).

[FYFFE, CHARLES ALAN], 'Study and Opinion at Oxford', *Macmillan's Magazine*, 21 (Dec. 1869), 184–92.

GADAMER, HANS-GEORG, *Reason in the Age of Science*, trans. Frederick G. Lawrence (Cambridge, Mass.: MIT Press, 1981).

330 BIBLIOGRAPHY

GARDNER, W. H., *Gerard Manley Hopkins: A Study of Poetic Idiosyncrasy in Relation to Poetic Tradition*, 2 vols. (Oxford: Oxford University Press, 1949; repr. 1958).

GAY, PETER, *Freud: A Life for our Time* (London: Dent, 1988).

[GILCHREST, ANNE], 'The Indestructibility of Force', *Macmillan's Magazine*, 6 (Aug. 1862), 337–44.

GIOVANNINI, MARGARET, 'Hopkins' "God's Grandeur"', *The Explicator*, 24/4 (Dec. 1965), item 36.

GOMBRICH, E. H., *The Sense of Order: A Study in the Psychology of Decorative Art*, 2nd edn. (Ithaca, NY: Cornell University Press, 1979).

GRANT, ALEXANDER (ed.), *The Ethics of Aristotle*, 2nd edn., 2 vols. (London: Longmans, Green, & Co., 1866).

GREEN, THOMAS HILL, *Works of T. H. Green*, ed. R. L. Nettleship, 3 vols. (London: Longmans, 1888; repr. 1911).

GREGOR, MARY J., 'Kant's Conception of a "Metaphysics of Morals"', *Philosophical Quarterly*, 10 (1960), 238–51.

—— *Laws of Freedom: A Study of Kant's Method of Applying the Categorical Imperative in the* Metaphysik der Sitten (Oxford: Blackwell, 1963).

GRIFFITHS, ERIC, *The Printed Voice of Victorian Poetry* (Oxford: Clarendon Press, 1989).

GROSZ, ELIZABETH, *Volatile Bodies: Toward a Corporeal Feminism* (Sydney, Allen & Unwin, 1994).

GROTE, GEORGE, *A History of Greece*, 3rd edn. (London: John Murray, 1851).

GROTE, JOHN, *Exploratio Philosophica: Part I* (Cambridge: Cambridge University Press, 1865; repr. 1900).

HARMAN, P. M. [as P. M. Heimann], 'Conversion of Forces and the Conservation of Energy', *Centaurus*, 18 (1974), 147–61.

—— *Energy, Force, and Matter: The Conceptual Development of Nineteenth-Century Physics* (Cambridge: Cambridge University Press, 1982).

—— *Metaphysics and Natural Philosophy: The Problem of Substance in Classical Physics* (Brighton: Harvester, 1982).

HARVIE, CHRISTOPHER, *The Lights of Liberalism: University Liberals and the Challenge of Democracy 1860–86* (London: Allen Lane, 1976).

[HATCH, EDWIN], review article of 'The Ethics of Aristotle ... By Sir Alexander Grant ...', *North British Review*, 29 (Aug. 1858), 367–95.

[HEATH, DOUGLAS DENON], 'Professor Bain on the Doctrine of the Correlation of Force in its Bearing on Mind', *Contemporary Review*, 8 (May 1868), 57–78.

HEGEL, G. W. F., *Hegel's Science of Logic*, trans. A. V. Miller (London: George Allen & Unwin, 1969).

—— *Phenomenology of Spirit*, trans. A. V. Miller (Oxford: Clarendon Press, 1977).

—— *The Philosophy of History*, trans. J. Sibree (New York: Colonial Press, 1899; repr. New York: Dover, 1956).

—— *Philosophy of Mind*, trans. William Wallace (Oxford: Clarendon Press, 1971).

—— *Philosophy of Nature*, trans. Michael John Petry, 3 vols. (London: Allen & Unwin, 1970).

—— *Science of Logic*, trans. W. H. Johnston and L. G. Struthers (London: George Allen & Unwin, 1929).

HEIDEGGER, MARTIN, *Early Greek Thinking*, trans. David Farrell Krell and Frank A. Capuzzi (New York: Harper & Row, 1984).

HELMHOLTZ, HERMANN VON, *Popular Lectures on Scientific Subjects, First Series*, trans. E. Atkinson, 2nd edn. (London: Longmans, Green, & Co., 1895).

HENDRY, JOHN, *James Clerk Maxwell and the Theory of the Electromagnetic Field* (Bristol: Adam Hilger, 1986).

[HERSCHEL, J. F. W.], 'On the Origin of Force', *Fortnightly Review*, 1 (July 1865), 435–42.

HESSE, MARY B., *Forces and Fields: The Concept of Action at a Distance in the History of Physics* (London: Nelson, 1961).

HIEBERT, ERWIN N., 'The Uses and Abuses of Thermodynamics in Religion', *Daedalus*, 95 (1966), 1046–80.

HIGGINS, LESLEY J., 'Hopkins and the "Jowler"', *Texas Studies in Literature and Language*, 31/1 (Spring 1989), 143–67.

—— 'Fixity versus Flux: Hopkins and the Discourse of Development', *The New Welsh Review*, 2/3 (Winter 1989–90), 25–9.

HILL, GEOFFREY, ' "Perplexed Persistence": the Exemplary Failure of T. H. Green', in *The Lords of Limit: Essays on Literature and Ideas* (London: Deutsch, 1984), 104–20.

HINCHLIFF, PETER, *Benjamin Jowett and the Christian Tradition* (Oxford: Clarendon Press, 1987).

HOLTON, GERALD, 'The Thematic Imagination in Science', in id. (ed.), *Science and Culture* (Boston: Houghton Mifflin, 1965), 88–108.

HOPKINS, GERARD MANLEY, *The Correspondence of Gerard Manley Hopkins and Richard Watson Dixon*, ed. Claude Colleer Abbott, 2nd (rev.) impression (London: Oxford University Press, 1955).

—— *The Early Poetic Manuscripts and Note-books of Gerard Manley Hopkins in Facsimile*, ed. Norman H. MacKenzie (New York: Garland, 1989).

—— *Further Letters of Gerard Manley Hopkins*, ed. Claude Colleer Abbott, 2nd (rev.) impression (London: Oxford University Press, 1959).

—— *Journals and Papers*, ed. Giuseppe Castorina (Bari: Adriatica, 1974).

—— *The Journals and Papers of Gerard Manley Hopkins*, ed. Humphry

House and Graham Storey, 2nd. edn. (London: Oxford University Press, 1959).

—— *The Letters of Gerard Manley Hopkins to Robert Bridges*, ed. Claude Colleer Abbott, 2nd (rev.) impression (London: Oxford University Press, 1955).

—— *The Poetical Works of Gerard Manley Hopkins*, ed. Norman H. MacKenzie (Oxford: Clarendon Press, 1990).

—— *The Sermons and Devotional Writings of Gerard Manley Hopkins*, ed. Christopher Devlin (Oxford: Oxford University Press, 1959).

HOPKINS, MANLEY, *Spicilegium Poeticum: A Gathering of Verses* (London: The Leadenhall Press, 1892).

HUGHES, ROBERT, *The Shock of the New*, 2nd edn. (London: BBC, 1991).

HUME, DAVID, *A Treatise of Human Nature*, ed. L. A. Selby-Bigge (London: Clarendon Press, 1888).

HUTCHISON, KEITH, 'W. J. M. Rankine and the Rise of Thermodynamics', *British Journal for the History of Science*, 14/46 (1981), 1–26.

HUXLEY, THOMAS HENRY, *Man's Place in Nature and Other Essays* (London: Dent, 1906).

INMAN, BILLIE ANDREW, *Walter Pater's Borrowings from the Queen's College Library, the Bodleian Library, the Brasenose College Library, and the Taylor Institution Library, 1860–1894* (Tucson, Ariz.: University of Arizona, 1977).

JASPERS, KARL, *Anaximander, Heraclitus, Parmenides, Plotinus, Lao-Tzu, Magarjuna*, ed. Hannah Arendt, trans. Ralph Manheim (New York: Harcourt Brace Jovanovich, 1974).

JENKYNS, RICHARD, *The Victorians and Ancient Greece* (Oxford: Blackwell, 1980).

JONES, E. E. CONSTANCE, 'Green's Account of Aristotle's Ethics', *Hibbert Journal*, 1 (1903), 802–5.

JOULE, JAMES PRESCOTT, *The Scientific Papers of James Prescott Joule*, 2 vols. (London: Physical Society of London, 1884).

JOWETT, BENJAMIN, et al., *Essays and Reviews*, 11th edn. (London: Longman, Green, Longman, Roberts, & Green, 1863).

—— *The Dialogues of Plato: Translated into English With Analyses and Introductions*, 5 vols. (Oxford: Clarendon Press, 1871); 2nd edn., 5 vols. (Oxford: Clarendon Press, 1875); 3rd edn., 5 vols. (Oxford: Clarendon Press, 1892).

—— *The Interpretation of Scripture and other Essays* (London: George Routledge & Sons Ltd., n.d.).

—— *The Republic*, 2nd edn. (Oxford: Clarendon Press, 1881).

KANT, IMMANUEL, *Critique of Judgement*, trans. James Creed Meredith (Oxford: Clarendon Press, 1928; repr. 1952).

—— *Critique of Pure Reason*, trans. Norman Kemp Smith (London: Macmillan, 1933).

—— *Kant's Critique of Practical Reason and Other Works on the Theory of Ethics*, trans. Thomas Kingsmill Abbott, 4th edn. (London: Longmans, Green, & Co. 1889).

KENNY, ANTHONY, *Aristotle's Theory of Will* (London: Duckworth, 1979).

KESSLER, EDWARD, *Coleridge's Metaphors of Being* (Princeton: Princeton University Press, 1979).

KIRK, G. S., RAVEN, J. E., and SCHOFIELD, M., *The Presocratic Philosophers*, 2nd edn. (Cambridge: Cambridge University Press, 1983).

KNICKERBOCKER, WILLIAM S., *Creative Oxford: Its Influence in Victorian Literature* (Syracuse, NY: Syracuse University Press, 1925).

KNIGHT, DAVID, *The Age of Science: The Scientific World-view in the Nineteenth Century* (Oxford: Blackwell, 1986).

KOOISTRA, LORRAINE JANZEN, ' "The Proportion of the Mixture": Stress and Slack in the Perception and Poetics of Hopkins', *Hopkins Quarterly*, 17/4 (Jan. 1991), 113–25.

KÖRNER, S., *Kant* (Harmondsworth: Penguin, 1955).

KRISTEVA, JULIA, *Desire in Language: A Semiotic Approach to Literature and Art*, trans. Thomas Gora, Alice Jardine, and Leo S. Roudiez (Oxford: Blackwell, 1981).

KUHN, THOMAS S., 'Energy Conservation as Simultaneous Discovery', in *Critical Problems in the History of Science*, ed. Marshall Clagett (Madison: University of Wisconsin Press, 1962), 321–56.

LAHEY, G. F., *Gerard Manley Hopkins* (Oxford: Oxford University Press, 1930).

LAUER, QUENTIN, *A Reading of Hegel's* Phenomenology of Spirit, 4th (rev.) repr. (New York: Fordham University Press, 1976; 1987).

LEAR, JONATHAN, *Aristotle: The Desire to Understand* (Cambridge: Cambridge University Press, 1988).

LETTERS, F. J. H., *The Life and Work of Sophocles* (London: Sheed & Ward, 1953).

LEWES, GEORGE HENRY, *The Biographical History of Philosophy: From its Origin in Greece down to the Present Day* (London: John W. Parker & Son, 1857; repr. Farnborough: Gregg International Publishers, 1970).

LIDDELL, HENRY GEORGE, and SCOTT, ROBERT, *A Greek–English Lexicon*, 8th edn. (Oxford: Clarendon Press, 1891).

'Literae Humaniores, VII', *Oxford Magazine*, 27/16 (11 Mar. 1909), 247–8.

LOCKE, JOHN, *The Conduct of the Understanding*, in *The Works of John Locke*, iii (London: printed for Thomas Tegg, W. Sharpe & Son, *et al.* 1823; repr. Aalen: Scientia Verlag, 1963).

LOCKE, JOHN, *An Essay Concerning Human Understanding* (London: Ward, Lock, & Co., n.d.).

LOOMIS, JEFFREY B., *Dayspring in Darkness: Sacrament in Hopkins* (Toronto: Associated University Presses, 1988).

MACKENZIE, NORMAN, 'Hopkins and Science', *Studies in the Literary Imagination*, 21/1 (Spring 1988), 41–56.

—— *A Reader's Guide to Gerard Manley Hopkins* (London: Thames & Hudson, 1981).

MANSEL, HENRY LONGUEVILLE, 'Modern German Philosophy', *Bentley Quarterly*, 1 (July 1859), 413–32.

—— *Letters, Lectures, and Reviews, Including The Phrontisterion*, ed. Henry W. Chandler (London: John Murray, 1873).

MANSER, ANTHONY, *Bradley's Logic* (Oxford: Blackwell, 1983).

MARIANI, PAUL, *A Commentary on the Complete Poems of Gerard Manley Hopkins* (Ithaca, NY: Cornell University Press, 1970).

MAX MÜLLER, FRIEDRICH, *Lectures on the Science of Language*, 1st ser., 2nd edn. (London: Longman, Green, Longman, & Roberts, 1862).

MAXWELL, JAMES CLERK, 'The "Encyclopaedia Britannica"' (a review of the 9th edn., xvi. Men–Mos), *Nature*, 29 (15 Nov. 1883), 51–4.

—— *The Scientific Papers of James Clerk Maxwell*, ed. W. D. Niven, 2 vols. (Cambridge, Cambridge University Press, 1890; repr., New York: Dover, 1965).

Merton College, Oxford, F. H. Bradley MS Notebook I-A1, Notes on T. H. Green's Lectures on Moral Philosophy, 1867.

MILL, J. S., *A System of Logic, Ratiocinative and Inductive*, ed. J. M. Robson, 2 vols. (London: Routledge & Kegan Paul, 1973).

—— *Autobiographical and Literary Essays*, ed. John M. Robson and Jack Stillinger (London: Routledge & Kegan Paul, 1981).

MILLER, J. HILLIS, *The Disappearance of God: Five Nineteenth-Century Writers* (Cambridge, Mass.: Belknap Press of Harvard University Press, 1963; 1975).

—— *The Linguistic Moment: From Wordsworth to Stevens* (Princeton: Princeton University Press, 1985).

MONTAG, GEORGE E., 'Hopkins' "God's Grandeur" and "The Ooze of Oil Crushed"', *Victorian Poetry*, 1/4 (Nov. 1963), 302–3.

MOYER, DONALD FRANKLIN, 'Energy, Dynamics, Hidden Machinery: Rankine, Thomson and Tait, Maxwell', *Studies in the History and Philosophy of Science*, 8/3 (1977), 251–68.

MURE, G. R. G., 'Oxford and Philosophy', *Philosophy (The Journal of the British Institute of Philosophy)*, 12 (1937), 291–301.

NEWMAN, JOHN HENRY, *Essays Critical and Historical*, 2 vols. (London: Longmans, Green & Co. 1871; repr. 1910).

NEWSOME, DAVID, *Two Classes of Men* (New York: St Martin's Press, 1974).

NIXON, JUDE V., *Gerard Manley Hopkins and his Contemporaries: Liddon, Newman, Darwin, and Pater* (New York: Garland, 1994).

NUTTALL, A. D., *A Common Sky: Philosophy and the Literary Imagination* (London: Sussex University Press, 1974).

OGILVIE, R. M., *Latin and Greek: A History of the Influence of the Classics on English Life from 1660 to 1918* (London: Routledge & Kegan Paul, 1964).

OLDROYD, D. R., *Darwinian Impacts: An Introduction to the Darwinian Revolution*, 2nd edn. (Sydney: New South Wales University Press, 1983).

—— *The Arch of Knowledge: An Introductory Study of the History of the Philosophy and Methodology of Science* (Sydney: New South Wales University Press, 1986).

ORSINI, G. N. G., *Coleridge and German Idealism: A Study in the History of Philosophy with Unpublished Materials from Coleridge's Manuscripts* (Carbondale: Southern Illinois University Press, 1969).

'Oxford Studies—Mr. Pattison and Dr. Gillow', *The Month*, 11 (July 1869), 101–9.

PAGET, STEPHEN (ed.), *Henry Scott Holland: Memoir and Letters* (London: John Murray, 1921).

Papers Relating to the University, 1864, Bodleian Library, Oxford, G. A. Oxon. C. 80, item 175.

Papers Relating to the University, 1865, Bodleian Library, Oxford, G. A. Oxon. C. 81, item 43.

Papers Relating to the University, 1866, Bodleian Library, Oxford, G. A. Oxon. C. 82, item 38.

Papers Relating to the University, 1867, Bodleian Library, Oxford, G. A. Oxon. C. 83, items 5, 13, 16, 17, 104, 236, 250, and 262.

PATER, WALTER, 'Coleridge's Writings', *Westminster Review* (Jan. 1866), 106–32.

—— *The Renaissance*, ed. Kenneth Clark (London: Collins, 1961).

PATTISON, MARK, *Memoirs* (London: Macmillan, 1885).

—— 'Philosophy at Oxford', *Mind*, 1 (1876), 82–97.

—— *Suggestions on Academical Organisation with Especial Reference to Oxford* (Edinburgh: Edmonston & Douglas, 1868).

PENDEXTER, HUGH, 'Hopkins' "God's Grandeur"', *The Explicator*, 23/ 1 (Sept. 1964), item 2.

PETERS, W. A. M., *Gerard Manley Hopkins: A Critical Essay towards the Understanding of his Poetry* (London: Oxford University Press, 1948).

PIPPIN, ROBERT B., *Hegel's Idealism: The Satisfactions of Self-Consciousness* (Cambridge: Cambridge University Press, 1989).

PLOTKIN, CARY H., *The Tenth Muse: Victorian Philology and the Genesis of the Poetic Language of Gerard Manley Hopkins* (Carbondale: Southern Illinois University Press, 1989).

POINCARÉ, HENRI, *Science and Hypothesis*, trans. W. J. G. (London: Walter Scott Publishing Co., 1905; repr. New York: Dover, 1952).

PRICKETT, STEPHEN, *Coleridge and Wordsworth: The Poetry of Growth* (Cambridge: Cambridge University Press, 1970).

—— 'On Reading Nature as a Romantic', in *Papers and Synopses from the 22nd. Congress of the Australasian Universities Language and Literature Association* (Canberra: Australian National University, 1984), 56–70.

QUINTON, A. M., *Absolute Idealism*, Dawes Hicks Lecture on Philosophy, British Academy, 1971 (London: Oxford University Press, 1972).

RANDELL, JOHN HERMAN, 'T. H. Green: The Development of English Thought from J. S. Mill to F. H. Bradley', *Journal of the History of Ideas*, 27 (1966), 217–44.

RANKINE, W. J. M., *A Manual of Applied Mechanics* (London: Charles Griffin, 1858).

—— *Miscellaneous Scientific Papers of W. J. Macquorn Rankine* (London: Charles Griffin, 1881).

REIMAN, DONALD H., 'Hopkins' "Ooze of Oil" Rises Again', *Victorian Poetry*, 4/1 (Winter 1966), 39–42.

RILKE, RAINER MARIA, *Duino Elegies*, trans. J. B. Leishman and Stephen Spender (New York: Norton, 1939).

RITTER, H., and PRELLER, L., *Historia Philosophiae Graecae*, 7th edn. (Gotha: Andr. Perthes, 1888).

ROBERTS, GERALD (ed.), *Gerard Manley Hopkins: The Critical Heritage* (London: Routledge & Kegan Paul, 1987).

ROGERS, JAMES E. THOROLD, *Education at Oxford* (London: Smith, Elder & Co., 1861).

ROLL-HANSON, DIDERIK, *The Academy 1869–79: Victorian Intellectuals in Revolt*, Anglistica, 8 (Copenhagen: Rosenkilde & Bagger, 1958).

ROSEN, MICHAEL, *Hegel's Dialectic and its Criticism* (Cambridge: Cambridge University Press, 1982).

ROSENBLUM, ROBERT, and JANSON, H. W., *Art of the Nineteenth Century* (London: Thames & Hudson, 1984).

RUSKIN, JOHN, *The Elements of Drawing*, ed. E. T. Cook and Alexander Wedderburn (London: George Allen, 1904).

—— *Modern Painters*, ed. E. T. Cook and Alexander Wedderburn (London: George Allen, 1904).

SANDEEN, ERNEST P., *The Roots of Fundamentalism: British and American Millenarianism 1800–1930* (Chicago: Chicago University Press, 1970).

SARTRE, JEAN-PAUL, *The Age of Reason*, trans. Eric Sutton (London: Hamish Hamilton, 1947).

—— *Being and Nothingness: An Essay on Phenomenological Ontology*, trans. Hazel E. Barnes (New York: Philosophical Library, 1956).

SCHMIDT, CARL, 'Classical Studies at Balliol in the 1860s: The Undergraduate Essays of Gerard Manley Hopkins', in John Prest (ed.), *Balliol Studies* (London: Leopard's Head Press, 1982), 160–84.

SERRES, MICHEL, *Hermes: Literature, Science, Philosophy*, ed. Josué V. Harari and David F. Bell (Baltimore: Johns Hopkins University Press, 1982).

SHAW, W. DAVID, *The Lucid Veil: Poetic Truth in the Victorian Age* (London: Athlone Press, 1987).

SIEGEL, DANIEL M., 'Thomson, Maxwell, and the Universal Ether in Victorian Physics', in G. N. Cantor and M. J. S. Hodge (eds.), *Conceptions of Ether: Studies in the History of Ether Theories 1740–1900* (Cambridge: Cambridge University Press, 1981), 239–68.

SKORUPSKI, JOHN, *John Stuart Mill* (London: Routledge, 1989).

SMITH, C. A., 'T. H. Green's Philosophical Manuscripts: An Annotated Catalog', *Idealistic Studies*, 9/2 (May 1979), 178–84.

SMITH, CROSBIE, 'A Chart for British Natural Philosophy: The Development of Energy Physics in the Nineteenth Century', *History of Science*, 16 (1978), 231–79.

SMITH II, PHILIP E., and HELFAND, MICHAEL S. (eds. and intro.), *Oscar Wilde's Oxford Notebooks: A Portrait of Mind in the Making* (New York: Oxford University Press, 1989).

SOLL, IVAN, *An Introduction to Hegel's Metaphysics* (Chicago: University of Chicago Press, 1969).

Special Report from the Select Committee in the Oxford and Cambridge Universities Education Bill, together with the Proceedings of the Committee, Minutes of Evidence, and Appendix [and] Index ([London:] n.p., 1867).

SPENCER, HERBERT, *The Principles of Psychology*, 3rd edn. (London: Williams & Norgate, 1881).

SPRINKER, MICHAEL, *'A Counterpoint of Dissonance': The Aesthetics and Poetry of Gerard Manley Hopkins* (Baltimore: Johns Hopkins University Press, 1980).

STIRLING, JAMES HUTCHISON, *The Secret of Hegel: Being the Hegelian System in Origin, Principle, Form, and Matter*, 2 vols. (London: Longman, Green, Longman, Roberts, & Green, 1865).

SULLOWAY, ALISON (ed.), *Critical Essays on Gerard Manley Hopkins* (Boston: G. K. Hall & Co., 1990).

—— *Gerard Manley Hopkins and the Victorian Temper* (London: Routledge & Kegan Paul, 1972).

TAIT, PETER GUTHRIE, 'The Dynamical Theory of Heat', *North British Review*, 40/79 (Feb. 1864), 40–69.

—— 'Energy', *North British Review*, 40/80 (May 1864), 337–68.

TAYLOR, CHARLES, *Hegel* (Cambridge: Cambridge University Press, 1975).

TAYLOR, MICHAEL, 'Hopkins' "God's Grandeur"', *The Explicator*, 25/8 (Apr. 1967), item 68.

THOMAS, ALFRED, *Hopkins the Jesuit: the Years of Training* (London: Oxford University Press, 1969).

THOMAS, GEOFFREY, *The Moral Philosophy of T. H. Green* (Oxford: Clarendon Press, 1987).

THOMSON, WILLIAM, and TAIT, PETER GUTHRIE, 'Energy', *Good Words* (1862), 601–7.

—— *Treatise on Natural Philosophy* (Oxford: Clarendon Press, 1867).

TURNER, FRANK M., *The Greek Heritage in Victorian Britain* (New Haven: Yale University Press, 1981).

URMSON, J. O., *Aristotle's Ethics* (London: Basil Blackwell, 1988).

[VAUGHAN, HERBERT], 'English Catholic University Education', *Dublin Review*, 9 (Oct. 1867), 381–440.

VINCENT, A. W., and PLANT, R, *Philosophy, Politics and Citizenship: The Life and Thought of the British Idealists* (Oxford: Blackwell, 1984).

WALKER, RALPH C. S., *Kant* (London: Routledge & Kegan Paul, 1978).

WALLACE, ALFRED RUSSEL, *The Wonderful Century: Its Successes and Its Failures*, 4th edn. (London: Swan Sonnenschein & Co., 1901).

WARD, ANTHONY, *Walter Pater: The Idea in Nature* (London: MacGibbon & Kee, 1966).

WEIL, SIMONE, *Gravity and Grace*, trans. Emma Craufurd (London: Routledge & Kegan Paul, 1952).

WELLEK, RENÉ, *A History of Modern Criticism: 1750–1950*, vi: *American Criticism, 1900–1950* (London: Jonathan Cape, 1986).

WEMPE, BEN, *Beyond Equality: A Study of T. H. Green's Theory of Positive Freedom* (Delft: Eburon, 1986).

WHEWELL, WILLIAM, *On the Philosophy of Discovery, Chapters Historical and Critical; Including the Completion of the Third Edition of the Philosophy of the Inductive Sciences* (London: Parker, 1860).

—— *The Philosophy of the Inductive Sciences, Founded Upon Their History*, 2nd edn., 2 vols. (London: John W. Parker, 1847; repr. Frank Cass & Co. Ltd., 1967).

WHITE, NORMAN, *Hopkins: A Literary Biography* (Oxford: Clarendon Press, 1992).

WILKERSON, T. E., *Kant's Critique of Pure Reason: A Commentary for Students* (Oxford: Clarendon Press, 1976).

WILLIAMS, L. PEARCE, *Faraday: A Biography* (New York: Simon & Schuster, 1971).

WINDELBAND, WILHELM, *A History of Philosophy*, trans. James H. Tufts, 2nd edn. (New York: Macmillan, 1901).

WINTERS, YVOR, *The Function of Criticism: Problems and Exercises* (London: Routledge & Kegan Paul, 1962).

WITTGENSTEIN, LUDWIG, *Philosophical Investigations*, trans. G. E. M. Anscombe, 2nd edn. (Oxford: Blackwell, 1958).

YOLTON, J. W., *Locke: An Introduction* (Oxford: Blackwell, 1985).

ZANIELLO, TOM, *Hopkins in the Age of Darwin* (Iowa City: Iowa University Press, 1988).

—— 'The Sources of Hopkins' Inscape: Epistemology at Oxford, 1864–1868', *Victorian Newsletter*, 52 (Autumn 1977), 18–24.

Index

aesthetics 82–91, 125, 206
analogy 204–6, 208–13, 230, 238–40
Aristotle 44
  and Hegel 135, 190
  and Kant 74, 95, 113, 115,
    117–18, 131, 136, 143–5
  moral ontology 100–5, 113–17,
    128–9, 255
  ontology 44, 63, 70–1, 74, 143–5,
    154, 190, 192, 256–7, 287
  his principle of τὰ λεγόμενα 99,
    106, 108, 293
  WORKS:
  Nicomachean Ethics 94–5, 100–1,
    113–18, 128–31
  Physics 171
associationism 5–6, 46, 68–9, 73
atheism 30, 36, 37

Bacon, Francis 45, 47
Bain, Alexander 5–6
Being 142, 148, 298, 320
  analogous to a sphere 171, 178,
    229, 284, 291
  and knowing 131, 182–6
  and Not-being 176–80, 219–20,
    224–30
  see also instress; stress
being, determinate 170, 226, 288
  see also concrete universal
Benjamin, Walter 294, 299, 314, 319
Blake, William 325–6
breath 301–6, 309, 312, 319, 322,
    326
burl, the 229–31
Butler, Joseph 94–5

catching, metaphor of 163, 290–1
causation 67–73, 75
  and induction 48–51
  mechanical 110, 247–8, 253, 285
Challis, H. W. 183 n.
Christ 178, 251–4, 256–7, 284,
    289–90, 302, 305, 310, 312–13

his blood 172–3, 225, 244
  see also Crucifixion; λόνος; Trinity
Coleridge, S. T. 24, 90, 131 n.
Comte, I. A. M. F. X. 2, 36
concrete universal 146–9, 154–5, 174
Crucifixion, the 172–3, 304, 311

Darwin and Darwinism 3, 4, 19–20,
    39, 195, 196, 203, 248–9
determinism 118–20

electromagnetism 257–8, 269–70
  see also field theory
Eliot, T. S. 200, 324
energy 230
  the mind's 81–2, 88–90, 250
  potential and actual 192–3
energy physics 41, 192, 202–3,
    240–1, 272
  and romanticism 193–5
  and theology 195–7, 203–6
Essays and Reviews 13, 14, 17
Eucharist 18, 305
expressivism 235, 236, 242, 272, 314

Faraday, Michael 211–12, 238
  see also field theory
Fechner, G. T. 3–4
field theory 211–12, 216–17,
    238–43, 245, 250, 278
'flushness' 171, 173–4, 182, 222–3,
    302
freshness 161–4, 306–7
Freud, S. 272

geology, Lyellian 19–20
God the Father 246, 251
  see also Trinity
grace 203–4, 261–3, 265, 267,
    270–1, 305
Grant, Alexander 50, 95, 101
  on Aristotle and Kant 113–15,
    117–18, 142–3
  on ἐνέργεια 135–7